Praise for *Blood Sisters*

"Once again, Sarah Gristwood proves that she is at the top of her field with *Blood Sisters.* . . . It's the book that I wish I had written." —Alison Weir, *BBC History Magazine*

"Arguing persuasively for the existence of a 'female network,' . . . Gristwood details the paths of seven royal women who transcended their roles as diplomatic pawns and heir producers." —*The New Yorker*

"Most of the leading players in the Wars of the Roses have traditionally been thought to be the men. Historian Sarah Gristwood . . . stands this on its head. She examines seven women, whose lives were bound together across the best part of a century, and tries to see the wars from their points of view." —*Sunday Times* (London)

"A revolutionary approach. For too long, history has been the purview of men, of kings and their battles, wars, conquests, murders and thirst for power. . . . Gristwood's perspective and lively writing are refreshing. . . . Certainly there have been individual biographies of each of these seven powerful women but by tracing the connections among them, Gristwood digs into motives and aspirations of royals too long overlooked. . . . Through them, she gives an unconventional history of the wars between relations, arguing that their actions mattered as much as battles, and certainly played a significant role in ending the war and establishing the peace." —*Toronto Star*

"This is the true story of the most important women of the period, their travails and suffering; but also of the links between them, their friendships and ambitions, their cooperation, their courage and pragmatism. It is a different way of looking at this complex period, and Gristwood weaves the story with considerable skill. The battles and bloodshed that led to the loss of so many of the old nobility of England form a backdrop to the narrative, but the real emphasis is on half-a-dozen women whose extraordinary experiences of triumph and disaster, often in a bewilderingly short period of time, brought them to the edge of despair but did not, in the end, lessen their commitment to their families. They provided continuity as the world fell apart around them. . . . Gristwood is to be congratulated for her highly readable account of their lives." —*Literary Review*

"Gristwood has written a compelling narrative of what went on behind the scenes and away from the battlefields. . . . [*Blood Sisters*] is an engaging, well written, and thoroughly-researched page turner that should delight academics as much as fans of Philippa Gregory's historical novels about several of the same notable women." —*Publishers Weekly*

"[*Blood Sisters*] deftly navigates a period of shifting alliances in a clear, concise fashion." —*Library Journal*

"As Gristwood amply proves in this shrewd, rewarding study, alliances and ambitions involved women as much as men. . . . [Gristwood] nimbly makes sense and relevance out of the confoundingly entangled dynasties of the Yorks and Tudors." —*Kirkus*

BLOOD SISTERS

ALSO BY SARAH GRISTWOOD

BLOOD SISTERS

The WOMEN BEHIND the
WARS of the ROSES

Sarah Gristwood

BASIC BOOKS

A Member of the Perseus Books Group

New York

Copyright © 2013 by Sarah Gristwood

Hardcover first published in 2013 by Basic Books,
A Member of the Perseus Books Group

Paperback first published in 2014 by Basic Books

Designed by Cynthia Young

The Library of Congress has cataloged the hardcover as follows:

Gristwood, Sarah.
Blood sisters : the women behind the Wars of the Roses / Sarah Gristwood.
    pages cm
Includes bibliographical references and index.
ISBN 978-0-465-01831-4 (hard cover : alk. paper) —
ISBN 978-0-465-06598-1 (e-book)
1. Great Britain—History—Wars of the Roses, 1455–1485. 2. Great Britain—History—Henry VII, 1485–1509. 3. Plantagenet, House of. 4. Margaret, of Anjou, Queen, consort of Henry VI, King of England, 1430–1482. 5. York, Cecily, Duchess of, 1415–1495 6. Elizabeth, Queen, consort of Edward IV, King of England, 1437?–1492. 7. Anne, Queen, consort of Richard III, King of England, 1456–1485. 8. Margaret, of York, Duchess, consort of Charles the Bold, Duke of Burgundy, 1446–1503. 9. Elizabeth, Queen, consort of Henry VII, King of England, 1465–1503. 10. Beaufort, Margaret, Countess of Richmond and Derby, 1443–1509. I. Title.
DA250.G75 2013
942.04092'52—dc23

                                                2012044813
ISBN 978-0-465-06098-6 (paperback)
ISBN 978-0-465-03868-8 (paperback e-book)

10 9 8 7 6 5 4 3 2 1

CONTENTS

GLOSSARY OF SELECT NAMES

Anne: The name borne by **Anne Neville** (1456–1485), daughter to the Earl of Warwick, wife first to Edward of Lancaster and then to Richard III. Her mother was another Anne, the heiress Anne Beauchamp, Countess of Warwick (1426–1490). Anne was also the name given to the Duchess of Exeter (1439–1476), eldest daughter of Richard, Duke of York, and Cecily Neville, and sister to Edward IV and Richard III. Other noblewomen bearing the name include one of Cecily's sisters, who became Duchess of Buckingham; one of Edward IV's daughters; and Anne Mowbray, who was married in childhood to Edward's youngest son.

Beaufort: The family name of **Margaret Beaufort** (1443–1509), mother to Henry VII, and of the Dukes of Somerset, one of whom was Margaret's father. The Beaufort family also included Cardinal Beaufort, adviser to Henry VI.

Butler, Eleanor (?–1468): Born Eleanor Talbot, the woman who was later said to have been secretly married to Edward IV.

Catherine (or Katherine) of Aragon (1485–1536): Daughter of the Spanish monarchs Ferdinand of Aragon and Isabella of Castile, she was brought to England to marry Arthur, son to Henry VII and Elizabeth of York. She subsequently became the first wife of Arthur's brother Henry VIII.

Cecily Neville (or Cicely, 1415–1495): Matriarch of the York dynasty; wife to Richard, Duke of York; and mother to Edward IV and Richard III. The name was also shared by Cecily's granddaughter (Edward IV's daughter, 1469–1507).

Clarence, George, Duke of (1449–1478): Son to Cecily Neville and Richard, Duke of York. The second of their sons to survive into maturity, Clarence was famously executed on the orders of his brother Edward IV.

Dorset, Marquis of (1455–1501): The title bestowed on Thomas Grey, the eldest son of Elizabeth Woodville by her first husband, John Grey.

Edmund, Earl of Rutland (1443–1460): Second son to Richard, Duke of York, and Cecily Neville, killed young in battle.

Edward: This name was borne most importantly by Edward IV (1442–1483), eldest son to Richard, Duke of York, and Cecily Neville, and by his own eldest son (1470–1483?), the elder of the "Princes in the Tower," who would have reigned as Edward V. The name Edward was also bestowed, however, on the eldest sons both of Henry VI ("Edward of Lancaster," 1453–1471) and of Richard III ("Edward of Middleham," 1476?–1484). Both were, in their time, also Prince of Wales. The name Edward may have been considered particularly suitable for kings or prospective kings, perhaps because the last undisputed king of England had been the mighty Edward III. Henry VIII, in the next century, would also call his son Edward.

Elizabeth: The name borne by **Elizabeth Woodville** (1437–1492), queen to Edward IV, and by their daughter **Elizabeth of York** (1466–1503), who would marry Henry VII. It was also the name borne by Edward IV's sister (1444–1503), who became Duchess of Suffolk.

George: *See* **Clarence.**

Gloucester, Richard, Duke of: The title borne in early adulthood by the future Richard III.

Henry: The name borne by successive Lancastrian and later Tudor kings: Henry V (1387–1422), Henry VI (1421–1471), Henry VII ("Henry Tudor," 1457–1509), and Henry VIII (1491–1547).

Isabel Neville (1451–1476): Daughter to the Earl of Warwick and elder sister to Anne Neville; wife to George, Duke of Clarence.

Jacquetta Woodville (1415?–1472): Born Jacquetta of Luxembourg, mother of Elizabeth Woodville, wife to Sir Richard Woodville, subsequently created Earl Rivers. She had previously, by her first marriage, been Duchess of Bedford.

Katherine: The name borne by one of Edward IV's daughters, sometimes used for Catherine of Aragon and also given to Katherine Gordon, wife to the pretender Perkin Warbeck.

Lancaster: The name of one of the two great rival houses, the other being York. Sometimes identified by the symbol of the red rose.

Margaret: Besides Margaret Beaufort, the name was borne by **Margaret (or Marguerite) of Anjou** (1430–1482), queen to Henry VI and mother to Edward of Lancaster. Margaret (**Margaret "of Burgundy"** or "of York," 1446–1503) was also the name of the youngest daughter of Cecily Neville and Richard, Duke of York, sister to Edward IV and Richard III, who was married to Charles, Duke of Burgundy. Yet another Margaret was Margaret Tudor (1489–1541), eldest daughter of Elizabeth of York and Henry VII, who was married to the king of Scots.

Mary: The younger daughter of Henry VII and Elizabeth of York was Mary Tudor (1495/6–1533), who would be married to the king of France. The name also belonged to Mary of York (1467–1482), one of Elizabeth of York's sisters, as well as to Mary of Burgundy.

Neville: Name of the great northern family to which Cecily and Anne both belonged, Anne's father, Warwick, being the son of Cecily's brother Salisbury. The Neville family was a particularly extensive one, not all of whose members would necessarily be on the same side.

Paston: Name of the Norfolk gentry family whose letters, down the generations, provide an invaluable background to this period.

Richard: Name borne by Richard, Duke of York (1411–1460); by his youngest son, Richard III (1452–1485); and by the younger of the two "Princes in the Tower" (1473–1483?).

Somerset, Dukes of: John Beaufort, Earl (later first Duke) of Somerset (1404–1444), was Margaret Beaufort's father. He was succeeded by his brother Edmund Beaufort, second Duke of Somerset (1405–1455), who in turn was succeeded by his son Henry, the third duke (1436–1464). When Henry was executed, his younger brother, another Edmund (1439–1471), assumed the title of fourth duke, although it was never formally granted to him.

Stafford, Sir Henry (1425?–1471): Second husband of Margaret Beaufort, a son to the Duke of Buckingham.

Stanley, Thomas, Lord Stanley, Earl of Derby (1435?–1504): Third husband of Margaret Beaufort and a powerful magnate.

Suffolk, William de la Pole, Duke of (1396–1450): Favorite minister of Henry VI and Marguerite of Anjou. He was married to Alice Chaucer (1404–1475), a granddaughter of the poet Chaucer. William was succeeded by his son John (1442–1491), who, despite the family's Lancastrian affiliations, was married to Elizabeth, sister to Edward IV and Richard III, daughter of Richard, Duke of York, and Cecily Neville.

Tudor: Family name of Henry VII; his father, Edmund (1428–1456); and his uncle Jasper (1431–1495). The Welsh Tudors were a comparatively obscure family until Edmund's father, Owen (1400–1461), became the second husband of Henry V's widow.

Warwick, Richard Neville, Earl of (1428–1471): Known as the "Kingmaker" for the prominent role he played in placing the house of York on what had previously been a Lancastrian throne. He was the father of Isabel and Anne Neville, both of whom he married to York brothers.

Woodville (or Wydeville): The birth family of Elizabeth Woodville, Edward IV's queen. Notable among her numerous siblings was her eldest brother, Anthony (1440?–1483), who became Earl Rivers on his father's death.

York: As in Richard, Duke of. The second of the two great warring families, often identified by the symbol of a white rose.

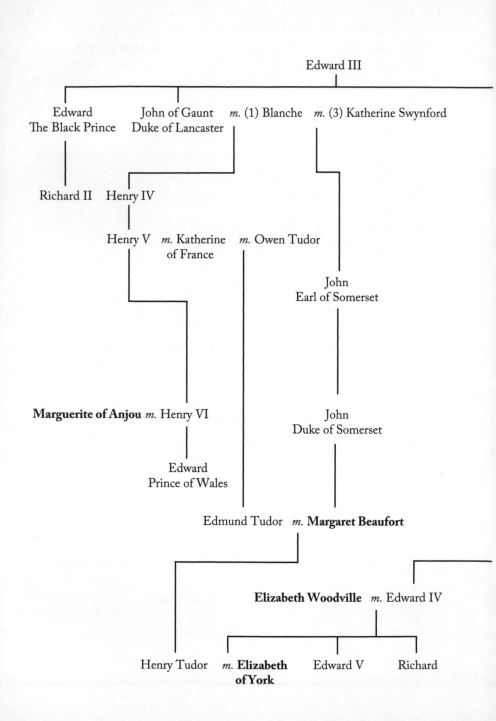

Edward III

Edward
The Black Prince

John of Gaunt
Duke of Lancaster

m. (1) Blanche

m. (3) Katherine Swynford

Richard II   Henry IV

Henry V   *m.* Katherine
of France

m. Owen Tudor

John
Earl of Somerset

Marguerite of Anjou *m.* Henry VI

John
Duke of Somerset

Edward
Prince of Wales

Edmund Tudor   *m.* **Margaret Beaufort**

Elizabeth Woodville   *m.* Edward IV

Henry Tudor   *m.* **Elizabeth
of York**

Edward V   Richard

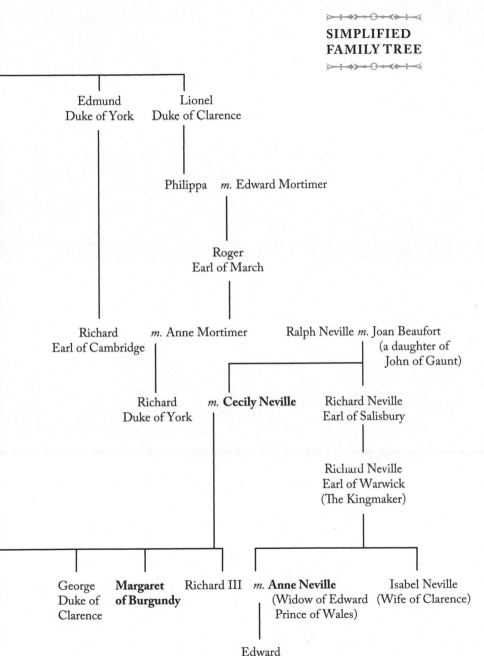

Edmund
Duke of York

Lionel
Duke of Clarence

Philippa *m.* Edward Mortimer

Roger
Earl of March

Richard
Earl of Cambridge

m. Anne Mortimer

Ralph Neville *m.* Joan Beaufort
(a daughter of
John of Gaunt)

Richard
Duke of York

m. **Cecily Neville**

Richard Neville
Earl of Salisbury

Richard Neville
Earl of Warwick
(The Kingmaker)

George
Duke of
Clarence

**Margaret
of Burgundy**

Richard III

m. **Anne Neville**
(Widow of Edward
Prince of Wales)

Isabel Neville
(Wife of Clarence)

Edward
of Middleham

England in the fifteenth century

PROLOGUE

February 1503

She had died on her thirty-seventh birthday, and the figure thirty-seven would be reiterated throughout the ceremony: thirty-seven virgins dressed in white linen, wreathed in the Tudor colors of green and white, stationed along the great market street of Cheapside holding burning tapers, thirty-seven palls of rich cloth to be draped across the effigy. The king's orders specified that two hundred poor people in the procession from the Tower of London through the City to Westminster Abbey should each carry a "weighty torch," the flames flickering wanly in the February day.

It was a public display of grief to match that almost five hundred years later when another wildly popular royal bride was carried to her grave (another who died in her thirty-seventh year—another people's princess). Elizabeth of York had been one of London's own. Her mother, Elizabeth Woodville, had been the first English-born queen consort for more than three centuries, and if she had been in other ways a figure of scandal, in the person of her less controversial daughter that heritage had come into its own. Elizabeth of York was a domestic queen, whose expenses reveal a woman of careful practicality: she paid out money for presents given her of apples and of woodcocks and bought silk ribbons for her girdles, while thriftily she had repairs made to a velvet gown. She had been a family queen, who rewarded her son's schoolmaster, bought household hardware for her newly married daughter, and tried to keep an eye out for her sisters and their families. The trappings of the hearse showed she was a queen who'd died in childbed, a fate feared by almost every woman in the fifteenth century.

She had been, too, a significant queen: the white rose of York who married red Lancaster in the person of Henry Tudor, ending the battles over the crown. Double Tudor roses, whose red petals firmly encircled the white, were carved all over the chapel where she would finally be laid to rest. Indeed, the very presence of foreign worthies at her funeral (for not even grief could get in the way of diplomacy) showed that by 1503, it was accepted the Tudors were here to stay.

The Spanish ambassador had reported that the queen was "beloved because she was powerless," and many thought she had been sidelined by her husband, Henry. But the anonymous manuscript that provides a detailed record of her funeral tells a different tale. It describes how on her death, Henry "took with him certain of his secretest, and privately departed to a solitary place to pass his sorrows and would no man should resort to him." Henry left behind orders for bells to be rung, and church services said, throughout the land. The loss of his queen was "as heavy and dolorous to the King's Highness as hath been seen or heard of." It was the end of the partnership that had given birth to the Tudor dynasty.

Elizabeth had been at the Tower when she "travailed of child suddenly" and was there delivered on Candelmas Day of a baby daughter who may have come prematurely. The records of her own Privy Purse expenses show boatmen, guides, horses sent suddenly to summon a doctor from the country, linen purchased to swaddle a new baby who would outlive her mother by only days. On February 11, Elizabeth— "the most gracious and virtuous princess the Queen"—died, unexpectedly, a grievous loss not only to her husband but also to her country.

Her corpse was carried to the Tower's own church, to lay there for eleven days. Mourning garments were hastily ordered for her ladies, and while these were being prepared they put on their "most sad and simplest" clothes. Elizabeth's body would, immediately after death, have been disemboweled; prepared with spices, balm, and rose water; and tightly wrapped in waxed cloth, before the body was placed in a wooden chest, covered in black and white velvet with a cross of white damask. On the Sunday night, the body was ready for removal to the chapel. The queen's sister Lady Katherine Courtenay acted as chief mourner at the requiem mass, a ritual repeated daily as long as the body lay in the Tower.

It was Wednesday, February 22, when the coffin was placed on a bier covered in black velvet and drawn by six horses, themselves decked in black. The cushions must have helped secure the coffin in place, and helped the gentlemen ushers who knelt, braced against the horses' motion, at either end of the moving construction. Above the coffin was an effigy of the queen, clothed in "the very Robes of Estate," with her hair about her shoulders and her scepter in her right hand. The funeral effigy symbolized the dual nature of Elizabeth's royal personage: the immortal office and the mortal body.

The banners at the corners of the bier were painted on a white background, to show this was the funeral of a woman who died in childbed, while behind the bier came the ladies of honor, each mounted on a palfrey, the chariots bearing other senior ladies, a throng of servants, and citizens of London. In front of the bier went the choirs and the English and foreign male dignitaries. Companies of foreign merchants—French, Spanish, Venetian—bearing their country's arms stood among the craft guilds and fellowships of London, whose members held literally thousands of torches along the way. Bells rang, choirs sang, and incense scented the cold air from each parish church as the body passed by, from the Tower to Temple Bar, to Charing Cross and then on to Westminster, the same route that had been taken for Elizabeth's coronation.

In the churchyard of St. Margaret's, where the peers assumed their robes, the body was once again censed and then borne into the abbey shoulder high for the first of many more religious services. Elizabeth rested for the duration of the Dirige—conducted by the abbot and nine bishops—and then Lady Katherine, escorted by her nephew the Marquis of Dorset and by the Earl of Derby, led the lords and the ladies to a supper of fish in the Queen's Great Chamber. Watched that night in the abbey by her ladies and men of all ranks, lit by hundreds more heavy tapers, Elizabeth's corpse waited for the next day. Body and soul could not be left unprotected through the dark night hours: each one of those tapers might serve to drive a demon away.

The long list of services offered for the dead woman reflects the importance of church rites in the daily life of the fifteenth century. Lauds were said at six the next morning, followed by Our Lady's Mass at seven, the Mass of the Trinity, and then the requiem mass. As the ceremony moved toward its close, the mourners, in order of precedence, laid more lengths of costly fabric across the effigy. The blue and green, the bright strands of metal in the weave, would have stood out against the funereal scene. After the sermon, the ladies left for men to do the physical work of burial. The queen's chamberlain and ushers broke their staves of office and cast them into the grave with ritual tears, in token that their service to Elizabeth of York was ended. Perhaps the emotion was real—Elizabeth had been a gentle mistress and loyal to those who served her and her family.

The manuscript description of Elizabeth's funeral details a lavish distribution of alms after the funeral: money given to "bed-rid folks, lazars, blind folks," to churches, to hospitals, to charitable foundations. And, all in all, with more than nine thousand yards of black cloth coming out of the great wardrobe, King Henry handed out "the greatest livery of black gowns that ever was seen in our day." Elizabeth's funeral had cost some three thousand pounds, twice that of her father's and five times that of her eldest son's. Henry must indeed have loved her, even though he had taken great pains to deny that her bloodline was the source of his political legitimacy.

As was customary for a female corpse, the funeral had been a predominantly female ceremony—partly because the one mourned was a woman, and partly because concern for the dead was always first a female duty. But those women who were not there are almost as interesting as those who were. Queen Elizabeth was survived by four of her sisters, though only two are recorded as having been present. Absent also were Elizabeth's young daughters, her husband, and her surviving son, Prince Henry. The royal family did not attend funerals; it was as though this most carefully protected family in the country feared that death itself might prove contagious.

Elizabeth's mother-in-law, Lady Margaret Beaufort, was likewise absent, though her husband, Thomas Stanley, Earl of Derby, had ridden immediately ahead of the bier and had escorted Lady Katherine to the Westminster supper. Perhaps Margaret was with the king, the son she adored, to comfort him in privacy. Perhaps, simply, she was at her home of Collyweston in Northamptonshire, having been unable to journey so fast along the sodden winter roads. Or perhaps it was that My Lady the King's Mother had always claimed status almost equal to that of the queen herself. If royalty did not attend funerals, then neither would she.

Rather than presenting herself at the funeral, Margaret occupied herself in laying down a set of ordinances for royal mourning to be used for any future deaths—prescribing precisely the court's costume and comportment, "apparel for princesses and great estates," moving down the scale in their order. A queen was to wear a surcoat with a train before and behind; the king's mother (though Margaret was technically only a countess) was "to wear in every thing like to the queen."

It was said, too often for it to be wholly a lie, that Margaret's concern for rank and dominance came between her and Elizabeth; if so, they were not the only mother- and daughter-in-law to have had problems in our story. Elizabeth's own mother, Elizabeth Woodville—the beautiful widow who had captured the heart of King Edward IV—had been bitterly resented by Edward's mother, Cecily Neville. Mother also to Richard III, Cecily had been the matriarch of the Yorkist clan, just as Margaret Beaufort was a leader of the Lancastrian. Both were mothers of kings who could never quite forget that Fortune had snatched their own queen's crowns away. Cecily's youngest daughter, Margaret, was living in Burgundy, but as the sister of two Yorkist monarchs, her determination to take a hand in the affairs of England had never quite disappeared.

Poor Anne Neville, Richard III's wife, had been too shadowy a figure to have quarreled with her mother-in-law. But the seventh woman in our story had quarreled with half the world and—in political terms, at least—had been the most potent of all the ghosts hovering around Elizabeth of York's head as she had lain awaiting burial. This was Marguerite of Anjou, Henry VI's wife and the Lancastrian queen under whose determined rule the "Wars of the Roses," the civil wars that reshaped British history in the mid- to late fifteenth century, first got under way.

The events that caused the Wars of the Roses and finally brought into being the Tudor dynasty were above all a family saga—a

"Cousins' War," as the conflict is also known.* Indeed, although the white rose was indeed a popular symbol for the house of York, one line of descendants from the ruling Plantagenet family, the red rose was never widely identified with their opponents in the house of Lancaster until the moment when Henry VII, poised to take over the country, sought an appropriate and appealing symbol. And in some ways, moreover, the attractive iconography of the two roses does the real history a disservice, encouraging us to look no further than the idea of a neat two-party, York-Lancaster divide.

The "Cousins' War" is a more accurate name, since all the protagonists were bound together by an infinite number of ties. And rather than a series of clear-cut disputes, these conflicts should really be seen in terms of politics, in all its many shades of gray, and with its secret alliances, queasy coalitions, public spin and private qualms, and marriages of convenience in the political as well as the literal senses. It was an era in which positions were under constant readjustment and alliances changed from day to day.

One affiliation, however, was shared on both sides of the struggle. Both houses claimed descent from the last undisputed king of England, who when the wars erupted had been dead for nearly eighty years. He had been the powerful and prolific Edward III, one of the long line of Plantagenet kings who had ruled England since the Norman Conquest. But in 1377 Edward was succeeded by his grandson (the son of his dead eldest son), the ten-year-old Richard II. Richard was deposed in 1399 by his cousin, Shakespeare's "Bolingbroke," who became Henry IV and was succeeded by his son Henry V, who in turn was succeeded by his son, Henry VI. This so-called Lancastrian line (Henry IV's father, John of Gaunt, had been created Duke of Lancaster) would successfully hold the throne for more than a half century.

There had, however, been an alternative line of succession lowering from the wings, in the shape of the Yorkists—descended, like the Lan-

---

*The name "Wars of the Roses" is variously credited to historian David Hume in the eighteenth century and novelist Sir Walter Scott in the nineteenth.

castrians, from Edward III's younger sons. The Yorkists had arguably a better claim than the Lancastrians (depending on how you felt about a woman's ability to transmit rights to the throne), since while the Lancastrian progenitor, John of Gaunt, had only been Edward's third son, the Yorkists were descended in the female line from his second son, Lionel, as well as in the male line from his fourth son, Edmund. From the beginning, then, the dispute between the Lancastrians and Yorkists hinged as much upon the women in both families—mothers, daughters, sisters, and wives—as it did upon the men who vied for the throne.

The circle of women behind the conflicts and resolutions of the late fifteenth century was locked into a web of loyalty and betrayal as intimate and emotional as that of any other domestic drama, albeit that in this dispute—almost literally a game of thrones—a kingdom was at stake. The business of their lives was power, their sons and husbands the currency. The machinations were those you might see in the Mafia story *The Sopranos,* the stark events worthy of Greek tragedy. Cecily Neville had to come to terms with the fact that her son Edward IV had ordered the execution of his brother George, Duke of Clarence, and the suspicion that her other son, Richard III, had murdered his nephews, the so-called Princes in the Tower. Elizabeth Woodville is supposed to have sent her daughters to make merry at Richard III's court while knowing that he had murdered her sons, those same princes. Elizabeth of York, as the decisive battle of Bosworth unfolded, could only await the results of what would prove a fight to the death between the man some say she had incestuously loved—her uncle Richard III—and the man she would in the end marry, Henry VII.

The second half of the fifteenth century is, in the tales of conflicted maternity and monstrous births, alive with female energy. Yet the lives of the last Plantagenet women remain a subject comparatively unexplored by historians. The events of this turbulent time are usually described in terms of men, under a patriarchal assumption as easy as that which saw Margaret Beaufort give up her own blood right to the throne in favor of her son, Henry, or which saw Anne Neville, an important heiress, passed from one royal family to the other as though she were as insentient an object as any other piece of property.

Of the seven women who form the backbone of this book, the majority have already been the subject of at least one biographical study, although these are still fewer than the drama of their lives might justify, and much of the work has tended to be academic in intent. (Popular history has traditionally preferred to deal in certainties that, for this period and this subject, tend to be in short supply.)

The aim of this book, unlike those that have come before it, is to interweave these women's individual stories and thereby trace the connections between them—connections that sometimes ran counter to the allegiances established by their men—and demonstrate the ways in which the patterns of their lives often echoed each other. It is also to attempt to understand their daily reality, to see what these women saw and heard (and read, smelled, and even tasted): the bruised feel of velvet under the fingertip, or the silken muzzle of a hunting dog; the discomfort of furred ceremonial robes on a scorching day, a girl's ability to lose herself in reading a romantic story.

These women and their contemporaries left many clues about their world: the stamping feet of the "maid that came out of Spain" (as the queen's list of expenses put it) and danced before Elizabeth of York, and the roughened hands of Mariona, the laundress listed in Marguerite of Anjou's accounts who kept the queen's personal linen clean; the tales of Guenivere and Lancelot, popularized in these very years by a man who knew these women; the ideal of the virginal saints whose lives they studied so devotedly. To ignore these things is to treat history as disaster tourism—to focus (and admittedly, in the earlier years it sometimes seems inevitable) so exclusively on the wild roller-coaster ride of events as to get only a distorted picture, stripped of the context of daily problems and pleasures that must have altered the impact of the events to some degree.

The attempt to tell the story of these years through women is beset with difficulties, greater even than those that face other historians of the notoriously challenging later fifteenth century. To insist that the women were equal players with the men, on the same stage, is to run the risk of claiming more than the facts can bear, but the only alternative might seem to be to accept the deal the women themselves apparently made (and generations of historians have followed) and chronicle them only through those men. We have to find some way of negotiating this rocky terrain, where reliance on the few known public facts seems almost to get in the way.

We have to acknowledge the profound difference between their ideas and our own, and then, conversely, admit emotions we recognize: Elizabeth of York's frantic desire to find a place in the world, Margaret Beaufort's obsessive love for her son. We have to borrow from our own emotional reality, our own understanding of the world, to imagine how it felt to be flung quite as abruptly as these women were, up to the top point of the turn of Fortune's Wheel, and then back down again, to take the wearying list of battles and grasp, emotionally, that although the tactics of the field are not the subject of this book, each one meant the worst loss of all for wives, daughters, mothers—women whose destinies would be decided, and perhaps unthinkably altered, in an arena they were not allowed even to enter. Only then can we attempt to approach these women and these years in another way.

The women of the Cousins' War should be legends, their names bywords. In a time not only of terror but of opportunity as well, the actions of these women would ultimately prove to matter as much as the battles in which cousin fought cousin. It had been the alliances and ambitions of these women that helped get that new world under way.

They were the mothers and midwives of the Tudor dynasty—of modern England, you might say. The Tudors would rule England throughout the sixteenth century, and the reigns of monarchs like Henry VIII and his daughter Elizabeth I would see not only a great flowering of art and literature, adventures in trade and exploration, and the establishment of the Protestant religion in the country, but also a new sense of national identity.

The Tudor age would also, of course, see—in Elizabeth I and her sister Mary—the first women to rule England, and Elizabeth in particular is one of the best-known characters in history. But even the Tudor wives of the early sixteenth century have a much higher profile than the Plantagenets in popular currency. Yet the stories of these other, earlier, figures are even more dramatic, riper with possibility—if we could but find the right way to tap it. For all that these women have often been hidden from history, it is possible to bring them center stage, as central as was Elizabeth of York, that February day.

NOTE ON NAMES

Of the seven women whose stories I explore, the fashion of the times means that two are called Elizabeth and three Margaret. I have therefore referred to the York princess who married the ruler of Burgundy as Margaret "of Burgundy," while giving Margaret of Anjou the French appellation she herself continued sometimes to use after marriage—Marguerite. The family originally spelled as "Wydeville" has been given its more familiar appellation of "Woodville," and other spellings and forms have sometimes been modernized. The quotations at the top of each chapter have been drawn from Shakespeare's history plays.

PART I

1445–1460
Lancaster

FATAL MARRIAGE

O peers of England, shameful is this league,
Fatal this marriage, cancelling your fame

HENRY VI, PART 2, 1.1

I t was no way for a queen to enter her new country, unceremoniously carried ashore as though she were a piece of baggage—least of all a queen who planned to make her mark. In her later courage and conviction, her energy and her ruthlessness, Marguerite of Anjou would be in part what the times and the circumstances of her life in England had made her. But no doubt as she first set foot on the English shore on April 9, 1445, her character and ambition were already there to see.

The ship that brought her across the Channel, the *Cock John*, had been blown off its expected course and so battered by storms as to have lost both its masts. Marguerite arrived, as her new husband, Henry VI, put it in a letter, "sick of ye labour and indisposition of ye sea." Small wonder that the Marquess of Suffolk, the English peer sent to escort her, had to carry the seasick fifteen-year-old ashore. The people of Porchester, trying gallantly to provide a royal welcome, had heaped carpets on the beach, where the chilly April waves clawed and rattled at the pebbles, but Marguerite's first shaky steps on English soil took her no farther than a nearby cottage, where she fainted. From there she was carried to a local convent to be nursed, making her first English impressions ones of sickrooms and austerity.

This would be the woman Shakespeare, in *Henry VI, Part 3*, famously dubbed the "she-wolf" of France, her "tiger's heart wrapped in a woman's hide." Italian chronicler Polydore Vergil, by contrast, would look back on her as "imbued with a high courage above the nature of her sex . . . a woman of sufficient forecast, very desirous of renown, full of policy, counsel, comely behaviour, and all manly qualities." But then Vergil was writing for the Tudor king Henry VII, sprung of Lancastrian stock, and he would naturally try to praise the wife of the last Lancastrian king, the woman who would, in her later years, fight so hard for the Lancastrian cause. Marguerite was, from the beginning, a controversial queen. Few queens of England have so divided opinion; few have suffered more from the propaganda of their enemies.

Marguerite of Anjou was niece by marriage to the French king Charles VII, her own father, René, having been described as a man of many crowns but no kingdoms. He claimed the thrones of Naples, Sicily, Jerusalem, and Hungary as well as the duchy of Anjou in the region of the Loire Valley, titles so empty, however, that early in the 1440s he had settled in France, his brother-in-law's territory. At the beginning of 1444, the English suggested a truce in the seemingly endless conflict between England and France known as the Hundred Years' War, the temporary peace to be cemented by a French bride for England's young king, Henry VI. Unwilling to commit his own daughters, Charles had proffered Marguerite as pledge. Many royal marriages were made to seal a peace with an enemy, the youthful bride as passive a potential victim as any princess of story. But in this case, the deal making was particularly edgy.

In the hopes of finally ending the long hostilities, the mild-mannered Henry VI—so unfitting a son, many thought, to Henry V, the hero of Agincourt—had agreed not only to take his French bride virtually without dowry but also to cede allegiance of the territories Anjou and Maine in France, which the English had long occupied. Suffolk, as England's negotiator, knew how unpopular this would be, but when he had sent home for instructions after receiving the French demands, Henry had sent word to accept them, a decision with which many of his advisers would disagree. Now, the weather seemed to echo English sentiment about the union. The thunder and lightning that greeted Marguerite's arrival had been a repeated trope in the arrival of foreign royal brides, a disproportionate number of whom seem to have had a stormy passage across the sea. All the same, it seemed an ominous sign to contemporaries.

Marguerite had been ill since she set out from Paris several weeks before, progressing slowly toward the coast while distributing Lenten alms, making propitiatory offerings at each church where she heard mass, dining with dignitaries, and saying good-bye one by one to her relations along the way. Slowly, though, in the days after her arrival in England, she recovered her health in a series of Sussex convents, amid the sounds and scents of the church's rituals, with all their reassuring familiarity. On April 10, the records of the royal finances show a payment of 69s 2d* to one "Master Francisco, the Queen's physician," who provided "divers aromatic confections, particularly and specially purchased by him, and privately made into medicine for the preservation of the health of the said lady."

If Suffolk's first concern had been to find a convent where Marguerite could be nursed, his second was to summon a London dressmaker to attend to her, before the English nobility caught sight of her shabby clothes. Again, the financial records tell the tale: 20s, on April 15, to one Margaret Chamberlayne, dressmaker, or "tyre maker," as it was then phrased. Among the various complaints the English were preparing to make of their new queen, one would be her poverty.**

Before Marguerite's party set out toward the capital, there was time for something a little more courtly, if one Italian contemporary, writing to the Duchess of Milan three years later, was to be believed. An

---

*The letter *s* was used for shillings and the letter *d* for pennies.

**A more generous payment of 3l 6s 4d was made to John Fouke, perhaps understandably. The galleyman was ordered to take charge of one of Marguerite's wedding presents—a lion.

Englishman had told him that when the queen landed in England, the king had secretly taken Marguerite a letter, having first dressed himself as a squire. "While the queen read the letter the king took stock of her," the correspondent wrote, "saying that a woman may be seen very well when she reads a letter, and the queen never found out it was the king because she was so engrossed in reading the letter, and she never looked at the king in his squire's dress, who remained on his knees all the time."

It was the same trick Henry VIII would play on Anne of Cleves almost a century later, a game from the Continental tradition of chivalry. But this time it ended more happily. When Marguerite, afterward, was told of the pretense, she was vexed at having paid the supposed squire no attention. But she must at least have reflected that there was nothing noticeably repulsive about her twenty-three-year-old bridegroom, and nothing intimidating, either. And Henry VI, if the Milanese writer is to be believed, saw "a most handsome woman, though somewhat dark"—and not, the Milanese tactfully assured his duchess, "so beautiful as your Serenity." (The Englishman, he reported, "told me that his mistress was wise and charitable, and your Serenity has the reputation of being equally wise and more charitable. He said that his queen had an income of 80,000 gold crowns.")

At the French court Marguerite had already acquitted herself well enough to win an admirer in the courtly tradition, Pierre de Brézé, to carry her colors at the joust and to move the Burgundian chronicler Barante to write that she "was already renowned in France for her beauty and wit and her lofty spirit of courage." The beauty conventionally attributed to queens features in the scene when Shakespeare's Marguerite first meets Henry VI; the lofty spirit, on the other hand, was to prove a difficulty in the years ahead. Vergil too wrote that Marguerite exceeded others of her time "as well in beauty as wisdom," and though it is usually hard to guess real looks from medieval portraiture, it is hard not to read determination and self-will in the swelling brow and prominent nose of the medallion of Marguerite of Anjou by Pietro di Milano.

The royal couple officially met five days after Marguerite had landed and had their marriage formalized just over a week later in Titchfield Abbey. The first meeting failed to reveal either the dangerous milkiness in the man or the capacity for violence in the young woman, traits that would eventually shape their respective lives and legacies. But the first of the problems they would face was—as Marguerite moved toward London—spelled out in the very festivities.

Marguerite's queenship would be dogged by problems of faction within the English court and by her own controversial relationship with France, and both were reflected in the ceremonies that ushered her into London. Her impoverished father had at least persuaded the clergy of Anjou to provide for a white satin wedding dress embroidered with silver and gold marguerites and to buy violet and crimson cloth of gold and 120 pelts of white fur to edge her robes. As she approached the city, she was met outside London on Blackheath by Henry's uncle Humfrey, the Duke of Gloucester, with five hundred of his retainers and conducted to his Greenwich Palace of Placentia—a reception doubtless the more effulgent for the fact that he had opposed the marriage, seeing no advantage for England in it.

Her entry into London on May 28, having rested the night before at the Tower of London, was all it should be: nineteen chariots of ladies and their gentlewomen to accompany her, the conduits running with wine white and red, and a coronal of "gold rich pearls and precious stones" on the bride's head. The livery companies of the City turned out to meet her resplendent in blue robes, with a red hood, and the council had ordered the inspection of roofs along the way, anticipating that the crowds would climb onto them to see the new queen pass by. The surviving documentation details a truly royal provision of luxury goods for Marguerite's welcome. A letter from the king to his treasurer orders up "such things as our right entirely Well-beloved Wife the Queen must necessarily have for the Solemnity of her Coronation," including a pectoral of gold garnished with rubies, pearls, and diamonds; safe conduct for two Scotsmen and their sixteen servants, "with their gold and silver in bars and wallets"; a present of ten pounds each to five minstrels of the king of Sicily (the nominal title of Marguerite's father) "who lately came to England to witness the state and grand solemnity on the day of the Queen's coronation"; and twenty marks' reward to one William Flour of London, goldsmith, "because the said Lord the King stayed in the house of the said William on the day that Queen Margaret, his consort, set out from the Tower."

The cost of the marriage was reckoned at an exorbitant fifty-five hundred pounds. All the same, Marguerite had had to pawn her silver plate at Rouen, to pay her sailors' wages, and as details of the marriage deal began to leak out, the English would feel justified in complaining they had bought "a queen not worth ten marks." In the years ahead, they would discover something more: that they had a queen who—for better or worse—would try to rewrite the rules, and indeed the whole royal story.

As Marguerite rode into her new capital of London, the pageantry with which she was greeted spelled out her duty. In the first pageant that greeted her, to the south side of London Bridge, the actor impersonating the figure Peace prophesied hopefully that, through Marguerite's "grace and high benignity,"

Twixt the realms two, England and France
Peace shall approach, rest and unite,
Mars set aside, with all his cruelty.

This was a weight of expectation placed on many a foreign royal bride. Earlier in the century, the famous Frenchwoman Christine de Pizan had written in *The Treasury* [or *Treasure*] *of the City of Ladies* that women, being by nature "more gentle and circumspect," could be the best means of pacifying men: "Queens and princesses have greatly benefitted this world by bringing about peace between enemies, between princes and their barons, or between rebellious subjects and their lords," just as, after all, the queen of heaven, Mary, interceded for sinners. Marguerite would be neither the first nor the last such princess to find herself uncomfortably placed between the needs of her adopted and her natal countries. The Hundred Years' War had been a conflict of extraordinary bitterness, which Marguerite, by her very presence as a living symbol, was supposed to soothe. It would have been a position of terrifying responsibility.

Luckily—or perhaps unluckily—for Marguerite, she responded eagerly (if sometimes misguidedly) to such demands. Her kinsman the Duke of Orléans wrote that Marguerite seemed as if "formed by Heaven to supply her royal husband the qualities which he required in order to become a great king." But the English expectations of a queen were not necessarily those of a Frenchman. Marguerite's female forebears had taken an active role in governing; her mother, Isabelle of Lorraine, had run the family affairs while René of Anjou spent long years away on military operations or in captivity. Her grandmother Yolande of Aragon, in whose care she spent many of her formative years, had acted as regent for her eldest son, Marguerite's uncle, and been one of the chief promoters of Joan of Arc, who had helped sweep the French Dauphin, the heir apparent, to victory against the English in their long war against the French. ("I have not raised this [child] . . . for you to let him die . . . to send him mad . . . or to make him English," Yolande had written, when the Dauphin's own mother tried to regain possession of the boy.) The English, by contrast, expected their queens to take a more passive role. Uncomfortable memories still lingered of Edward II's wife, Isabella, little more than a century before, that other "she-wolf of France" (as she was later dubbed, and as Marguerite too would become known), who was accused of having murdered her husband to take power with her lover.

Had Marguerite's new husband been a strong king, the memories might never have surfaced—but Henry showed neither inclination nor ability for the role he was called to play. Henry VI had been crowned while in his cradle and had grown up a titular king under the influence of his elderly male relatives. Perhaps that had taught him, oddly, to equate kingship with passivity. As Henry matured in years, he still, at twenty-three, showed no aptitude for taking the reins of government himself.

There was and is considerable debate over what, if anything, was actually wrong with Henry. Some contemporaries (the reports differ wildly) described him as both personable and scholarly; others suggest he may have been simple-minded or inherited a streak of insanity. He was certainly notably pious and prudish—a papal envoy described him as more like a monk than a king—and seemed reluctant to make any kind of decision or take any lead. He was the last man on earth, in other words, who should rule what was already a turbulent country. Shakespeare, at the end of *Henry VI, Part 2*, vividly dramatizes the moment at which the new Henry V, this Henry's father, moves from irresponsible princedom to the harsh realities of kingship. There was, however, no sign of Henry VI's reaching a similar maturity—a situation that left Marguerite herself to confront the challenges of monarchy.

It can be difficult to get a picture of Marguerite, or her husband, in the first few years of their marriage. Anything written about them later is colored by hindsight, and the early days of Marguerite's career—any picture of her daily life—tend to be lost in the urgent clamor of events just ahead. There is no reason to doubt, however, that when she entered London, she had expected to enjoy a normal queenship, albeit one cast in perhaps slightly more active a mode than the English were wont to see. Though her husband's finances may have been depleted, though English manners might not compare to those across the Channel, her life must at first have been one of pleasant indulgence.

Christine de Pizan in her *Treasury* gives a vivid picture of life for a lady at the top end of the social tree in a morality tale of an idle and prideful lady: "The princess or great lady awaking in the morning from sleep finds herself lying in her bed between soft, smooth sheets, surrounded by rich luxury, with every possible bodily comfort, and ladies and maids-in-waiting at hand to run to her if she sighs ever so slightly, ready on bended knee to provide service or obey orders at her word." Marguerite surely enjoyed the same comforts, and more. The list of estates granted to her as part of her dower entitlement lasts for pages, an evocative litany:

> To be had, held and kept of the said Consort of Henry, all the appointed Castles, Honours, Towns, Domains, Manors, Wapentaches, Bales, county estates, sites of France, carriages, landed farms, renewed yearly, the lands, houses, possessions and other things promised, with all their members and dependencies, together with the lands of the Military, Ecclesiastic advocacies, Abbotcies, Priories, Deaneries, Colleges, Capellaries, singing academies, Hospitals, and of other religious houses, by wards, marriages, reliefs, food, iron, merchandize, liberties, free customs, franchise, royalties, fees of honour . . . forests, chaises, parks, woods, meadows, fields, pastures, warrens, vivaries, ponds, fish waters, mills, mulberry trees, fig trees.

It is the same genial picture of a queen's life that can be seen in a tapestry that may have been commissioned for Marguerite's wedding. There are *M*s woven into the horses' bridles and marguerites (daisies), her personal symbol, sported by some of the ladies. It depicts a hunting scene bedecked with flowers and foliage, the ladies in their furred gowns, hawk on wrist, with the characteristic headdress, a roll of jeweled and decorated fabric pecking down over the brow and rising behind the head. Hunting along with "boating on the river," dancing, and "meandering" in the garden were all recreations allowed by Christine de Pizan in a day otherwise devoted to the tasks of governance (if relevant), to religious duties, and to charity. Visiting the poor and sick, "touching them and gently comforting them," as de Pizan wrote, sounds much like the comportment of modern royalty, "for the poor feel especially comforted and prefer the kind word, the visit, and the attention of the great and powerful personage over anything else." Letters written by Marguerite show her asking the archbishop of Canterbury to treat a poor widow with "tenderness and favour" and seeking alms for two other paupers, "poor creatures and of virtuous conversation."

But Marguerite had been reared in an idea of queenship that went beyond simple luxury and Christian charity. Not only were there the examples set by her mother and grandmother, but her father, René, was also one of the century's leading exponents of the chivalric tradition. He was more besotted even than the majority of his contemporaries with that great fantasy of the age, the Arthurian stories, and his example surely influenced his daughter. (Indeed, when Thomas Malory wrote his English version of the tales, the *Morte d'Arthur*, completed in 1470, his portrayal of Queen Guenivere may have been influenced by Marguerite to some degree.) It may have been on the occasion of Marguerite's betrothal that René organized a tournament with knights dressed up as Round Table heroes and a wooden castle named after Sir Lancelot's castle of Joyeuse Garde. A bound volume of Arthurian romances was presented to the bride.

René was the author not only of a widely translated book on the perfect management of the tournament, but also of the achingly romantic *Livre du coeur d'amour épris* (Book of the heart as love's captive). René may also have been the illustrator, and the book's images of the figure of Hope—who repeatedly saves the hero—were possibly modeled on Marguerite. Queens in the Arthurian and other chivalric legends were active and sometimes ambiguous creatures. Ceremonious consorts and arbiters of behavior, they were also capable of dramatic and sometimes destructive action; it was Guenivere, after all, who brought down Camelot.

The two visions of queenship came together in the *Shrewsbury* [or *Talbot*] *Book* presented to Marguerite on the occasion of her marriage by John Talbot, Earl of Shrewsbury. Talbot was one of England's most renowned military commanders, though he would play comparatively little part in the political tussles ahead. On the book's illuminated title page, Henry and Marguerite are seated crowned and hand in hand, her purple cloak fastened with bands of gold and jewels, the blue ceiling painted with gold stars behind her. At her feet kneels Talbot, presenting his book, which she graciously accepts, the faintest hint of a smile lurking under her red-gold hair. All around are exquisite depictions of the daisy, Marguerite's personal symbol. The image is at once benign and stately, an idealized picture of monarchy; the facing page, more controversially, traces Henry VI's genealogical claim to be king of France as well as of England. An anthology of Arthurian and other romances, poems, and manuals of chivalry, the book also includes Christine de Pizan's treatise on the art of warfare and one on the art of government—a textbook, if you like, not only on how to conduct your emotional life, but on how to run a country as well.

Despite the heavy responsibilities weighing on Marguerite, her daily life was lived in the lap of luxury. Henry had had his palaces revamped for his bride—the queen's apartments must have fallen out of use before he came of age. Marguerite employed a large household and paid them handsomely, exploiting all the financial opportunities open to a queen in order to allow her to do so. Regulations for a queen's household drawn up in the year of her arrival listed 66 positions, from a countess as senior lady with her own staff down to two launderers, from a chamberlain down to three chaplains, three carvers, and a secretary. She had a personal gardener, pages of the beds and of the bakery, and of course squires. Less than ten years later, the council had to suggest that the queen's household be cut *down* to 120.

Marguerite's personal staff was extensive, composed largely of Englishmen and -women. She had brought no relations and few French attendants with her, something that eliminated one potential source of controversy. (There had been trouble two hundred years before, for example, when too many of the followers of Eleanor of Provence, queen consort of King Henry III, were given generous pensions and her uncles given too much prominence in the country.) But what at first looked like a blessing meant only that she would attach herself to new English advisers, ardently and unwisely.

On the journey from France, Marguerite had learned to trust her escort, Suffolk, the preeminent noble that Burgundian chronicler Georges Chastellain called England's "second king." She never saw any reason to change her mind—or to hide her feelings of affection for the older man. Suffolk, for his part, perhaps from a mixture of genuine admiration and policy, flattered and encouraged the young queen, even writing courtly verses playing on her name, the marguerite, or daisy:

> *For wit thee well, it is a paradise*
> *To see this flower when it begins to spread*
> *With colours fresh enewed, white and red.*

Although by the standards of courtly love poetry this was tame stuff, there were inevitably those who suggested there was something more than friendliness between the girl in her teens and the man in his late forties— and those who saw in the ostensible betrayal of England's king the betrayal of England as a country. More than a century later, the scandalous rumors were still sufficiently in currency that Shakespeare has Suffolk, on their first meeting in France, falling for Marguerite's beauty before he learns her identity. But even Shakespeare's Suffolk mixes self-interest with sexual attraction, hoping to rule the king through Marguerite, and in reality the queen had become notably close not only to the duke but also to his wife the duchess (born Alice Chaucer, granddaughter of the poet), which surely argues against an affair.

Suffolk had not been the only man among the king's advisers to support the French marriage. It also had the support of Cardinal

Beaufort, the king's great-uncle and one of the men who had governed the country before he came of age. Beaufort shared Suffolk's personal regard for Marguerite, and she also enjoyed the support of the cardinal's relatives, including the more immediate family of another soon-to-be-prominent Lancastrian, the young Margaret Beaufort.

Other powerful figures, however, had been against the marriage—notably the Duke of Gloucester, the king's uncle, who had welcomed Marguerite so lavishly along her route to London. In many ways, his was the voice of the Francophobe English people.

All too soon, within weeks of Marguerite's arrival and coronation, the question of England's ceding Maine and Anjou in France came to a head. As word of Henry's secret, and as yet unfulfilled, promise leaked out, angry talk centered on the rumor that Henry had been persuaded to cede the territories at "the request of his wife." As one angry reporter, Dr. Thomas Gascoigne, put it later, "That aforesaid queen of ours begged the King of England that [the lands] so be given to her father at the urging of William [de la] Pole, duke of Suffolk, and his wife"—Alice Chaucer again—"who earlier had promised to request it." Partisan though Gascoigne may have been, his was but one voice among many railing against the new queen.

In a sense, Gascoigne was right; Marguerite does seem to have agitated for the English withdrawal. In a letter written before the end of 1445 to the king of France, her uncle, Marguerite promised, "And as to the deliverance which you desire to have of the Comte of Maine, and other matters contained in your said letters, we understand that my said lord has written to you at considerable length about this: and yet herein we will do for your pleasure the best that we can do." A letter of Henry's own volunteers to give up territory in Maine, at least partly because of "our dear and well-beloved companion the queen, who has requested us to do this many times." But Marguerite's efforts need not be read as a betrayal of her new kingdom, for wasn't reconciliation, urging the peace, what a queen was supposed to do? Even the pageants had said so.

Marguerite herself, while badgering Henry, had been under sustained pressure from her relatives in France to achieve the promised release of Maine and Anjou, neither the first nor the last princess, of course, to suffer such a clash of loyalties.* Popular blame for England's predicament fell largely on the head of Suffolk, the official negotiator of the marriage deal, but the controversy did not help Marguerite's popularity.

Neither did the enmity of the old Duke of Gloucester. As Polydore Vergil wrote later, the queen determined herself to take over the important role Gloucester had once played in forming Henry's opinions, "lest she also might be reported to have little wit who would suffer her husband, now of mature years, to be under another man's government." This, however, came close to crossing a dangerous boundary. Christine de Pizan had urged that a wife's task should always be to preserve "the honour of her husband," and Marguerite was trying to protect her husband's reputation. But her determined entry into the fray wound up aligning her with one of the two major court parties. This was unacceptable—in England, though not in France. In the French court, faction was the modus operandi, and it was normal for the crown to align itself with one or another party. The monarchy in England, on the other hand, was supposed to be above such disputes.

The difficult relationship between England and France underpinned the first years of Marguerite of Anjou's queenship—it was both the reason for her presence in England and the source of her troubles there. The fallout from the long dispute also dominated the lives of women from the English families on either side of the political divide.

---

*Ferdinand of Aragon would find an unusual solution in designating his daughter Catherine of Aragon as his official ambassador at the court of her father-in-law, Henry VII.

2

"THE RED ROSE
AND THE WHITE"

The red rose and the white are on his face,
The fatal colours of our striving houses

HENRY VI, PART 3, 2.5

In 1445, the year Marguerite arrived in England, none of the other six women who are central to this story were yet major players on the national scene. Indeed, neither Anne Neville nor Margaret of Burgundy had been born, let alone Elizabeth of York. Elizabeth Woodville—about eight years old, though no one had bothered to record her precise date of birth—was growing up in country obscurity.

Only two others of the group showed any hint of their future prominence, and only one, Cecily Neville, was a woman of full maturity. Margaret Beaufort, meanwhile, was just a toddler, though her bloodline meant she was already a significant figure—a prize for whom others would compete. As an important carrier of the Lancastrian claim, she (or, rather, any son she might bear) might be considered as possible heir presumptive to the throne, until children came to her kinsman Henry VI.

Margaret Beaufort had been born in 1443 at Bletsoe in Bedfordshire, to a comparatively obscure widow who already had children by her first husband, Sir Oliver St. John. Margaret's father, however, was the Earl (later Duke) of Somerset, and from him she inherited a debatable but intriguing relationship to the throne.

Somerset's father, the first Earl of Somerset, had been a son of John of Gaunt, the first Lancastrian forebear. Although the first Earl of Somerset had been born to Gaunt's mistress Katherine Swynford, Gaunt's nephew Richard II confirmed by binding statute that all the children of the pair were rendered legitimate by their subsequent marriage and were able to inherit dignities and estates "as fully, freely, and lawfully as if you were born in lawful wedlock." When John of Gaunt's eldest son (by his first wife, Blanche of Lancaster) seized Richard's throne and had himself declared Henry IV, this first Earl of Somerset thus became half brother to the king. But when in 1407 Somerset requested a clarification of the position laid down in that earlier legitimation, the resultant letters patent (a less binding form of documentation than a statute) confirmed his entitlement to estates and noble rank with one very crucial exception: *"excepta dignitate regali"*—excepting the dignities of the crown.

Margaret from her very birth thus occupied an equivocal position. Less controversially, she was also heiress to great lands. But by the time of her birth, the anomalies of her family's position—royal, but yet possibly excluded from ruling—had been further compounded by her father's checkered career.

Somerset's life had been blighted by the accident that had him captured as a young man in the wars with France and held captive there for seventeen long years. When he returned to England only a few years before Margaret's birth, he set about trying to assume the position to which he felt his blood entitled him—but, as the author of the Crowland Abbey chronicles put it, "his horn was exalted too greatly on high." In 1443 his closeness in blood to a king short of relatives had seen Somerset appointed to lead England's army in fresh wars against the French. The campaign was a disaster, and Somerset was summoned home in disgrace, his daughter having been born while he was away. Only a few months later, in May 1444, he died, the Crowland chronicler asserting ("it is generally said") that he had committed suicide—a heinous sin in the fifteenth-century Catholic Church. The rumors surrounding his death only added to the dubiousness of the baby Margaret's position, and perhaps later increased her well-documented insecurities.

Somerset's brother Edmund, who succeeded to the title, was able to ensure that the Beaufort family retained their influence, not least because of the friendship he would strike up with the new queen. It was this friendship that would bring him into conflict with the Duke of York, and York's wife, Cecily.

Born in 1415, the beautiful Cecily Neville (nicknamed the "Rose of Raby" for the castle where she entered the world) was the daughter of Ralph Neville, the powerful Earl of Westmorland, by his second marriage to Joan Beaufort—Beaufort, as in Margaret Beaufort's notably Lancastrian family. Cecily would later become the matriarch of the ruling house of York, but in 1445 those fateful political divisions had not fully taken shape, and in fact Cecily's father had originally supported the Lancastrian usurpation by John of Gaunt's son Henry IV.

Indeed, while Margaret Beaufort's royal blood made her line a potential pathway to the throne, Cecily's connection was even more direct. Joan Beaufort was daughter to John of Gaunt by Katherine Swynford, and one wonders if Cecily, John of Gaunt's granddaughter, would not in later years come to find it galling that Margaret Beaufort could be regarded as inheriting John of Gaunt's Lancastrian claim when she was only his great-granddaughter. The vital difference was that although Margaret herself was just as much a female as Cecily, her claim had come through her father and her father's father, by way of the male line. Unlike Cecily, Margaret's connection to John of Gaunt was through one of his sons, not his daughter.

By the time Cecily was born in May 1415, the Neville family was enormous. Joan Beaufort had made a first marriage with a mere knight and borne two daughters, and when she married Ralph, he had a large family already; nevertheless, he and Joan had ten more surviving children. By contrast Cecily's husband, Richard of York, had just one sister. His marriage would bring him an almost unparalleled number of in-laws, who in the fifteenth century figured as potentially trustworthy allies and were perhaps to be considered more a blessing than a curse. Certainly, the Nevilles would—in many ways, and for many years—do Richard proud.

Richard had been born in 1411, grandson to Edward III's fourth son, Edmund. In 1415 his father (another Richard) was executed for his involvement in a plot against Henry V. The young boy eventually became Ralph Neville's ward. By that time, Richard had inherited the dukedom of York from a childless uncle, and in the years ahead another childless uncle died, leaving Richard heir to the great Welsh and Irish lands of the Mortimer family.

Whether or not there was already any thought that he might also be king in waiting, York was an undoubted catch, and it was inevitable Ralph Neville would hope to keep this rich matrimonial prize within his own family. York's betrothal to Cecily took place just a year after he came into the Nevilles' care. The following year, Ralph himself died, but York's wardship passed into the hands of Cecily's mother, Joan. Full, consummated marriage would have been legal when Cecily was twelve, in 1427, and had certainly taken place by 1429, when permission was received from the papacy for them jointly to choose a confessor.

In medieval terms, Cecily was lucky. She would have known Richard well, and he was only four years her elder. And since Richard, like Joan, had moved south, into the glittering world of the royal court, it seems probable Cecily would have done so, too—unless we are to deduce separations from the fact that their first child was not born until ten years into the marriage, though after that they came with notable frequency.

Cecily gave birth to that first child—a daughter, Anne—in 1439 and a first son, Henry, in February 1441, at Hatfield. But the baby Henry soon died, so it was just as well, perhaps, that Cecily had the distraction of an imminent move to France that summer. York had been appointed governor of the English territories there, a swath of land still haunted by the specter of Joan of Arc, the holy maid, burned there by the English occupiers only a decade before. In Rouen, the capital of English Normandy, the couple set up home in a state so nearly regal that an officer of the household had to be appointed to overlook Cecily's expenditures: lavishly jeweled dresses and even a cushioned privy. Their second son, Edward, the future Edward IV, was born there in April 1442; another son, Edmund, in May 1443; and another daughter, Elizabeth, the following year.

At the time, there seems to have been no whisper of the future rumors concerning Edward's paternity. But in the years ahead, there would be debate about the precise significance of the date of Edward's birth, about where his father had been nine months before it, and about the hasty and modest ceremony in which he was christened. It is true that Edward was christened in a private chapel in Rouen Castle, while his next sibling, Edmund, was christened in the far more public arena of Rouen Cathedral—but that may have meant no more than that the child Edward seemed sickly, an explanation that would be all the likelier, of course, if he were indeed premature. It is true, too, that whereas Edward, the "Rose of Rouen," was notably tall and as physically impressive as his grandson Henry VIII, Richard of York was dark and probably small. But perhaps Edward simply took after his mother, Cecily, several of whose other children would also be tall.

The basic fact remains that York himself showed no sign of querying his son's paternity. Indeed, he and the English government proposed and sustained lengthy negotiations for a match between Edward and a daughter of the French king, which hardly suggests suspicion about his status. This was not, moreover, the first time an allegation of bastardy had been leveled at a royal son born abroad: John of Gaunt, born in Ghent, had been called a changeling. In the years ahead, Cecily's relationship with Richard of York would give every sign of being notably close and strong. And there is the question of the identity of her supposed lover—an archer called Blaybourne. For a woman as conscious of her status as Cecily—the woman who would be called "proud Cis"—that seems especially unlikely. There are certainly queries as to how the story spread. The Italian Dominic Mancini, visiting England years later at a time when it had once again become a matter of hot debate, said that Cecily herself started the idea when angered by Edward. A continental chronicler has it relayed by Cecily's son-in-law Charles of Burgundy. But sheer political expedience apart, it was not at all uncommon for women in this era—even, and perhaps especially, the highborn—to be slurred through their sexual morality.

Certainly, Cecily was still queening it in Rouen as Duchess of York when, in the spring of 1445, the young Marguerite of Anjou passed through the city on her way to England and marriage with Henry VI. It may have been here that the thirty-year-old woman and the fifteen-year-old girl struck up a measure of friendship that would survive their husbands' future differences—one example among many of women's alliances across the York-Lancastrian divide. But at this point Marguerite's role was far the grander, albeit beset with difficulty.

3

"A WOMAN'S FEAR"

If it be fond, call it a woman's fear;
Which fear, if better reasons can supplant,
I will subscribe, and say I wronged the duke.

HENRY VI, PART 2, 3.1

When Marguerite of Anjou had arrived in England, her recent acquaintance, Cecily, was not far behind her. In that autumn of 1445, Cecily's husband's term of office in France came to an end. Richard and Cecily had returned to England and settled down. Another daughter, Margaret (the future Margaret of Burgundy), was born to the Yorks in May 1446, probably at Fotheringhay, while the two eldest boys were likely to have been given their own establishment, at Ludlow. But the couple were now embittered and less wealthy, since the English government had never properly covered their expenses in Normandy.

York had hoped to be appointed for another spell of office but was balked, not least by Cardinal Beaufort and his nephew Somerset. It was this, one chronicler records, that first sparked the feud between

York and the Beauforts, despite the fact that the latter were Cecily's mother's family. The Burgundian chronicler Jean de Waurin sheds some light on this, writing that Somerset "was well-liked by the Queen. . . . She worked on King Henry, on the advice and support of Somerset and other lords and barons of his following, so that the Duke of York was recalled to England. There he was totally stripped of his authority." York had now a long list of grievances, dating back a decade to the time when a sixteen-year-old Henry VI had begun his own rule without giving York any position of great responsibility.

York belonged to the "hawks" among the country's nobility, who believed in pursuing an aggressive policy against France. So too did the king's uncle, the aging Humfrey of Gloucester. By the autumn of 1446, King Charles was demanding the return of ever more English holdings in France, and Henry VI, under Marguerite's influence, was inclined to grant it. But Humfrey, who would be a powerful opponent of the policy, would have to be gotten out of the way in order for the deal to go through. In February 1447—under, it was said, the aegis of Marguerite, Suffolk, and the Beaufort faction—Gloucester was summoned to a Parliament at Bury St. Edmunds, only to find himself arrested by the queen's steward and accused of having spread rumors that Suffolk was Marguerite's lover. He was allowed to retire to his lodgings while the king debated his fate, but there, twelve days later, he died. The cause of his death has never been established to this day, and though it may well have been natural, inevitably rumors of murder crept in—rumors, even, that Duke Humfrey, like Edward II before him, had been killed by being "thrust into the bowel with a hot burning spit."

Gloucester had been King Henry's nearest male relative and therefore (despite his advanced age) his heir. His death promoted the disaffected York to that prominent, tantalizing position. The following month Cardinal Beaufort also died. The decks were being cleared, and the way was open for younger men—and women. Marguerite did not miss her opportunity.

Over the next few years, Marguerite could be seen extending her influence through her new English homeland, albeit often in a specifically female way. A letter from Margery Paston—a member of the Norfolk gentry family whose correspondence gives us so many insights into the era—tells of how when the queen was at Norwich, she sent for one Elizabeth Clere, "and when she came into the Queen's presence, the Queen made right much of her, and desired her to have a husband." Marguerite the matchmaker was also active for one Thomas Burneby, "sewer for our mouth," telling the object of his attention (vainly, this time) that Burneby loved her "for the womanly and virtuous governance that ye be renowned of," and writing to the father of another reluctant bride, sought by a yeoman of the Crown, that since his daughter was in his "rule and governance," he should give his "good consent, benevolence and friendship to induce and excite your daughter to accept my said lord's servant and ours, to her husband." Other letters of hers request that her shoemaker might be spared jury service "at such times as we shall have need of his craft, and send for him" and that the game in a park where she intended to hunt "be spared, kept and cherished for the same intent, without suffering any other person there to hunt."

For a queen to exercise patronage and protection—to be a "good lady" to her dependents—was wholly acceptable, and so many of Marguerite's queenly activities would not have raised any hackles in England. But Marguerite was still failing in her more pressing royal duty—and for this, she would once again find herself struggling to stay on the right side of her people. In contrast to the fertile Yorks, and despite her visits to Thomas Becket's shrine at Canterbury, the royal Marguerite's marriage was bedeviled by the lack of any sign of children.

A prayer roll of Marguerite's, unusually dedicated to the Virgin Mary rather than to the Saviour, shows Marguerite kneeling hopefully at her feet, probably praying for a pregnancy. One writer expressed, on Marguerite's arrival, the psalmist's hope that "thy wife shall be as the fruitful vine upon the walls of thy house," and the perceived link between a fertile monarchy and a fertile land* only added to the weight of responsibility. When Marguerite failed to deliver, many an Englishman's suspicion of the foreign-born queen turned to open scorn—or worse. As early as 1448, a farm laborer was up before

---

*This was the theory behind the Arthurian legend of the Fisher King.

the lords declaring that "our Queen was none able to be Queen of England . . . for because that she beareth no child, and because that we have no prince in this land."

The problem was probably with Henry, whose sexual drive was not high. The young man, who had famously left the room when one of his courtiers brought bare-bosomed dancing girls to entertain him, may also have been swayed by his spiritual counselor, who preached the virtues of celibacy. But it was usually the woman who was blamed for infertility, as Marguerite must have known. On the other hand, a child would have aligned the queen more clearly with English interests and perhaps removed from her the pressure of making herself felt in other, less acceptable, ways. Letters written by the king were now going out accompanied by a matching letter from the queen, and it was clear who was the more forceful personality.

Despite the petitions of his wife, Henry VI had never managed to enforce his promise to return Anjou and Maine to France, and in 1448 a French army had been dispatched to take what they had been promised. The following year, a temporary truce was broken by a misguided piece of militarism on the part of Somerset, now (like his brother before him) England's military commander in France and (like his brother before him) making a woeful showing in the role. The French retaliation led them to Normandy. Rouen—where York and Cecily had ruled—swiftly fell, and soon Henry V's great conquests were but a distant memory. Only Calais remained English property into the next century (and when that too was lost in the reign of Mary Tudor, the queen declared that when she died, they would find the word *Calais* engraved on her heart). York would have been more than human had he not cited this as one more example of his rivals' inadequacies, while Suffolk (now elevated to a dukedom) did not hesitate to suggest that York aspired to the throne itself. Suffolk had the ear of both king and queen, and in 1449 York was sent to occupy a new post as governor of Ireland—or, as Jean de Waurin had it, "was expelled from court and exiled to Ireland." Cecily went with him, giving birth to a son, George, in Dublin.

The place was even then known as being a graveyard of reputations for any Englishman sent to control it; still, given the timing, the Yorks may have been better off there, in comfortable exile. English politics were becoming ever more factionalized, and some of the quarrels could be seen swirling around the head of the young Margaret Beaufort, at the time only six years old.

After her father had died, wardship of the valuable young heiress, with the right to reap the income of her lands, had been given to Suffolk, although (unusually for the English nobility) baby Margaret was at least left in her mother's care. Her marriage, however, was never going to be left to her mother to arrange. By 1450 she was a pawn of which her guardian, Suffolk, had urgent necessity.

Most of the blame for recent disasters in England's long war with France had been heaped on Suffolk's head, though there was enmity left over and to spare for Marguerite, whose father had actually been one of the commanders in the French attack. Suffolk was arrested at the end of January 1450, and at some time over the next week, to protect the position of his own family, he arranged the marriage of the six-year-old heiress, Margaret, to his eight-year-old son, John de la Pole. Presumably in this, as in everything else, Suffolk had Queen Marguerite's support.

The marriage of two minors, too young to give consent, and obviously unconsummated, could not be wholly binding: Margaret herself would always disregard it, speaking of her next husband as her first. Nonetheless, it was significant enough to play its part; when, a few weeks later, the Commons brought charges against Suffolk, prominent among the other charges—of corruption and incompetence and of selling out England to the French—was that he had arranged the marriage "presuming and pretending her [Margaret] to be next inheritable to the Crown."

Suffolk was placed in the Tower, but appealed directly to the king. Henry, to the fury of both the Commons and the Lords, refused to proceed to extremes against Suffolk. Absolving him of all capital charges, he sentenced him only to a comparatively lenient five years' banishment. Shakespeare has Marguerite pleading against even this, with enough passion to cause her husband concern and to have the Earl of Warwick declare it a slander to her royal dignity. But in fact, the king had already gone as far as he felt able in resisting the pressure from peers and Parliament alike, who would rather have seen Suffolk executed. And indeed, when at the end of April Suffolk finally set sail, having been granted a six-week respite to set his affairs in order, his departure did become a final one. He was murdered on his way into exile, his body cast onshore at Dover on May 2.

It had been proved all too clearly that Henry VI, unlike his immediate forebears, was a king unable to control his own subjects (just as Marguerite, despite her forcefulness, had none of the power that, a century before, had enabled Isabella of France to rule with and protect for so long her favorite and lover, Mortimer). It has been said that when the news reached the queen—broken to her by Suffolk's widow, Alice Chaucer—she shut herself into her rooms at Westminster to weep for three days. In fact, king and queen were then at Leicester, which casts some doubt on the whole story—but tales of Marguerite's excessive, compromising grief would have been received with angry credence in the country.

It was said at the time that, because Suffolk had apparently been murdered by sailors out of Kent, the king and queen planned to raze that whole county. Within weeks of Suffolk's death came a populist rising lead by Jack Cade, or "John Amend-All," as he called himself, a colorful Yorkist sympathizer backed by three thousand (mostly) Kentish men. The rebels demanded an inquiry into Duke Humfrey's death and insisted that the Crown lands and common freedoms given away on Suffolk's advice should all be restored. (They also made particular complaint against the Duchess of Suffolk; indeed, her perceived influence may have been the reason that, the next year, Parliament demanded the dismissal of Alice Chaucer from court.)

By the middle of June, the rebels were camped on Blackheath, just to the south of London. In the first days of July, they entered the city, joined initially by many of the citizens. Several days of looting and riot changed that. The rebellion collapsed, and Cade himself fled to Sussex, where he was killed. But it had exposed even more cruelly than before the weakness of the government. The royal pardons offered to the rebels were declared, as was customary (if in this case unlikely), to have been won from Henry by "the most humble and persistent supplications, prayers and requests of our most serene and beloved wife and consort the queen."

Even as the authorities were horrified by the Cade rebellion, they also had a stream of bad news from France with which to contend. In May the Duke of Somerset had been forced to follow the surrender of Rouen by the surrender of Caen. Even as Cade died, other English citadels were falling. When Cherbourg too fell on August 12, 1450, England had now, as one Paston correspondent put it, "not a foot of ground left in Normandy." But Somerset's favor with the queen survived his military disasters. It was Marguerite who protected Somerset, on his return to London, from demands that he should be charged as a traitor, but this flamboyant partisanship was itself a potential source of scandalous rumor (despite the fact that Somerset's wife, Eleanor Beauchamp, was herself [like Suffolk's widow, Alice Chaucer] also close to the queen, which might seem to make illicit relations the less likely).

In the vacuum left by Suffolk's death, meanwhile, two leading candidates arose to vie for the position of the king's chief councilor. One was indeed the Duke of Somerset, Margaret Beaufort's uncle. The other candidate was Cecily's husband, Richard Plantagenet, Duke of York, now making a hasty, unannounced return from Ireland and intensely aware of his position both as the king's ranking male kinsman and as the progenitor of a flourishing nursery, "the issue that it pleased God to send me of the royal blood," as he put it, pointedly.

York's dissatisfaction with the current regime was no doubt partly personal—he had been left seriously out of pocket by his experiences abroad—but at the start of the 1450s, he could be seen at the same time as heading a call for genuine reform. Six years into Marguerite's queenship, the Crown of England was in a lamentable state, so poor the Epiphany feast of 1451 had reputedly to be called off because suppliers would no longer allow the court food on credit, while the king's officials had recently been petitioning Parliament for several years' back wages. This was certainly no new problem—the financial position had been markedly serious a decade before Marguerite arrived in England—but it was now worse than ever. By 1450, the Crown was almost four hundred thousand pounds in debt.

The military campaign in France had been disastrously expensive, and the war inevitably caused disruption to trade—but the costs of maintaining the royal court were also now conspicuously far greater than the revenues available, especially under the influence of a high-spending queen, while there was widespread suspicion that her favorites were being allowed to feather their nests too freely. On Marguerite's arrival in England, Parliament had voted her the income usually bestowed on queens—ten thousand marks, or some sixty-seven hundred pounds—but the parlous state of her husband's finances meant that, in particular, those sums due her from the Exchequer were often not forthcoming. The surviving accounts show her making determined efforts to claim her dues, but they also show a formidable expenditure of money—not just the seventy-three pounds she might give to a Venetian merchant for luxury cloths, or the twenty-five pounds to equip a Christmas "disguising," or masque, but sums of money clearly used to reward, in gifts and in high wages, her allies.

With the king and those around him thus looking vulnerable, York moved to act. The Parliament of May 1451 saw a petition for York to be named as heir presumptive to the childless Henry VI and his and Cecily's sons after him. Everything we know about her would suggest Cecily stood right alongside her husband, whose allies were by the beginning of 1452 claiming that the king "was fitter for a cloister than a throne, and had in a manner deposed himself by leaving the affairs of his kingdom in the hands of a woman who merely used his name to conceal her usurpation."

Although it is unclear whether the enmity between Marguerite and York was as instinctive and began as early as has popularly been supposed, there is no doubt that by this point, real conflict was on the way. By February 1452, both sides were raising troops. On March 2, the two armies drew up, three miles apart, near Blackheath, from which Jack Cade's rebels had launched their attack less than two years before.

Neither party, however, was yet quite ready to fight. A royal delegation of two bishops and two earls was sent to command York, in the king's name, to return to his allegiance. Prominent among York's demands was that Somerset should be arrested and York himself acknowledged the king's heir. Back in the royal camp (so one story goes), the bishops saw to it that the queen was kept occupied while they spoke to the king, who was persuaded to agree to all of York's demands. But the next morning, in a dramatic scene, Marguerite intercepted the guards who were leading Somerset away and instead led him to the king's tent so that York, arriving a few minutes later to make his peace with his monarch, found himself also confronting a furious queen. Somerset was clearly in as much favor as ever, and York understandably felt he had been fooled. He had no option, however, but to make a humiliating public pledge of his loyalty before being allowed to withdraw to his estates in Ludlow.

Armed conflict had been averted for the moment, but the divisions in the English nobility were deeper even than they had been before. The resentful York and his adherents remained a threat for a king and a court party anxious to strengthen their position in any possible way. One of the ways most favored by the age was marriage, and so, in February 1453, Margaret Beaufort's mother was commanded to bring her nine-year-old daughter—Somerset's niece—to court.

Margaret Beaufort, during the first years of Marguerite's queenship, had been raised at her own family seat of Bletsoe, as well as at Maxey in the Fens, the great marshy region of eastern England. Her mother had remarried, and though she was growing up without a biological father—a pattern that would be repeated with her own fatherless son—there is evidence from her later life both that Margaret developed an enduring closeness with her five half siblings from her mother's first marriage with Sir Oliver St. John and that she learned to share several traits with her mother: piety and a love of learning, matched by an ambition for money and property. On April 23, 1453, she and her mother attended the Garter celebrations that marked St. George's Day; on May 12, the king put through a generous payment of one hundred marks for the arraying of his "right dear and well beloved cousin Margaret." But Margaret Beaufort had not been invited to court just for a party. The king had decided both to dissolve her espousal to Suffolk's son and to give her wardship to two new guardians: his half brothers, Edmund and Jasper Tudor.

Margaret Beaufort's new Tudor guardians were the sons of Henry VI's mother, the French-born Katherine de Valois, by her second, secret, alliance with a young Welshman in her service, the lowly Owen Tudor—or "Tydder," as the family's enemies would spell it slightingly. More to the point, they were half brothers whom the still-childless Henry had begun to favor, having still no son of his own to succeed him and with the older relations who had once been his mentors now dead.

It seems certain that when the king had the marriage with Suffolk's son dissolved, he already had it in mind to marry Margaret and her fortune to Edmund Tudor, the elder of his two half brothers. This could take place in just over two years' time, as soon as she turned twelve and reached the age of consent. It is possible he envisaged it as a step to making Edmund his heir, though of course Edmund's own lineage gave him no shadow of right to the English throne. (Edmund Tudor had royal blood in his veins all right—but it was the blood of the French, not the English, royal house.) But marriage might allow him to absorb Margaret's claim—a claim that, of course, would certainly be inherited by any sons of the marriage. And the fact that Henry had neither children nor royal siblings meant that even comparatively distant claims were coming into prominence. It was a situation comparable to that preceding the death of Margaret's great-granddaughter Elizabeth I, in 1603.

The formal changes in her marital situation required some participation from the nine-year-old Margaret herself. She would later imagine it as a real choice and an expression of manifest destiny, claiming that she had prayed to Saint Nicholas to help her choose between the two putative husbands. Later in life, Margaret would describe to her chaplain John Fisher how, the night before she had to give her formal assent to her marriage, as she lay in prayer at about four in the morning, "one appeared unto her arrayed like a Bishop, and naming unto her Edmund, bade take him unto her husband. And so by this mean she did incline her mind unto Edmund, the King's brother, and Earl of Richmond."

Perhaps Margaret, even then, was trying to invent for herself a scenario to mask the unpalatable fact that, in reality, she would have had no choice in the matter. She was, essentially, fooling herself—likely struggling with the realities of a girl's destiny, or simply trying to cast the glow of divine approval over her son, Henry. Perhaps, indeed, the story was only later Tudor propaganda, designed to reinforce the message that they were a divinely ordained dynasty. Between the annulment of Margaret's marriage and the ascension of the Tudors some thirty years later, there would be a great many turns in the Wheel of Fortune—turns that might have produced an entirely different outcome for England.

4

"NO WOMEN'S MATTERS"

Madam, the king is old enough himself
To give his censure. These are no women's matters.

HENRY VI, PART 2, 1.3

The court party of Henry VI was about to get another, unexpected, boost—one that, ironically, made Margaret Beaufort's marriage a matter of a little less urgency. That spring of 1453, Queen Marguerite was, at long last, able to announce a pregnancy—the news that the king's "most dearly beloved wife the Queen was *enceinte*," to his "most singular consolation," as his official proclamation had it.

Marguerite can have had no doubt to whom to give thanks. She had recently been on pilgrimage to Walsingham, where the shrine of Our Lady was believed to be particularly helpful to those trying to conceive, and she had already made a new year's offering of a gold tablet with the image of an angel, bedecked with jewels. On the way back, she had stayed a night at Hitchin with Cecily Neville, wife of the still alienated Richard of York. Now, in the summer of 1453, Cecily wrote to Marguerite praising "that blessed Lady to whom you late prayed, in whom aboundeth plenteously mercy and grace, by whose mediation it pleased our Lord to fulfil your right honourable body of the most precious, most joyful, and most comfortable earthly treasure that might come unto this land."

But Cecily was not writing only to congratulate Marguerite—nor even to lament the infirmity of her own "wretched body," which she bemoaned in the same letter. Cecily was indeed recovering from the birth of her son Richard; Thomas More wrote that it was a breech birth, and Cecily could not be delivered "uncut." But also on the forefront of Cecily's mind was her husband's fall from favor, which caused her to be "replete with such immeasurable sorrow and heaviness as I doubt not will of the continuance thereof diminish and abridge my days, as it does my worldly joy and comfort." She would have made her plea to Marguerite earlier had not "the disease and infirmity that since my said being in your highness presence hath grown and groweth" caused her "sloth and discontinuance." In this long, elaborate, and convoluted letter, Cecily renews the suit she had made at Hitchin: that her husband, the Duke of York, should no longer be "estranged from the grace and benevolent favour of that most Christian, most gracious and most merciful prince, the king our sovereign lord."

It is unclear whether York, estranged from court and out of favor, asked Cecily to intercede, or whether this advance was on Cecily's own initiative. The lists of the gifts Marguerite gave each year show presents made to Cecily and her servants, and we can choose to see such female recipients being used as a less politically coded conduit to their husbands, or as another kind of female alliance, based on sisterhood and liking. Either way, Cecily's letter may possibly have had some effect. When a great council was summoned that autumn, York did, belatedly, receive an invitation to attend. One of the signatories on the document was Marguerite's confessor.

The council was first summoned by Margaret Beaufort's uncle Somerset on October 24, 1453. But in the weeks before that date, several important things had happened, as Cecily may or may not have been aware when she wrote to Marguerite. On October 19, the French king's forces had entered Bordeaux, leaving England only Calais as a foothold in France and ending the "Hundred Years' War" with France's resounding victory. Six days earlier, on October 13, Queen

Marguerite had given birth to a healthy baby boy, named Edward, after Edward the Confessor, whose feast day it was. But while proclamations of the joyous news were read around the country, at court at least the joy was muted. The man to whom the news should have been most welcome of all, the baby's father, Henry VI, had fallen into a catatonic stupor.

It had been the middle of August when the king, after complaining one evening of feeling unusually sleepy, had awoken the next morning with a lolling head, unable to move or to communicate with anybody. Over the days and then weeks ahead, as his physicians and indeed priests tried the full panoply of fifteenth-century remedies—bleedings, purgings, and cautery on the one hand, exorcism on the other—he seemed not entirely to lose consciousness, but to be utterly incapable. Modern medicine has tentatively diagnosed his condition as catatonic schizophrenia, or alternatively a depressive stupor—triggered, perhaps, by the news from France or just possibly by the thought of Marguerite's pregnancy, which may have come as an unpleasant shock to the notoriously ascetic king.

Every effort was made, at first, to conceal the king's condition, not only from the country at large but also from York himself. And it was in this tense climate that, sometime before the expected birth, Marguerite, as custom dictated, had withdrawn into her apartments at Westminster to await her child's birth, passing into an all-female world, which not even her priest was allowed to enter.

Never can withdrawal from the wider world have seemed less timely, and one can only wonder which, as she waited in the darkened rooms, seemed the more pressing danger—the unknowable outcome of the situation outside or the well-known dangers of the birth ahead. And although Marguerite weathered the birth as she had her other English trials, the situation outside was no less fraught when she emerged. After the baby had been delivered—and after the churching some forty days later at which Marguerite, wearing a robe trimmed with more than five hundred sables, was attended by the duchesses not only of Suffolk and Somerset but also of York—she had to accept the fact that Henry in his catatonic state could make no sign of acknowledging the baby as his. The king's obliviousness not only was something that could be presented as a personal slight, but also constituted a practical problem if the name of the little prince were to be invoked as nominal authority of a council to rule during his father's incapacity.

There would, perhaps inevitably, be rumors about the baby's paternity, whispers that Marguerite had been guilty of adultery with the Duke of Somerset.* If it were indeed the news of Marguerite's pregnancy that had triggered the king's collapse, then the question is whether he were horrified by the first indisputable evidence of his own sexuality or, conversely, by awareness the child could not be his and that his wife must have been unfaithful. It was the same slur that would be leveled at Cecily, but this time—given the unhappiness of Marguerite's marital situation, her husband's presumed lack of virility, and the more suitable choice of the alleged partner—it does seem at least a more realistic possibility.

Adultery in the queen would be an outrage to the whole country. It is true that by the traditions of courtly love, adultery could be a forgivable, even in some senses a laudable, route to emotional fulfillment. Thomas Malory's celebrated character Guenivere was guilty of adultery with Lancelot (while her husband, Arthur, soon to fall into his own magic sleep below the lake, stood by; because Guenivere was Lancelot's true lover, however, she was therefore able to be redeemed—to have "a good end"). In the world of practical politics, however, it was a different story. When chroniclers such as Robert Fabian wrote that "false wedlock and false heirs fostered" were the "first cause" of the ills in the body politic, they were making an equation between public well-being and private morality that would have seemed reasonable to any contemporary.

The whispers of unfaithfulness would be fanned into a flame of public debate toward the end of the decade, when Marguerite's Yorkist enemies found it convenient both to discredit the Lancastrian heir and to cast a slur on Marguerite herself in the field in which women were above all judged: her chastity. As Catherine de Medici would later warn Elizabeth I, her sexuality was always the way in which a

---

*The whispers were enduring enough to be echoed by Shakespeare in *Henry VI, Part 3*, 2.2.

powerful woman could be most successfully attacked. Christine de Pizan similarly suggested that a queen had less freedom of sexual action at least than a lower-ranking lady, for "the greater a lady is, the more is her honour or dishonour celebrated through the country."

But whatever the damage such rumors did her, the birth of little Prince Edward had significantly advanced Marguerite's standing—as she well knew. It transformed Marguerite into the first of several women in this story for whom their sons would be the ones to play. Marguerite would now not be prepared to sit back and allow others to rule the country during her husband's incapacity.

In January 1454, a Paston correspondent reported that the queen had made a bill of five articles—"whereof the first is that she desires to have the whole rule of the land." No wonder contemporaries saw her as, in the words of the sixteenth-century chronicler Hall, "a manly woman, using to rule and not be ruled." There was in England no very recent precedent for a woman's rule, or indeed a formal regency, albeit that, in the great fictional work of these years, when Malory's King Arthur went away to the wars, he had "resigned all rule" to certain of his lords "and Queen Guenivere." In sober fact, however, though several of the early Norman queens had acted as regent, memories of Isabella of France were not reassuring. The last woman to hold the reins of power, a century before, Isabella had deposed and perhaps murdered her husband, Edward II, taking over the whole rule of the country, with her lover, in the name of her young son. Marguerite's mother-in-law, Katherine de Valois, had taken no part in government during Henry VI's minority.

The lands across the Channel offered precedent aplenty. Marguerite's family tradition was of women taking control when necessary—deputizing for a husband during his absence, or a son during his minority. But severe disapproval, and perhaps more, awaited the woman who crossed the indefinable bound and seemed to seek rule openly. Perhaps Marguerite's very bid, influenced by the experience of her Continental family, would have repercussions when, almost thirty years later, the governors of England came to consider the position of another, a Woodville, queen during her son's minority.

Discussions as to how the country should be ruled dragged on for weeks, in Parliament and in the council chamber, which suggests that

Marguerite's claim was not instantly dismissed. When, one week at the end of February, both she and York were scheduled to make grand public arrivals in London, the mayor and aldermen of the City were faced with the problem of showing them both equal respect. They agreed to turn out in scarlet to give the queen a formal welcome on Wednesday—and to do precisely the same for the Duke of York on Friday. In the end, however, in the last days of March, the final decision was that the country would be governed, during the king's incapacity, by a council of nobles, with York as "protector" at their head. It was a decision on which all the men involved—even Henry VI's half brothers, Edmund and Jasper Tudor—could agree.

York was described also as "defensor" of the realm—a military role that could only have been held by a man. Somerset was disempowered—arrested in the queen's apartment—and Marguerite was sent to Windsor to be with her husband, as a wife, not a force in the land. She seemed to accept the decision, however, even when the council's money-saving reforms reduced her household and thus her power base. It is hard, indeed, to know what else she could have done. Certainly, she could not have stressed Henry's incapacity; she had no authority to act other than through him. Although some lords refused to serve on York's council on the grounds that they were "with the queen," either physically or otherwise, the normal business of administration seemed—except only for the continued opposition of Somerset—to be going comparatively smoothly.

Then, on Christmas Day 1454, Henry recovered his senses. On December 28, the queen brought her son to him and told him the baby's name, and (in the words of the Paston letters) "he held up his hands and thanked God therefore." Another account has it that he also, unhelpfully, said the child "must be the son of the Holy Spirit," which could not but fan the flames of any doubts about the boy's paternity.

The king's recovery was hailed as a relief to all. In truth, however, it only presented a new set of problems. York had been a capable governor, but now a weak king was back on the throne, and his recovery had also resurrected Somerset, boiling with fury. The weakened Henry would thenceforth be more susceptible than ever to his wife's petticoat government, which boded ill for York and perhaps for the country.

York could only ride back to his own estates for safety, and with him, this time—morally, if not physically—came a great affinity: notably, Cecily's brother, Richard Neville, Earl of Salisbury, and Neville's eldest son, the Earl of Warwick. Warwick was an impressive figure who would go down in history as "the Kingmaker" and whose wife, two years later, would give birth to the most obscure female protagonist of this story: Anne.

Up until the 1450s, the Neville family had continued to support the Lancastrian government, to which they were linked by the connections of Joan Beaufort. Cecily, married to York, must have found herself isolated within her own family. This had now begun to change, largely because of the repercussions of a feud with another great northern family. The Nevilles had long been locked into a land dispute with the Percy earls of Northumberland, and now Warwick, in particular, felt that Henry (and Somerset) was showing too much favor to the Percys. The result was that two different divisions of the Neville family were coming to be on opposite sides. Cecily, the former "Rose of Raby," was now closest to the Nevilles of Middleham, Salisbury, and Warwick, who were realigning themselves with her husband, while her half nephew Ralph, who held the Raby land and the Westmorland title, remained Lancastrian. Whatever the cause, the change of allegiance in at least some of her kin must have been welcome to Cecily.

The spring of 1455, and the recovery of Henry VI, triggered the start of what has come to be known as the "Cousins' War." In May 1455, the queen and Somerset held another great council charged with protecting the king "against his enemies." The standoff between the two opposed parties quickly gave way to armed conflict, as the king (supported by Somerset, though not by the queen, who had retreated to Greenwich with her baby) rode out of London at the head of a royal army, and York, following the principle of getting his retaliation in first, likewise mustered his forces. The battle of St. Albans was no major military engagement—an hour-long fracas through the marketplace and the town's principal street—but it was notable for two things. Contemporaries were shocked, not only by the fact that the victorious Yorkist soldiers were looting their way through an English town, but also by the fact that the king was slightly wounded, by an arrow from one of his English subjects. Notable too was the fact that a number of lords and gentlemen on the royal side were slain. Among them was the Duke of Somerset, cut down by an ax outside the Castle Inn. Once again Marguerite had lost a great ally (and Margaret Beaufort her uncle and the head of her family).

It was York's and the Nevilles' victory. But the battle of St. Albans was significant in yet another way. There may not have been one single turning point in Marguerite of Anjou's progress toward political activism, but this was the moment when the process was completed, surely. With her main supporter cut down in battle and her weak husband unable to offer any further resistance, Marguerite would have to take the fight to her enemies herself, and in whatever way she could.

By and large, with a few notable exceptions, the battlefield was not part of a lady's experience in the fifteenth century. Some thirty years before, legend had it, Margaret's grandmother Yolande had donned silver armor and led her troops against the English at the battle of Baugé. Although the century of Joan of Arc may have given minimal lip service to the idea of the woman warrior, even Isabella of Castile, Catherine of Aragon's mother, often pictured as leading her own troops into battle, in fact confined herself to strategy and the supply of arms, planning, and provisioning. Certainly, most of the ladies whose husbands or sons were involved in conflict would have heard of the event only days or even weeks later. News traveled only at a horse's pace, and in an age before mass media (before, even, the dissemination of official printed reports), they may never have known as much about the progress of each battle as we know today. The history of the "Wars" of the Roses has usually been told in terms of the men who alone could take part in its physical conflicts. But the lives of the women behind them could be affected as profoundly.

As the Yorkists took over the reins of government, there was no overt breach of loyalty—everything was done in the king's name. Past wrongs were blamed on the dead Somerset and his allies. But Marguerite at least was mistrustful and unhappy, leaving the court to take refuge in the Tower with her baby. The fact that Henry resumed his role as king almost as York's puppet must have frightened as well as angered her.* More uncertainty lay ahead: that autumn the king fell ill again, though this time only for three months, and for that period, from November 1455 to the next February, York resumed his protectorship of the country.

But as York set about a policy of, among other things, royal financial retrenchment, the queen was working to try to make the king's nominal rule something closer to a reality. "The queen is a great and strong laboured woman, for she spares no pain to sue her things to an intent and conclusion to her power," wrote one observer named John Bocking, a connection of the Paston family. Early in 1456, as the king's recovery put an end to York's protectorship yet again, Marguerite herself left London, taking her baby son to the traditional Lancashire stronghold of Tutbury.

Marguerite had decided to take action. From Tutbury, she rallied support and persuaded the king to remove the court from London to the Midlands, where her own estates lay. In September of that year, her chancellor was entrusted by the king with the privy seal, which gave her access to the whole administration of the country.

Marguerite postured herself always as the king's "subordinate and adjunct," which was what was needed in the short term. In the long term, however, this both acted to the detriment of her authority and left her vulnerable to charges of exceeding her brief. It was as Marguerite managed to accrue more power to herself that the rumors really began to circulate about her sexual morality, as if the two things were two sides of the same unnatural coin. It was increasingly said that the prince was not the king's son but perhaps Somerset's—or not even Marguerite's child, but a changeling. In February 1456, one John Helton, "an apprentice at court," was hung, drawn, and quartered "for producing bills asserting that Prince Edward was not the queen's son."

The pageants that welcomed Marguerite into the city of Coventry on September 14, 1456, reflected the confusion about her role. The

---

*Again, there would perhaps be repercussions ahead when another queen, Elizabeth Woodville, had to contemplate the prospect of another Richard, another Yorkist duke, holding the effectual reins of the country.

bulk of them saw her figured as traditionally female—mother and wife—and praised particularly for her "virtuous life." (Considering the aspersions that had been cast upon her sexual virtue, it is likely a point was being made, if, as is possible, Marguerite herself had any hand in framing the images.) She was hailed, hopefully if inappropriately, as a "model of meekness, dame Margaret," and though the ending made a show of the famously sword-wielding and dragon-slaying Saint Margaret, it was not before six famous conquerors had promised to give the saint's less well-armed namesake their protection—of which, as a female, she clearly stood in need.

BUT THAT AUTUMN the king called a council from which (so a correspondent of the Pastons wrote) the Duke of York withdrew "in right good conceit with the king, but not in great conceit with the Queen." And when the next spring Marguerite paid another visit to Coventry, she was at the insistence of her officers escorted back out of the city by the mayor and sheriffs with virtually the same ceremonies that would have been accorded to the king, or so the city recorder noted with shock: "And so they did never before the Queen till then." Only the parade of the king's sword was missing.* By January 1457, while a council was appointed for Marguerite's baby son, the queen herself ordered a huge stock of arms to the Midlands castle of Kenilworth. Marguerite was showing her hand ever more openly. With attention on Marguerite, no one at the time would have been inclined to look elsewhere, to another recent event—to others who, as they grew to womanhood, would later be important in the country's history.

On June 11, 1456, in Warwick Castle, just a few miles away from Kenilworth, the Earl of Warwick's wife, Anne Beauchamp, had given birth to their second daughter, Anne. Anne Beauchamp had come

---

*Eighteen years later, Ferdinand of Aragon was shocked to hear that his wife, Isabella, had not only had herself proclaimed hereditary monarch of Castile, but also paraded through Segovia with a drawn sword carried before her. "I have never," he protested, "heard of a queen who usurped this masculine attribute."

unexpectedly (and not without familial strife) into a vast inheritance, and since the Warwicks never produced sons, their daughters, Isabel and Anne Neville, were early marked out as among the greatest heiresses of their day. Anne's future would take her from one side to another of the York-Lancaster dispute, but at the moment (however close geographically they may have been to Marguerite), her father and her family were prominent in the Yorkist cause. It was in far-off Wales, at Pembroke Castle, that young Margaret Beaufort—Queen Marguerite's namesake and fellow Lancastrian—was also about to have to take control of her own destiny.

5

"CAPTAIN MARGARET"

Where's Captain Margaret to fence you now?

HENRY VI, PART 3, 2.6

Almost two years earlier—in 1455, shortly after her uncle Somerset had been killed in the queen's cause—Margaret Beaufort had reached her twelfth birthday. Until this time, in the absence of evidence to the contrary, it is likely that the young Margaret had been left still in her mother's care. But when the king's half brother Edmund Tudor was sent to Wales as the king's representative late that year, he had almost certainly been able to take Margaret with him as his wife.

Popular opinion would have suggested that consummation of the marriage should be delayed, even though it was now legal—the more so since Margaret was slight and undeveloped for her age. But other factors weighed more heavily on Edmund: the fact, perhaps, that fathering a child with Margaret would give him a life interest in her lands, or that although there was now a Lancastrian heir, there was still not a spare. She became pregnant in the first half of 1456, sometime before her thirteenth birthday. It would at the best have been an anxious time for her, but worse was to follow. Edmund did not live to see the birth of his child. Captured at Carmarthen by an ally of the Duke of York's, he was soon released, but died there of plague in November 1456.

ISOLATED IN PLAGUE-RIDDEN WALES, heavily pregnant, and thirteen, a terrified Margaret had only one ally close at hand: her brother-in-law Jasper Tudor, who, himself only in his early twenties, was called on to take on this quasi-paternal role. She fled to his stronghold of Pembroke, and it was there that on January 28, in the forbidding chill of a Welsh winter, she gave birth to a boy.

The ceremony that was supposed to surround the birth of a possible heir to the throne was described in ordinances Margaret Beaufort herself would lay down in later life for the birth of her first grandchild, and though there was obviously more ritual about the confinement of a queen than a mere great lady, the essential goals were the same. The pregnant mother should go apart, some weeks before the birth, into the rooms carefully prepared: "Her Highness's pleasure being understood as to what chamber it may please her to be delivered in, the same to be hung with rich cloth or arras, sides, roof, windows and all, except one window, which must be hanged so that she have light when it pleases her." She took communion at a solemn mass, then progressed in state to her apartments, took wine and sweetmeats with her (male) officers, and then bade them farewell. As she entered her chamber, she passed into a world of women, where "women are to be made all manner of officers, butlers, sewers and pages; receiving all needful things at the chamber door." A roughly contemporary illustration shows a world of color and comfort, with three ladies tending to the mother, while a fourth nurses the child before a blazing fire.

After the birth, a new mother was to stay in bed, then to be allowed to walk around the room, then the rest of the house, until she went for her "churching," or purification, some forty days after her accouchement, accompanied by midwives and female attendants, bearing a lighted candle, to be sprinkled with holy water. Christine de Pizan gives a description of the lying-in of one woman—a mere merchant's wife, shockingly—who arranged that awestruck visitors should walk past an ornamental bed and a dresser "decorated like an altar" with silver vessels before even reaching her own bedchamber, "large and handsome," with tapestries all around, and a bed made up with cobweb-fine display sheets, and even a gold-embroidered rug "on which one could walk" (this at a time when carpets were too expensive usually to placed on the floor). "Sitting in the bed was the woman herself, dressed in crimson silk, propped up against large pillows covered in the same silk and decorated with pearl buttons, wearing the headdress of a lady." But it seems likely Margaret Beaufort's circumstances militated against any such pleasurable feminine display.

We know that women were as anxious then as now to take any precaution they could against the perils of childbirth, from a favorite midwife to the Virgin's girdle. Even in a lower sphere of society, Margaret Paston was so eager to get the midwife she wanted that the woman— though incapacitated by a back injury—had to reassure her she'd be there, even if she had to be pushed in a barrow. What we do not know is to just what degree the conditions of the year or the remoteness of the place changed things for Margaret. But we know the birth did not go easily.

The labor was long and difficult. Both Margaret and the child were expected to die, and were there to be a choice, some church authorities urged that those in attendance should prioritize the unbaptized baby, even if it was not a valuable boy. There seems little doubt her physical immaturity was part of the problem—as Fisher would later put it, "It seemed a miracle that of so little a personage anyone should have been born at all." She herself thought so, at least: in later years, she would combine forces with her daughter-in-law, Elizabeth of York, to ensure that her young granddaughter and namesake, Margaret, was not sent to Scotland too early, lest her new husband, the king of Scotland, would not wait to consummate the marriage "but injure her, and endanger her health."

There seems little doubt that Margaret Beaufort was indelibly marked by her early experiences—perhaps physically (since neither of her two subsequent marriages produced any children) and certainly mentally. Contemporaries remarked on her sense of vulnerability. The image of Fortune's Wheel was as impossible to avoid for contemporary commentators on this period as it is today. "But Fortune with her smiling countenance strange / Of all our purpose may make sudden change" ran the popular jingle, and no one was more aware than Margaret Beaufort of its lethal possibilities.

For the rest of her life, the pall of mortality would hang heavily on Margaret Beaufort. After her death, her confessor, John Fisher, would say, in the *Mornynge Remembraunce* sermon he preached a month after her death, that "she never was yet in that prosperity but the greater it was the more always she dread the adversity." Whenever "she had full great joy, she let not to say, that some adversity would follow." (And this was despite the fact that the other early Tudor biographer, the court poet Bernard André, claimed that she was "steadfast and more stable than the weakness in women suggests.") Perhaps, even, it would not be surprising if Margaret the devout turned with a sense of angry recognition to the religious theories of the day that held maidenhood and virginity to be the most perfect time of a woman's life—or if she attempted, in her later rejection of the married state, almost to re-create it. Certainly, the iconography was all around: the Virgin Mary, the Maid of Orléans, the Pearl Maiden of poetry, even Galahad and the Grail. The nobly born virgin martyrs—Saints Catherine of Alexandria, Cecilia, Barbara, Agnes, Agatha, and Margaret—had become the most popular saints in the England of the day.

But even the trauma she had suffered did not long subdue the young mother's determination. We have few early proofs of Margaret Beaufort's character, but this, if true, is one of them, surely: the sixteenth-century Welsh chronicler Elis Gruffydd claimed that Jasper had the baby christened Owen, but Margaret forced the officiating bishop to christen him again with a name allied to the English throne—Henry. The next few months—the time of her official period of mourning—would be spent at Pembroke and on the care of her delicate baby. But she had no intention of leaving the tides of the times to pass her by, at a moment when she must have known that they were flowing swiftly.

The birth of her son impelled Margaret into speedy action. In March, almost as soon as she was churched and received back into public life, she and her brother-in-law Jasper were traveling toward Newport and the home of the Duke of Buckingham. A new marriage had to be arranged for her and an alliance that would protect her son.

The choice fell on Henry Stafford, a mild man some twenty years older than she but, crucially, the second son of the Duke of Buckingham, a staunchly Lancastrian magnate and a man almost as powerful as the Duke of York (who, ironically, was his brother-in-law, since Anne, Duchess of Buckingham, was Cecily Neville's sister). A dispensation was needed, since the pair were second cousins; by April 6 it had been applied for and granted, although the actual marriage ceremony would not take place until Margaret's mourning was complete, on January 3, 1458.

The bride, still only fourteen, would keep the grander title her first marriage had won her, Countess of Richmond, but she brought with her estates now enriched by her inheritance from Edmund Tudor. Her son, Henry Tudor, by contrast, would at first probably remain in Wales and in his uncle's care. Nonetheless, this appears to have been a happy familial relation, with Margaret and her new husband visiting Jasper and baby Henry at Pembroke, with the elder Buckinghams welcoming their new daughter-in-law (Duchess Anne would bequeath Margaret several choice books), and—despite the absence of any further children—with every sign of contentment, at least, between the pair. Margaret would seem to have found a safe haven—except that events would not leave any haven tranquil and unmolested for long.

IN THE SPRING OF 1458 the adversarial parties in the royal dispute were brought to the ceremony of formal reconciliation known as a "Loveday." It was in everyone's interest that some unity should be restored to the country. Queen Marguerite and the Duke of York walked hand in hand into church, to exhibit their amity before God. The pose showed queenly intercession, peacemaking, but it also cast Marguerite as York's equal and political match. Ironically, what might sound to modern ears like a tribute to her activities was actually a devaluation of her status: as queen, she was supposed to be above the fray. To remain on that pedestal might keep her immobile, but to step down from it exposed her vulnerability.

The pacific image was, moreover, misleading. The summer and autumn of 1458 saw fresh clashes between Marguerite and the Yorkists. She had Warwick summoned to London to account for acts of piracy he had committed while governor of Calais, to which post he had been appointed the previous year. He arrived with a large force of armed retainers wearing his livery, and his supporters rallied protests in the city against the queen and the authorities. Tensions deepened when Warwick narrowly escaped impalement on a spit as he passed through the royal kitchens. He claimed that the queen had paid the scullion to murder him. Later that year, Marguerite left London. She was assembling a personal army—what one report described as "queen's gallants," sporting the livery badge of her little son.

A RANDOM LETTER PRESERVED in the archives of Exeter cathedral, concerning a snub to the Crown's candidate for the deanery, gives a taste of Marguerite's mood at this time. It had been reported that some of the chapter were inclined to set aside the royal recommenda- tions "to our great marvel and displeasure if it be so," she wrote. "Wherefore we desire and heartily pray you forthwith that for rever- ence of us . . . you will . . . be inclined and yield to the accomplishment of my lord's invariable intention and our in this matter." It is notable that Henry's letter of confirmation was shorter and feebler and that the officer sent down to see that the royal will was done was Mar- guerite's own master of jewels. But it is also notable, of course, that she was only able ever to act in the name of her husband—or even of her tiny son.

Vergil says that the queen (who was, "for diligence, circumspec- tion and speedy execution of causes, comparable to a man") believed a plan was afoot to put the Duke of York on the throne itself, "Where- fore this wise woman [called] together the council to provide remedy for the disordered state of things." A meeting of the council in Coventry in the summer of 1459 saw York, Warwick, and their ad- herents indicted for their nonappearance "by counsel of the queen." Nominally, of course, the council was the king's council, and it was he who was still ruling the country. But the queen's dominance must have made it hard for many loyal Englishmen to be sure just where their loyalties lay.

The anonymous *English Chronicle* declares that it was at this point that the Yorkists really began spreading rumors. "The queen was defamed and denounced, that he that was called prince, was not her son, but a bastard gotten in adultery." That, the chronicler believed, was why she felt it necessary to raise support for his claim, holding an "open household" among all the knights and squires of Cheshire.

One anomaly of female leadership in the fifteenth century was about to be made clear. Even in the context of armed conflict, Marguerite's power was far from negligible, but here she could act only by proxy. One chronicle describes how it was "by her urging" that the king—nominally—assembled an army. But as that army met the York-Neville forces in the autumn of 1459, at Blore Heath, Marguerite could only wait for news, a few miles away. She would have to wait to hear, among other things, that Thomas, Lord Stanley, whose forces were promised to her, had in fact held them neutral and outside the fray. Shakespeare's Clarence in *Henry VI, Part 3* mocks "Captain Margaret," but in fact the inability to lead their own army would be a problem for female rulers through the time of Elizabeth I, in the next century.* Blore Heath was a massive victory for the Yorkist forces: it was after this battle that Marguerite reputedly told a local blacksmith to put the shoes of her horse on backward, to disguise her tracks as she rode away.

But Marguerite was far from without influence, even in this arena. When the two armies faced off outside Ludlow a couple of weeks later, one source records that the Lancastrian soldiers would fight "for the love they bare to the King, but more for the fear they had of the Queen, whose countenance was so fearful and whose look was so terrible that to all men against whom she took displeasure, her frowning was their undoing and her indignation their death." On this occasion, the Yorkist forces ultimately backed off from armed conflict with their

---

*Christine de Pizan wrote that a baroness should know the laws of arms and the tactics necessary to defend her castle against attack; her queen, however, was expected to take a more passive role. Even at the Paston level, a man could be found sending his wife to preserve their claim to the house and she ordering crossbows. But Margaret Paston was eventually to find that "I cannot well guide nor rule soldiers," who did not heed her as they would a man.

monarch, and the resultant flight has come to be called the rout of Ludford Bridge.

Warwick and Salisbury fled across the Channel to Calais, where their family was waiting. With them went Edward, Earl of March, the eldest son of York and Cecily. York himself and his second son, Edmund, fled to Ireland. Cecily with her younger children had most likely remained at Ludlow: a comfortable castle fitted out for the York family with the fifteenth-century luxuries of window glass and privacy, but now no sanctuary. Several sources record that she and her two youngest sons were taken prisoner there, but in an age that prided itself on chivalry, it was never likely that any personal, physical reprisal would be taken against her, a woman (and indeed there would be widespread disapproval when anyone did break the unspoken rules that meant a lady, whatever her husband had done, might still be assured not only of her personal safety, but perhaps even of control of some of the family's property). One chronicle does say that while the town of Ludlow was robbed to the bare walls, "the noble Duchess of York was entreated and [de]spoiled," but the absence of any other sign of outrage suggests that the damage was only to her goods.

When a Parliament held at Coventry—packed with Marguerite's supporters and known as the "Parliament of Devils"—attainted the Yorkist lords, Cecily went to the city on December 6 and submitted herself to royal mercy. *Gregory's Chronicle* recorded that "the Duchess of York came unto King Harry and submitted her unto his grace, and she prayed for her husband that he might come to his answer to be received unto his grace; and the king full humbly granted her grace, and to all hers that would come with her." Attainder meant not only that the men were convicted of treason, but also that their lands were now the property of the Crown. Cecily, however, was given a grant of a thousand marks per annum—income derived from some of those confiscated lands—"for the relief of her and her infants who had not offended against the king," as the official wording put it, carefully. Her sister-in-law, the Countess of Salisbury, was personally attainted; Cecily was not. She was placed in custody, but the custodian was her own sister, Anne, the Duchess of Buckingham, Margaret Beaufort's mother-in-law, whose husband had declared for the queen's side and who seems to have kept her own natal Lancastrian sympathies. It is speculated that the comparative leniency with which Cecily was treated was the result of her friendship with Queen Marguerite—though the chronicles also report that "she was kept full straight with many a rebuke" from her sister—and by January she was free to move southward again. All the same, it was a low moment for Cecily.

No wonder the German artist Albrecht Dürer drew Fortune frequently, in many different guises, blind and pregnant, wounded or weaponed. In future years, when Cecily's family had left this low point long behind them, the poet John Skelton would lament Cecily's son Edward IV as Fortune's fool:

> *She took me by the hand and led me a dance,*
> *And with her sugared lips on me she smiled,*
> *But, what from her dissembled countenance,*
> *I could not beware till I was beguiled . . .*

At this moment, however, the future prominence of Cecily's son had never looked more unlikely.

6

"MIGHTINESS
MEETS MISERY"

then, in a moment, see
How soon this mightiness meets misery
THE LIFE OF KING HENRY
THE EIGHTH, PROLOGUE

E ven by the standards of these tumultuous years, the ups and
downs of these few months were extraordinary. Cecily had
reached what must surely have felt like her nadir at the end of
1459, but by the following summer, 1460, her Yorkist menfolk were
back with a fresh army.

The Earl of Warwick, and Cecily's son Edward, had returned from
Calais, and at Northampton, in July, their forces again met those of
the king and queen. This time the victorious Yorkists were able to
seize the person of Henry VI and bring him back to London as their
puppet or prisoner, all the while proclaiming their loyalty.

The London chronicler Gregory described Marguerite's flight after Henry's capture: "The queen, hearing this, voided unto Wales

but . . . a servant of her own . . . spoiled her and robbed her, and put her so in doubt of her life and son's life also." The servant was one John Cleger, but as he was rifling through her luggage, the queen and her son managed to escape. "And then she come to the castle of Harlech in Wales," wrote Gregory, "and she had many great gifts and [was] greatly comforted, for she had need thereof." The queen had with her only four companions, the chronicler reports in horror (a great lady's household might be a hundred and fifty; the Duke of Clarence would regularly take almost two hundred people with him from house to house), and she was forced most often to ride pillion behind a fourteen-year-old boy.

Marguerite was not the only woman whose fortunes had changed overnight. Everything was changing, once again, for Cecily, too. In this latest battle, her brother-in-law, the Duke of Buckingham, was among the casualties; the widowed Anne had only recently been rebuking Cecily for being on the wrong side of the fight, an irony that could not have been far from her mind now. While her nephew, Warwick, returned to Calais in triumph to fetch his family home, Cecily and her younger children moved to London, to await word from her husband. As Queen Marguerite fled westward, York sent for Cecily (traveling in a chair of blue velvet "and four pair coursers therein," as Gregory described her) to come and meet him in Hereford, so as to share his triumphal progress, heralded by trumpeters and displaying the royal arms, back into London.

It surely says something about their relationship that York wanted Cecily by his side, riding in victory through the green summer country. But in fact the very flamboyance of the entry "proud Cis" shared with her husband may have worked against them. Citizens and nobles alike were pleased enough to welcome York: he had during his previous stints as protector proven himself a steady hand, to keep anarchy at bay. But when it looked as though York would claim the throne itself, it was clear they were no more ready to accept this usurpation than they had been Marguerite's proxy sovereignty. One monastic chronicler, the abbot of St. Albans, John Whethamsted, has a long and vivid description of the misstep into which York's "exaltation of mood" led him, right down to a record of the distribution of the major players around Westminster palace. York strode to the parliamentary chamber and laid his hand upon the throne as if to claim it. He waited for the applause that, however, failed to come, and then proceeded to the principal chamber of the palace, smashing the locks to gain his entry.

But people of all "estates and ranks, age, sex, order and condition" had, Whethamsted says, begun to murmur against York's presumption. When York continued to press his own claim to the throne, even his friends were horrified. By the end of October 1460, the matter had gone to Parliament, and under the auspices of the Lords a deal was hammered out. Henry would keep the throne for his lifetime but would be succeeded not by his son, but by York and York's sons—an idea presumably made more plausible by that long whispering campaign suggesting Marguerite's infidelity. Such a prospect, with its huge advancement for her children, must have been acceptable to Cecily. But of course Marguerite, whose own young son had been disinherited, was never going to accept it quietly.

Toward the end of the year, she took a ship northward from Wales. Marguerite's plan was to appeal for help from the Scots—over whom, ironically, another woman, Mary of Guelders, was commencing her rule as regent on behalf of her eight-year-old son, James, her husband having recently been killed by an exploding cannon while besieging Yorkist sympathizers at Roxburgh. Mary sent an envoy to escort Marguerite and her young son to Dumfries and Lincluden Abbey, where they were royally entertained while Mary herself came down to meet them. The two queens spent twelve days together at the abbey, and Mary promised military aid, offering the hospitality of the Scottish royal palaces while it was assembled. Moving into England with a foreign army would do little to increase her popularity, but Marguerite was in no mood to worry.

With Henry's captivity, she had now become the undisputed leader of the Lancastrian party: stripped of much she had once enjoyed, but liberated for the first time to act openly on her own initiative. The Yorkist lords, recognizing her importance, tried—according to *Gregory's Chronicle*—to lure Marguerite south to London with faked messages from her husband, "for she was more wittier than the king."

As the Duke of York moved north to meet the impending Lancastrian threat, Marguerite's name was being invoked by friends and enemies alike—even before she was ready to leave Scotland. York, inside his own Sandal Castle, was advised (says the Tudor writer Hall, whose grandfather had been the adviser concerned) not to sally out, but answered it would be a dishonor to do so "for dread of a scolding woman, whose only weapons are her tongue and her nails." The Lancastrian herald, to provoke York into taking a dangerous offensive, sneered that he should allow himself "to be tamely braved by a woman."

York should have heeded all the warnings. Now, once again, the time was coming when it would be Cecily's turn to drink a bitter cup. No wonder she, like Margaret Beaufort, would remember the image of Fortune's Wheel, and would, perhaps ironically, bequeath a bed decorated with that image to the Tudor dynasty. An anonymous poem neatly captures the vicissitudes with which she must by now have been familiar:

> *I have seen fall to men of high nobleness—*
> *First wealth, and then again distress,*
> *Now up, now down, as fortune turneth her wheel—*

On December 30, the royal forces (under the command of the third Duke of Somerset, Margaret Beaufort's cousin, who shared his father's and uncle's strong Lancastrian loyalty) met the Yorkists at the battle of Wakefield and were soundly defeated. Casualties of the rout included York himself, pulled from his horse in the thick of the fray, and his seventeen-year-old son, Edmund, with whose death Shakespeare would make such play. Salisbury (whose son had also died) was killed the next day. Their heads were set on spikes on the gates of York, the duke's capped with a paper crown. Tudor chroniclers like Hall and Holinshed, followed by Shakespeare, had the heads presented to a savagely vengeful Marguerite. But in fact Marguerite left Scotland only after news of the victory, traveling southward in an outfit of black and silver lent to her by the Scottish queen, Mary.

Cecily had lost a husband, a son, a brother, and a nephew. The news must have reached her and her three youngest children, in London and probably at Baynard's Castle, with the taste of the Christmas feasts still in their mouths. A house like Baynard's Castle with its gardens and terraces—and its great hall and its courtyards capable of holding the four hundred armed men the duke had once brought with him from Ireland—must have seemed a place of refuge in a treacherously shifting world. But the Duke of York's death brought to an end a long and in many ways happy union. It had also narrowly deprived Cecily of her chance of being queen, and she would not forget it easily.

Marguerite's party were once more in the ascendant. As the queen came south with her forces, sometime in January or early February 1461, she sent letters—writing once on her own behalf, and once in the name of her young son—to the authorities of London, demanding the City's loyalty. The letter nominally from the seven-year-old prince presents him as the active avenger, heading his own army. Even Marguerite's own letter, forcefully written though it is, can only suggest that she is acting in tandem with her young son, "praying you, on our most hearty and desirous wise, that [above] all earthly things you will diligently intend [attend] to the surety of my lord's royal person in the mean time; so that through malice of his said enemy he be no more troubled, vexed, or jeoparded. And, by so doing, we shall be unto you such a lady as of reason you shall largely be content."

As her army swept ever southward, her troops pillaged the land and she did nothing to halt them, aware that she was unable to offer the alternative of pay. The pillaging did much to sour her subsequent reputation, besides providing fuel for Yorkist propaganda that implicitly linked this catastrophic "misrule" with the parallel reversal of right order represented by a woman's leadership.

But despite their marauding, the Lancastrian troops seemed unstoppable with the queen at their head. After the second battle of St. Albans, on February 17, 1461, the reports are full of mentions of the queen or the queen's party. One source, the Milanese Prospero di Camulio, seems even to suggest that this one time she was in the thick of the fray: "The earl of Warwick decided to quit the field, and . . . pushed through right into Albano [St. Albans], where the queen was with 30,000 men." The chronicler Gregory wrote that in the midst of the battle, "King Harry went to his queen and forsook all his lords, and trust[ed] better to her party than to his own." One anecdotal report of a speech she made to her men is as heroic in its own way as Elizabeth I's at Tilbury: "I have often broken [the English] battle line. I have mowed down ranks far more stubborn than theirs are now. You who once followed a peasant girl [Joan of Arc] now follow a queen. . . . I will either conquer or be conquered with you."

Marguerite had by now experienced far more warfare than most ladies of her time. She would have known the tension beforehand, mounting to a fever pitch; the fear that each step of her horse's hoof could bring it down on the sharp point of a hidden caltrop, before men rushed out from ambush in the bushes to claim her as their prey; the roads, afterward, crammed with the bodies of horses and with bleeding, dying men who lacked even the strength to crawl away.

King Henry had been brought under guard to the second battle of St. Albans by Warwick, and after the battle he was found seated under an oak tree. Marguerite was reunited with her husband, and together they headed for the capital. As the couple halted outside London, the City officials requested that a delegation of trusted ladies should act as go-betweens, interceding with Marguerite "for to be benevolent and owe goodwill to the city," which had until recently been host to the pretender York.* The ladies were Ismanie, Lady Scales, who had been among those escorting Marguerite from France and who had remained in her household; the widowed Duchess of Buckingham (Cecily of York's sister and Margaret Beaufort's mother-in-law, Anne, whose husband had been killed the previous summer fighting in the Lancastrian cause); and Jacquetta, dowager Duchess of Bedford. Born a scion of the princely house of Luxembourg, married in her youth to Henry VI's uncle John, Jacquetta had been widowed in 1435 at the age of just nineteen, and "minding also to marry rather for pleasure than for honour, without council of her friends," had promptly married "a lusty knight, Sir Richard Woodville." Originally sent to France as one of the party escorting Marguerite to England, Jacquetta had remained close to the queen; indeed, her eldest daughter, Elizabeth, may have been one of Marguerite's ladies. Now not only was Jacquetta's own

---

*Women, of course, traditionally had an intercessionary or conciliatory function. Margery Paston was urged to persuade the Duchess of Norfolk to support her family, for "one word of a woman should do more than the words of twenty men."

husband with the queen's force, but so too, until recently, had been her daughter's husband and father to her two young sons, John Grey. John Grey had died at the second battle of St. Albans, leaving Elizabeth Woodville a widow—a development that would soon propel her into national history.

A letter reported that the delegation returned to London on Friday, February 20, with news that "the king and queen had no mind to pillage the chief city and chamber of their realm, and so they promised; but at the same time they did not mean that they would not punish the evildoers." But the message was ambiguous enough that there was still the danger of panic in the streets, and the ladies were sent out again on Sunday to negotiate that the Lancastrian leaders might enter the City without the main body of their army. The queen agreed.

Ironically, Marguerite's decision to send only a small symbolic force into London, and her subsequent withdrawal back to Dunstable with her husband and the bulk of her forces, would prove to be arguably the mistake of her life. The wheel was about to turn yet again. In another of the huge overturns of fortune that had already marked this young war, the upset was not heralded in any way. In the weeks after the battle of Wakefield, Cecily Neville had been so afraid as to send her two younger sons, George and Richard, abroad, to the safety of Burgundy. Yet almost as she did so, her eldest son, Edward, and her nephew, the Earl of Warwick, with their armies, were preparing to approach London from the west. They encountered no opposition due to Marguerite's northerly withdrawal, and on February 27 they were welcomed into the City, and Edward went to his mother's house of Baynard's Castle.

This time, there was no talk of loyalty to King Henry, or of wishing only to rid him of his evil counselors. On Sunday, March 1, the Bishop of Exeter, Warwick's brother and, like him, cousin to Edward, asked the eager Londoners whether they felt that Henry deserved to rule, "whereunto," as the *Great Chronicle of London* reported, "the people cried hugely and said Nay. And after it was asked of them whether they would have the Earl of March [Edward] for their king and they cried with one voice, Yea, Yea."

Cecily Neville's eldest son, the "fair white rose" of York, was still only eighteen, but when, three days later, he was acclaimed and enthroned, his huge stature and glowing golden looks made him seem every inch the king. The youthful Edward with his royal bloodline not only was the favorite candidate backed by Warwick and the Neville party, but had also recently proved his mettle by leading his army to a decisive victory at Mortimer's Cross. And it would have seemed appropriate to the Yorkists at least for his royal title—Edward IV—to have such closeness and continuity with that of the great Plantagenet progenitor, Edward III.

The Yorkists had finally succeeded in putting one of their own on the throne, but they had not yet completely won. London was not England. On March 13, with Warwick already engaged recruiting men in the Midlands, King Edward marched his army north to a fresh fight. There was still another king alive, with Henry and Marguerite in the North still commanding the loyalty of a majority of the nobility. Prospero di Camulio, the Milanese ambassador in France, erroneously heard that Marguerite had given her husband poison, after persuading him to abdicate in favor of their son. "However," he equivocated, "these are rumours in which I do not repose much confidence." Very soon, however, after the dreadful battle of Towton, di Camulio was writing less cautiously.

Fought outside York in the worst of wintry weather, on an icy Palm Sunday, Towton is still probably the bloodiest battle ever fought on English soil. No detailed description survives, and the numbers of those involved, as estimated by contemporary reporters and later historians, vary wildly. But what is agreed is that this was a ten-hour endurance test in which men slogged each other to exhaustion, one in which King Edward told his men to give no quarter, and one in which the opposing Lancastrians, with the wind against them, suffered snow and arrows blowing together into their faces.

Before the battle had begun, both sides were already worn and frozen, after a bitter night spent in the biting wind. Nonetheless, the fighting went on until ten o'clock, long after it was dark. By dusk the Lancastrian forces had been driven backward to a deep gully of the River Cock, and many who were not hacked down were drowned as they tried to cross.

It was, says the *Great Chronicle of London*, "a sore and long and unkindly fight—for there was the son against the father, the brother against brother." Crowland talks of more than thirty-eight thousand dead, and though that is probably an exaggeration, "many a lady," said *Gregory's Chronicle,* lost her beloved that day.

For others, of course, the news was good. Cecily had word of the Yorkist victory early, on April 3, as William Paston wrote: a "letter of credence" bearing Edward's own sign "came unto our said lady this same day . . . at xi clock and was seen and read by me." The Bishop of Elphin was, as he subsequently told the Papal Legate, actually in her house when she received the glad news. "On hearing the news the Duchess [returned] to the chapel with two chaplain and myself and there we said 'Te Deum' after which I told her that the time was come for writing to your Lordship, of which she approved."

Now it was Marguerite, her husband, and her son who were to flee, leaving York, where they waited for news, with only what they could carry. The Lancastrian army had been scattered, and the Yorkists held London. Whatever the future held in store for the family, it was sure to be brutal—all the more so given the distinct lack of public affection for Marguerite in most corners of England. As Prospero di Camulio wrote, "Any one who reflects at all upon the wretchedness of that queen and the ruins of those killed and considers the ferocity of the country, and the state of mind of the victors, should indeed, it seems to me, pray to God for the dead and not less for the living."

PART II

1460–1471

7

"TO LOVE A KING"

Lady Grey: Why stops my lord? Shall I not hear my task?
Edward: An easy task: 'tis but to love a king.

HENRY VI, PART 3, 3.2

A new regime had come in, a new ruling house held the throne, and everything had changed. But none of the protagonists could have failed to be aware that, where Fortune's Wheel had spun once so dramatically, it could spin again just as easily.

The fortunes of Marguerite of Anjou had turned dramatically for the worse, though it had been such a brief time since she had been graciously receiving humble petitioners. After the battle, she, with her husband and son, had fled north back to Scotland, where they would remain for the next year. The refugees were forced again to promise the perpetually contested border town of Berwick to the Scots as the price of their entertainment, while any further attempt to recruit French aid was temporarily thwarted by the death that summer of the French king, Charles. His successor, Louis, would have to be wooed afresh. Attainted in the first Parliament of November 1461 for transgressions and offenses "against her faith and Liegance" to

King Edward, Marguerite was being destroyed as only a woman can be. A ballad from the time sums up the campaign against her:

> *Moreover it is a right great perversion,*
> *A woman of a land to be a regent—*
> *Queen Margaret I mean, that ever hath meant*
> *To govern all England with might and power*
> *And to destroy the right line was her intent.*

The absent Marguerite was now everyone's choice of villain. Another ballad, a couple of years later, had Henry VI lamenting he had married a wife "that was the cause of all my moan." When the Tudor chronicler Polydore Vergil wrote later that "by mean of a woman, sprang up a new mischief that set all out of order," he was casting her as another Eve. Even Edward, for whom the still-extant Henry should surely have been the greatest enemy, wrote of him as having been moved "by the malicious and subtle suggestion and enticing of the said malicious woman Margaret his wife."

Elizabeth Woodville, the freshly widowed daughter of Jacquetta, Duchess of Bedford, had certainly suffered as well. She had endured the loss of her husband, John Grey, but she was also forced to confront the potential wreck of her whole family. She could no longer count on the security of a home on one of the Grey family's Midland estates. Not only would she have to fight her dead husband's family for her dower rights, but as leading Lancastrians the Woodvilles might well have found themselves ruined when Henry and Marguerite fell.

Margaret Beaufort too had suffered, to a lesser degree. The armed clashes that brought the Yorkists into power killed her father-in-law, the Duke of Buckingham, at Northampton in 1460 and brought the position of his family into question, threatening the bastion of support that Margaret had enjoyed since her marriage to Henry Stafford. They had also scattered her natal family. Her cousin Henry, the latest Duke of Somerset (son to Marguerite's ally), had to flee abroad after Towton with his younger brothers, as did Margaret's brother-in-law Jasper Tudor. In the autumn of 1461, Jasper followed Queen Marguerite into her Scottish exile and would spend almost a decade, there and in France, trying to rally the Lancastrian cause.

Margaret's husband, too, had fought for the Lancastrians at Towton; he, however, had been pardoned by a King Edward determined to heal breaches insofar as possible. Henry and Margaret were able to establish themselves in the castle of Bourne in the Fen country, part of Margaret's own Holland inheritance from her grandmother. The wardship of Margaret's son, the young Henry Tudor, however, was another matter. He was no threat to Edward (or, rather, with Henry VI and his son both living, he was hardly the greatest threat), but he and his lands did present a financial opportunity for anyone the king wished to reward.

Whereas Henry Tudor's lands were given to the Duke of Clarence, wardship of the four-year-old boy was given to the devoted Yorkist Sir William Herbert, the man who had once, in Wales, taken Edmund Tudor into custody, leaving the young Margaret Beaufort a widow. But for several years this arrangement, like Henry's previous wardship with his uncle Jasper, seemed a comparatively happy one; Henry, visited by Margaret and her husband, was raised with every advantage as one of Herbert's own family—which, with several young daughters to marry off, they may have planned he would one day become.

As for Cecily Neville, it must have been hard for her to work out where Fortune's Wheel had left her. The loss of her husband and her second son, a shattering personal grief, was only weeks behind her, but now another son, her eldest, sat on the throne, opening up a world of possibilities. As Edward set out north again, he recommended his mother to the burghers of London as his representative. The Bishop of Elphin concluded his letter about Cecily's reception of the battlefield news by urging the Papal Legate to take advantage of the new influence of the king's mother: "As soon as you can, write to the King, the Chancellor, and other Lords, as I see they wish it; also to the Duchess, who is partial to you, and [holds] the king at her pleasure." In the early days of Edward IV's reign, perhaps the bishop was not the only one to consider that Cecily could rule her son as she wished. Edward granted to her the lands held by his father and further subsidized her always lavish expenditure. She regarded herself as queen dowager, and she played the part. Edward, for his part, must have been aware that he had come to the throne by the efforts of her relations (whatever breaches between the Nevilles and the Yorkists had existed in the past, or might come later). And he was young enough to make it possible for everyone—perhaps even including his mother—to underestimate his capabilities.*

Cecily's sons Richard and George and her youngest daughter— fourteen-year-old Margaret "of Burgundy," as she would become— were now installed at Greenwich, the luxurious riverside pleasure palace that had been remodeled by Henry VI's uncle Humfrey, the Duke of Gloucester. Her two elder sisters were already established elsewhere, though both of their marriages reflected the problems women could face when their natal and their marital families wound up on different sides of the political divide. Anne, the Yorks' eldest child, had been matched in 1445 when she was six with Henry Holland, son of the great Duke of Exeter; her husband, however, was committed to the Lancastrian cause, and by the time she reached adulthood, it seems likely the couple were estranged to the point where Anne notoriously found consolation elsewhere, with a Kent gentleman called Thomas St. Leger. The next sister, Elizabeth, had recently been married to John de la Pole, Duke of Suffolk (who, as a child, had nominally been married to Margaret Beaufort). John's father had been the great minister of Henry VI (and great friend to Marguerite), murdered in 1450; his mother, the duchess, was the mighty Alice Chaucer, a natural Lancastrian who, despite her ties to the new king's enemies, doubtless found her son's marriage to the new Yorkist princess to be for her family's safety. Elizabeth quickly began to produce a string of children—at least five sons and four daughters— and with her husband converted to the Yorkist side, Elizabeth's future looked uncontroversial, the more so since John showed no aptitude for nor interest in active political office. But his new sister-in-law Margaret, while a mere two years younger than Elizabeth, was, crucially,

---

*If we want a suggestion of what Cecily might have hoped her relation to Edward would be, we could look to the letter Alice Chaucer's husband, Suffolk, had left for his son: "I charge you, my dear son, always, as ye be bounden by the commandment of god to do, to love, to worship your lady and mother, and also that ye obey always her commandments, and to believe her counsels and advices in all your works."

still unmarried when her brother Edward came to the throne—and her single status now became one more card for the new king to play.

Greenwich had once, under the so recent former regime, been adopted by Queen Marguerite as her own. Marguerite had decorated it with the daisy emblem (and new windows, a Great Chamber, an arbor in the gardens, and a gallery overlooking them) that was now fitting also for this other Margaret. The whole family would come to use Greenwich a good deal, but for the moment, Edward seized on it primarily as a suitable and healthy residence for his three youngest siblings, and those bonds between Margaret and her brothers Richard and George, which this proximity may have fostered, would play an important part in English affairs throughout the Tudor reign.

Here Margaret would have continued her education. A well-to-do girl's training usually centered on the religious and on the practical: reading, in case she had to take over business responsibilities; some knowledge of arithmetic; and an understanding of household and estate management that might even extend to a little property law. The technical skill of writing was rarer; even Margaret's own later signature was rough and unformed. And though a girl might be expected to read the psalms in Latin from an early age, to write Latin, by contrast, was so unusual that even the learned Margaret Beaufort, says her confessor, John Fisher, had later to regret she had not been taught.

But perhaps this York Margaret benefited to some degree from being brought up with her brothers and their tutors. In later life, her own books would be in French—a language she obviously was taught—but by then her collection of books (at least twenty-five of them, an impressive collection for a woman), and her habit of giving and getting books as gifts, shows notable literary interest. Printer William Caxton would later—tactfully, but presumably also truly—acknowledge her help in correcting his written English. Under her auspices, he published the first book ever printed in English, a translation from French of the tales of Troy, and wrote of how she had "found a defaut in my English which she commanded me to amend."

Those books Margaret later owned would be wonderfully illustrated in the lively modern style with flowers and fruit, animals and birds. Perhaps she got a full measure of enjoyment out of the gardens at Greenwich, but perhaps, too, the spirit of Duke Humfrey, a famed bibliophile, lingered on in the palace.

Margaret's pronounced interest in religion may have come from her mother, but although in her later life she would give particular support to those orders of religion that devoted themselves to practical good works, and had as ardent a passion for relics of the saints as any other medieval lady, she seems also to have boasted a more intellectual interest in the subject than Cecily Neville. If there was to be a darker, an almost hysterical, element in her religious faith, then perhaps it shows only that the travails of her family, at her most impressionable age, had not left her untouched.

Margaret's young relation Anne Neville, meanwhile, also found herself in a radically new position within Edward's England. Anne Neville's father, Warwick, Cecily Neville's nephew and cousin to the new king, was now the man most thought to be the real power behind the throne, though in fact there is much to suggest that Edward would be (from Warwick's viewpoint) finding his own feet much too quickly; the commons "love and adore [Edward] as if he were their god," wrote one Italian observer. But all the same, Warwick, having helped the new king to his throne, was riding high, restless and busy. The whereabouts of his daughters and wife, the countess Anne Beauchamp, are not often known for sure, though it is likely they visited the great northern stronghold of Middleham and the royal court. The countess's own family estates in the West Midlands are one possibility for their main base; a countess had her own household, as distinct from her husband the earl's, but events in this female-led world were not recorded as extensively.

Not that Anne Neville's world was always female. Edward's younger brother Richard was brought up in Warwick's household for three years, and in 1465 he and Anne were recorded as being at the feast to celebrate the enthronement of Anne's uncle George Neville as archbishop of York. By this point it would have been evident that the nine-year-old Anne would be a significant heiress, whether or not the thirteen-year-old Richard was mature enough to take note. The continental chronicler Waurin would record that even now, Warwick contemplated marrying his daughters to the king's two brothers.

Marriage was in the air, and not just for Edward's brothers. Cecily Neville was about to find out the truth behind the later adage "Your daughter's your daughter all of your life—your son's your son till he gets him a wife." And the young King Edward was about to make a choice based (most unusually for the times) on "blind affection," as Polydore Vergil describes it disapprovingly—a choice that would shape the future of his kingdom.

The story of how the widowed Elizabeth Woodville had originally met Edward IV is one of the best known from history. And it is just that—a story. No one knows much about Elizabeth's life before she made her royal match because no one was watching. Where fact was absent, fiction rushed in.

The sixteenth-century writer Edward Hall had Edward IV hunting in the forest of Wychwood near Grafton and coming to the Woodville home for refreshment. Other traditions say it was Whittlebury Forest, where an oak was long celebrated for the theory that Elizabeth—and the pleading figures of the two little boys she had borne her dead husband—stood under it to catch the king's attention as he rode by, so that she could petition to be granted the lands owed to her under the terms of her dowry. Either way, Elizabeth, Hall said, "found such grace in the King's eyes that he not only favoured her suit, but much more fantasised her person. . . . For she was a woman . . . of such beauty and favour that with her sober demeanour, lovely looking and feminine smiling (neither too wanton nor too humble) beside her tongue so eloquent and her wit so pregnant . . . she allured and made subject to her the heart of so great a king."

After Edward, Hall said, "had well considered all the lineaments of her body and the wise and womanly demeanour that he saw in her," he tried to bribe her into becoming his mistress (under the more flattering courtly appellation of his "sovereign lady") in the hopes of her later becoming his wife. She answered that "as she was unfitted for his honour to be his wife then for her own honesty she was too good to be his concubine"—an answer that so inflamed the king to a "hot burning fire" he determined indeed to marry her. The same technique, of course, worked again when Anne Boleyn practiced it on Elizabeth's grandson Henry, whose likeness to Edward has been much remarked.

Even when traced backward in time, the story does not lose much drama. Thomas More described the same scenario, the one Shakespeare too would echo almost exactly—the king struck by this woman "fair and of good favour, moderate of stature, well-made, and very wise," who claimed that if she was too "simple" to be his wife, she was too good to be his concubine, Elizabeth herself virtuously refusing Edward's advances, but "with so good manner, and words so well set, that she rather kindled his desire than quenched it." Hearne's "Fragment," written in the early sixteenth century by someone who was probably at Edward's court in its later years, similarly recorded that Edward "being a lusty prince attempted the stability and constant modesty of divers ladies and gentlewomen," but after resorting at "diverse times" to Elizabeth, he became impressed by her "constant and stable mind."

The Italian traveler Mancini, writing in 1483, even has Edward— so "the story runs"—holding a dagger to Elizabeth's throat; again, as More and Hall would have it, "she remained unperturbed and determined to die rather than live unchastely with the king. Whereupon Edward coveted her much the more, and he judged the lady worthy to be a royal spouse." One of the most dramatic versions occurs in Italy very soon after, in Antonio Cornazzano's *De Mulieribus Admirandis* (Of admirable women). This reverses the scenario, to have Elizabeth holding the king off with a dagger; the very stuff of melodrama.

These are stories that equate the nobility of virtue—which could be allowed to Elizabeth—with the blood nobility she did not possess. The question is, of course, whether they are all only stories. There is a very real possibility that the tale of the Grafton meeting under the tree is a myth. Certainly, the dating of it is confusing. It had been as far back as 1461, after Towton, that Edward had ridden slowly south and first found the Woodville family, with their widowed daughter, Elizabeth Grey, licking their wounds; one account suggests that the romance started there, because when the king left the district two days later, he had not only "pardoned and remitted and forgiven" Elizabeth's father all his offenses—Woodville and his son had fought on the Lancastrian side at Towton—but also "affectionately" agreed to go on paying Jacquetta her annual dowry of "three hundred and thirty three marks four shillings and a third of a farthing."

Woodville was indeed pardoned in June 1461, and the king agreed in December that Jacquetta should receive her dowry. Jean de Waurin early claimed that it was Edward's love for Woodville's daughter that had gotten Woodville his pardon, but the timing of events complicates this interpretation, suggesting a more prolonged and more pragmatic story.

From that record of the Woodville pardon in 1461, it is well into 1463 before Elizabeth Woodville next appears in the records, and then it is in the context of a property dispute over her dowry from her first husband. Indeed, in mid-April 1464, Elizabeth Woodville was still negotiating for her dower lands as if she had no idea she was about to become queen.

It is possible that Elizabeth did indeed stand by the side of the road, but in 1464 instead of 1461; however, since her father had by then been restored to royal confidence as a member of Edward's council, she would surely have had better ways to put her plea. It may be Elizabeth simply met Edward at court after Woodville had been restored to favor. Caspar Weinreich's *Chronicle* of 1464 claims that "the king fell in love with [a mere knight's] wife when he dined with her frequently." This would in many ways make sense. In the first years of the 1460s, his advisers suggested various foreign marriages for the new king, and Edward seemed quite content that negotiations should begin. This suggests that it was indeed several years into his reign when he met Elizabeth and changed his mind.

The circumstances of the marriage between Edward and Elizabeth Woodville are not much clearer. Hall and More have Edward first determining to marry Elizabeth and then taking secret counsel of his friends; the more popular, and more dramatic, version, however, suggests a marriage made in total secrecy. Robert Fabian (contemporary compiler of the *New Chronicles of England and France* and probably also of the *Great Chronicle of London*) describes a marriage made at Grafton early in the morning of May Day, "at which marriage no one was present but the spouse, the spouses, the Duchess of Bedford her mother, the priest, two gentlewomen and a young man to help the priest sing."

After the spousals ended, he says, the king "went to bed and so tarried there upon three or four hours," returning to his men at Stony

Stratford as though he had merely been out hunting but in fact going back to Grafton, where Elizabeth was brought to his bed nightly "in so secret manner that almost none but her mother was council." May Day is a suitably romantic date—as Malory put it, "all ye that be lovers, call unto your remembrance the month of May, like as did Queen Guenivere." May 1 is also Beltane, an important date in the witches' calendar, and there would later be suggestions that witchcraft had been used to produce so unexpected a match between the king and a relatively obscure noblewoman.

Although the marriage is cloaked in so many uncertainties, the ceremony was sufficiently covert that Richard III's first Parliament, when the time came, would be able to denounce it as an "ungracious pretensed marriage" by which "the order of all politic rule was perverted," a marriage that had taken place privately "and secretly, without Edition of Banns, in a private Chamber, a profane place." The fact, however, was that the secrecy of this marriage did not make it illegal (there would be other reasons brought in to support that allegation); indeed, even the mere consent of the two parties before witnesses might have been enough to make the match a valid one. But the surreptitiousness did give the union an odd aura, at a time when the church was endeavoring to regulate marriage ceremonies—an aura all the odder, of course, in view of the very different style in which a king's wedding would usually be celebrated.

Elizabeth's mother, Jacquetta, would be blamed for her part in making this marriage, but there were two mothers in this story, and however much Jacquetta might have wanted the match, Cecily was equally set against it. Whether Cecily heard before the event and failed to dissuade her son, or learned of the marriage afterward, she was furiously angry—"sore moved," as More would put it, and "dissuaded that marriage as much as she possible might." It is hard not to think of Elizabeth Woodville when one reads of Thomas Malory's Merlin trying to dissuade King Arthur from marrying Guenivere: "As of her beauty and fairness she is one of the fairest alive. But an ye loved her not so well as ye do, I should find you a damosel of beauty and of goodness that should like you and please you, and your heart were not set. But there as man's heart is set, he will be loath to return." Edward's heart was similarly set upon Elizabeth, as Cecily was about to find out: More's account of her arguments against Elizabeth goes on for pages, showing her urging her son upon the vital importance of marrying for foreign alliance and objecting "that it was not princely to marry his own subject, no great occasion leading thereunto, no possessions, or other commodities, depending thereupon, but only as it were a rich man would marry his maid, only for a little wanton dotage upon her person."

Elizabeth Woodville's person, of course, was very much the question—what she looked like and what about her could have been so seductive. The urge to know these things is to some degree the same with all of these women, of course, but information is scarce and sometimes confusing. Margaret Beaufort's later associate John Fisher revealed that she was small and slight; Cecily, meanwhile, was apparently a beauty (and since her husband was slight and dark, her son tall and golden, we can guess she was a statuesque blonde). Elizabeth of York's full bust was described by ambassadors, and her long yellow hair was admired at her coronation; Anne Neville was sufficiently similar to Elizabeth for them to be noted as wearing the same clothes. Margaret of Burgundy was described by the chronicler Jean de Haynin as notably tall "like her brother Edward" and having "an air of intelligence and wit." Portraits of her show an oval face, straight nose, firm lips, and a receding chin—not a beauty, but someone you might be glad to know.

The same ideal of female beauty probably held sway throughout the whole medieval era: gold hair, black eyebrows, white skin, high forehead, small but slightly swelling lips—eyes sparkling and usually gray—small high breasts, narrow waist, long arms, slim white fingers. (Perkin Warbeck—a pretender but nonetheless well equipped with princely graces—would write to the noble lady he was courting of her "eyes, as brilliant as stars . . . your white neck, easily outshining pearls . . . your peerless brow, the glowing bloom of youth, the bright gold hair.") To quote one contemporary writer, Geoffrey of Vinsauf, "Let the upper arms, as long as they are slender, be enchanting. Let the fingers be soft and slim in substance, smooth and milk-white in appearance, long and straight in shape. . . . Let the snowy bosom present both breasts like virginal gems set side by side. Let the waist be slim, a mere handful. . . . [L]et the leg show itself graceful, let the

remarkably dainty foot wanton with its own daintiness." Osbern Bo-
kenham in the mid-fifteenth century, writing a life of female saints for
Isabella, the Countess of Essex and Richard of York's sister, described
Saint Margaret:

> *her forehead lily white*
> *Her bent brows black and her grey eyen*
> *. . . her chin, which as plain*
> *Polished marble shone, & cloven in twain.*

Marguerite of Anjou was depicted in an illustration with honey-
blonde hair, despite the Milanese description of her as dark—but
queens usually were shown as blonde: fairness was attributed to the
Virgin Mary. The trouble is that the depiction or description of
queens might then owe more to the ideal than to reality.

But unlike most of the other women here, Elizabeth Woodville
can boast enough of a legacy of recognizable portraiture to suggest a
beauty that shines down the centuries as well as conforming to that
early ideal, beauty enough that the trying fashion for a high shaven
forehead and hair drawn plainly back only illuminates its smooth regularity. A 1470s depiction shows her with red dress beneath blue cloak,
like that of the Virgin Mary—red for earthly nature, blue for heavenly
attributes, with roses (virginity) and gillyflowers (virtuous love, moth-
erhood). Elizabeth would choose the deep-red gillyflower as her personal symbol; the name also meant "queen of delights."

So even her prospective mother-in-law, Cecily, had to admit that
there might be "nothing to be misliked" in the person of "this widow."
But she (and many others among Edward's advisers) found plenty else
of which to complain. First, of course, there was the simple difference
in rank and the fact that Elizabeth brought no great foreign alliance.
Warwick—convinced that only a French marriage would put an end to
French support for Marguerite of Anjou—had been in the process of
negotiating for Bona, daughter of the Duke of Savoy, when Edward
apparently broke the news of this other contract. The Italian visitor
Mancini would later claim that Cecily declared Edward was illegitimate, his choice of a woman of lower rank proof he could not be of the
blood of kings.

It is debatable just how far from suitable Elizabeth actually was. Certainly, she was not the princess a king might usually have been expected to marry, but her mother, Jacquetta, did, after all, come from the cadet branch of the Luxembourg family that gave her connections with the emperors of Germany and the kings of Bohemia. Obviously, a woman's status came from her father, and a mother could not give to her husband and children her superior rank. That said, women through the medieval period frequently chose—in the modes of expression open to them, most notably in the arms displayed on their seals—to reflect their maternal heritage, showing that this part of their lineage could still be significant. Indeed, much play would be made, when the time came for Elizabeth's coronation, of her connections with European royalty. Then again, there may also have been some popularity value in Elizabeth's very Englishness—Marguerite had arguably soured the market for French princesses—and even a reconciliatory gain from her family's attachment to the Lancastrian cause.

But Elizabeth's widowhood was another problem. There was at the very least a strong sentiment (More and Mancini put it higher and make it a custom) that the king's bride should be a virgin, not a widow, the more so if she was to provide the children who would inherit the throne. Decades later Isabella of Castile was still throwing up the fact that Edward had refused her for "a widow of England," and the king's brother Clarence, said Mancini, would go so far as to declare the marriage illegal because of this. More reports (or imagines) Cecily as declaring that "it is an unfitting thing, and a very blemish, and high disparagement, to the sacred majesty of a prince . . . to be defiled with bigamy in his first marriage," and it *may* have been that Elizabeth's previous marriage was enough to make this one seem bigamous. Later, another, more serious, issue would raise its head.

The king's heart, however, was set. Edward answered his mother, More says, that "he knew himself out of her rule." Playing to Cecily's well-known religiosity, he added that surely, "marriage being a spiritual thing," it should follow the guidance of God who had inclined these two parties "to love together" rather than be made for temporal advantage. But perhaps attitudes were changing—or perhaps they had, indeed, never been that clear-cut. The writers of the courtly love tradition, and Malory in their wake, may not necessarily have envisaged love as located in the context of a marriage, but they certainly had no problem in crediting women with romantic feelings and sexual desires. And Edward III had allowed several of his children to make a love match, as his namesake may very well have now pointed out.

As for Warwick and his French schemes, Edward added, surely his cousin could not be so unreasonable as "to look that I should in choice of wife rather be ruled by his eye than by my own, as though I were a ward that were bound to marry by the appointment of a guardian." This was perhaps the crunch—that Edward was getting tired of his mother's, and his mentor's, governance. And anyway, the deed was done; in the face of mounting rumors, Edward admitted as much to his council in September 1464, albeit, said Waurin, in a "right merry" way that surely bespoke embarrassment. Elizabeth was presented to the court on September 30, Michaelmas Day, in the Chapel of Reading Abbey, led in by Edward's brother Clarence and the Earl of Warwick, in a ceremony that may have been aimed at re-placing the big public wedding that would usually have made a queen.

The only Englishwoman to become queen consort since the Nor-man Conquest, Elizabeth Woodville was crowned the following spring, in a ceremony of great magnificence in the presence of her un-cle Jacques of Luxembourg—careful reminder that although Elizabeth might not be a foreign princess, her mother, Jacquetta, could still boast of a European royal kin. Edward had been ordering from abroad "divers jewels of gold and precious stones, against the Coronation of our dear wife the Queen," silk for her chairs and saddle, plate, gold utensils, and cloths of gold. Other expenses show a more homely touch: the bridge master of London Bridge was purchasing paints, glue, and colored paper, "party gold" and "party silver." Elizabeth would be greeted by eight effigies in the pageant as she crossed the river, coming from Eltham to the south. Six of the effigies were of women—virgins—with kerchiefs on their heads over wigs made of flax and dyed with saffron; two were angels, their wings resplendent with nine hundred peacock feathers. Elizabeth made her way to the Tower, where tradition dictated she would spend the night, along streets espe-cially sprinkled with sand, through air alive with song. The next day she was carried in a horse litter to Westminster, where she was to spend the night, her arrival heralded by the white and blue splendor of several dozen newly made knights.

Details of the coronation survive in a contemporary manuscript. Elizabeth entered Westminster Hall under a canopy of cloth of gold, in a purple mantle, flanked by bishops and with scepters in her right hand and her left. Removing her shoes before she entered sacred ground, she walked barefoot, followed by her attendants, led by Cecily's sister, Anne, the dowager Duchess of Buckingham; with Edward's sisters, Elizabeth and Margaret; the queen's own mother, Jacquetta; and more than forty other ladies of rank.

As the procession moved up to the high altar, the queen first knelt, and then prostrated herself, for the solemnities. She was anointed with the holy unction and escorted to her throne "with great reverence and solemnity." This (for a queen as well as to a greater degree for a king) was a ceremony that not only acknowledged but actually created the sacred nature of monarchy.

After mass was sung, the queen processed back into the palace, where Elizabeth retired into her chamber before the banquet begun. It was to be a meal of three "courses," each of some fifteen or twenty dishes, followed by wafers, hippocras (a wine), and spices, served with the utmost ceremony. Before it the queen washed, while the Duke of Clarence held the basin. For the entire duration of the meal, the Duke of Suffolk (husband to the king's sister Elizabeth) and the Earl of Essex knelt beside her, one on either side. To signal each course trumpets were sounded, and a procession of mounted knights made the rounds of the great Westminster Hall. Musicians played solemn music, and the festivities ended with a tournament the next day, the victor of which was Lord Stanley, now in good graces with the Yorkists after abandoning Marguerite at the battle of Blore Heath.

The king had not been present at the ceremonies, and this was normal procedure: the queen was always the most important person present at her own coronation day. But there is another whose name does not appear in the records: the king's mother, Cecily.

It was at this time that Cecily elaborated her title of "My Lady the King's Mother"—used by her, though more often accorded to Margaret Beaufort—into "Cecily, the king's mother, and late wife unto Richard in right king of England and of France and lord of Ireland," or, more directly, "Queen by Right." Though she spent less time now at court, she still kept an apartment—the "queen's chambers"—in one of the royal palaces. Rather than attempt to dispossess his mother, Edward built a new one for his wife.

According to at least one report—admittedly made to Elizabeth's brother—the marriage was, broadly speaking, acceptable in the country: Marguerite, and the turmoil for which she was blamed, had put the people off foreign royalty. But a newsletter from Bruges reported differently, that the "greater part of the lords and the people in general seem very much dissatisfied." In court circles, the marriage was certainly unwelcome. Woodville ascendancy was bound to upset both actual royal family and the great magnate Warwick—more mouths to feed at the royal trough, never mind any differing views on policy. This was all the more true, of course, since those who had shed blood for York had now to see a household of Lancastrians exalted so high.

8

"FORTUNE'S PAGEANT"

And, being a woman, I will not be slack
To play my part in Fortune's pageant

HENRY VI, PART 2, 1.2

While discord was sprouting within the young Yorkist regime, Edward had another, more pressing, cause for concern. The previous queen, the deposed Marguerite, had long since ceased nursing her wounds and was on the move once again. Although Henry had never been the most capable of leaders at even the best of times, Marguerite had proven herself an active queen. It was a role she had no intention of walking away from now.

In April 1462, before most people in England had even heard the name Elizabeth Woodville, Marguerite had made her way from Scotland to France. A register of the city of Rouen, in July, describes her as being received "with much honour, by the gentlemen of the King's suite," and lodging in the hotel of the Golden Lion, belonging to a lawyer of the city. She had since the year before been using her old admirer Pierre de Brézé to negotiate a loan and a fleet with which to seize the Channel Islands and make a bridgehead from France to

England. The idea of inviting their traditional enemies, the French, to launch an armed invasion would have appalled Marguerite's English subjects. "If the Queen's intentions were discovered, her friends would unite with her enemies to kill her," de Brézé said. Foreseeing "good winnings," the French king, Louis (possibly under pressure from his mother, Marguerite's aunt), did eventually give her aid, with Marguerite, in another gesture that would have horrified most Englishmen and -women, promising to cede him Calais in return. In the autumn of 1462, she had sailed back to Scotland, bringing forty ships and eight hundred French soldiers provided by the French king and under de Brézé's command. Collecting some Scots led by Somerset (and nominally by the deposed king Henry VI), she pushed across the border into northern England, where she made "open war," as the *Great Chronicle of London* puts it.

Her campaign was unsuccessful. When the Yorkist guns on England's northern coast were trained upon her, she was forced to flee in a small sailing ship, a carvel. But the *Great Chronicle* relates how, as a violent storm came up, she was compelled to abandon even that attempt to find safety and land again at Berwick, leaving the carvel, with all her goods on board, to go down at sea. Edward himself rode north to confront her. The next spring, as *Gregory's Chronicle* describes it, she was still fighting on in the North.

In the summer of 1463, there came one of the few episodes from the Cousins' War in which the conflicts and their heroines have been converted into story. As Marguerite and her party were fleeing back toward Bamburgh, the stronghold on the Northumberland coast, she and her son were separated from their followers. Suddenly, a gang of robbers leaped out of the bushes, seized the baggage, tore the very jewels from around her neck, and dragged her before their leader. He had drawn his sword to cut her throat when she threw herself on her knees and implored him not to disfigure her body past recognition, for, as she said, "I am the daughter and wife of a king, and was in past times recognized by yourselves as your queen." In the best tradition of monster-taming myth, the man ("Black Jack") in turn fell on his knees before her and led her and her son to a secret cave in Deepden Woods, where Marguerite sheltered until de Brézé found her.

The Duke of Burgundy's official "historiographer," Georges Chastellain, had the opportunity of hearing the gist of the tale from Marguerite herself only a few months later—but Chastellain was a poet and rhetorician as much as a chronicler, and for him the message may have been more important than the factual reality. Less romantic if perhaps also exaggerated is the fact that, as Chastellain tells it, Marguerite was now so poor she had to borrow a groat from a Scottish archer to make an offering on Saint Margaret's feast day. So poor was she that for five days, she and her husband and son were forced to subsist on a single day's ration of bread and "one herring between the three."

There is, of course, an air of unreality about Chastellain's story, but there is no doubt about what happened next: Marguerite was forced to flee back to the Continent, leaving her husband behind to roam as a fugitive in the North, hiding in friendly houses. Even then, Marguerite did not give up so easily, attempting, over the next few years, to rally support from the rulers of Brittany, Burgundy, Germany, and Portugal, as well as France. Chastellain describes not only her forcible pleading with the European monarchs but also the "wonder" caused by her arrival in Burgundy, since she had once been the duke's mortal enemy. "Wherefore were heard divers murmurs against her in many mouths, and many savage comments on the nature of her misfortune."

Marguerite, Chastellain says, arrived in Burgundy

poor and alone, destitute of goods and all desolate; [she] had neither credence, nor money, nor goods, nor jewels to pledge. [She] had her son, no royal robes, nor estate; and her person without adornment befitting a queen. Her body was clad in one single robe, with no change of clothing. [She] had no more than seven women for her retinue, and whose apparel was like that of their mistress, formerly one of the most splendid women of the world and now one of the poorest; and finally she had no other provision nor even bread to eat, except from the purse of her knight. . . . It was a thing piteous to see, truly, this high princess so cast down and laid low in such great danger, dying of hunger and hardship.

For all his sympathy, it is hard not to feel that the Burgundian chronicler was relishing the drama of her "lowliness and abasement" as he describes how the English in Calais were trying to capture Marguerite, how she had been forced to travel in a country cart "covered over with canvas and harnessed with four mares like a poor woman going unknown."* The Burgundian duke tried to dodge her for a time, but Marguerite sent word that "were my cousin of Burgundy to go to the end of the world I would follow him." He gave way and after meeting her did send her both financial aid and his sister the Duchess of Bourbon as a companion. The two women struck up an eager friendship, with Marguerite recounting adventures that, she said, outdid any in story. The duchess agreed that if a book were to be written on the troubles of royal ladies, Marguerite's would be acknowledged as the most shocking of catastrophes.

Marguerite was finally forced to retreat to her father's land at St. Michel-sur-Bar, living on an inadequate pension and paying visits to her European relatives. Letters from her officers detail the extreme shortage of ready money—hardly enough coins to pay the messenger—"but yet the Queen sustaineth us in meat and drink, so as we be not in extreme necessity." Early in 1465 she tried again to get help from King Louis, warning that if he refused her, "she will take the best course she can." The king's response was to marvel to his court: "Look how proudly she writes . . . "

But if Marguerite still had all her pride, it—and her claim to any power in England—would soon suffer a further blow. In July 1465, just months after Elizabeth Woodville's elaborate coronation ceremony in London, the fugitive Henry VI was finally taken captive, the news reaching Edward in Canterbury some five days later. After a humiliating journey south, with his legs tied to his horse's stirrups and a straw hat on his head, Henry was placed in comparatively lenient imprisonment in the Tower, welcome to receive visitors, albeit Lancastrian chroniclers complained he was not kept as cleanly as a king should be. He would remain in captivity for the next five years while—

---

*He adds how she came to see the duke disguised "in the garb of a chambermaid": it would prove to be repeated as a contemporary trope.

with England settling into Edward's rule and Elizabeth's queenship—Marguerite, on the Continent, was a threat that refused to go away.

Abroad, Marguerite's own mood must have been made the more desperate by news that in England, things were going well, especially when she learned it was the daughter of her old friend Jacquetta who had now turned sides and supplanted her as queen, with Jacquetta's active connivance. In 1465 Elizabeth was asked to become patroness of the college (now Queens' College) Marguerite herself had founded in Cambridge, "to laud and honour of sex feminine." Patronage was an established function of queenship; royally born or not, Elizabeth Woodville was settling into her new role.

As if to add to Marguerite's miseries, in the summer of 1465, hard on the heels of her coronation, came evidence that Queen Elizabeth was pregnant. February 1466 saw the birth at Westminster of the couple's first child, Elizabeth of York. The physician and astrologer Master Dominic, who would have been canvassed for his predictions, had been convinced this would be a prince, says the chronicler Fabian; when it turned out, instead, to be a lady princess, the Archbishop of York was substituted for that of Canterbury at the christening. But there was no other diminution of ceremony. A visitor from Bohemia, one Gabriel Tetzel, who came in the train of the Lord of Rozmital, left an account of the queen's churching that followed some forty days after the birth.

Tetzel was already convinced that this was "the most splendid court that one can find in all Christendom" when he saw the procession that headed to Westminster Abbey—forty-two singers, twenty-four heralds, sixty lords before the queen, and sixty-two ladies after. The banquet that followed—or, rather, banquets, since the king and queen kept their separate state—survives as the most striking example of court etiquette. Some have taken it as an example of the upstart Elizabeth Woodville's personal grandiosity, but in fact it may have been no more than the reverence the English were expected to pay to majesty.

Leo von Rozmital and his train were carefully seated (King Edward would have wanted reports of this to spread) in an alcove of "a particularly splendid and decorated hall" where Elizabeth sat alone at a table on a costly golden chair, with her own mother and the king's sister standing below her. If the queen talked with either of them, so Tetzel reported, they had to kneel down until, by taking a drink of water, she gave them the signal to rise. It was even worse for her ladies: they had to remain on their knees for the whole time that the queen was eating—no light undertaking, since the meal lasted three silent hours.

Edward's sister Elizabeth took the new queen's right: his youngest sister, Margaret, was on her left. (No accounts mention the king's eldest sister, Anne, and his mother, Cecily, presumably chose to absent herself.) After the banquet came the dancing: Tetzel writes that Margaret danced with two dukes "in stately dances, and made impressive courtesies to the queen such as I have never seen elsewhere; nor have I witnessed such outstandingly beautiful maidens."

Edward's charm offensive, designed to increase his reputation around the European courts, had clearly worked spectacularly well, and his queen was proving adept, new to the task though she might be. She was helping Edward to shore up his position in other ways as well. Elizabeth of York's birth in February 1466 was followed quickly by the delivery of a second daughter, Mary, in August 1467. The royal family was growing fast—although as yet there were no direct male heirs to inherit the throne in the case of Edward's death.

Elizabeth Woodville was also busy in other ways. The only surviving accounts for her date from 1466–1467, and though it is tempting to concentrate on the colorful details (£14 for sable furs, £18 7s 6d for medicines), they make it clear that to be a queen was not only to be a diplomatic pawn, a breeding machine, or a decorative accessory. It was to be the head of an important household, the mistress of wide estates, and an employer of laborers, craftsmen, and professionals in many different capacities.

Elizabeth's income during this period was £4,541 (as opposed to the extravagant Marguerite of Anjou's £7,563, fourteen years before), but she ended the year in profit, unlike Marguerite, employing fewer servants—seven maids to Marguerite's ten—and paying more cautiously. (Marguerite had paid one of her principal ladies in waiting, Barbalina, 40 marks a year. Elizabeth paid her principal ladies 20.) Her husband did not charge her, as Marguerite's had done, for the time her household spent living with his—some recompense for the fact that he could not afford to grant her dower lands on the scale her predecessor had enjoyed. And Elizabeth was sharp when she needed to be in the pursuance of the rights on which much of her income depended: an undated letter to Sir William Stonor chastises him for the fact that he had taken it upon himself "to make masteries within our forest and chace of Barnwood and Exhill, and there, in contempt of us, uncourteously to hunt and slay our deer within the same, to our great marvel and displeasure."

Elizabeth did not hesitate to exercise influence, sometimes using a specifically female network to do so. In 1468 instructions of the king's, concerning the Pastons' affairs, were echoed by letters of the queen to the Duchesses of Norfolk and Suffolk; she had already written more directly to the Earl of Oxford on the same point. On the other, it begs the question of when and how the use of that influence might be seen as inappropriate by her contemporaries.

A queen was allowed and even expected to intercede on behalf of those to whom she owed protection. It was part of the symbiotic relationship the phrase "good ladyship" implied. But Elizabeth's advancement of her family over the years did leave both herself and her husband vulnerable to attack. These very years saw a cementing of Woodville alliances, in a way that seemed threatening to other members of the nobility—not least to Edward's brother Clarence, who might otherwise himself have hoped to enjoy greater benefits from his brother's regime. Five Woodville brothers and five sisters married into the nobility, the men given influential posts; Elizabeth Woodville's two sons by her first marriage benefited handsomely from their mother's new position as well. The Milanese envoy's later report that since her coronation, Elizabeth "had always exerted herself to aggrandise her relations . . . they had the entire government of the realm" might have been based on her enemy Warwick's propaganda, but it did reflect a popular and influential perception. When Warwick turned later against Edward, proclaiming him guilty of choosing a life of "pastime, pleasure, and dalliance" among base companions ("men descended of low blood and base degree"), he was using the Woodville connection as a stick with which to beat Edward, as well as invoking the trope of scapegoats—"evil counselors"—that the would-be king-makers of these years had so frequently invoked.

Up to a point, Elizabeth had just been doing what anyone would have done. In many ways, Warwick and his associates had been just the same, and there is a case for suggesting that Edward had consciously elevated the Woodvilles to balance the Warwick affinity, constructing an alternative power base—one dependent on him, rather than on his mentor, Warwick, and one he could control. Elizabeth's family, after all, had now become his. The Woodville rise had been, however, both flamboyant and somewhat roughshod—in 1466 Elizabeth's sister Katherine, for example, was married to the youthful Duke of Buckingham, who in later years was said to have resented a bride he felt beneath him. One of her brothers, John, himself no more than twenty, had attracted widespread disapproval by making a marriage, purely for money, with the Duchess of Norfolk, well past her sixtieth birthday.*

The Woodvilles' elevation was becoming the stuff of bitter parody, even making its way into the royal court. The king's fool promenaded through the court one day, dressed for passing through water. When the king asked why, he punned that he'd had difficulty passing through many parts of the realm because the "Rivers"—the recently bestowed title of the queen's father, the Earl Rivers—were running so high.

More trouble arose in the late 1460s because of the prominent part the Woodvilles were said to have played in arranging the marriage between Charles, Duke of Burgundy, and Edward's twenty-year-old sister, Margaret, who since the queen's arrival had been living at court as one of her ladies. Indeed, Crowland says that the enmity between the

---

*Of course, as so often is the case, a look at the personalities offers a slightly different perspective: this Duchess of Norfolk, Katherine Neville, Cecily Neville's elder sister, had been married off by her father in 1412, in the chapel of Raby Castle to the Duke of Norfolk. She swindled his estates after he died, then married a servant in the household, and then married a third time to a Viscount Beaumont. She would outlive all her husbands, the last included. It is just possible she was not entirely the passive victim here.

Woodvilles and Warwick really began when the latter heard that they ("in conformity with the King's wishes") were promoting the Burgundian match, instead of the marriage he himself had been urging, with one of several possible candidates in France. The Woodvilles were probably only carrying out Edward's wishes. Nonetheless, the pageantry notably associated with the marriage was a field in which the Woodvilles (with the Continental inheritance they had from their mother, Jacquetta) could shine.

The marriage of Charles and Margaret was bookended by legendary tournaments, both of which showed just how far the Woodvilles had climbed. At Smithfield in London in June 1467, Elizabeth Woodville's brother Anthony—his train of horses variously decked out in white cloth of gold; in damasks of purple, green, and tawny; blue and crimson velvet; and crimson cloth trimmed with sables—fought the "Bastard of Burgundy," the half brother of Duke Charles, in a ritual battle carefully brought to an end by the king before the knights could do real damage to each other, or to Edward's diplomacy. The Woodvilles had been all over this fantastical adventure, first mooted soon after the coronation. Anthony Woodville made a chivalric tale of how the queen's ladies pounced on him (while he was speaking to his sister on his knees, "my bonnet off my head, according to my duty") and tied a jeweled band to his leg, with a letter bidding him to attend the tournament. The emphasis on courtly parade in the reign of Edward IV deliberately evoked his inheritance from Edward III, and thus provided a king who had seized his crown with an aura of legitimacy. *

Underneath the chivalric pageant lurked something darker, as became clear during a second tournament held in the leading city of Bruges, after Margaret's arrival in Burgundy. Louis of France—who had no wish his two enemies, England and Burgundy, should ally— had been spreading rumors about Princess Margaret's chastity. The

---

*Chivalric spectacle, with the ritual parade of homage paid by knights to ladies, also gave to women the semblance of authority. There is considerable debate over whether it, and the whole ideal of courtly love, improved their actual lot in any way.

rumors seem actually to have originated with the Milanese ambassador at the French court, who had passed on stories that Margaret was "somewhat attached to love affairs and even, in the opinion of many, has had a son"; there is no reason to believe there was any truth in the tale, but Edward's own love affairs and colorful marriage must have lent some air of plausibility to it. Despite the rumors about the bride, the tournament when Margaret arrived in Bruges was no less splendid than the one at Smithfield had been, and possibly more genuinely perilous. (Burgundy paid full lip service to the courtly ideal, and Charles genuinely loved warfare; in the end, Margaret had to wave her handkerchief to ask him to call off the bloodshed.) She was, so John Paston reported, "received as worshipfully as all the world could devise."

Elizabeth Woodville's brothers were prominent both among the escort who accompanied Margaret across the Channel and among the participants in the tournament. In Bruges, Edward Woodville was declared prince of the tourney. Anthony Woodville was Margaret's chief presenter at the Burgundian court. Perhaps he reminded her of the proper etiquette when, meeting her new mother-in-law for the first time, the two ladies knelt to each other for the appropriate duration; perhaps he reassured her after her new husband, the first time he clapped eyes on her, stared into her face for "a tract of time," "avising" her, or checking out her possibilities.

It was lucky the English government had granted expenses to send Margaret off generously equipped with £1,000 of silks and £160 of gold, silver, and gilt dishes, for the nine-day celebrations were lavish enough to have eclipsed the new bride. The Tournament of the Golden Tree in Bruges was built around a specially created fantasia with all the tropes of quests and mysterious ladies so beloved of chivalry and formed only part of the nine-day celebrations. The guests at each day's feast delighted in gilded swans and stags carrying baskets of oranges, or unicorns bearing baskets of sweets; monkeys threw trinkets to the company, and a court dwarf on a gilded lion competed for attention with a wild man on a dromedary. John Paston wrote, "As for the Duke's court as of ladies and gentlewomen, knights, squires and gentlemen I heard never of none like to it save King Arthur's court . . . for such gear and gold and pearl and stones they of the Duke's court, neither gentlemen or gentlewomen they want none." A crown still survives in Aachen inscribed MARGARIT[A] DE [Y]O[R]K, of silver-gilt, enamel, precious stones, and pearls, ornamented with white roses, most likely made either to celebrate Margaret's wedding or as a votive offering, to be worn by the statue of the Virgin that still carries it on major feast days.

There is no reason to doubt that, on the other side of the royal family, Cecily too approved her daughter's marriage. Charles was, in Edward's words, "one of the mightiest Princes in the world that beareth no crown," and queens (the position to which Cecily aspired) expected to send their daughters away. But whatever Cecily Neville's thoughts on the matter, it is impossible to separate the acknowledgment of the Yorkist dynasty that Margaret's marriage represented from the success of the Woodville family.

The prominence of the unpopular Woodvilles was helping to ensure that the Lancastrian threat never went away. As long as the Yorkist regime was open to such piercing criticism, a viable alternative would hold some degree of appeal for the people of England. These were paranoid years for Edward and his family. From abroad, messengers were still being captured, bringing instructions from Marguerite to her partisans in England, and one of these letters even seemed to have revealed a plot close to the heart of the new regime. One Cornelius, a shoemaker serving one of Marguerite of Anjou's gentlemen, had been captured carrying incriminating letters from Lancastrian exiles and tortured, so the "Worcester" chronicler puts it, "by burning in the feet until he confessed many things." He named a man called John Hawkins as a Lancastrian supporter. Hawkins, in turn, accused a London merchant called Sir Thomas Cook. As for the cause for Cook's opposition to the Yorkist dynasty, the *Great Chronicle of London* suggests that he had been the object of a vendetta by Jacquetta, Elizabeth Woodville's mother, to whom he had refused to sell, at an unreasonably low price, a fine tapestry. Clearly, the Woodvilles were stirring up trouble in more ways than one.

Jasper Tudor, for his part, had never flagged in his support for the cause of Henry VI, and in the summer of 1468—just weeks after Princess Margaret had set sail for Burgundy—he landed in Wales with three ships provided by King Louis of France. It was too small a force for a serious invasion, but it represented, as it was intended to, an embarrassment for King Edward. As one of Edward's chief supporters in Wales, William Herbert—also Henry Tudor's guardian—was ordered to raise troops and ride against Jasper Tudor. Herbert took the twelve-year-old Henry with him, for his first taste of action. Jasper Tudor and Henry Tudor, uncle and nephew, were on opposite sides of the battlefield, but luckily neither saw dreadful consequences that day. But the thought of her son's danger, when she heard of it, must have been terrifying for Henry's mother, Margaret Beaufort.

Indeed, Margaret Beaufort's position had already been undermined by the actions of other members of the Beaufort family. King Edward had from the start of his reign shown her and her husband a certain amount of conciliatory favor, granting them the great moated manor house of Woking where they made a luxurious home. In the first days of Edward's reign, it had looked as if the Beaufort fortunes were slowly rising again. In 1463 Margaret's cousin Henry, the third Duke of Somerset, had accepted a pardon and received many favors from the new king. But only the next year, Somerset had betrayed Edward and been summarily executed. His younger brother and heir, the fourth duke, became a leader of the Lancastrian exiles. After that, the king could hardly be blamed if he looked on all Beauforts warily.

9

"DOMESTIC BROILS"

. . . and domestic broils
Clean over-blown, themselves the conquerors
Make war upon themselves, brother to brother

THE TRAGEDY OF RICHARD
THE THIRD, 2.4

I t would swiftly become apparent that the threat from surviving Lancastrians was not the only one that Edward IV and Elizabeth Woodville faced. The Yorkist dynasty would soon be in greater danger from divisions within than it would be from the impoverished queen in France or her supporters plotting in England.

The great Warwick had been growing steadily more dissatisfied with his position under Edward's rule and with Woodville's prominence in the new regime. As the ally of Edward's father, York, and as the guiding spirit of Edward's own military takeover, he had naturally expected to play not only a leading but a preeminent part in the management of the country. But as Edward settled ever more firmly into the seat of power, Warwick found himself increasingly alienated.

Warwick began to move against Edward—and as he did, he found an extraordinary ally within the king's immediate family.

George, Duke of Clarence, was likewise disaffected, resentful of his position as a mere adjunct to his brother's regime. For a while, he had hoped to find an alternative sphere of influence. There was talk of a second Burgundian marriage, with the Duke of Clarence marrying Charles of Burgundy's daughter and heiress presumptive Mary. But that came to nothing, perhaps because Edward would have been dubious about giving the jealous Clarence a foreign crown and access to a foreign army.

Instead of following in his sister Margaret's footsteps, Clarence pursued a match much closer to home—and one that would prove just as disastrous for Edward as any Burgundian alliance. On July 12, 1469, the nineteen-year-old Clarence married Warwick's eldest daughter, Isabel, Clarence's second cousin and a woman just a year younger than he. History suggests she got a bad bargain, but to contemporaries like John Rous, Clarence was "seemly of person and well-visaged," as well as "right witty." This was another advantageous marriage for Clarence of which his brother the king disapproved: the Worcester chronicle suggests that two years earlier he had forbidden it, had indeed blocked attempts to secure the papal dispensation necessary for two relatives to marry. The erratic Clarence would, after all, be a potential weapon in Warwick's hands. Yet, so long as the king had no son, Clarence was still his likeliest heir, and the king had a strong vested interest in arranging his marriage for the benefit of the country.

Clarence's position in the line of succession was obviously of prime importance to Warwick, who now began the machinations that would one day earn him his nickname, the Kingmaker. It was around the time of Clarence's marriage into Warwick's family that, on the Continent and among Warwick's allies, rumors of Edward's bastardy—rumors that implied Clarence was the true heir of the Yorkist monarchy—can first be traced with certainty. It has been suggested that Clarence's mother, Cecily, had recently told him this was true: that his older brother Edward had been conceived in adultery. In 1469, the year of Clarence's marriage, Edward asked his mother to exchange the castle of Fotheringhay, into which she had poured both money and effort, for the run-down Berkhamsted in Hertfordshire. It could have been punishment for spreading damaging rumors, or simply for a too visible partiality on Cecily's part.*

In view of Edward's disapproval, the marriage ceremony and the celebration took place in Warwick's own jurisdiction of Calais, away from the king's eye, and Cecily traveled to Sandwich, from whence the wedding party was leaving. She may have done so to give them her blessing. Not only was Clarence her son, but Isabel was her goddaughter, an important connection in the fifteenth century. But she may, alternately, have been hoping to dissuade Clarence from a plan that could only divide her family.

Whatever Cecily's role in the matter, Edward had been right to worry about his brother's closeness to their cousin. Warwick and Clarence now issued a proclamation inveighing against certain "seditious persons" prominent at Edward's court: notably, Elizabeth Woodville's father, brothers, and mother, Jacquetta—interestingly, the only woman named. (To have named the queen herself would have been a little too close to the bone.) The very day of the marriage, they declared their support for a rebellion in northern England—a rebellion Warwick had secretly been fostering. The next day, Warwick and Clarence sailed to England, almost certainly leaving their womenfolk to follow them later. Arriving in Kent, they set about raising an army.

On July 26, at the battle of Edgecote Moor, Edward's main army was defeated. The king himself was with a separate, smaller, force farther north, but on July 29 he was captured and taken to imprisonment in Yorkshire. Immediately thereafter, in August 1469, Margaret Beaufort—ever the opportunist—visited the London residence

---

*Berkhamsted—today an impressive ruin cradled in the surrounding hills, and with a thriving market town at its foot—had been used before as a home for queens dowager, the role Cecily felt was hers, and the venerable building had an impressive history. First built soon after the Conquest, subsequent residents and remodelers had included Thomas Becket and Piers Gaveston. But the last of those remodelings had been some time ago. Cecily would be its last inhabitant, and the fact that it became a ruin in the year after her death hardly suggests a widely desired residence.

of the newly prominent Clarence, hoping to negotiate over those lands of Henry Tudor's that Clarence held, and surely to regain custody of her son.

The terrible news of Warwick's betrayal and Edward's capture hit Queen Elizabeth while she was making a formal visit to Norwich, only four months after the birth of her third daughter, named Cecily for the child's paternal grandmother. Then came even worse news—that Warwick had captured her father, and her brother John, after the battle of Edgecote and executed them without trial.

As Elizabeth retreated to London, in terror for her husband, she also had to face the accusations of witchcraft brought against her mother (possibly as a precursor to declaring invalid the marriage Jacquetta had helped to make, through such dubious means). The official documents, the *Patent Rolls,* show a Northamptonshire gentleman called Thomas Wake producing "an image of lead made like a man of arms the length of a man's finger broken in the middle and made fast with a wire," along with two other images, of a man and a woman, which he tried to prove Jacquetta had commissioned, presumably as a means of binding the king and her daughter together. Witchcraft was a serious allegation—one of the few from which even royal rank would not protect a woman.*

Jacquetta, however, had allies behind her, and not only her relations. Her intercession with Marguerite on behalf of London almost a decade before had won her friends in the City, and now she appealed to the City authorities for support. The Wheel of Fortune was about to spin again.

There was not enough support for Warwick's coup. Edward was allowed to escape on September 10 and reached London in October, making a triumphal entry into the City. He commanded that the

---

*Henry IV's dowager queen, Joan of Navarre, in 1419 had been briefly imprisoned on the accusation of it. Eleanor Cobham, Humfrey of Gloucester's wife (and thus once Jacquetta's sister-in-law, in the days when she had been Duchess of Bedford), was charged in 1441 by her husband's enemies and sentenced to imprisonment for life, as well as humiliating public penance.

charges against his mother-in-law be examined, but it was January 1470 before Jacquetta was cleared of this "said slander." If Thomas Wake were, as seems likely, a pawn of Clarence and Warwick, Jacquetta had been another woman to suffer for the friction between the York brothers.

In December at Westminster, King Edward staged a deliberately public reconciliation with his brother Clarence and cousin Warwick, but in private the tension seems to have continued. As John Paston reported, though the lords claimed now to be the king's best friends, "his household men have other language, so what shall hastily fall I cannot say." Cecily and her daughters were surely working for a real rapprochement, and efforts were made, too, to reconcile the cousinship: Edward's young daughter Elizabeth of York was betrothed to Warwick's nephew, thus possibly suggesting that if Edward didn't have a son, the crown might pass to his daughter rather than to Clarence in the collateral male line. If this were the suggestion, however, then it surely pushed Clarence even further, the more so since there was also now discussion of restoring young Henry Tudor to his father's earldom of Richmond, greatly to the detriment of Clarence, who had been holding the lands.

The peacemaking attempts were of course in vain. Clarence and Warwick quickly returned north, and perhaps the only real gainer was Marguerite, since Louis of France had responded to the Yorkist confusion by inviting the Lancastrian queen to his court, where as the year turned she enjoyed not only a reunion with her father, but also the promise of French support. Back in England, in the early months of 1470, more rebellions broke out. In March Cecily invited Edward and Clarence both to Baynard's Castle, her London home, trying to bring about an agreement between her two sons, but to no avail. Warwick and Clarence instituted fresh uprisings. When Edward rode out to deal with them, Margaret Beaufort's husband, the peaceable Henry Stafford, was summoned to arm himself and ride out with him. After Margaret's misguided attempt to negotiate with Clarence the autumn before, there was need for a proof of loyalty.

In April 1470, Warwick (and the wife and daughters who had now joined him and Clarence) was forced to flee back across the Channel, confident of finding safe haven in Calais. The confidence was misplaced: Warwick's lieutenant had received orders from England, and Calais was now closed against them, dreadful news for everybody but disastrous for Clarence's wife, the heavily pregnant Isabel, who, on the tiny heaving ship, with probably only her mother and sister for attendants, went into labor, with only two flagons of wine sent by the Calais commander for her relief.

Isabel did not die, but her baby was stillborn. It was the beginning of May before the party was allowed to make landfall in Normandy and then perhaps only because Louis had decided the diplomatic treaties that prevented him from openly helping Warwick permitted him to give refuge to the ladies. Spare a thought for Isabel's younger sister, Anne Neville, here; besides the general wreck that had befallen her family, she must have known that her own hopes of making a good marriage had declined dramatically—until, that is, she heard what fortune (or her father) had in store.

Edward in England now had two enemies in exile: Warwick and Marguerite of Anjou. As far back as 1467, it was claimed, some abroad believed the earl "favoured Queen Margaret's party"; assuming that this was untrue, it may now have been the serpentine brain of Louis— the "Spider King" whose machinations Machiavelli observed before writing *The Prince*—that conceived the idea of making alliance between these two, themselves long the bitterest of enemies. And the age knew only one good way of cementing that sort of improbable alliance: marriage.

Arranging this would be no simple matter. True, Marguerite had a son, Edward; Warwick had one unmarried daughter, Anne. But the parents' long enmity was bound to create problems along the way. The Milanese ambassador to the French court gives a long account of the French king persuading Marguerite to the Warwick marriage and how she had shown herself "very hard and difficult," keeping the earl on his knees before her as she railed. Another account, *The Manner and Guiding of the Earl of Warwick at Angers in July and August 1470*, agrees that she was "right dificyle." Not only, as she exploded, had Warwick "injured her as a queen, but he had dared to defame her reputation as a woman by divers false and malicious slanders."

Anne's own feelings about the plan can only be guessed at. The little we hear of her prospective bridegroom is not attractive. The

Milanese envoy reported that, as a child, he talked of nothing but the cutting off of heads. Still, despite the boy's bloodthirstiness, Hall would describe him as having matured into "a goodly girlish looking and well featured young gentleman," and in the nature of diplomacy, a high-ranking girl was at least as likely to be married to an enemy as a friend. And of course it was a splendid match—one that might make Anne queen someday, if Henry VI's throne could but be regained for him, and if she was someone who cared for that. But even in an age when most aristocratic marriages were bargains, few brides (Elizabeth Woodville apart) can have had to face quite such a furious reception from their prospective mothers-in-law.

The two accounts vary a little over the timing, but *The Manner and Guiding* claims that Queen Marguerite held out for fifteen days against every argument the king of France could show her. "Some time she said that she saw never honour nor profit for her, nor for her son the Prince. In other [times] she [al]ledged that and she would, she should find a more profitable party, and of more advantage, with the King of England. And indeed, she showed unto the King of France a Letter which she said was sent her out of England the last week, by the which was offered to her son My Lady the Princess"—that is, Elizabeth of York.

Even once Marguerite had given in, the marriage treaty was packed full of conditions, not least that "from thence forth the said daughter of the Earl of Warwick [Anne] shall be put and remain in the hands and keeping of Queen Margaret," and also that "the said marriage shall not be perfected to [until] the Earl of Warwick had been with an army over the Sea into England, and that he had recovered the realm of England." If he failed to do so, Anne was presumably to have been left high and dry. But the Milanese ambassador suggests rather that the marriage also had to be delayed by the need to wait for a papal dispensation, since this couple, like so many others, were distantly related by blood (Clarence's mother being brother to Anne's grandfather).

Warwick wasted no time in attempting to fill at least one of the conditions of the marriage contract. In mid-September 1470, he and Clarence set sail, landing in the West Country, claiming always to be doing so in the name of the captive King Henry and "by the assent of the most noble princess, Margaret, Queen of England," and her son.

King Edward was in the North, trying to put down a rebellion organized by Warwick's brother-in-law, having moved his pregnant wife
and daughters into the Tower (which Elizabeth, as the contemporary
Warkworth's Chronicle says, "well victualled and fortified") for safety
while he was away.

Soon Marguerite and her son at Amboise, along with the young
Anne, heard of a great victory. Warwick's army had moved south. The
mayor of London had tried to raise a defense, but a Lancastrian supporter had thrown open the Southwark jail, and a mob burst out. A
London contemporary left a vivid description of Queen Elizabeth re-
leasing the Tower to the mayor's control, he leading her family to the
waterside, she holding a chest of jewels while her daughters dragged
bedsheets stuffed with clothing behind them to the boats that would
carry them upriver to Westminster Abbey and sanctuary.

On October 1, the Tower fell to Warwick's forces. On October 3,
though Elizabeth and her daughters could not have known it from
their refuge in Westminster, Edward with his brother Richard (and
Elizabeth's brother Anthony Woodville, once the hero of the Smithfield tournament) commandeered a boat to the Low Countries and
eventually sought refuge with Edward's sister Margaret of Burgundy.
The Yorkist regime was over—for the moment, anyway.

"THAT WAS A QUEEN"

Thyself a queen, for me that was a queen,
Outlive thy glory, like my wretched self.

THE TRAGEDY OF RICHARD
THE THIRD, 1.3

A s the king fled the country and his queen cowered in sanctuary, Warwick's Lancastrian supporters came flooding up to London from Kent. When the earl himself finally entered the city, he did at least calm the rioting that had followed the opening of the South-wark jail. He also released King Henry from his imprisonment, although the fuddled king seemed hardly to care he had once again the throne.

It may not have mattered to Henry that he was once again king of England, but to the deposed Yorkists, the changeover meant every-thing. Elizabeth Woodville was (in official parlance) no longer queen, Cecily Neville no long the mother of a king, albeit another of her sons was prominent on the victorious side. Crammed into the mass of low-lying buildings between Westminster Abbey and the river, how much did the four-year-old Elizabeth of York and her younger sisters com-prehend? They probably lived in the abbot's house, where Abbot

Mylling certainly received them with kindness and offered occasional luxuries, while a London butcher provided "half a beef and two muttons" every week for the royal family's nourishment. Nonetheless, the official Yorkist narrative of these months, *The History of the Arrival of Edward IV in England,* describes Elizabeth Woodville at least as enduring "great trouble, sorrow, and heaviness, which she sustained with all manner patience that belonged to any creature."

Meanwhile, in Burgundy, Duchess Margaret, in warm remembrance of her Yorkist roots, sent letters to her fugitive brothers, Edward and Richard, while her husband, the duke, sent funds. She—like, presumably, their mother, Cecily—was concerned above all to heal the rifts in the family. But the appearance of these new exiles was nonetheless something of an embarrassment to a duke still anxious to keep peace with the rapacious French. It wasn't until Christmastime that the new arrivals were invited to join the Burgundian court, France's hostile intentions toward Burgundy having at last become unmistakable. Still, Margaret, delighted at being allowed to meet and help her two brothers, was active in raising money for their cause.

For Margaret Beaufort in England, the news of Warwick's takeover had been welcome. The Lancastrians were back, supported by her brother-in-law Jasper Tudor, who had sailed with Warwick's fleet in September, and Henry Tudor could be reclaimed from William Herbert and handed over into his uncle's custody. By the end of October, Jasper and Henry were in London, and Margaret, reunited with her son, took him to see his restored uncle, Henry VI, who (as Polydore Vergil later told it) prophesied future greatness for the boy. With her son and husband, Henry Stafford, she then traveled to Woking for what sounds very much like a joyous holiday, before Margaret once again handed her son back to his uncle Jasper, to be trained as a man should be, while she resumed negotiations with Clarence about his inheritance.

But Henry Tudor's standing in the contentious ranking of Plantagenet scions had just diminished considerably, for on November 2, 1470, Elizabeth Woodville, still in sanctuary at Westminster, had given birth to a boy, whom she named Edward, for his father. One Lady Scrope was allowed in to help her (or possibly to keep an eye on her), along with professional midwife Marjory Cobbe, on whom

Elizabeth placed enough reliance to see that she had, only the year before, been granted ten pounds a year for life. The arrival of a long-awaited son and heir should have been the moment of greatest triumph for Elizabeth, but at the moment no one could know what this boy's future would be. A prince should have had a cradle canopied in a cloth of gold, an ermine-trimmed blanket, and the grandest of christenings. Instead, with his grandmother Jacquetta and the abbot for godparents, he was baptized in the abbey with scant ceremony. There would indeed have been few funds to pay for anything more. While Henry VI's resumed government was notably restrained about reclaiming Yorkist lands, they did seize the dower properties of Elizabeth and of Jacquetta.

Elizabeth's treacherous brother-in-law Clarence had ridden behind Warwick as he entered London, but as the weeks wore on, he was once again becoming increasingly disaffected. The deal between Warwick and Marguerite had neatly cut him out; with Warwick's daughter Anne now married to the Lancastrian Prince of Wales (and the Yorkist king having now an infant son and heir in the cradle), it had become a matter of secondary importance that her sister, Isabel, was married to that king's brother Clarence, once his brother's heir.

Curiously, Marguerite—whose return to England would surely have confirmed the authority and permanence of the new regime—was still across the Channel. She and her son, with Warwick's wife and daughters, had spent the autumn at and around the French court, where the records of Louis's receiver of finance show moneys paid out for their maintenance, for their silverware, "for their pleasures." Marguerite's delay might seem to say something not only about her lack of eagerness to be reunited with her husband, but also about the way she thought, the way she had never gotten in touch with England emotionally. But it may instead have been simply that Louis demanded her (and Anne's) presence as a guarantee of Warwick's honesty—as hostages, in the nicest possible way.

Given the news of Warwick's success, Anne and Edward of Lancaster were finally married, in Amboise, on December 13. Anne's mother and sister, at least, were present. It is unclear whether the marriage was immediately consummated, the one way of making it irrevocable, but it seems possible that it was not; several years later, Crowland was still describing Anne as a "maiden." On the day after the wedding, they set out for Paris and a ceremonial entry into the city.

It was well after Christmas before Marguerite headed to Rouen, where she expected to find Warwick waiting to escort her across the Channel. But rather than crossing to France to escort her, Warwick had remained in England. He had other fish to fry. When Marguerite finally realized he was not coming and traveled to the coast, the winds had turned against her. It was almost the end of March before the party attempted to set sail, only to be delayed more than another two weeks by those contrary winds.

The delay was fatal. As Marguerite cooled her heels on the French coast, on March 11, 1471, Edward (with his brother Richard of Gloucester and his brother-in-law Anthony Woodville) had set sail back to England, with a new army. He landed north of the Humber on March 14, winning his welcome into York with the now-traditional announcement that he sought only his father's inheritance as Duke of York. Working their way southward, his forces set up camp outside the town of Warwick, where they found an opposing Lancastrian army led by Clarence.

Rather than setting upon each other, however, the two elder York brothers were reconciled. Clarence took a force of more than forty thousand men over to his brother's side. It was an extraordinary, and dramatic, turn of events. Clarence, who had just helped to drive Edward off the throne and out of England, was now allied with him once again. Marguerite of Anjou (and Anne with her) must have suffered the bitterness of knowing that if only they had arrived earlier, the pulls and fractures within the Lancastrian party, and the support in the country, might have played out very differently. Anne's sister, Isabel, had crossed the Channel to England earlier to be with her husband, Clarence, and it is tempting to wonder what part she played in his deliberations, the results of which now set her on the opposite side from her father, mother, and sister.

But Clarence—so the *Arrival* reports—had been under pressure from his own mother and sisters, with "the high and mighty princess my Lady, their mother; my lady of Exeter [their sister Anne], my lady of Suffolk [their sister Elizabeth] . . . and, most specially, my Lady of

Bourgoigne [Burgundy]" mediating between the two "by right covert ways and means." Other sources too record Margaret's "great and diligent efforts," her stream of messengers: Croyland says Clarence had been reconciled to his brother "by the mediation of his sisters, the Duchesses of Burgundy and Exeter," the former working on the king and the latter on the duke.

Some suspected a deal had been in negotiation for months, with Margaret of Burgundy as the go-between. When Clarence had been in Calais the previous year, says the continental writer Philippe de Commynes, he had been approached by a mysterious Englishwoman "of few words" who claimed she had come from England to serve the Duchess Isabel and requested a private interview. When they were alone, she produced a letter from Edward offering full forgiveness if he would return to the fold. Clarence gave an ambiguous promise that he would indeed return—sometime, as soon as it was possible—and the lady, "the only contriver of the enterprise," departed as mysteriously as she had arrived.

After the battlefield reconciliation, Margaret wrote a vivid description to her mother-in-law: "Clarence with a small company left his people behind him and approached my lord and brother who saw him coming and Lord Clarence threw himself on his knees so that my lord and brother seeing his humility and hearing his words, lifted him up and embraced him several times and gave him his good cheer."

Whatever role his female relatives had played in it, Clarence's defection was a catastrophe for the Earl of Warwick—and, of course, for all those women still tied to the Lancastrian side. Clarence tried to mediate a deal between his brother and his father-in-law, but to no avail. Edward retook London in a bloodless coup, taking care as he neared the city to send what the *Arrival* called "comfortable messages" to his wife, Elizabeth. Most of the Lancastrians powerful enough to stand against him were heading for the West Country to greet Marguerite when she finally made her way across the Channel, and the attempt to rally London against Edward was led by Sir Thomas Cook, he with whom Jacquetta had quarreled over the tapestry. Henry returned without argument to captivity in the Tower, while Edward moved in procession toward Westminster. His reunion with his family—now the richer by the all-important baby boy, his father's "most desired treasure"—was too great a propaganda opportunity to be done altogether privately. In the words of a later ballad:

> *The King comforted the Queen and the other ladies eke.*
> *His sweet baby full tenderly he did kiss.*
> *The young prince he beheld and in his arms did bear.*
> *Thus his bale turned him to bliss.*

But of course things were not quite that sunny. Fortune's Wheel could turn yet again. Despite the blow Clarence's defection had given him, Warwick could never be underestimated, and Marguerite, with a French army, was known to be on the way. Edward, still marching southward from the battlefield, sent word his family should take refuge in his mother's home of Baynard's Castle, just west of the City. Clarence and Gloucester joined them for the night: it was only a few days before Easter, but Elizabeth Woodville's feelings must surely have been less than Christian as she looked at Clarence, the man who had helped put her through so much.

Edward was intent on meeting the growing Lancastrian threat head-on. On April 11, he entered London to public applause, but it was to urge his family to the Tower for safety while he rode out again. On Easter Sunday, April 14, his force met Warwick's at Barnet, just to the north of London, in a fog so dense there were suggestions it must have been raised by witchcraft or, as the chronicler Fabian put it, "incantations." The fighting was intense and bloody—and among the many casualties was the Earl of Warwick.

Cecily's son had now killed her nephew: the Kingmaker had played his last hand in English politics. When Marguerite and her son at long last landed at Weymouth on the evening of April 14, the battle was already decided, although she could not know it. She had reached Cerne Abbey in Dorset before the news arrived—news that, when it did come, caused her to swoon with shock. But she rallied her courage and moved through the West Country, trying to rally support, cheered in Bristol by a reception warm enough to give her fresh courage.

Nor did those on the other side have it altogether easy. In London, the Lancastrians had not given up all hope of the city. The mayor and aldermen had to send a message to Edward, begging him to come back to the defense "of the Queen, then being in the Tower of London, my Lord Prince, and my Ladies his daughters . . . and of the city," all in "the greatest jeopardy." The royal women felt the Tower shake as the Bastard of Falconbridge, a kinsman of Warwick's, turned his guns on the city, and seven hundred men died under his onslaught.

Overall, though, the tide was still running the Yorkists' way. Philippe de Commynes heard that one reason London welcomed Edward back was his wife, Elizabeth. Not only had she borne a son in Westminster, but Londoners were grateful that she had retreated into sanctuary instead of expecting citizens to risk their lives and livelihoods to defend her position. As well as a private pleasure, she had become a political asset for Edward. The Parliament of 1472 would put forward a commendation "of the womanly behaviour and the great constance of the Queen." At the times of their marriages, Marguerite of Anjou had looked a more suitable queen of England than Elizabeth Woodville, but now the positions were reversed.

As for the other, Lancastrian, queen, the *Arrival* tells of the frantic, exhausting passage of Marguerite and her son around the West through the first days of May, Anne Neville perforce with them, though her state must have been pitiable—a fourteen-year-old cut off from her own family and now no use to her in-laws. On the afternoon of May 3, the Lancastrian army—powerful now in numbers, but exhausted by a thirty-six-mile march in "foul country"—had gotten as far as Tewkesbury. The ladies of the party retired to a nearby manor for the night, but the next morning—according, tellingly, to Hall, who also described Marguerite's terrified dismay after learning of Warwick's defeat—she rode around the field to encourage her soldiers.

The Duke of Somerset and Marguerite's son, Edward of Lancaster, led the Lancastrian forces; Edward IV and Richard of Gloucester (with Edward's friend Lord Hastings and Elizabeth Woodville's eldest son, now Marquess of Dorset) led the rather smaller but more experienced Yorkist troops. For the Yorkists, it was to be a flamboyant victory, albeit one so bloody that the fleeing Lancastrians were slaughtered even as they tried to cross the River Severn or seek sanctuary in Tewkesbury Abbey. Among the casualties was Marguerite's son—the Lancastrian prince and Anne Neville's husband—with question marks over whether he actually died in the battle or was put to death afterward, as other chroniclers suggest or state. Later historians long laid the deed at Richard's door, although there is no evidence for this, and in any case Edward the king would surely have to bear the ultimate responsibility.

Henry VI, Marguerite's husband, now died too, in the Tower and in Yorkist custody. The *Arrival* says he died of "pure displeasure and melancholy"; others, including Fabian and Commynes, say he was killed by the eighteen-year-old Richard of Gloucester. As he struck, Richard is supposed to have said, "Now there is no heir male of King Edward the Third but we of the House of York!" There is no hard evidence for Richard's involvement, let alone his words, but if they were true, Richard was ignoring Margaret Beaufort's son, Henry Tudor, possibly because of the legitimation issue, or because of doubts about the validity of a claim passed through a woman. But one thing is certain: with no son or husband to promote, Marguerite would now have been considered irrelevant.

Marguerite was found three days later, the *Arrival* reports, "in a poor religious house, where she had hidden herself, for the security of her person." She appears to have hidden Anne too, since a list of those taken and presented to the king included "Lady Margaret, Queen, Lady Anne, Princess." Whether or not Anne felt personal loss in her husband's death, as an example of the turning of Fortune's Wheel her year had been close to unrivaled. She now passed into the charge of her brother-in-law Clarence, who had been pardoned by his brother the king. By contrast, Crowland reports that when Edward made his triumphal entry into London, Marguerite was "borne in a carriage before the king," as the Roman emperor would have done to Shakespeare's Cleopatra. The last days had brought the loss of those closest to Marguerite, the wreck of all her hopes, but (in keeping with the treatment generally accorded to women in these wars) she suffered no more direct penalty.

Her father wrote his hope that God might help her with his counsels, "for rarely is the aid of man tendered in such a reverse of fortune." Some sort of aid did soon come to Marguerite: Edward IV's records show payment to one Bawder Herman "for the expenses and daily allowances to Margaret, lately called the Queen, and to other persons attendant upon the said Queen." In fact (and possibly at Elizabeth Woodville's persuasion), after the first few months of confinement Marguerite would be sent into the kindly custody of her old friend Alice Chaucer, the dowager duchess of Suffolk, at Wallingford, who was paid five marks a week for her expenses. She was probably even freed, at least to some degree; in 1475 she joined the London Skinner's Fraternity of the Assumption of the Virgin, on the same occasion as two of Elizabeth Woodville's ladies. (The queen herself was already a member.) Marguerite was, in other words, accepted back, if she had ever left them, into the networks of aristocratic women and by men accorded the half-patronizing, half-chivalric treatment seen time and again in the treatment of ladies.

The Lancastrian "Readeption," as it was called, was over, barely six months after it had begun.* This time—for this branch of the family—there would be no coming back. As one contemporary put it, "And so no one from that stock remained among the living who could claim the crown"—except, posterity would add, for Margaret Beaufort and any heirs of her body.

Margaret Beaufort had shown all too clearly her pleasure in that brief restoration of the Lancastrian dynasty. That she did not now suffer any penalty is due to the actions of her husband, and what she felt about them we cannot know. When Edward reentered London, Stafford had been there to welcome him; at Barnet, where Warwick was killed, Stafford had been wounded fighting for Edward's army. (In the last week of March, Margaret's cousin Somerset, having taken on his dead brother's role as one of the most prominent Lancastrian

---

Readeption, a term not readily found in the lexicon, was used by the Lancastrians themselves in official documents and has become the standard designation of Henry VI's brief resumption of rule.

leaders, had visited Woking, trying to persuade Stafford to fight for their cause, but in vain. After Tewkesbury, this latest inheritor of the Somerset title too had been dragged out of sanctuary and killed: evidence of Edward's determination and ruthlessness that Margaret would have taken seriously.)

Jasper and Henry Tudor had been in Wales when they heard of the disaster that had overtaken the Lancastrians. Jasper would have had no option but to flee abroad: Bernard André says it was Margaret who begged him to take with him her thirteen-year-old son, Henry. With the deaths of Henry VI and his son, Edward of Lancaster, Henry Tudor had suddenly assumed a dangerous importance. As the direct descendant of John of Gaunt, Henry was the only Lancastrian heir available in England since his mother was at once disabled and protected by her gender.* Margaret would surely have been in contact with her boy before he and Jasper set sail from Tenby, but it would be fourteen years before she saw him again.

---

*Several of the European royal families could also boast descent from John of Gaunt, but they would have seemed less pressing a concern to the Yorkists than a homegrown candidate.

PART III

1471–1483

"MY LOVELY QUEEN"

Clarence and Gloucester, love my lovely queen,
And kiss your princely nephew, brothers both.

HENRY VI, PART 3, 5.7

As the Yorkists returned to power, the Lancastrian threat, it seemed, had finally been eliminated. From now on, the only challenge would come from within. The years ahead would prove that was indeed a serious threat—but there was little sign of internecine strife in the summer of 1471. When the end of June saw the infant Edward, Elizabeth Woodville's long-awaited son, named Prince of Wales, it was more than a routine appointment. It was a symbol that this time—so they intended—the Yorkists were here to stay.

Just as significant, perhaps, was the fact that Queen Elizabeth was the head of the little prince's council and that all the others named— the king's brothers Clarence and Gloucester, the queen's brother Anthony Woodville, the leading bishops—were given power to advise and council him only "with the express consent of the Queen," as the official papers declared. Elizabeth Woodville could feel that the tribulations of the previous year were safely behind her. That September, king and queen went on pilgrimage to Canterbury, a favorite place, and at Christmas in Westminster they took care to display themselves going to mass in the abbey, "wearing their crowns," though for the Twelfth Night procession Elizabeth went uncrowned, "because she was great with child." This child, Margaret, was to die before the end of the year, a year that also saw the death of Elizabeth's mother, Jacquetta, on May 30. Joy was mixed with sorrow—but all the same, in her public capacity, Elizabeth was riding high. Her husband's opulent lifestyle gives some sense of what she herself would have enjoyed. The *Liber Niger* (Black book) of Edward IV, compiled between the summer of 1471 and the autumn of 1472, while intended in part to impose much-needed economies on the royal household, nonetheless described an impressive edifice, divided into two principal departments, the *domus providencie* (kitchens, buttery, laundry, and so on) and the *domus magnificencie* (the chapel, signet office, wardrobes, and those in closest attendance on the monarch).

The queen's household was on a smaller scale and would have included far more women. Even so, Elizabeth too had grooms and kitchen staff, clerks, auditors, carvers, almoners, attorneys who served on her council, butlers, bakers, pages and pursuivants, surgeons, and squires. Her offices—of course she had offices—at Westminster were in the New Tower, next to the king's Exchequer.

There is a good description from 1472 of the pleasure and state in which the royal family lived, in the great palaces close to the Thames: Greenwich, Eltham, Westminster, Windsor (so extensively remodeled by Edward III a century before), and Sheen. While Edward had been in exile in Burgundy, he had been entertained by Lord Gruuthuyse, whose palace is familiar to any visitor to Bruges today. Now it was the restored king's chance to reciprocate, and the details of the visit Lord Gruuthuyse made to the court at Windsor are preserved in the account by the so-called Bluemantle Pursuivant, one of the heralds whose job it was to concern himself with questions of precedence and ceremony.

After being greeted by the royal couple, and escorted to their chamber, the visiting party was offered dinner there, in the company of a number of English officers, and then taken back to the king. Afterward, the king led him to the queen's chamber, "where she had there her ladies playing at the marteaux [a game like bowls], and some of her ladies and gentlewomen at the Closheys [ninepins] of ivory, and Dancing. And some at divers other games, according." The king danced with his daughter Elizabeth, and so they parted for the night.

The next morning came Matins and mass in the king's own chapel, after which Edward gave Lord Gruuthuyse a gold cup garnished with pearl and with a great sapphire and "great piece of a Unicorn's horn." After breakfast came hunting, dinner in the lodge, and more hunting, with a half-dozen bucks pursued by hounds and killed near the castle. "By that time it was near night," the herald writes, "yet the King showed him his garden, and Vineyard of Pleasure, and so turned into the Castle again, where they heard evensong in their chambers."

Elizabeth did her part in honoring Gruuthuyse, ordering a great banquet in her own chamber, with dancing after it. "Then about nine of the clock, the King and the Queen, with her ladies and gentlewomen, brought the said Lord Gruuthuyse to three chambers of Pleasure, all hanged with white silk and linen cloth." The floors were covered in carpets—then a great luxury—and the counterpane of cloth of gold, furred with ermine, and the herald took care to record that the queen herself had given orders about the visitor's bed linen. Notable too (along with the charming description of Lord Gruuthuyse ending a wearing day by lingering in the bath, in company with the lord chamberlain) is the way that access to the queen's chambers was being set up as a privilege in the chivalric style, and also as a place where monarchy could be seen—and displayed—in its most accessible and human guise.

This was an age when greater privacy was in demand, and even the earlier generations of great noble builders such as Edward III or Lord Scrope at Bolton Hall had already started to use the great hall, once the all-purpose center of the house, only for big public functions. These great nobles had looked to their peers on the Continent for inspiration, daring to require more rooms (albeit still multifunctional), privies, fireplaces, and chimneys, more painted walls and tiled floors. But what cannot be seen today, when one goes around these palaces, is the sheer riot of color that would once have clamored inside them: textiles, tiles, painted glass, bright wooden roofs and corbels, to say nothing of clothes and livery.

In these ways and others, Elizabeth and Edward would have been anxious to follow the new trends, ushering in a newer and more modern style of life in England. Wood paneling instead of wall hangings was just coming into style, as was translucent glass. There was a new spirit of luxury and comfort in the air. Sir John Fastolf's fifty-room brick castle of Caister could boast feather beds and forty wall hangings, collections of jewels and plate, an astrolabe (or astrological instrument) in the owner's bedroom, and books in the bathing chamber. Back in 1456, so the Paston letters record, Cecily Neville had "sore moved" Sir John to sell her the place, so impressed was she.

The great houses each had their gardens: the formally enclosed plots with their herb beds and their rose bowers, their lavender and their lilies, and the half-wild meadow with the sweet scent of the elderflower in spring and the soapy smell of hawthorn. Smell was important in the medieval world: a sweet odor was one of the signs by which a saint could be identified—an indication that holiness was nearby. Sight, too, could be a way to God, and whereas in winter visitors to Windsor might have had to make do with the images in the chapel (Edward bought a fabulous gold statue of the Virgin for the chapel there), in summer, as they walked on short turf carefully dotted with violets and the daisies Chaucer loved, the blue of the columbine might have reminded them of the Virgin's robe, golden heart of a honey-scented oxlip the promise of her heavenly crown. In art and literature, even the paths through an orchard could become an allegorical rendition of a saint's mystical dialogue with God. When Gruuthuyse visited in autumn, the swell of the fruit on trees and grapes on vines would have brought their own message of God's favor, of promise and prosperity.

Even amid these cheery distractions, however, there were hints of foreboding. Not all symbols and allegories brought the promise of heavenly comfort. The year 1472 saw a comet that blazed across the sky for almost two months; no one knew what the ever-changing portent meant. The next year brought fevers and a bloody flux, and it was through a troubled landscape that in the spring of 1473 the two-and-a-half-year-old Edward was sent to Ludlow, on the borders of his Welsh principality, with Elizabeth's brother Anthony destined to be his governor. Anthony was, in Mancini's words, "a kindly, serious and just" man, one whose spiritual leanings reputedly led him to wear a hair shirt underneath his courtly garments. Both educated and gifted as a military commander, he was undoubtedly well suited to his task.

Anthony was not the only Woodville to be assigned to the young prince. Two of Elizabeth's other brothers were the young prince's counselors and another his chaplain, while her son by her first marriage—assisted by her cousin—became his comptroller and her brother-in-law by her first marriage his master of horse. Abbot Mylling, who had been so kind to Elizabeth in sanctuary, became his chancellor. In the years ahead, such a comprehensive placing of Woodville connections about the boy would come to prove a vulnerable point, creating mistrust among the nobility, but at the time it must have made Elizabeth feel safe. Still, when her son set out for Ludlow, she went with him, despite being once again pregnant, and stayed until autumn.

The instructions his father sent for the rearing of the little prince sound a lovely domestic note. He was to rise "at a convenient hour according to his age," hear Matins in his chamber and mass in the chapel, and then after breakfast "to be occupied in such virtuous learning as his age shall suffer to receive." Every care was to be taken as to his companions and his conversation at dinner, "so that the communication at all times in his presence be of virtue, honour, cunning, wisdom, and deed of worship, and of nothing that shall stir him to vice." No "swearer, brawler, backbiter, common hazarder or adulterer" was even to be admitted to the household. After two more hours of lessons, he might "be shewed such convenient disports and exercises as belong to his estate to have experience in," then after Evensong those about him were "to enforce themselves to make him merry towards his bed."

But Elizabeth's role on this journey was not purely domestic and maternal: when the little Prince of Wales was sent to visit Coventry, Elizabeth could be found making friendly overtures to its officials. Her letter to the city assured them that a servant of her husband's who had made a public disturbance there would receive no special treatment, "for as much as you shall now certainly understand that we do not intend in any way to maintain, support, or favour any of my said lord's servants or ours in any of their riots or unfitting behaviour."

Elizabeth and her husband were particularly mindful of what you might call the women's vote. When she visited Coventry in 1474, the city records show that she gave six bucks to the mayor and his colleagues—and six to their wives. The *Great Chronicle of London* relates how Edward, raising money for his wars, kissed an old lady to such effect that she changed her ten-pound donation into twenty pounds, and his welcome into London after the Readeption was said by Commynes to be in part due to the "ladies of quality and rich citizens, wives with whom he had formerly intrigued," and who forced their husbands to declare for his side.

Mindfulness, of course, could go too far—from a wife's viewpoint, anyway. Edward was always going to take the freedoms the age accorded to any wealthy husband, never mind a king, and avail himself of the services of mistresses. His wife, Elizabeth, must up to a point have accepted this, especially given the frequency of her pregnancies and retreats into confinement. But around this time, Edward began an affair that would become a matter of comment in the next reigns for its personal qualities, as well as its capacity for use in political propaganda—the affair with the beautiful merchant's wife "Jane" Shore, as she is usually known. (Her real name was Elizabeth.) Yet despite Edward's infidelity, these might be called the golden years for the Yorkist monarchy, for Elizabeth as much as for Edward. Their second son, Richard, was born on August 17, 1473, at the Dominican Friary in Shrewsbury, adding to the line of succession and surely making Edward more confident that his side of the Plantagenet family was secure on the throne.

But the rifts that caused the Readeption were still evident. Indeed, there were rumors of the troubles that lay ahead. In February 1472, the first February after Edward's resumption of the throne, Sir John Paston had written that the king and queen, with Clarence and Gloucester, had gone to Elizabeth's own palace of Sheen: "Men say not all in charity; what will fall men cannot say."

George of Clarence and Richard of Gloucester had recently been on different sides of a deadly dispute, but now they had a new cause of enmity. The death of Edward of Lancaster, Marguerite's son, had left his young wife, Anne, a widow—and potentially a hugely wealthy one. Warwick's treason and death meant his estates reverted to the Crown;

it seemed likely (though illegal) that his wife's huge Beauchamp and Despenser inheritance would also be taken from her. Clarence's wife, Isabel, was to be the first beneficiary. Warwick's other daughter, Anne, Isabel's younger sister, might also benefit—and, coincidentally or otherwise, Richard now showed a desire to marry her. But Clarence had no wish to see his brother share the bounty from the Countess of Warwick's estates. The Crowland chronicler claimed that Clarence spirited Anne away to a house in London, disguised as a kitchen maid. Richard, discovering Anne's whereabouts, moved her to sanctuary at the College of St. Martin-le-Grand while a deal was thrashed out. In April 1472, papal dispensation was granted for the marriage of two such close connections, Richard's mother being Anne's great-aunt. Richard had already had a clause put into the contracts ensuring him of Anne's inheritance even if the dispensation failed to arrive. It is not known exactly when or where the ceremony took place, but marry they did: with the support of Edward—who can now more than ever, after Clarence's recent treachery, have had no desire to see so much wealth and power concentrated in that brother's hands—and also, it seems, with that of the queen, who had made a point in the preceding months of renewing a grant Richard held from her.

None of the contemporary reporters hint at Anne's feelings, unless it is the Milanese ambassador in France who, sometime later, in February 1474, sent a patchily erroneous report of enmity between Richard (who "by force has taken to wife a daughter of the late Earl of Warwick") and Clarence (who feared this might deprive him of "Warwick's county"). The "force," of course, may well imply that the marriage was against Clarence's will, rather than against Anne's, but it would certainly be interesting to know how much say she really had in the affair.

She may not have wanted any other choices. She and Richard had known each other as children when, between 1465 and 1468, Richard had been brought up partly in Warwick's home of Middleham—so it is conceivable there was an element of affection involved. The early-seventeenth-century antiquarian George Buck, indeed, has Richard having held off from taking any part in the killing of Anne's first husband, Edward, "in regard of this prince's wife, who (as Johannes Meyerus saith) was [in the room with him and] was akin to the

Duchess of York his mother, and whom also he loved very affectionately, though secretly." Though there is no evidence for that, by the same token there is no evidence for the popular picture of Richard, perpetuated by Shakespeare, as a lank-haired hunchback, so deformed that the dogs bark as he limps by. Nothing else that is known of Richard—his prowess in battle, for example—suggests that there was anything about him that would have turned a girl away. And even Richard's sudden pursuit of Anne does not necessarily have to do entirely with venality. Rous describes Anne herself as "seemly, amiable and beauteous, right virtuous and full gracious"—but that might have been a family chronicler's partiality.

But even if there was any element of affection between Richard and Anne, it would not have been considered as of prime importance. Their marriage was primarily a matter of property. John Paston reported that Clarence told Richard that "he may well have my lady his sister-in-law, but they shall divide no livelihood"—that he was welcome to Anne herself, as long as he did not expect to get the lands with her. If so, Richard was clearly uninterested in the lady without the lucre.

With the royal brothers squabbling over the Neville lands, one woman was certainly robbed—Anne and Isabel's mother, the Countess of Warwick, who after her husband's death had fled to Beaulieu Abbey, only to find that on the king's orders she was not permitted to leave. The appalled widow wrote pleading letters (in her own handwriting, "in the absence of clerks," as she explained) not only to the king and to her sons-in-law themselves but also to "the Queen's good Grace, to my right redoubted Lady the King's mother, to my Lady the King's eldest daughter [the six-year-old Elizabeth] . . . to my Ladies the King's sisters, to my Lady of Bedford mother to the Queen, and to other Ladies noble of the realm." But on this occasion, the female network was powerless.

In June 1473, the countess was taken north to her new son-in-law's castle of Middleham in Yorkshire. Rous describes her as "locked up," by Anne as much as Richard. Her lands were to be shared out, in the chilling words of the Act of Parliament of May 1474, as though "she were naturally dead."

Middleham was a Norman keep, substantially modernized and impressive enough to earn the sobriquet Windsor of the North, but still built for war. The medieval age did not distinguish between castles and great houses—by this point houses were being built often with purely decorative crenellation and moats being converted into lakes. But Middleham was still a fully functional fortress. Northern houses were more likely to be for genuine defense, close as they were to England's only land frontier—the border with the often-hostile Scots.

It was in this imposing structure that Anne's only child, Edward "of Middleham," was presumably born, although the exact timing is unknown. One description of him might seem to suggest 1473, the date often given, but one chronicler would suggest 1476 to 1477, which is just before the first definite record of his existence, an instruction that he should be prayed for, along with his parents, in a chantry endowed for the purpose.

There are a huge number of question marks over Anne, more than any other woman in our story. Rous says she and Richard were "unhappily married," but there is little other evidence, and "unhappily" here may simply imply that it ended unfortunately. Still, to modern eyes, there is something worrying in Anne's notable absence from the records—notable even by the standards of a fifteenth-century wife. In order to create a power base for himself, Richard needed to make use of his wife's heritage and lineage—to present himself as the legitimate inheritor of Neville authority in the North. But perhaps that need made him all the more determined to limit her autonomy.

While Anne, and the share of her mother's fortune the 1474 act had granted her, was thus absorbed into the Yorkist structure, Margaret Beaufort had been working toward her own rehabilitation. Her unfortunate husband Stafford had died in October 1471 of the wounds he received at the battle of Barnet sometime earlier, and within eight months she had married again, this time in a match that would bring her into even better graces with the Yorkists.

Margaret had, it seems, been fond of Stafford—they celebrated their wedding anniversaries, feasting on plover and larks, sharing pleasures as well as property. If Edmund Tudor had been the father of her child, it was Stafford whose favorite house, in later years, she would painstakingly rebuild. After his death, she had for a time moved out of Woking and into the London home her mother owned—perhaps because she needed to put herself visibly on the market again.

Margaret could not afford to remain unprotected. It cannot be known for sure at what point Margaret Beaufort really did start to shape her own destiny—the records of her business affairs do not distinguish between her own decisions and those of a husband until much later in her life—but surely it would be fair to speculate that it was now. The leading Beauforts had all been executed, so there was only the king who might have been expected to exercise direct control over her affairs, and for his part Edward must have been only too glad to see her married to a man seemingly wholly reconciled to the Yorkist monarchy—a man like Thomas, Lord Stanley.

Margaret's third (or, technically, fourth) marriage would be a matter of business, a partnership that would years later be to some degree dissolved, by mutual consent, when need no longer required and opportunity offered. Nonetheless, it was in its own terms a success story, with every sign that Stanley respected his wife's abilities.

Lord Stanley, a hardheaded man of property, was distinguished chiefly for his success in having kept himself clear of firm commitment to either side of the unpredictable war that had ravaged England for the past two decades. He was therefore not wholly trusted; all the same, by this juncture he had achieved the position of lord steward of Edward IV's household. A widower, already with children, he was apparently content with the fact that no children would come from his marriage with Margaret. She, however, increased his status, while his position within the Yorkist regime fostered her security and that of her son, Henry.

Henry Tudor, however, was by now far enough away that any benefit of his mother's new alliance would be slow in reaching him. When Henry and his uncle Jasper had fled England, their ship, steering for France, had been forced by storms instead to make for Brittany. There Duke Francis received them courteously as guests—and bargaining chips, not permitting them to leave. Both Louis of France and Edward in England had tried to win Henry and Jasper out of Breton hands, Edward being convinced, Polydore Vergil says, that with them on the Continent he could never live "in perfect security." But Duke Francis had refused, and there, for the moment, the matter rested, while Margaret went on consolidating her policy of reconciliation.

A new war—waged, this time, outside England—would afford Margaret an opportunity to strengthen her ties with the Yorkists. When King Edward invaded France in 1475, in pursuance of England's long-standing claim to the French crown, Margaret Beaufort's husband, Stanley, was one of the lords accompanying him and selected to negotiate the final resulting treaty.

The French expedition marked a significant point for another woman also. Before he left for the war, Edward brought his four-year-old heir and namesake back from Ludlow as nominal ruler, with the title "Keeper of the Realm," all under his mother's charge. The will the king made before his campaign acknowledged Elizabeth's importance. His two eldest daughters were to have ten thousand marks each as a marriage dowry, so long as "they be governed and ruled in their marriages by our dearest wife the Queen and by our said son the Prince, if God fortune him to come to age of discretion"; otherwise—if the princesses should be so bold as to marry themselves, "so as they be thereby disparaged, (as God forbid)"—the dowry would be forfeited. The will also granted eighteen thousand marks (plus two thousand already paid) to Edward's third daughter, Cecily, but then her marriage to the heir of the king of Scots was already arranged, to secure the Scottish border before the fighting forces went to combat the French. The York lands would go to Edward's younger son Richard; the queen herself would have the revenues of all the lands she already possessed for her lifetime and also her personal property to dispose of as she would: "all her own goods, chattels, stuff, bedding, arrases, tapestries, verdours, stuff of household plate and jewels, and all other things which she now hath and occupieth." She was named first of his ten executors: "our said dearest and most entirely beloved wife Elizabeth the Queen . . . our said dearest Wife in whom we most singularly put our trust in this party."

Elizabeth was granted forty-four hundred pounds a year for the maintenance of the king's household, which she and her son Edward would now occupy. She was not in any sense given a regency of the sort that was well known in France, the sort Marguerite had sought; this was probably due partly to the memory of Marguerite, partly to the lack of recent precedent, and perhaps partly also to personality. Maybe Edward felt that Elizabeth's gifts were more suited to protecting the interests of her children, and handling their property, than to ruling a country. All the same, it was a declaration of trust.

The invasion of France had been planned in alliance with Burgundy, and Margaret of Burgundy had rushed to see her brothers Edward and Richard as they landed. But the war proved short-lived—to the annoyance of the more militant Richard—when Edward was easily persuaded to accept a peace treaty and a pension from the French, rather than pursue his claims to their throne. Margaret now had to mediate between her brother and her husband, who had been thus deprived of England's aid against their common enemy. Commynes described the French and English kings meeting on a bridge and embracing through a grate. Louis joked that if Edward wanted to come and meet the French ladies, he would lend him the Cardinal of Bourbon for his confessor, "who he knew would willingly absolve him, if he should commit any sin by way of love and gallantry."

The peace ultimately was cemented not by the amorous intervention of Edward himself, nor only by the pension Louis granted him, but also by the promise of a marriage between young Princess Elizabeth and the Dauphin. As the treaty declared: "For the inviolate observation of the friendship, it is promised, settled, agreed, and concluded that a marriage shall be contracted between the most illustrious Prince Charles, son of the most powerful prince of France, and the most serene lady Elizabeth, daughter of the most invincible king of England, when they shall reach marriageable years." Edward returned to his delighted capital, calling his eldest daughter Dauphiness and declaring she must have a new wardrobe in the French style. He would be losing one daughter, perhaps, but was gaining another: a fifth daughter, Anne (probably named for Anne Mortimer, through whom came Edward's best claim to the throne), was born to the royal couple on November 2 that year.

As part of the peace deal, the French king had offered Edward a ransom of fifty thousand crowns, ten thousand pounds, for Marguerite of Anjou, in exchange for her signing over to Louis all rights of inheritance in her parents' lands. The wording of the documents denies she had ever been a queen of England, let alone one of the most active in that country's history. Louis signed an agreement concerning "the daughter of the King of Sicily," and it was as "I, Margaret, formerly married in the Kingdom of England," that Marguerite herself was forced to renounce "all that I could pretend to in England by the articles of my marriage."

It was a new kind of humiliation, then, that Marguerite suffered as she made her way back to France. An entry in the roll of accounts reads, "To Richard Haute, esquire, paid as a reward for the costs and expenses incurred by him for conducting Margaret, lately called the Queen, from London to the town of Sandwich." At the beginning of 1476, Marguerite was returned across the Channel to live as Louis's pensioner, and this time there is no record of how she—who in the past had made her feelings so plain—felt about the decision. For a few years, she may at least have enjoyed a reunion with her father, but René of Anjou died in 1479. Holinshed, in his sixteenth-century chronicles, would take a moment to moralize on the subject, describing how "this queen" was "sent home again with as much misery and sorrow as she was received with pomp and triumph. Such is the instability of worldly felicity, and so wavering is false flattering fortune. Which mutation and change of the better for the worse could not but nettle and sting her with pensiveness, yea and any other person whatsoever that, having been in good estate, falleth into the contrary."

Hall describes an equally gloomy scenario: "And where in the beginning of her time, she lived like a Queen, in the middle she ruled like an empress, towards the end she was vexed with trouble, never quiet nor in peace, and in her very extreme age she passed her days in France, more like a death than a life, languishing and mourning in continual sorrow, not so much for herself and her husband, whose ages were almost consumed and worn, but for the loss of prince Edward her son." Marguerite seemed fated to live out the rest of her days in this strange purgatory, haunted by her lost hopes for herself and her family and taunted by events even then unfolding in the kingdom across the Channel.

12

"FORTUNE'S WOMB"

Some unborn sorrow, ripe in fortune's womb,
Is coming towards me, and my inward soul
With nothing trembles.
THE LIFE AND DEATH OF
KING RICHARD THE SECOND, 2.2

These were the mature years of Edward IV's kingship. Time would prove that fractures within the Yorkist dynasty had never entirely healed, but for the moment at least they were concealed. In 1476 came a chance for the celebration of the dynasty. An illustration probably made around that time shows the royal court and the royal family in what seemed like an earthly equivalent to the order of the sacred Trinity they reverenced. The king and his men kneel on one side, Elizabeth and her ladies on the other, with her mother-in-law, Cecily, behind Elizabeth wearing as a cloak the royal arms of England. Everything was set for an extraordinary scene—and the Yorkists did not disappoint.

The reburial of Richard, Duke of York, at Fotheringhay was meant in part to fulfill filial piety, but also—and more important—to show that the York dynasty he had spawned was here to stay. It began with the procession south, a public ten-day parade that would convey Richard's body from its initial grave in northern England to its final resting place in the church attached to the Midlands castle of Fotheringhay. The season was high summer, and the trailing black draperies must have turned brown with dust, as the days on the road went by— brush them at night though the servants may. In July the country people would be out in the fields to see the procession pass by, and every trade guild from every town could send their own little train of riders and banners to pay their respects, proudly carrying with them their crosses, their holy water, and their holy relics, without too much fear rain would spoil the local officials' best clothes or the glitter of the gold embroidery.

Of course, the noblemen escorting the bodies were going to sweat in their black cloaks—especially the officers of arms with their bright tabards over the mourning clothes. The black hoods were pulled forward over each face, and underneath the heavy folds each forehead must have been streaming, but no matter, these were (as Hamlet, more than a century later, would put it) but the trappings and the suits of woe. If the black clothes, and the black velvet stretched on hoops over the vehicle that bore the coffins, stood out like a stab of darkness against the blue and gold of the July fields, well, that was the point, surely.

Real, painful, grief must have been the one thing in short supply. It was, after all, more than fifteen years since the dead men—Richard, Duke of York, and his son Edmund—had perished at the battle of Wakefield and been buried there in the North with the scant ceremony accorded to those on the losing side of any war. It was high time that the king's father—once so shamefully mocked—should be reburied in an appropriately splendid tomb. A few sweaty foreheads, even if they were noble ones, a few horses chafing under the black trappings that swept the ground, were a small price to pay for such a conscious display of power and permanence.

It had been on or shortly before Sunday, July 21, that the bodies of the Yorkist duke and his son had been exhumed from the place where they had been buried—in the Priory of St. John the Evangelist near Pontefract Castle, probably. After the Dirige had been sung, the cortege had set out, with the correct order of precedence strictly observed and the candles flickering wanly in the bright light of day. Central to the ceremonials was a life-size effigy of the duke, an honor normally permitted only to kings, queens, and bishops—but then, a point was being made. A funeral was an important ceremony in the legitimization of monarchy. The effigy used in a king's funeral represented the public, symbolic body of the monarch, still present and active, even while the mortal body of the current incumbent might die. This duke's effigy was clad in dark blue, the color of a king's mourning, and an angel held a crown over his head in the same assumption of royal dignity that led his widow, Cecily, to call herself "queen by right."

As chief mourner, Richard, Duke of Gloucester, rode directly behind the coffins. His habitual residence in the North made him the natural choice to escort his father's body southward. Behind him rode the nobles and officers, then four hundred poor men on foot, each carrying a taper. The choir of the Chapel Royal was there, to sing at each church where the body rested overnight along the way. They traveled about thirteen miles a day, from Pontefract to Doncaster, Blyth to Tuxford, Newark on Trent, then Grantham, then the long leg to Stamford, and on to their final destination of Fotheringhay.

The church of Fotheringhay still stands, startling across the meadows. A three-story tower and belfry—probably odder, if less impressive, today than it used to be, since the chancel and cloisters were destroyed after the Reformation. The York tombs have been demolished and different ones rebuilt: only the greens and blues and gold of the restored pulpit originally commissioned by Edward IV give a hint of what the church's robust color must once have been, when the cloister alone glowed with the jeweled light of almost ninety stained-glass windows.

The castle that once stood near the church was built as a defensible structure, surrounded by a double moat: one of the country's finest, with a newer manor house as well as the ancient keep, and all the usual complexes of butteries and breweries, stables and chapels. Today only a grassy mound remains, and even the surrounding water, as shown in the old illustrations, has dwindled to a small river. But nothing can destroy the grandeur of the setting, looking south over the once great River Nene, surrounded by the hunting forest of Rockingham. Besides the castle complex, the church, and the surrounding market town, there was a collegiate establishment covering more than two and a half acres, large enough to boast twelve fellows or chaplains—a center of learning and piety. In 1476 Fotheringhay had only recently been relinquished by Edward IV's mother, Cecily, but whether or not she had willingly exchanged it for Berkhampsted, she would have approved Edward's intention for Fotheringhay—to make it into a mausoleum for the York family.*

King Edward, as described in a French text, written by Chestre le herault (the Chester herald), met his father's body at the entrance to the churchyard and "very humbly did his obeisance to the said body and laid his hand on the body and kissed it, weeping." With the corpse carried into the choir of the church and placed inside the hearse, the king "retired to his closet" while "Placebo" and "Dirige" began. "And at the moment of the Magnificat the king had his chamberlain offer to the body seven pieces of cloth of gold and each piece was five yards long, and the queen had five yards offered by her chamberlain and they were laid in the shape of a cross on the said body." It is the first time any woman has been mentioned—even acting by proxy and offering through her chamberlain—in the course of the ceremony.

That was on Monday, July 29, and that night the body would have rested in a blaze of candles, though it was in fact some years too late for them to light the path for the departing soul. On Tuesday, three high masses were sung and more cloth of gold offered on behalf of the king, the queen, and the dead man's younger sons. A horse, a courser, was led to the church door; as part of the traditional offering of the dead man's knightly trappings, his coat of arms, shield, sword, and helmet were each brought in by different noblemen.

Next, the royal family came to pay their respects, the queen "dressed all in blue without a high headdress, and there she made a

---

*Elizabeth of York would own Fotheringhay eventually, and her death would mark an end to its warm association with the royal family. Elizabeth of York's granddaughter Elizabeth I would have another of her descendants beheaded there, and now the name of Fotheringhay will forever be associated with that of the Scots queen Mary.

great obeisance and reverence to the said body, and next two of the king's daughters came to offer in the same way." The royal daughters are not named but would surely have been the eldest—ten-year-old Elizabeth of York (so recently betrothed to the French Dauphin) and Mary. That the queen, the former Elizabeth Woodville, came without a hennin—the tall pointed cone from which floated a flattering veil, or the veiled, backward-pointing "butterfly" headdress—was presumably a conventional token of grief.

There is a second French text, surviving in various sixteenth-century versions, that also gives an account of the reburial at Fotheringhay. It places a fourth woman at the requiem mass: "The king offered for the said prince his father and the queen and her two daughters and the countess of Richmond offered next." The "second French account" survives as a medley of late-fifteenth- and sixteenth-century documents, and it is always possible that a later hand added the name of Margaret Beaufort, Countess of Richmond—later, when her son, Henry, was on the throne, when she had become "My Lady the King's Mother," when her presence at any gathering would have become worth recording (and tactful to do so). This could account for the fact that she is the only woman, other than the queen and her two daughters, mentioned specifically in the document. But the blandly undescriptive words do show just how well Margaret Beaufort was doing in trying to placate the ruling Yorkist family.

And no one could fault this as a resplendent celebration of the Yorkist dynasty. The Chester herald describes the blend of liberality and charity—a penny given to everyone who came to mass and twopence to each pregnant woman. The accounts of John Eltrington, treasurer of the royal household, show a formidable provision of food: "49 cattle at 16s the piece, 210 sheep at 2s, 90 calves, 200 piglets." The bill from the Poultry Department recorded a payment of £67 13s 4d "to Thomas Cornyssh" for "capons, cygnets, hens, partridges, pheasants, herons, 'wypes' [lapwing or curlew], coneys, 'rabettes,' chickens, milk, cream, butter, eggs and other victuals bought for the burial feast."

Although many of the details of the menus have been lost, the names of some of the feast's suppliers have survived—even the name of the man who transported the chickens: "To William Strode for carriage of said poultry for 31 days with 5 horses £10 6s 8d." The names are invariably male; the heraldic, knightly aspect both of ceremonies and of the accounts kept of them by the Chester herald and his like meant that mentions of women's presence would be scarce. All the same, there are certain names whose absence is worth noting.

It is not recorded whether Anne Neville, Duchess of Gloucester, was at Fotheringhay, despite the conspicuous part played in the event by her husband, Richard. Her presence may have gone unremarked, as her doings so often did, though surely, had she been there, she would have made her offering before Margaret Beaufort. Her absence may simply have been due to a pregnancy. If it was around now that Anne's one child was born, and if she was newly delivered or even still pregnant, it might be good reason not to risk an arduous journey. The logistics, in any case, would have been against her coming; there had been no role for her in that stylized procession of a journey.

But for this period of Anne's marriage at least, there are mentions of her in other records. In 1475–1476 there is a message from her to the city of York, conveyed by one of her husband's councilors and suggesting—as would indeed be the norm—that she was able to deputize for him in his absence. In 1476 she was admitted to the sisterhood of Durham cathedral priory; the following year, she and Richard would both join the guild of Corpus Christi at York, and she joined her husband in funding a chantry at Queens' College Cambridge. At the beginning of December 1476, some of Richard's payment warrants, issued from London, show purchases of furs and silk for "the most dear consort of the lord duke." So there is probably no reason to read anything sinister into Anne's absence—but one other omission from the list of attendees, however, does look more pointed.

It is hard not to read something into the apparent absence, from the Fotheringhay ceremony, of the woman with most reason of all to be there—Cecily, Duchess of York, the dead man's widow. It is true that royalty did not customarily attend funerals and that a woman might in any case have no place at the actual funeral ceremony of a man. But this was not a funeral as such, and neither the king nor the queen felt obliged to stay away from the occasion.

Cecily may simply have been ill; she was, after all, past sixty—old for the day. Alternatively, it is possible that she simply watched the ceremony, instead of taking part. But when Margaret Beaufort, for example, would watch rather than participate in similarly important ceremonies during her son's reign, her presence would be recorded. If Cecily had indeed been absent entirely, the question has to be why. It is possible "proud Cis" couldn't stand having to play second fiddle to the daughter-in-law she despised as a lowborn interloper—not at this of all ceremonies. Cecily and Elizabeth Woodville would not, in this story, be the only mother- and daughter-in-law who did not always agree.

There are signs from this same year of possible strains in Cecily's relationships, not only with her daughter-in-law but with her own children as well. It is tempting to read between the lines of a letter written in October 1476 by a member of the Stonor family. Elizabeth Stonor writes to her husband of how she had attended the Duchess of Suffolk—the king's sister Elizabeth—on a visit to Cecily Neville. "And also on Saturday last was I waited upon [the duchess] again, and also from thence she waited upon my lady her Mother, and brought her to Greenwich to the King's good grace and the queen's: and there I saw the meeting between the King and my lady his Mother. And truly me thought it was a very good sight." It sounds almost as though Cecily failed to meet her daughter-in-law, even though Elizabeth Woodville was obviously at Greenwich at the time of Cecily's visit. Worse, it sounds as though Edward's sister had to "bring" Cecily to see her son and that her meeting her son was thought worth commenting on—an indication that all was not well at the very highest levels of the house of York.

But there are signs also that Cecily had been trying to mend the rifts within her family. One letter of Cecily's perhaps written in 1474 had been to her son Richard, and there is the sound of a mother's finger-wagging in its lines. "Son," Cecily wrote, "we trusted you should have been at Berkhamsted with my lord my son [Edward] at his last being there with us, and if it had pleased you to come at that time, you should have been right heartily welcome. And so you shall be whensoever you shall do the same, as God knoweth, whom we beseech to have you in governance." Though this need not reflect anything more than a mother's natural desire to see as much as possible of her son, one could also perceive a desire to bind ties in what had long been shown to be a dangerously fractured family.

The ranks of Cecily's children had been diminished, at the start of 1476, by the death of her eldest daughter, Anne, in childbirth. Four years before, in 1472, Anne had obtained what the sixteenth-century chronicler John Stow called a divorce (probably an annulment) from her estranged husband, the Duke of Exeter, and married her long-standing lover, the Kentish gentleman Thomas St. Leger. By contrast, Cecily's second daughter, Elizabeth, the Duchess of Suffolk mentioned by Elizabeth Stonor, was enjoying an access of independence and influence after the death of *her* formidable mother-in-law, Alice Chaucer, in 1475, just the year before. But this particular scion of the York family seems, nonetheless, to have taken little personal part in political affairs.

Political affairs, on the other hand, were the daily concern of Cecily's youngest and grandest daughter, Margaret of Burgundy. And as 1477 dawned, Cecily must have been worried about her daughter across the Channel as much as, if not more than, her other children.

When she had married Duke Charles in 1468, Margaret had entered a court, and a political system, where the duchess was expected to play a comparatively active role, this despite the fact that her new husband was more than a decade older than she, a man strongly committed to his own rule, ferocious in war and frequently away, relaxing into the company of his fellow soldiers. Attention at first was likely to have focused on how she would do with a consort's prime duty: the provision of heirs. This Margaret would never manage, for reasons we do not know, and Charles' existing daughter, Mary, remained his sole heiress. Although before her arrival he had told his subjects as a matter of prime importance that his bride was "ideally shaped to bear a prince," there is no sign of the kind of frantic and reproachful flailings after a male heir in which Margaret's great-nephew Henry VIII of England would indulge.

It seems possible Charles adapted with the readiness of relief to the idea of a more distant marriage. Only a few years into the alliance, records of their movements show the pair were quite literally almost never together, though relations seem to have been amicable. With Charles at the wars, Margaret nonetheless retained enough hope to make offerings to those saints associated with childbirth and fertility: Waudru, Margaret of Antioch, Colette, Anne. In 1473 she made an unusual two-month trip to a palace especially designated as a place of cure and recovery; her trouble may possibly have been the loss of a child.

Alone or in company with the stepdaughter (with whom, as with her mother-in-law, she seems to have gotten on well), Margaret traveled indefatigably, raising men and money for her husband's campaigns and receiving petitions and ambassadors in his frequent absences. Her secure position survived not only the childlessness that would destroy Henry VIII's queens, but also the political turmoils in England that cast into doubt her other prime function, as living guarantor of the Anglo-Burgundian alliance.

Margaret's security, however, would not last. Duke Charles, having made his own truce with the French, had been fighting on his other frontiers throughout 1476. In the frozen month of January 1477 came news—filtering only slowly, though, to his womenfolk and to his foreign allies—that he was dead. Immediately, King Louis of France laid claim to a significant part of his lands.

It was lucky Margaret at thirty-one already had considerable experience of the swift reverses of fortune, for she had quickly to play an active role in Burgundian affairs. She and her stepdaughter (Mary as the new ruling duchess and Margaret under the title of Duchesse Mère) acted together to summon the Burgundian parliament, the Estates-General, and urge the individual cities and provinces that made up Burgundy to resist the French invaders, to buy diplomatic time by a letter to Louis pleading for the protection due to "widows and orphans." (Louis's first response was to suggest a marriage between the twenty-year-old Duchess Mary and his seven-year-old son, the Dauphin—who, of course, had two years before been betrothed to Elizabeth of York as part of that peace treaty.)

In the course of a fraught spring and summer, the two women would pull off the deal, but things got worse before they got better. Margaret and Mary had to cope with the arrest and execution, by the Estates-General, of their most trusted advisers; the former had also, like so many widows, to battle for her dower rights, withheld on the grounds her brother had never paid all the dowry he had promised. That battle finally ended when Mary intervened on behalf of Margaret—a woman who, she said, had always held "our person and our lands and lordships in such complete and perfect love and goodwill that we can never sufficiently repay and recompense her."

But Margaret also had two other things with which to cope. The first was a whispering campaign against her sponsored by the French king. Before her marriage, he had spread rumors about her chastity. Now, he spread a different story, which would have repercussions in England in the year ahead. The second, and more pressing, fact was that her brother Edward was not going to send military support or risk his own rapport with (and pension from) the French to support her, now that Louis was attacking her dower lands.

Margaret wrote to Edward in the strongest terms, protesting that although he had once made her "one of the most important ladies in the world," she was now "one of the poorest widows deserted by everyone, especially by you." She implored him to send a thousand or more English archers "to rescue me from the King of France who does his best to reduce me to a state of beggary for the rest of my days."

Although Edward did write to Louis on her behalf, Margaret was deeply dissatisfied with her brother, and, as events would prove, she was not a woman to take dissatisfaction lightly. Nor was she the only one of the York siblings to feel aggrieved. Just two years after the triumphant symbolism of the Fotheringhay ceremony, the Yorkist dynasty and its matriarch, Cecily, were wracked by the fate of her second son, Clarence.

MOTHER OF GRIEFS

Alas, I am the mother of these griefs;
Their woes are parcelled, mine is general.

THE TRAGEDY OF RICHARD THE THIRD, 2.2

George, Duke of Clarence, had long been a disaffected stirrer of trouble. For ten years, he had been his brother's heir, which had given him what in modern terms would be called an exaggerated sense of entitlement. History, however, sees him less kindly. Clarence has gone down as, in Shakespeare's words, "false, fleeting, perjured Clarence," and this reputation is bound up with the story of the women around him.

Clarence's wife, Isabel Neville, had died at the end of 1476, just before Christmas, less than three months after giving birth to a son. This baby, Isabel's third living child, very shortly followed her, and (though a local chronicler definitely links the event to the childbirth) rumors would soon accrue around their deaths.

The first effect of Isabel's death was to make Clarence an available widower. The Crowland chronicler reports that Margaret of Burgundy, "whose affections were fixed on her brother Clarence beyond any of the rest of her kindred," now devoted her energies to reviving the old idea of a match between him and the heiress Mary of Burgundy, the same woman whom the French king Louis wanted as a match for his young son. But, just as when the idea had first been mooted almost a decade before, King Edward refused his permission.

Perhaps it is true that, as Crowland claims, Margaret was deeply attached to her brother Clarence, though there is no particular evidence for it. (One suspects that those relatives who did retain most affection for Clarence were those at some distance from him.) They may indeed have suffered from a common anger, a shared sense of disillusionment with Edward insofar as he had seemed to put their welfare second to other concerns. Clarence too had been in favor of the military intervention in Burgundy rejected by Edward—a thwarted hope that may have given him an additional bond with his sister.

What wasn't said in Crowland was that the siblings may all to some degree have been victims of the French king, who was still trying to break up the anti-French alliance established between England and Burgundy. Now French envoys, keen to weaken the new Duchess Mary by disabling one of her most powerful advisers, spread the story that Margaret and certain English lords might have Mary kidnapped and taken to England to marry Clarence; the same envoys whispered into Edward's ear the poisonous suggestion that Margaret and Clarence, this marriage with the heiress made, would use Burgundian troops to seize the English throne. (Burgundy itself, in the person of Mary, had a claim to that crown, as she was descended through her grandmother from John of Gaunt.)

There is no reason to believe the charges; within a couple of months of Duke Charles's death, Margaret and Mary alike were actively seeking the long-planned marriage between Mary and Maximilian, the Archduke of Austria and son of the Holy Roman Emperor, which finally took place in summer 1477 to the satisfaction of all parties immediately concerned.

But Clarence's past history must have made even the most damaging rumors all too credible. Any whispers of a stronger Anglo-Burgundian link could—assuming they had not been instituted by the French king himself—have broken the fragile peace with France and thrown that country back on their old alliance with the ever-troublesome Scots.

Whatever the rumors, no intervention by either Louis or Margaret may have been necessary: Clarence had an almost unparalleled capacity for making trouble on his own.

In the spring of 1477, Clarence was involved in two bizarre trials. The first was the result of his accusing one Ankarette Twynho, formerly a servant to Clarence's wife but now perhaps come into the Woodvilles' sphere, of having given Isabel poisoned ale (given on October 10, though improbably not causing death until December 22). Two others were accused of having joined with her to poison also Isabel's baby, which died ten days later. Ankarette was snatched from her home by Clarence's men and taken across three counties to Warwick, where Clarence held sway. There, despite the absurdity of the charges, she was found guilty by a jury, who later pleaded that Clarence had left them no choice, and executed on the spot.

A few weeks later, in an apparently unrelated case, three men were tried and convicted in London for "seeking the destruction of the King and Prince," as Crowland reported, by seditious means but also by necromancy—witchcraft. At least one of the men was a close associate of Clarence's, who later, in May, stormed out of the king's council, having had the men's declarations of their innocence read.

Clarence was displaying a flagrant lack of respect for the due process of the law and also for the king's authority. Crowland relates how the king summoned the duke to Westminster and inveighed against his behavior "as derogatory to the laws of the realm and most dangerous to judges and jurors throughout the kingdom." The two had, as the continuator describes, come to look upon each other with "unbrotherly" regard. In June, Clarence was himself arrested and sent to the Tower.

At the beginning of 1478, Clarence was attainted on a rhetorically elaborate charge of treasons past and present. The parliamentary sessions in which he was tried began on January 16. The date reflects the complicated life of the York family, for January 15 had seen, by contrast, a resplendent wedding ceremony. Early in 1476, the last Mowbray Duke of Norfolk had died, leaving only an infant daughter as heir, and Edward had immediately collared the heiress, Anne, for betrothal to his younger son, the four-year-old Richard. Now, two years later, he seized on the chance to have the marriage formally celebrated—despite the youth of the participants—in the presence of many of his nobles assembled for a very different purpose.

It was Elizabeth Woodville's brother Anthony, Earl Rivers, who led the little girl into the king's Great Chamber, where the whole court was gathered to receive her—a daunting experience for a five- or six-year-old. The next day, followed by a train of ladies and gentlewomen, she was led by Earl Rivers, again, and the "Count of Lincoln," son to Edward's sister Elizabeth, in procession through the queen's chamber, the king's Great Chamber, the White Hall, and into St. Stephen's Chapel, hung with blue tapestry decorated with gold fleurs-de-lis, where under a canopy the royal family waited to receive her.

The king gave the bride away, coins were flung to the crowd from gold and silver bowls brought in by the Duke of Gloucester, and after more spices and wine the banquet saw her seated at the head of the first table and honored as Princess of the Feast. A few days later, there was a great tournament, at which the queen's brother Anthony appeared as Saint Anthony the hermit, with a hermit's house of black velvet—complete with a bell tower and a bell that rang—built into his horse's trappings. The little duchess had to award the prizes—although she was assisted, in the interests of practicality, by the princess Elizabeth and a council of ladies.

But beneath the ceremony, the Mowbray marriage is also noteworthy in the way it showed Edward's own sometimes cavalier attitude toward the law. The king's son had already been created Duke of Norfolk, anticipating presumably that it would be in the right of his tiny wife, and two Acts of Parliament were now passed to ensure that if she died before bearing children, her lands would pass to her "husband" rather than to her heirs-at-law. Anne Mowbray's mother, the Duchess of Norfolk, Elizabeth Talbot, urged or forced out of much to which she was entitled, seems barely to have figured in the wedding ceremony. Neither, of course, did Clarence himself; he was in the Tower, only a few miles away from his family.

Convicted by Parliament in a trial begun amid the merriment of his nephew's wedding celebrations, Clarence was sentenced to death in the early days of February. When Edward hesitated for ten days before ordering that the sentence be carried out, the Speaker of the

Commons asked the House of Lords to impose the penalty. He was executed on February 18—drowned, or so it is always said, in a butt of Malmsey wine. The story was certainly considered plausible enough that it was quickly repeated all over Europe, by de Commynes and the *Great Chronicle* among others. Clarence's daughter would be painted with a wine cask as an emblem on her bracelet. The wine has served to lend a note of comic horror to Clarence's death—but the bare facts of the case open the door to a wealth of speculation, not least as to who might have been involved in plotting Clarence's downfall.

Thomas More—writing in the next century and always Richard III's detractor—claimed that some "wise men" believed Richard, acting in secret, "lacked not in helping forth his brother of Clarence to his death." It is true that several of Richard's men were in the Parliament that nodded through the attainder (as well, of course, as many of the Woodvilles' adherents); it is true too that, inheriting some of Clarence's titles and offices as well as his place in the succession, he greatly benefited from Clarence's fall. But then, so too did Edward, who got Clarence's great estates and needed the money; Margaret Beaufort must have noted with interest that the Richmond earldom—which in 1471 had been granted to Clarence for his life—was once again up for grabs after the execution. Almost everybody benefited from Clarence's death.

Mancini placed the blame for the events of 1478 very differently from More. Visiting England in Richard's reign and perhaps susceptible to his propaganda, Mancini wrote that at this time, "Richard Duke of Gloucester was so overcome with grief for his brother, that he could not dissimulate so well, but that he was overheard to say that he would one day avenge his brother's death." Mancini clearly blames the queen, who had "concluded that her offspring by the king would never come to the throne, unless the duke of Clarence were removed; and of this she easily persuaded the king." Indeed, More too would postulate as another possible cause of Clarence's fall "the Queen and the lords of her blood, which highly maligned the king's kindred (as women commonly not of malice but of nature hate them whom their husbands love)."

Elizabeth Woodville and her kindred were, of course, always blamed for greed, and certainly the Woodvilles not only were prominent in the weeks and the councils that led up to Clarence's trial, but also joined in the general harvest of Clarence's goods and offices. Mancini says it was now, with Clarence dead and Richard lying low on his own lands, that Elizabeth Woodville really started to ennoble her relatives. "Besides, she attracted to her party many strangers and introduced them to court, so that they alone should manage the public and private businesses of the crown, surround the king, and have bands of retainers, give or sell offices, and finally rule the very king himself." But as Mancini was also suggesting, there could have been another reason for Elizabeth's particular animosity toward Clarence at this time. Mancini's suggestion of "calumnies" against her—"namely that according to established usage she was not the legitimate wife of the king"—may have been just another rehashing of the old outcry against the secrecy of her marriage, her position as a widow. But it is also possible that Clarence was holding dangerous knowledge over his brother's and sister-in-law's heads.

One theory suggests that Clarence had been dropping hints about a lady called Eleanor Butler to whom, it was alleged, Edward had been precontracted or indeed actually married in the early 1460s—a situation that would have made his subsequent marriage to Elizabeth Woodville invalid. Eleanor, who had died in 1468, had been daughter to the great Earl of Shrewsbury and a widow of rank and notable piety, whom Edward would have met at the very beginning of his reign. (More says that Edward boasted of having three concubines— the merriest, the holiest, and the wisest harlots in the kingdom. If Jane Shore was the merriest, Eleanor might have been the holiest.) Commynes says that Edward "promised to marry her, provided that he could sleep with her first, and she consented"—the same technique he practiced on Elizabeth Woodville. Commynes says also that Robert Stillington (later the Bishop of Bath and Wells) "had married them," though his involvement would hardly have been necessary: witnessed consent and consummation alone would have done it. Mancini and Vergil also make reference to the story. The implication is that Stillington (who seems now briefly to have been cast into prison, possibly for something to do with the Clarence affair) had passed this lethal information either directly to Clarence or else to Eleanor's sister the Duchess of Norfolk and her husband, friends of his, and the same couple whose little daughter, Anne Mowbray, had just been snapped up as a royal bride.

The evidence in favor of this theory is circumstantial: for example, Eleanor's arranging for the disposition of her property in the form open to a married woman, rather than that possible only for a widow, as well as the suggestive coincidence of Stillington's imprisonment. Against that, there are no signs that Edward and Elizabeth, after Eleanor's death, attempted to regularize their liaison, as it would then have been possible to do. Thomas More, after all, muddied the waters considerably by saying that Edward was precontracted not to Eleanor but to another of his mistresses by whom he had had a child, a married woman of lower rank called Elizabeth Lucy; the question is whether More did so from ignorance or deliberately, in order to discredit a theory so potentially damaging to the Tudor dynasty under which he served.

The most that can be said for sure is that Edward's pattern of behavior with his women makes it impossible simply to dismiss the tale. But whether the allegation was true or false, if Clarence was indeed spreading this rumor, it lends added weight to the suggestions that Elizabeth Woodville believed him a threat to her children. The story of Edward's prior relationship with Eleanor Butler would certainly reappear, greatly to the detriment of Elizabeth's sons, a few years down the line.

How did the other women in the family respond to this lethal rift between the York siblings—and what, more particularly, was Cecily Neville's attitude? There can be no wholly authoritative answer. Crowland recalled after the event that in Parliament, "not a single person uttered a word against the duke [Clarence], except the king; not one individual made answer to the king except the duke." It is said that Edward himself also later lamented that "not one creature" interceded for Clarence. But women, of course, would not be speaking in a Parliament anyway; whatever was said by them was said behind closed doors and was not recorded.

But this needn't quite be the end of the matter. A detective story teaches that one should look at what everybody did, not what they said, and it would appear that Cecily did nothing at the time—or at least failed to protest her son's execution loudly enough to catch the ear of any reporters. It is often said that it was Cecily's pleading that won Clarence the right to choose his own manner of death, but evidence is hard to find. (The contemporary chronicler Jean de Roye wrote in his journal, the *Chronique scandaleuse*, that the dreadful sentence of hanging, drawing, and quartering had been commuted "by the great prayer and request of the mother," but his nineteenth-century editor, Bernard de Mondrot, points out that the words *of the mother* were added between the lines, and in a later hand.) Certainly, Cecily had been conspicuous with the rest of the royal family when, the very day before the beginning of the Parliament that was to try Clarence, the little Duke of York was married to Anne Mowbray.

Perhaps Cecily had at last given up on this particular branch of the Yorkist tree. It was, after all, Clarence who had impugned her chastity; one of the grounds on which Clarence was accused was that he had "upon one of the falsest and most unnatural coloured pretences that man might imagine, falsely and untruly noised, published and said, that the King our Sovereign Lord was a Bastard, and not begotten to reign upon us." Others have seen this very differently. One theory is that it was Cecily who actually offered Clarence the idea of her adultery, in pursuit of the family good. This was arguably a world where loyalty to the family as a whole might sometimes take precedence over loyalty to an individual, and that question would be even more crucial for the York family in the years ahead. These were the stark choices Cecily would have to contemplate—not once, but repeatedly.

It would seem Cecily accepted Clarence's death—but it may also have significantly altered her life. From this point it becomes increasingly hard to find mention of Cecily taking part in court rituals. Naturally, the business of running her estates continued. Besides her main residence, "our Castle of Berkhamsted," letters are signed from "our place at Baynard's Castle" and from the priory at Merton.

She never ceased to exercise her good ladyship: to administer her lands and insist on her dignities. One letter, to an officer she felt had failed her over the administration of her East Anglian lands, warns him of "the awful peril that may ensue with our great displeasure and heavy ladyship." She can be glimpsed licensing seven men in Thaxted to form a fraternity in 1481, joining in Edward's petition on behalf of a Carthusian monastery outside London's walls.

In the retirement of Berkhampsted, Cecily seems to have adopted a life of increasing piety. A few years later, Cecily's daily regime was recorded at length for posterity. By the time this description was written, Cecily had chosen to lead what was in many ways the life of a nun, albeit without retiring to a convent. This was a choice made by a number of wealthy widows, an increasing number of whom, in the last decades of the fifteenth century, were choosing to become "vowesses." But in Cecily's case, it is tempting to speculate that the traumas she had experienced during her life at court had led her, instead, to choose this almost cloistered existence.

"She is accustomed to arise at seven o'clock and has ready her chaplain to say with her matins of the day, and matins of Our Lady; and when she is full ready she has a low mass in her chamber." After all those early devotions, she would eat—she "takes something to recreate nature," as the account puts it—before returning to chapel for three more services before the dinner that was the main meal of the day.

After dinner, at last, there came a time for other business and for recreation. "After dinner she gives audience to all such as has any matter to show to her by the space of one hour; and then she sleeps one quarter of an hour, and after she has slept she continues in prayer to the first peal of evensong; then she drinks wine or ale at her pleasure." She heard several more Evensongs before supper, and it was only after the repast that Cecily "disposes herself to be familiar with her gentlewomen, to the following of honest mirth; and one hour before her going to bed, she takes a cup of wine, and after that goes to her private closet, and takes her leave of God for all night." By eight o'clock she was in bed. The account gives a rare and fascinating picture of how a medieval lady might actually divide up her day—but it also, of course, shows a level of religious observance that would have been excessive for an ordinary laywoman even in that day.

Cecily had chosen what the age called the mixed life: the "medled [*sic*] life that is to say sometime active sometime contemplative," as it was described by the late-fourteenth-century northern cleric and author Nicholas Love, a translation by whom of the *Life of Christ* was in Cecily's library. So too was the *Letter on the Mixed Life*, written by

Love's associate Walter Hilton, while another of her volumes, *The Abbey of the Holy Ghost* (of which Cecily's daughter Margaret of Burgundy owned a copy), was written to teach those "unable to leave the world how they might build an abbey in their soul and keep the rules of an order in their heart."

Cecily's books, indeed, reveal a great deal about the workings of her mind and heart, particularly the intense religious aspect of her later years. She owned copies of *De Infantia Salvatoris* (apocryphal stories of the miracles of Christ's infancy) and of the ever-popular *Legenda Aurea,* the Golden Legend. But she also owned copies of the lives and visions of the great female mystics like Matilda of Hackenborn, Saint Bridget of Sweden, and Saint Catherine of Siena. It was Saint Catherine who advised those who wished to follow her example, but were still constrained by the demands of the world: "Build a cell inside your mind, from which you can never flee."

Cecily's piety has traditionally been seen almost as a psychological alibi that allowed her tranquilly to sail above the turmoils of her family. She must often in her life have needed the sense of a special relationship with God and might have reflected on the biblical stories of brothers' struggles: Esau and Jacob, whose mother, Rebecca, showed the latter how to snatch his elder brother's birthright; Joseph, whose brothers collaborated to kill him; and David, king of Israel above his elder brother.

It is conceivable that Cecily too found in her faith at least an angry affirmation of and vindication for the vicissitudes imposed upon her family and those they had imposed upon themselves. Nicholas Love, in his early-fifteenth-century *Mirror of the Life of Christ,* has Christ tell his pilgrims, "If the world hate you, witeth [knoweth] well that it hated me first before you." In the years of Cecily's childhood, Thomas à Kempis had written in his *De Imitatione Christi* of the rashness of relying on anyone but God, of the triumph in the Last Judgment of the oppressed over the oppressor: "Then shall rightwise men stand in great [constaunce] against them that have anguished them and oppressed them." At the very least, Cecily must have needed the power of prayer to clear and focus the mind—to achieve that state of integration and acceptance that modern-day observers would couch in psychological, and medieval Europeans in spiritual, terms.

Like many devout women, Cecily probably made a particular identification with the Virgin Mary, an empathy that would have been particularly relevant for a mother who had lost two sons to political strife. Saint Bridget's prayer *The Fifteen Oes* specifically encourages the devout to share the pain of Christ and of the Virgin; a few years later, Margaret Beaufort would collaborate with Elizabeth of York to commission a printed version from Caxton. A shared religious enthusiasm was a very powerful link between almost all of the most powerful women in the Cousins' War: a socially and morally acceptable way, perhaps, of evading or triumphing over other divides. But in the case of Cecily—more even than of any of the others—Bridget's urging that one would thus be able to feel another's pain was surely unnecessary. Cecily had more than enough pain of her own.

14

"A GOLDEN SORROW"

I swear, 'tis better to be lowly born,
And range with humble livers in content,
Than to be perked up in a glist'ring grief,
And wear a golden sorrow.

THE LIFE OF HENRY THE EIGHTH, 2.3

The saga of Clarence's death had shown the divisions in the ruling York family—but it had also shown the important and at times divisive role played in English affairs by Margaret, the dowager Duchess of Burgundy. Margaret would become a significant meddler in English dynastic concerns, but even the visit she made to her natal country in 1480 had a political purpose, one that, perhaps, highlighted the comparative lack of interest Edward IV's other sisters seemed to play in public affairs.

The life she had developed in Burgundy since her husband's death in 1477 was, on a day-to-day level, a good one, despite the turmoils that had followed Duke Charles's passing. She and her stepdaughter, Mary, had faced down the problems presented by internal disputes and French hostility, and they had won—and Burgundy was a prize worth fighting for: replete with the profits of trade; rich in tapestries, each one of which could cost a whole year's income from a wealthy landowner; and cultivated with books. Tapestries and drawings show Margaret at falconry and the hunt; one, entitled *The Bear Hunt*, shows her sidesaddle on a horse led by a groom.

As her stepdaughter Mary's marriage to Archduke Maximilian bore fruit, Margaret stood godmother to her children. Her dower lands gave her a prosperous and well-maintained collection of villages and towns. She chose to make her main residence in Malines in Brabant, purchasing there a collection of adjoining houses that she extended and rebuilt, in redbrick decorated with white stripes, with a balcony on which she could display herself to the people. She installed gardens designed to be seen from her palace windows, as well as a tennis court, a shooting gallery, and hot baths. She had a chair of state, in the vast council chamber, upholstered in fine black velvet, and a study hung with violet taffeta, its beautiful books and manuscripts protected by a wrought-iron grill. She had her volumes on chess, her knives of ebony and ivory, her knight of honor and her doctors, her dogs, her horses, and her maker of preserves.

All the same, it seems likely Margaret had also an abiding sense of grievance (not least about her brother's failure ever fully to pay her dowry): a touchy imperiousness, or a tendency to see herself as the beleaguered heroine of the story. She was a complex character, and there was a hint of mysticism about her religious feeling, despite the crusading practicality with which she tackled the reform of religious orders in her domain. In an odd echo of the dream Margaret Beaufort once claimed, Margaret of Burgundy claimed she had been visited in her chamber by the risen Jesus. The scene is described in a book written at her request soon after her marriage. She also had the encounter painted: in the vaulted bedchamber, by her blue and scarlet bed, Margaret kneels fully dressed on a rug, waiting to kiss the bleeding hand extended to her so delicately.

A "beatific and uncovered vision" he was: naked under his crimson cloak, displaying his wounds, instructing her to make ready the bed of her heart—a bed in which she was to lie with him "in purest chastity and pure charity," ready to receive his instruction that she should look well upon the fires of hell and the glory of God. Christ had entered her bedchamber so quietly that even her greyhound did not wake, but she was so wholly convinced of his coming that she kissed the covers of her bed his body had touched until the color was worn away.

The same fanaticism that Margaret displayed toward religion could also surface in her secular affairs, skilled and competent though she might usually be. This trait would prove particularly disruptive in her dealings with her brother Edward, to whom Margaret—and Burgundy—now looked as an ally.

Margaret returned to England in the summer of 1480 to encourage her brother in his goodwill toward Burgundy, to turn him away from the French, and to negotiate a match between Edward's daughter Anne and Mary of Burgundy's little son. The visit can be spelled out in fabric as described in the expenses of the Wardrobe Department: two pieces of arras "of the story of Paris and Elyn [Helen]" to help furnish a house for her use; forty-seven yards of green sarcenet, garnished with green ribbon for curtains; bed linen; and "great large feather beds." A hundred servants were given new "jackets of woollen cloth of murrey and blue," the Yorkist colors. Edward Woodville—he of the famous tournament in Bruges—returning across the Channel to escort Margaret back home, was given a yard of blue velvet and a yard of purple for a jacket; the twenty-four men who rowed her up the Thames in the king's barge after she disembarked from the *Falcon* at Gravesend wore jackets embroidered with white roses (an embroiderer named Peter Lambard was paid a penny for each small rose). The horses Edward gave Margaret were harnessed in green velvet, garnished with gold and silver; the reins were of crimson velvet. They must have been easy on the hands, but Margaret's mind would probably have been too busy to notice.

Few princesses returned to their native land, unless they were like Marguerite of Anjou, disgraced and desperate or, in their widowhood, as surplus to the requirements of their marital country. This situation, however, was different; whatever Margaret's brother may have thought, as he had contemplated arranging for her a fresh match in Scotland, she returned to carry out the agenda of her adopted land. As she was rowed upstream and into London, she must have been taut with a mixture of excitement, nostalgia, and tension. Past Greenwich, around the great loop of the river, her impatience would have grown as the City itself began to come into view.

The cities of Burgundy had their own more ordered display of wealth, but there must have been a magic of memory in the very brawl of the streets that Margaret's mind's eye traced behind the forest of masts, streets where the shopkeepers sold everything from silks to strawberries, hot sheep's feet to Paris thread, peasecods and pie, where an Italian visitor two decades later would write that in the fifty-two goldsmiths' shops of one street alone there was such a magnificence of silver vessels that in Rome, Venice, and Florence together one might not find its equivalent. The Tower, London Bridge with its tall rows of houses, Baynard's Castle: each of the sites would have come into view, and farther ahead, past another green burst of country, the spires and turrets of Westminster. This was her own old home city, each building surely familiar (had any more been put up, did she wonder, craning her neck to see?) and the vista surely colored with the special excitement London can bring.

It was high summer, when the smell of rubbish and sewage from the open drains in the streets and the risk of infectious diseases that always mounted in the warmer months urged nobles out of the town, but Margaret was traveling the other way, into the stew of London. There was a house prepared for her at Coldharbour in Thames Street, near her mother's Baynard's Castle, and along the river from the apartment in Greenwich, her home in the first years of her brother's reign. Edward gave a banquet at Greenwich in honor of her and of their mother; Richard even came down from the battles with Scotland to see her. Margaret's sister Elizabeth visited too and must have been struck by her younger sister's glory. Perhaps their presence made the absence of Clarence the more poignant; perhaps, too, there was some awkwardness in the adjustment of positions and protocols that had changed the youngest daughter of the house of York into the dowager duchess of a foreign power. But the reforging of relationships (which most princesses must have preserved, as in aspic, from the time they went away) would be important in the next reigns.

The celebrations went well; the diplomacy was more edgy. If he yielded to Margaret's persuasions and agreed to marry his daughter Anne to his sister's stepgrandson, Edward stood to lose his French pension and that flattering match between the five-year-old Princess Elizabeth and the Dauphin. As far back as August 1478, Edward had been pushing for Elizabeth's French marriage to go ahead, but Louis, at that time, was less than keen; a son and heir's marriage was too important a tool of diplomacy to be squandered lightly. So it was surely no coincidence that Louis now chose this moment to attempt to placate the English royal family, not only sending over a delegation with Edward's annuity of fifty thousand crowns but also offering an additional fifteen thousand a year for Elizabeth until she and the Dauphin were actually wed.

The match Margaret was offering may have been all in the family, but that didn't mean it was not keenly bargained over. Edmund asked whether Burgundy would compensate him, if promising them his daughter Anne cost him his French pension. He also proposed that Anne should come without a dowry. Margaret had to send home for Maximilian and Mary's opinion, and the result was a compromise: Edward would allow English archers to reinforce the Burgundian troops and would actually declare war on France if they did not restore the plundered lands by Easter the following year; Burgundy would pay his pension if the French withdrew it. Anne would bring a dowry, albeit only half the one hoped for, but Burgundy would pay her an annuity until the marriage could be finalized. Margaret, meanwhile, gave her four-year-old niece a wedding ring set with diamonds and pearls and a chain on which—until her fingers grew—it could be hung.

But no sooner had Margaret (by this time well into the second month of her visit) sorted out the details than she had word Maximilian in Burgundy had negotiated his own truce with the French, doubtless using the English rapprochement Margaret was negotiating as leverage. She feared that Maximilian's duplicity would have angered her brother (who in fact took it with the calm of one who would have done exactly the same thing). One can only hope she did not take the double-dealing personally, but rather as evidence a woman's diplomatic work is never done.

The visit ended as it had begun, however, on a note of personal happiness. Edward accompanied Margaret as she rode out of London, on her way to Canterbury to visit the shrine of Thomas Becket. Before leaving from Dover, she spent a week at the Kent estate of Anthony

Woodville, talking books and philosophy. Margaret had sent the printer William Caxton (who in Bruges had served also as her financial adviser) to England a few years before, and in 1476, Anthony had become Caxton's patron, translating books for him to print. A stream of books emerged from Caxton's press in the yard of Westminster Abbey: Chaucer, Malory's stories of King Arthur, Boethius's *Consolation of Philosophy*, *The Mirror of the World*, Higdon's *Polychronicon*, *The Golden Legend*, *Aesop's Fables*, and *The Life of Our Lady*.

After this agreeable intellectual interlude, Edward's "well-beloved sister," as he wrote to Maximilian, went home. She would continue to look across the Channel, as one of Edward's successors would discover all too painfully. But, for the moment, England seemed established in comparative tranquillity.

The years that followed, the first of the 1480s, saw business as usual for King Edward and his family. Elizabeth Woodville was now well established as a wielder of influence and distributor of patronage, endowing, for example, a chapel dedicated to Saint Erasmus in Westminster Abbey. The Merchant Adventurers had cause to be grateful for the "very good effort" she put into helping them to negotiate a reduction in the amount of subsidy demanded of them by the king. Effort had been made by several nobles, their records noted, "but especially by the Queen." It is a useful reminder that these women were consumers and negotiators, patrons as well as parents, readers and (on their own estates) rulers. Even the young Princess Elizabeth had long had her own lands. (On November 4, 1467, the *Calendar of the Patent Rolls* records a "grant for life to the King's daughter the Princess Elizabeth of the manor of Great Lynford, county of Buckingham.")

Sometime in 1477, Elizabeth Woodville had given birth to a third son, George, who died in infancy in 1479. Her sixth daughter, Katherine, was born in 1479, at Eltham, a favorite residence, and her last child, too, was born there in November 1480. This last baby was named Bridget after Saint Bridget, the former court lady turned *religieuse* who founded the Bridgettine order, turning from matters of the world to matters of the soul, as, perhaps, Cecily was doing. Margaret Beaufort was asked to carry the royal couple's daughter when the child was christened at Eltham, a mark of high favor that showed how far she had come since having turned her back on the Yorkists during the Lancastrian Readeption:

> First 100 Torches born by Knights followed by Esquires and other honest Persons.
> The Lord Maltravers [Matraners], Bearing the Basin, having a Towel about his neck.
> The earl of Northumberland bearing a Taper not lit.
> The earl of Lincoln, the Salt.
> The Canopy born by 4 Knights and a Baron.
> My Lady Maltravers [Queen Elizabeth's sister] did bear a rich Chrysom pinned over her left breast.
> The Countess of Richmond did bear the Princess.

The godmothers were the baby's grandmother Cecily Neville and elder sister Elizabeth of York.

The visitor to Eltham today can see the Great Hall built by Elizabeth Woodville's husband, Edward. Though their walls are only ruins today, it is possible to trace also the pattern of the surprisingly tiny rooms Elizabeth would have used when she visited her children here—for Eltham was always in favor as a nursery palace (even when it came time for Elizabeth of York to rear her own children). It was a fit setting for a happy family.

And such the king's family had been, through the 1470s. Crowland—with pleasure and perhaps relief in the queen's fecundity?—described the court as filled with "those most sweet and beautiful children." A visitor to the court in 1482 described the young Richard, Duke of York, as singing with his mother and one of his sisters and playing the game called sticks and with a two-handed sword. There had been sadnesses, of course, as when in November 1481 Richard's eight-year-old bride, Anne Mowbray, died, followed six months later by Elizabeth Woodville's fourteen-year-old daughter, Mary, buried in royal state that reflected her family's now established status, as well, perhaps, as her own recent betrothal to the king of Denmark. But by and large, even after the new decade dawned, the glimpses history affords of the family are cheerful ones: a visit to Oxford, where they were joined by the king's sister Elizabeth, the Duchess of Suffolk; a set of signatures in a book, an early-fourteenth-century manuscript of an Arthurian romance, "E Wydevyll" on the back and "Elysabeth, the kyngs dowther" and "Cecyl the kynges dowther" on the flyleaf, suggesting as one possibility that Queen Elizabeth's daughters were reading the book she had once owned as a girl.

A stained-glass window in Canterbury Cathedral still survives, a symphony of singing, stinging color showing the royal family diminished slightly in number, but still in all its glory. It can be dated to 1482 or later by the fact that Cecily is shown as the king's second daughter: until her elder sister Mary died earlier in 1482, she had been the third. The king and queen, each kneeling at a prayer desk, face each other in the two central panels, with their children, similarly posed, lined up in order and dwindling in size behind them. The two surviving boys, like their parents, wear a royal purple cloak over a robe of cloth of gold, collared in ermine; the girls wear matching purple dresses girdled in gold, with flashes of jewels and fur at neck and hem and long yellow hair hanging down their backs. All crowned or coroneted, all with an open book on the prie-dieux before them, it was a family who knelt only to God. The panels would once have flanked an image of the Crucifixion, under a depiction of the seven holy joys of the Virgin Mary, before that window became the target of Cromwell's wreckers in 1642. The window shows Elizabeth of York kneeling directly behind her mother. She was growing up fast. After the great reburial ceremony at Fotheringhay, it seems Elizabeth of York had been considered old enough to join her mother on other ceremonial occasions: in the Garter procession that marked the feast of Saint George in April 1477, the Garter records note that the queen came to mass "on horseback in a murrey gown of Garters. Item: the lady Elizabeth, the King's eldest daughter, in a gown of the same livery."

From her later tastes and abilities, something can be intuited about the education of the younger Elizabeth, Elizabeth of York. Her Latin was not fluent—she would later request that her prospective daughter-in-law Catherine of Aragon would be taught French before her arrival, since English ladies did not usually understand the other tongue—but she learned to write, something that was not by any means a given even for ladies of the highest rank. But Elizabeth's was an educated family: her father collected books, and her uncle Anthony's literary interests seem to some degree to have been shared by the wide Woodville family.

Later in life, Elizabeth of York would hunt and shoot, would keep her own musicians, play at games of chance, sew expertly. Those last were expected of ladies; what was perhaps less usual was the degree to which Edward's daughters learned to fill their imaginations with the world of written thought and story.

Of course, children had always grown up with story, from the biblical world and the lives of saints, as well as from the allegories and spectacles of pageantry. Christine de Pizan had in *The Treasure of the City of Ladies* urged that "a young girl should also especially venerate Our Lady, St Catherine, and all virgins, and if she can read, eagerly read their biographies." But Elizabeth and her sisters would have had an unusual opportunity to get their information and stories directly, thanks both to the advent of printing, which was making books more available, and to their family's literary interests. Their uncle had translated the *Dictes or Sayengis of the Philosophers* and the *Moral Proverbs* of Christine de Pizan; their mother too was a patron of Caxton's. Elizabeth would have gotten to know the Arthurian stories, with their wildly mixed messages about a woman's love and a queen's duty, their tales of Guenivere and the other Arthurian heroines maying and feasting, shamed and repenting. (Such books were dangerous, declared a contemporary at the Castilian court, "causing weak-breasted women to fall into libidinous errors and commit sins they would not otherwise commit.") Elizabeth and her sister Cecily also wrote their names on a French story of the world and the funeral rites of an emperor of the Turks. They would have read therein about mosques and minarets, slaves and strange palaces. And they may have found a like-minded woman during the course of their reading: Saint Catherine of Alexandria, after all, was described in various of the many narrations of her life as having "held her household in her palace with full Christian governance"—but she had also a tower built for her by her father to allow uninterrupted study under "the best masters and highest of cunning that might be found in that end of the world."

But underneath the pleasures of daily life, it became apparent as the 1480s wore on that Elizabeth of York's future was less secure than it had seemed. Perhaps this early experience of uncertainty, indeed, would influence her sometimes controversial actions in the years ahead, for King Edward's diplomatic affairs—those affairs in which the royal children were such useful pawns—were going less than smoothly.

When Edward arranged what seemed to be yet another good alliance for his children, betrothing his eldest son, the Prince of Wales, to Anne, the young heiress of Brittany, Louis of France struck back by encouraging the Scots to attack northern England. This war compelled Edward, in 1481, to excuse himself to the pope for not joining a crusade against the Turks, on the grounds that "the acts of our treacherous neighbours" kept him fully occupied during "this tempestuous period." But things were about to get more tempestuous: in March 1482, Mary of Burgundy died after a riding accident, an event that gave her Flemish subjects the chance to decide they preferred peaceful relations with the French to Mary's husband, the Archduke Maximilian, and his English treaty.

On her deathbed, Mary begged her stepmother, Margaret, to protect her two surviving children, and she must at first have hoped that Mary's widower, Maximilian, would be able to keep the children in a country he proposed to rule himself. But in the course of the year, political necessity dictated otherwise. Although the little boy, Philip, remained largely in Margaret's care, after Christmas news reached England that Mary's three-year-old daughter was to be sent into France, another princess sent off to cement a peace treaty. The little girl was to be married to the French Dauphin, who—as had so often been threatened before—would jilt Elizabeth of York as a consequence. At seventeen, comparatively late for a royal girl to be unmarried, Elizabeth in England would certainly have been old enough to feel both the slight and the pangs of uncertainty about her future.

Edward's marital plans for his daughters were not going well. In October 1482, just months before receiving the bad news about Elizabeth's engagement, he had also to call off Cecily's arranged marriage with the ever-hostile Scots. The betrothal between Anne and the Burgundian heir, Philip, too, would founder on Edward's parsimony over Anne's dowry, which allowed Philip's father, Maximilian, when the chance arose, to abandon it for a better match elsewhere.

In this difficult diplomatic climate, Edward suggested for his eldest daughter a match that would once have seemed most unlikely—a match with Henry Tudor, still living in exile in Brittany. An agreement had already been drawn up to return Henry home, "to be in the grace and favour of the king's highness," and to enjoy a portion of the lands recently left to him by the death of his grandmother, Margaret Beaufort's mother. Now Edward mooted also the possibility of a marriage that would attach Henry to the Yorkist family.

The Tudor chronicler Holinshed says that a marriage between Henry Tudor and Elizabeth of York had been suggested several years before, even while Margaret Beaufort had been participating in the great Fotheringhay ceremony. If so, at that point Edward's offer may not have been sincere—just a lure to get Henry back to England—and when the ruler of Brittany was persuaded to hand Henry over, he may well, as Vergil would later have it, have been handing "the sheep to the wolf," since Edward's intentions toward Henry may not have been benign. Henry had been entrusted to the English envoys, but when he reached St. Malo to board a ship for England, he feigned illness, slipped into a church, and claimed sanctuary, from whence he was able to slip back to a remorseful Duke Francis in Brittany; he had been warned, says the Tudor poet Bernard André, by his mother, Margaret, who had scented a deception.

But now times had changed. With the new alliance between France and Burgundy, and with the danger that England might once again be at war with the French, King Edward may have found the thought of Henry Tudor—a potential English claimant—as a loose cannon at the French court too dangerous to contemplate. Marrying him into the royal family would be a way to neutralize the threat and bring him into the fold. To Margaret Beaufort, in any event, this new plan may well have seemed a reasonable advancement for her son. Her acquiescence may have represented an acceptance of the status quo and an admission that Henry's Lancastrian claim had no immediate prospect of bearing fruit. But as had happened so many times before, events were about to overthrow all plans.

The marriage arrangements were the calm before another storm, one that no one could have foreseen. Edward's way of life had long been intemperate enough to affect his health. Mancini wrote that "in food and drink he was most immoderate: it was his habit, so I have learned, to take an emetic for the delight of gorging his stomach once more." He had now "grown fat in the loins, whereas previously he had been not only tall but rather lean and very active." What is more, the legendarily beautiful and loving Elizabeth Woodville had always to deal with her husband's flagrant infidelity, a fault, More said, that "not greatly grieved his people," though it may in private have grieved his wife.

Mancini wrote, "He pursued with no discrimination the married and unmarried, the noble and lowly: however he took none by force. He overcame all by money and promises and having conquered them, he dismissed them. Although he had many promoters and companions of his vices, the most important and especial were three of the afore-mentioned relatives of the queen, her two sons and one of her brothers." If true, the abetment of Edward's stepsons and brother-in-law may throw an interesting light on Elizabeth Woodville's attitude, suggesting that actual infidelity as such, and any distress that might cause Elizabeth, took second place to the urgent necessity of keeping it in the family, so to speak, ensuring that no rivals had the chance of promoting their candidate into the king's bed and gaining influence that way. The question of Edward's relations with women, licensed or unlicensed, would become political dynamite. But Edward's mistresses were important in another, more immediate, sense as well: they reflected the king's rampant self-indulgence, which was taking a serious toll on his health.

On the outside, at least, Edward appeared to be carrying on as usual as the year drew to an end. Christmas 1482 had been kept in great state at Westminster, with Edward, as Crowland reported, "frequently appearing clad in a great variety of most costly garments, of quite a different cut to those which had been usually seen hitherto in our kingdom. The sleeves of the robe were very full and hanging, greatly resembling a monk's frock, and so lined within with most costly furs, and rolled over the shoulders, as to give that prince a new and distinguished air to beholders." The king "kept his estates all the whole feast in his Great Chamber and the Queen in her Chamber where were daily more than two thousand persons served." It was a time of great opulence and merriment, with the affairs of the royal court holding no sign of the troubles to come.

It looked—and was meant to—as if the royal family was here to stay, in prosperity and stability. On Candelmas 1483, the king and queen went in procession from St. Stephen's to Westminster Hall. Business went on, with a grant to the king's mother, Cecily, among the many financial matters listed in the records for the first month of the year.

But in the spring of 1483, Edward IV fell sick. Mancini said that he had been out fishing in a small boat and allowed the damp cold to strike his vitals; Commynes (with a certain credibility from other foreign reports) says that it was apoplexy following a surfeit. Some even put it down to chagrin at the failure of his attempts to marry his children advantageously. The English reports as to cause are all sixteenth century and inevitably include the suspicion of poison, but Hall says that since the French campaign of 1475, Edward had suffered from an ague "which turned to an incurable quarten," a type of fever.

On April 9, at the age of just forty, Edward IV died. Poet John Skelton summed up the shock many must have felt, at the unexpected collapse of so towering a figure, but the words he puts into Edward's mouth also speak eloquently of the distress that must have been felt in his immediate family:

> *Where is now my conquest and victory?*
> *Where is my riches and my royal array?*
> *Where be my coursers and my horses high?*
> *Where is my mirth, my solace, and my play?*
> *As vanity, to naught all is wandered away.*
> *O lady Bess, long for me may ye call!*
> *For now we are parted until doomsday;*
> *But love ye that Lord that is sovereign of all.*

If Edward IV had lived longer, the events that followed his death would surely have unfolded differently. The young Prince Edward, his heir, might not have been perceived as being so dangerously under Woodville influence. There would not have been the same shock to a country only a decade away from the last throes of civil war and still in recovery from the long-term effects of the minority rule of Henry VI.

The question of Edward's male heir was of course first in most people's minds, but Edward's death had bereaved more than just his little son. Mancini noted that Edward IV left two sons. "He also left daughters, but they do not concern us." In the Latin, the last part sounds even more chillingly dismissive—he left daughters, *sed de iis nihil ad nos*—but it was to prove a poor prophecy.

Less than a year before Edward's death, the woman who had done most to challenge the patriarchal assumptions of these years had also left the scene. Marguerite of Anjou had died in France at the Château de Dampierre near Saumur on August 25, 1482. She had, according to her Victorian biographer Mary Ann Hookham, been visited there by Henry Tudor, whom she urged to continue his struggle against the house of York—an ironic gesture, given that a marriage was about to be arranged between Henry and the daughter of the Yorkist king.

Marguerite died so poor, as her will recorded, that King Louis took her hunting dogs as the only things she had left of value. The document reflects how far she had fallen. The "few goods" that God and King Louis had allowed her were, she wrote, to be used to pay for her burial: "And should my few goods be insufficient to do this, as I believe they are, I implore the king meet and pay the outstanding debts as the sole heir of the wealth which I inherited through my father and mother and my other relatives and ancestors." These last lines reflect Marguerite's resentment of her poverty and her old pride in her lineage—a pride never quite extinguished, even by all she had undergone.

Marguerite's political life had long been over, but she had been one of the most forceful women in a century not short of them. Shakespeare has her at the beginning of *Richard III* returned from exile like a vengeful ghost to curse Elizabeth Woodville:

> *Long mayst thou live to wail thy children's death*
> *And see another, as I see thee now,*
> *Decked in thy rights, as thou art stalled in mine.*
> *Long die thy happy days before thy death,*
> *And after many lengthened hours of grief,*
> *Die neither mother, wife, nor England's queen.*

And in deed and in truth perhaps, Marguerite's ghost did live on—lived on, for example, in the mind of Richard of Gloucester, eyeing the accession of a twelve-year-old to the throne with all the paranoia of one born into the time of Marguerite's battles to rule the country for her infant son, in the time of Henry VI's insanity. Such a young ruler as Edward would surely be susceptible, as Marguerite's own son had been, to his mother's influence.

The stories of the next few years are usually told in terms of men: their battles, betrayals, and brutality. But women's choices, women's alliances—the accommodations they had already made and the slights and losses they had already suffered—would play a crucial part in the events ahead. They would, in time, help to steer England out of the carnage of the Cousins' War and into a new era.

PART IV

1483–1485

15

"WEEPING QUEENS"

For my daughters, Richard,
They shall be praying nuns, not weeping queens
THE TRAGEDY OF RICHARD THE THIRD, 4.4

T he marriage of Elizabeth Woodville and Edward IV had
been one of the great royal love stories, combining physical
passion with warm domesticity. It had rewritten the rules of
royal romance, with all the implications that would have in the next
century, when Henry VIII used passion as often as policy in choosing his brides. There can be little doubt that under normal circumstances, Elizabeth would have allowed herself to mourn most
sincerely. But the circumstances were far from normal, and there was
no time for mourning, for a queen fighting for position in her son's
minority.

Edward IV's death left a twelve-year-old boy to be declared the
new king—a difficult transition in any but the most stable country.
"Woe unto the kingdom where the king or lord is a child," thundered Ecclesiastes, in a warning that now may well have darkened
many an English outlook. England had looked relatively secure in

the preceding years, but its happy exterior had masked ongoing internal divisions, fractures that could only have been mended by the accession of a strong and adult king. Politics that were viable while Edward IV was alive were now a potential catastrophe.

Christine de Pizan took special pains to provide advice for the princess in a war-torn land, widowed while her son was still a minor, that she should "employ all her prudence and her wisdom to reconcile the antagonistic factions." It was good advice, but hard to know how Elizabeth Woodville was to follow it. Richard of Gloucester was riding high; the Parliament of January 1483 had acknowledged and rewarded his efforts against the Scots. Perhaps it had been in response to his high profile that in the same month, Anthony, Elizabeth Woodville's brother, seemed to be trying to bolster Woodville power. In February and March, Anthony had been making sure that his appointment as Prince Edward's governor was renewed and requesting confirmation of his right as such to raise troops in Wales.

In the blame game that has lasted more than five centuries since Edward IV's death, the question of who took the aggressive initiative—or who was merely getting their retaliation in first—has been argued endlessly. The main protagonists, after these last decades, all brought with them the memory of experiences enough to make anyone wary. Elizabeth's recollections, perhaps, were of the downturn in fortune that had followed the death of her first Grey husband and of her feeling when her second husband's crown had been snatched back from him in 1470. Richard, Duke of Gloucester, for his part must have remembered that the last two Dukes of Gloucester, Henry VI's uncle Humfrey and Richard II's uncle Thomas Woodstock, both holders of the reins during a royal minority, had both died imprisoned, amid rumors that their deaths had not been natural. Richard must, moreover, have remembered all too clearly the time of Henry VI's insanity, when Marguerite of Anjou attempted to take over in her infant son's name. With Elizabeth Woodville maneuvering in London, it must have seemed a most alarming precedent.

Richard, as the ranking, the only royal, uncle of the new boy king, had recent custom on his side: during the infancy of Henry VI, the country had been run by Henry's uncles. But Edward IV's death caught his brother Richard unawares, in the distant North of England,

and for the moment he was powerless to act. Still, Richard was aligned with the "king's men," led by the deceased sovereign's great friend Lord Hastings, the Duke of Buckingham, the Duke of Suffolk, and the Earl of Lincoln (the latter two being respectively brother-in-law and nephew to Edward IV through his sister Elizabeth). Buckingham had reputedly never forgiven Elizabeth Woodville for marrying him, as a child, to another Woodville sister he considered beneath him and may also have felt that the Woodvilles had deprived him of the influence in Wales his Marcher lordships should have allowed him to enjoy. Hastings and the queen had a different quarrel, says More: she was resentful of not only "the great favour the King bare him [but] also for that she thought him secretly familiar with the King in wanton company." Some of these men had been at court and clustered around the deathbed when Edward IV died. The king had bade them to "each of you love other," and, for the moment at least, they had agreed. The royal council met immediately, and Elizabeth Woodville met with them. There was, however, to be no question of her having an actual regency, nor of her having even the measure of influence she'd been given when her husband went to France in 1475, or the generous allowance of control given to her when her son's council as Prince of Wales had been set up. Her husband was dead, his wishes no longer paramount.

Perhaps there was never any question of anyone having a regency as such. What Henry VI's senior uncle had held in the king's infancy was a protectorate, which allowed the incumbent to "protect" prince and state without giving him regal powers. It would be said by some that Edward IV had wanted his brother Richard to occupy such a position. But Richard was not in London to make any such claim; he must have felt that events had overtaken him, just as Elizabeth must have felt herself cast adrift by the sudden loss of the man from whom all her influence had derived. But arguably for the wider Woodville clan—those not suffering her intimate grief—this looked like an opportunity to grasp even greater power. It was, after all, they in whose company and under whose guidance the new young king had been reared.

The council, in any event, made a decision that they hoped would neatly evade these problems. The dead king's son, who should soon be

crowned Edward V, might become a legal adult with his coronation—
he was, after all, twelve, and Henry VI had been declared adult when
not that much older—a device that would allow the council to govern
under the boy king's nominal rule. It looked like a balanced and a viable decision (the system had been used for Richard II), but it ignored
one thing. A twelve-year-old was inevitably going to fall under somebody's sway, and he would have ever more opportunity to respond to
their influence as he neared maturity and exercised more actual governance. And of course, that somebody, or those somebodies, was likely
to be the maternal line of his family, which had surrounded him since
infancy.

Dominic Mancini, the man who dismissed Edward's daughters,
was, ironically, the man who describes how Richard (incited thereto by
Hastings) wrote to the council after news of his brother's death, urging
his rights and his long tradition of loyalty. "He had been loyal to his
brother Edward, at home and abroad, in peace and war, and would be,
if only permitted, equally loyal to his brother's issue, even female (*eciam
mulieribus*), if perchance, which God forbid, the youth should die."

Prince Edward had received the news of his father's death on April
14, just five days after the king's passing; two days later, a letter declares his intention of setting out from Ludlow for London "in all convenient haste." There was considerable debate as to the number of
men who should accompany him on his journey, Mancini said: some
"suggested more, some less." All who were present, Mancini added,
keenly desired that this prince should succeed his father in all his
glory, but they also feared that, if the Woodvilles were allowed to escort young Edward to his coronation "with an immoderate number of
horse," it would be impossible subsequently to get rid of them.

Hastings particularly, who had always been at odds with the
Woodvilles, warned that for them to bring young Edward to London
with an army would send the wrong signal, and Elizabeth got the
point. Indeed, Crowland describes how "the Queen most beneficently
tried to extinguish every spark of murmuring and disturbance, and
wrote to her son, requesting him on his road to London, not to exceed
an escort of two thousand men."

It was April 24 before young Edward, with his uncle Anthony
Woodville and his half brother Richard Grey, finally left Ludlow for

London. Richard of Gloucester was also on his way south, leaving his wife, Anne Neville, behind in the North. It may seem strange—or significant—that Anne herself was not on the way down to take part in her nephew's coronation, scheduled for less than a week away. But there is no way to know just how far, at this stage, Richard's own plans went, let alone how much he had confided in his wife.

When young Edward's party diverted to meet his uncle Richard on April 29, in Northamptonshire, there was no apparent reason to fear. Richard, after all, had already written "so reverently, and to the Queen's friends, there so lovingly," says More, that they "nothing earthly" mistrusted. He had moreover himself sworn, and required all northerners to swear likewise, an oath to the new king, Edward V.

With the young King Edward left at Stony Stratford for the evening, Richard (and Buckingham, who had joined him) invited Rivers to dine where they were staying at Northampton, some eleven miles away. The party made, More says, "much friendly cheer" and parted with "great courtesy." But the next morning when Rivers came to leave, he found he was locked in, arrested by Richard's men. Meanwhile, Buckingham rode to Stony Stratford to inform Edward that his uncle Anthony and both of Edward's half brothers (among others) stood accused of attempting to rule him and to cause dissension in the realm.

Edward, if Mancini is to be believed, answered courageously and to the point: these were the ministers his late father had given him, and he trusted his father's judgment. Concerning the government of the kingdom, "he had complete confidence in the peers of the realm and the queen."

If it was a comment intended to placate Buckingham, it didn't work. "On hearing the queen's name," says Mancini, "the duke of Buckingham, who loathed her race, then answered, 'It was not the business of women but of men to govern kingdoms, and so if he cherished any confidence in her he had better relinquish it.'" Anthony Woodville and Richard Grey were sent north, to be held in one of Richard's castles.

When Elizabeth heard the news, Richard's actions must have seemed to her the opening moves of a great coup, and her first reaction was to strike back. "When this news was announced in London the unexpectedness of the event horrified every one," Mancini reported. Elizabeth and her eldest Grey son, Dorset, began collecting an army, "to defend themselves, and to set free the young king from the clutches of the dukes." Unfortunately for them, they found their fellow nobles reluctant to answer their call and "perceived that men's minds were not only irresolute, but altogether hostile to themselves." Some people said openly that it was more appropriate for the young king to be with his paternal uncle than with his maternal uncles and uterine brothers.

Other sources suggest instead that Elizabeth with her children fled into sanctuary at Westminster the minute she heard the news—and flee she certainly did. She surely cannot be blamed for hiding, though it has often been seen as hysterical and unnecessary, a move designed to put Richard, whom she saw as her enemy, at a disadvantage. Not all observers, however, are so skeptical about her motivations. More describes how Elizabeth escaped into sanctuary "in great flight and heaviness, bewailing her child's ruin, her friends' mischance, and her own infortune, damning the time that ever she dissuaded the gathering of power about the king." Her eldest son, Dorset, and her brother Lionel, the bishop, were to join her. Edward IV had confirmed Westminster's sanctuary rights after the queen's last residence there. But Edward himself had not respected sanctuary rights, when it suited him to choose differently.

Thomas Rotherham, Archbishop of York and Lord Chancellor of England, had gone to Elizabeth in the midst of her flight, and described a scene of chaos: "much heaviness, rumble, haste and business, carriage and conveyance of her stuff into Sanctuary, chests, coffers, packs, fardels, trusses, all on men's backs, no man unoccupied, some loading, some going, some discharging, some coming for more, some breaking down the walls to bring in the next way." The queen herself, as More reports Rotherham's finding, "sat alone low on the rushes all desolate and dismayed."

Rotherham comforted Elizabeth in the best manner he could, and, he gave into her custody the privy seal—the royal stamp, used to authenticate official documents—of which he was keeper. It showed there was still a game to play. But the archbishop regretted his impetuous move and the next day sent to ask for his seal back. After all, Richard had not moved against the Crown as such. Hastings (who, in

Crowland's words, was congratulating himself that the whole affair had been accomplished with no more bloodshed than "might have come from a cut finger") was reassuring those in London that Richard was still faithful to his brother's wishes and that nothing whatsoever had been done save a transfer of power from one to another side of the new king's family. And his excuse worked, to some degree.

On May 4, the young Edward entered London, riding in blue in a splendid procession, obsequiously attended by Richard, who had technically done nothing to breach his oath of loyalty. This should have been the day of Edward's coronation, but that event was now postponed to the end of June.

On May 7, a meeting was held at Baynard's Castle, Cecily Neville's London residence, at which the most powerful lords of the country, spiritual and temporal—Richard of course among them—officially took possession of Edward IV's goods, seals, and jewels on the grounds that they were executors of his will. Richard, says Mancini, had arrived in London preceded by four wagons loaded with arms and bearing the Woodville emblems, which he claimed were designed to be used against him. The excuse was obviously a fake—Mancini says everyone knew the weapons had really been collected back in Edward IV's day, as part of the government's preparation for a possible war with Scotland—but Richard's move must have appeared as another ominous sign to Elizabeth in sanctuary.

While Elizabeth's power was draining away, Richard's was growing. At a council meeting of May 27, Richard was declared the man most fitting to be declared protector of the realm. He would hold the post, however, only until Edward was crowned and declared of age just four weeks later, an impending development that opened up the prospect of fresh dispute and may have played a part in pushing Richard to seek a more definitive solution.

Sometime in the few weeks after his arrival, the young king was moved, at Buckingham's suggestion, from the Bishop of London's palace (too small for a full royal retinue) to the Tower. There was nothing sinister in that, necessarily—the place was a regular royal residence and traditionally used by monarchs in the run-up to their coronation. Moreover, it is hard to think where better Edward could have gone; the out-of-town palaces like Sheen and Eltham were too distant, and Westminster was ineligible because of his mother self-immured there such a short distance away.

Whether or not Richard had originally been opposed to his nephew's rule, his hostility was becoming more apparent. There does seem to have been a tentative plan for Richard to have continued his role at the head of government beyond the coronation, but there must also have been a fear that a king once declared of age would recall his mother and her family to his side. And the Woodvilles still represented a threat: Elizabeth's brother Edward had been commanding a fleet in the Channel to guard against the French, but now the English authorities ordered his soldiers to desert, while he himself was to be seized; in fact, he escaped with two ships and made his way to Henry Tudor in Brittany.

It is possible that Richard was already taking steps toward claiming the throne for himself. It has been suggested that, in the early days of June, Bishop Stillington told the council that he had married Edward IV to Eleanor Butler before his marriage to Elizabeth Woodville, which was thus rendered invalid. One chronicle describes doctors, proctors, and depositions being brought in to the lords. A case was being prepared.

Still, London seems to have maintained an eerie calm. A letter from Simon Stallworthe to Sir William Stonor on June 9 reports that the queen "keeps still at Westminster." "My Lord Protector, My Lord of Buckingham with all other lords as well temporal as spiritual were at Westminster in the Council Chamber from 10 to 2, but there was none that spoke with the Queen." There was, he says, "great business" about the young king's coronation, which was scheduled for just two weeks away, and when he adds that "My Lady of Gloucester"—Anne Neville—came to London "on Thursday last," the assumption must still have been that it was to attend this ceremony. The Parliament that always followed a coronation had been called, a sign that government was functioning normally. But there is perhaps a hint that even outside the Protector's rooms, other possibilities were being mooted, when Stallworthe urges Stonor to come to town "and then shall you know all the world."

What tranquillity lingered over London, however, would soon be shattered. On June 10 and 11, Richard wrote respectively to the city of York and to Lord Neville of Raby asking them to bring troops from the North with all diligence "to aid and assist us against the Queen, her bloody adherents and affinity; which have intended and daily doth intend to murder and utterly destroy us and our cousin the Duke of Buckingham and the old royal blood of the realm." It would have been reasonable for Richard to assume that Elizabeth was still hoping—plotting—to overthrow him, although her Grey son and her brother, hostages in Richard's custody, may have given her pause. But it is hard to believe Richard really feared she still had the means to put her hopes into effect—the more so because of what happened on June 13.

The exact circumstances of the story, as described by Thomas More, have served to build the legend of Richard's villainy. Richard arrived smiling at a council meeting, praising the strawberries from the Bishop of Ely's garden. This was Bishop Morton, already an ally of Margaret Beaufort's and later one of her closest friends. But soon after Richard left the room, he returned with a frowning face and a ritual parade of accusation on his lips—accusation directed first at the absent Elizabeth Woodville.

More's account has Richard pulling up his sleeve to show a withered arm, telling the lords to see what "that sorceress" (Queen Elizabeth) and "others of her counsel, [such] as Shore's wife with her affinity," had done to him by their "sorcery and witchcraft." "Jane" Shore, once Edward IV's "merriest harlot," was now the lover of Lord Hastings, and More shows his skepticism about that part of the story in particular. Would Elizabeth really have joined forces, he asks, with her husband's mistress? But Richard's fury was not directed only at the absent women. Hastings and Morton were both arrested, on a vague and unsubstantiated charge of having plotted to destroy Richard, and Hastings, hitherto Richard's ally, was (so the dramatic tale goes) unceremoniously beheaded the same day.

This looks like the first indisputable evidence that Richard, whether or not he had always done so, now sought the crown itself. It is hard to see why else he would have wished to dispatch Hastings, a mutual enemy of the Woodvilles. But although Hastings had supported Richard so far, doubtless believing the country would be better governed in Edward V's minority by Edward IV's loyal and able

brother than by the queen and her family, he would surely have balked
at what was now to follow.

After this, events moved swiftly. At the next meeting of the council, Richard insisted that his namesake, Elizabeth Woodville's second
son, had to be brought out of sanctuary—nominally to attend his
brother's coronation. On June 16, the council sent a delegation to visit
Elizabeth in sanctuary, and More details at length their arguments.
Some were technical: that an innocent child such as Richard could
have no reason to claim—could have no reason to be given—sanctuary, which was for those who had done wrong or those who had reason
to hide, that it was as reasonable for the council to fear to leave the
prince in the queen's hands as it was for her to fear to hand him over,
since he might be spirited away. Some were political: that Elizabeth's
evident refusal to trust the council was causing division in the realm
and would cause distrust outside it. One, at least, was directly gen-
dered: that her refusal sprang from what the senior cleric present char-
itably called "womanish fear" but the Duke of Buckingham called
"womanish frowardness." Other of the delegation's arguments for
handing over Richard were designed to appeal directly to a mother's
heart. Elizabeth was, the delegation said in a shrewd blow, like Medea
avenging herself at the expense of her own children by thus keeping
them shut up. They said that sanctuary was no place for a child, full as
it was of "a rabble of thieves, murderers, and malicious heinous traitors" (not to mention "men's wives [who] run thither with their husbands' plate, and say they dare not abide with their husbands for
beating"). They said that young Edward V needed his brother's company and that a life without play was unsuited to "their both ages and
estates." The saga of argument and counterargument runs on for
pages, and Elizabeth could only have been worn down by the barrage.

But More has her answering fluently and bravely. If the young
King Edward needed company, why should not he, as well as Richard,
be placed in her care (he more so since the younger boy had been ill,
and needed his mother's attention)? (It was, of course, the last thing to
which the councilors were likely to agree.) If not, then why not find
other peers' sons for Edward to play with, rather than his still ailing
brother? She said that the law made her as Richard's mother his
guardian ("as my learned counsel shows me").

The widowed Elizabeth mustered point after point to keep her younger son by her side. "You may not take hence my horse from me; and may you take my child from me?" she asked. It was another telling point. She also defended her decision to take her children into sanctuary, adding that the imprisonment of her brother and younger Grey son hardly led to confidence, that protection for herself or her other children could not be ensured in a time of "greedy" men, and that, yes, her son did have the right to claim sanctuary: Richard had a nerve, had come up with "a goodly glose"—a clever misinterpretation—to claim that "a place that may defend a thief may not save an innocent."

But the real point of the discussions, of course, was an unspoken one: the fear that if Elizabeth refused to hand over her boy, then he would simply be snatched away. Sanctuary was a moral rather than a physical concept; this was the middle of Westminster, with the Protector himself waiting in another part of the palace only a few hundred yards away. Indeed, Mancini says that "with the consent of the council [Richard] surrounded the sanctuary with troops," a sign that he may have been preparing for just such a maneuver.

As More tells it, the question of taking the boy by force was a matter of some dissent among the peers themselves, some of the lords spiritually holding back, but the majority agreeing to do whatever was necessary to get ahold of the boy. In the end, it was Thomas Bourchier, the Archbishop of Canterbury (and a relative of the York brothers through their father's sister), who broke the deadlock, telling Elizabeth that if she sent the boy now, he himself would guarantee the prince's safety, but that if she refused, he would have nothing more to do with a woman who seemed to think that "all others save herself lacked either wit or truth." The threat found its mark. "The Queen with these words stood a good while in a great study," More said.

More's pages have, up to a point, to be decoded, for he surely, at the very least, polished Elizabeth's words in his account of what happened next. "And at the last she took the young duke by the hand," More explains, "and said to the lords, 'my Lord,' quod she, 'and all my lords, I am neither so unwise [as] to mistrust your wits, nor so suspicious to mistrust your troths [promises].'" It may have been More's hindsight that makes her add, "We have also had experience that the desire of a kingdom knows no kindred. The brother has been the brother's bane.

And may the nephews be sure of their uncle?" But whenever these pre-
scient words were first strung together, they are considerations of which
everyone must, in any case, have been aware at the time; the Cousins'
War had, by now, turned many a brother against their own blood.
More has her giving the lords a warning, saying that she begged them
just one thing: "that as far as you think that I fear too much, be you well
ware [careful] that you fear not as far too little."

And then Elizabeth said good-bye to her youngest son. More describes how "she said to the child, 'Farewell my own sweet son, God
send you good keeping. Let me kiss you once yet before you go, for
God knows when we shall kiss together again.' And therewith she
kissed him, and blessed him, turned her back and wept and went her
way, leaving the child weeping as fast." When the lords brought the
little boy through the palace to his uncle, waiting in Star Chamber,
Richard received him kindly, welcoming him "with all my very
heart." The Stonor Letters report confidently that the child had gone
with the archbishop to the Tower, where he was known to be
"merry."

With both of his nephews—the two immediate heirs to the
throne—tucked away in the Tower under his watchful eye, Richard's
hands were now free. Immediately, the coronation and Parliament
were both deferred until November. When Elizabeth heard the news,
she must (with good reason) have feared the worst—that whatever he
said, Richard had no intention of crowning her son, in November or at
any other time.

On June 21, Simon Stallworthe, he who had previously urged Sir
William Stonor to come to London, was writing that "I hold you
happy that you are out of the press, for with us is much trouble and
every man doubts other." The Archbishop of York and Morton, the
Bishop of Ely, were in the Tower, but he hoped "they shall come out
nevertheless"; Mistress Shore was in prison, and "what shall happen
her I know not"; twenty thousand of Richard's and Buckingham's men
were expected in the city, "to what intent I know not but to keep the
peace." Crowland too wrote of armed men "in frightening and unheard of numbers." The same chronicle also wrote that the detention
of Edward V's servants and relatives had been causing widespread concern, "besides the fact that the Protector did not, with a sufficient

degree of considerateness, take measure for the preservation of the dignity and safety of the Queen."

But the dignity of Elizabeth Woodville was about to suffer a far worse insult. On Sunday, June 22, the popular London preacher Dr. Ralph Shaa delivered a sermon at St. Paul's Cross—"Bastard Slips Shall Never Take Deep Root"—that directly attacked the immediate family of the dead king. Many were eager to give a précis of the theme of that and other sermons Richard's agents surely caused to be preached around the City that day.

The most serious—because more plausible—of the various allegations made that Sunday raised the same specter that Clarence had invoked during his rebellion: the accusation that Edward IV's marriage to Elizabeth Woodville had been invalid, because he was already contracted to another lady, Eleanor Butler. The debate still runs today as to whether there might be any truth in the suggestion and whether invalidity in the parents' marriage would necessarily have debarred Edward V from the throne.

After the sermons had first mooted the idea, Richard's supporters took care to ram the point home. On Tuesday, June 24, the Duke of Buckingham addressed a Guildhall convocation with a secular version of the story: the tale of a precontract, with the old slurs that Edward's marriage to Elizabeth Woodville was in any case "not well made" since her blood "was full unmeetly to be match with his" and a general deprecation of Edward's sexual appetite. There was, More represents him as saying, no woman who caught Edward's eye "but without fear of God, or respect of his honour, murmur or grudge of the world, he would importunately pursue his appetite," so that "more suit was in his days to Shore's wife, a vile and abominable strumpet than to all the Lords in England." Commynes declares it was Bishop Stillington— the same official who had perhaps married Edward IV to Eleanor Butler as well—who told Richard the truth about his brother's marriage; it has been suggested, by those who believe the allegation, that he now displayed some proof.

But there was another allegation in the air, one on which, More said, Buckingham touched only lightly in his speech before the Guildhall convocation, since Richard had asked him to avoid it, because "nature requireth a filial reverence to the Duchess his mother." The allegation, of course, was that other specter Clarence had once raised: that Edward (and indeed, it was now hinted, also Clarence himself) was the bastard fruit of Cecily's adultery.

Not everyone, however, had treated this scandalous notion with such delicacy. More has Shaa having declared that neither Edward IV nor Clarence was "reckoned very surely" as the Duke of York's child, as both more closely resembled other men. Vergil has Shaa having declared simply that their bastardy "was manifest enough, and that by apparent argument."

Of course, there are doubts over just who did say what. Both More and Vergil were writing some years later, and it has been suggested that the whole notion of Richard's having raised the issue—the persistent myth of, as Vergil puts it, the "madness" of his "wicked mind"— was simply a Tudor slur. The Tudors, of course, did need to find alternative grounds for Richard's complaint, since the allegation about Edward's own marriage touched Elizabeth of York too nearly. But Mancini does say that "corrupted preachers" declared Edward "was conceived in adultery," in no way resembling his supposed father—and Mancini was writing within months of the event.

As far as the question of the adultery itself is concerned, there is no real evidence available from Cecily's time at Rouen on which to judge the veracity of her supposed affair with the archer, Blaybourne, who was rumored to be Edward's true father. More than a decade after Edward IV's death, writing on the edge of eternity, Cecily in her will would declare herself "wife unto the right noble prince Richard late Duke of York, father unto the most Christian prince my Lord and son King Edward the iiiith." She did not so boast of Richard, but then to do so in Henry VII's reign would have lacked tact. But it may also be significant that she made no bequests to Clarence's children as she did to her other grandchildren, a fact that militates against the idea that she had herself originated the claim he had made. Vergil states that Cecily, "being falsely accused of adultery, complained afterwards in sundry places to right many noble men, whereof some yet live, of that great injury which her son Richard had done her."

Another theory, however, says she was entirely supportive of Richard's takeover, if not actually the orchestrator of it, even going so far as to let her name be trampled in the dirt in order for his design to succeed. There is, however, little firm evidence for this. Richard did base himself at Baynard's Castle—his mother's house in London—for some of this time, but it has not been conclusively proven that Cecily was actually there. The Archbishop of Canterbury recorded that the first, early-May, meeting at which it was agreed to take possession of Edward's seals was held at the *"solite"* (accustomed, wonted) residence of the great duchess; indeed, it is a fair deduction that, in the irregular state of affairs, the archbishop drew some comfort from the connection of the plan with so respected a lady. But the London house was not Cecily's only regular residence, and if she was in the house at the time, then the archbishop's phraseology is oddly oblique. The list of those present at the meeting—senior clerics and officials, all male— does not mention her name. Mancini says that the lords gathered "at the house of Richard's mother, whither he had purposefully betaken himself, that these events might not take place in the Tower, where the young King was confined." But it is possible that in using Baynard's Castle, Richard hoped to echo the pattern of the offer of the crown to Edward IV (which had also taken place at Baynard's Castle), or indeed to invoke the idea of Cecily's support.

THERE REMAINS, OF COURSE, the matter of Cecily's grandsons, the Princes in the Tower. It is conceivable that Cecily's animosity toward Elizabeth Woodville extended to the queen's sons, but if Cecily was truly involved in a plot against her daughter-in-law, she might also have convinced herself that the boys were not in any great danger. Arguably, the simple substitution of an adult for an underage male— a step designed to ensure the family of York maintained the power it had only recently attained—might not have seemed so outrageous at the time. The right of inheritance to the throne was not necessarily as clearly defined in the fifteenth century as it might seem to later generations; witness, indeed, the relative flexibility in the manner of choice that had allowed one ruler to depose another with comparative impunity in the decades preceding this one. In such a climate, to replace a juvenile member of the family by a more viable candidate from the same house might seem a simple matter of practicality, at a time when the welfare of the family was seen as dependent not on the safety and welfare of the individual, but on the progress of the entity as a whole.

Moreover, if Cecily did indeed collaborate with Richard to any degree, she may have seen her function as that of a brake—a mediating, emollient influence, intercessionary even—since part of the role of a medieval lady was to stop her men from going far too far: witness the way in which the intercessionary function was always urged on queens. Cecily must have given a measure of acquiescence, since she did not cut off contact with Richard (the next spring, the grant of her manors and lands, and of Berkhampsted, was confirmed), but possibly she gave his campaign no more than tacit support. If she was indeed by now living largely retired from the world, she may have taken refuge in her solitude and distance. And if she was absent or anything less than totally committed to Richard's plan, then Vergil's report that she "complained afterwards" about the slur on her virtue has a certain ring of probability. It would surely have been easier for Shaa to preach that sermon if Cecily and Cecily's servants weren't in London to hear it. By the time report of it spread, it could be softened or explained slightly.

There is no doubt, at least, about where Cecily was not on one significant occasion in these few weeks. When her son Richard was crowned king, Cecily would be absent. That is far from conclusive, of course; the widow of a deceased monarch did not normally attend the coronation of his successor, and some such prohibition may have inhibited Cecily.* Margaret Beaufort, similarly, would be recorded as observing, rather than playing an active part in, her son's coronation ceremony. But Cecily is not mentioned at any point during the extensive records of Richard's lengthy festivities.

Whatever Cecily's role, on June 25 in northern England, Anthony Woodville was executed, as was Elizabeth Woodville's son Richard Grey. On the same day, Buckingham, with a deputation of London officials, went to Baynard's Castle to beg Richard to assume the throne.

---

*When the rule was finally broken by Queen Mary in 1937, her attendance at the coronation of George VI was taken as evidence of her strong views on his brother's abdication.

"INNOCENT BLOOD"

Rest thy unrest of England's lawful earth,
Unlawfully made drunk with innocent blood

THE TRAGEDY OF RICHARD THE THIRD, 4.4

On June 26, 1483, Richard proceeded to Westminster Hall to take the royal seat in the Court of the King's Bench. It was from this day that he dated his accession. On July 6, he was crowned—and Anne Neville, with whatever different expectation she may (or may not) have had, arrived in London and was crowned as his queen.

Unusually, it was to be a joint ceremony, the first double coronation for almost two centuries. Anne's inclusion in the ritual could be taken as a gesture of genuine affection on Richard's part, or simply as a suggestion that he needed to reinforce the commitment of the northerners loyal to Anne's family. It could, by contrast, also be taken to mean that he did not want to give her a separate ceremony and the suggestion of authority that might bring.*

---

*Henry VII, though, under those circumstances, would delay his wife's coronation.

Provision would in any case have had to be remarkably speedy—some of the preparations set in place for the boy Edward's coronation could still be used, though there were certainly robes to be made for the new, differently proportioned participants. At the same time, however, there must have been a particular, contradictory, concern that in these most unusual circumstances, everything should be done by the book, literally: a special document, the *Little Device,* laying down the formalities, was drawn up in addition to the more generally applicable *Liber Regalis.* The list of accounts for, and goods provided by, the Great Wardrobe department is in itself an extraordinary document: page after page recording everything from the commission of silk fringe and buttons of Venice gold from two silk women, Alice Claver and Cecily Walcote, to the "slops" of Spanish leather, the banners, and the saddlery. The records show the provision of garments to Anne—"a robe of crimson velvet containing mantle with a train, a surcoat and a kirtle made of xlviii yards of crimson velvet," furred with "cxxi timbers of wombs of miniver pure"—and also for the ladies of rank, Margaret Beaufort among them, who might be expected to attend the coronation. (Margaret would have appeared in two long gowns: one of crimson velvet "pufiled" [bordered] with white cloth of gold and another of blue velvet with crimson cloth of gold.) Anne herself is first sighted on July 3, when she and Richard exchanged formal gifts. He gave twenty-four yards of purple cloth of gold, with seven yards of purple velvet; she gave twenty yards of purple velvet decorated with garters and roses. The next day, they traveled to spend a night in the royal apartments at the Tower, as tradition dictated. Their proximity to those whose places they had taken (for the Princes were presumably still in the Tower at this time) may well have made this an uncomfortable stay for Richard and Anne, and some of the normal pomp and circumstance of the occasion was missing as well; the hurried and joint nature of the proceedings, and the shortness of the journey from Baynard's Castle, meant that Anne did not receive the usual pageants that would not only honor her queenship and lay down her specific role, but also acknowledge her ancestry and her own identity.

Richard, Mancini says, had summoned six thousand men from his estates and Buckingham's and now stationed them "at suitable points" around London, in case of "any uproar." The next day, they set out for the abbey, Anne wearing her hair loose under a jeweled circlet in the symbol of virginity that had become linked to the coronation ritual, however inappropriate it might be for the long-married Anne (and for Elizabeth Woodville before her). Seated on a canopied litter of white damask and white cloth of gold, fringed and garnished with ribbon and bells, her train followed Richard's. She was dressed, too, in white cloth of gold, tasseled and furred (in July!) with ermine and miniver. Two of her gentlemen ushers and her chamberlain went in front; her henchmen, her horse of state, and three carriages bearing twelve noblewomen came behind.

They reached Westminster Palace and took wine and spices in Westminster Hall. As they did so, and as they took supper in the Great Chamber of the palace, Elizabeth Woodville—demoted now from the dowager Queen Elizabeth to Dame Elizabeth Grey—cannot have been far away, still in sanctuary. But then, just as when the couple had stayed near the Princes at the Tower, it might have seemed like an admission of weakness to omit any part of the usual ceremony.

On July 6, the Sunday of the coronation, the procession assembled at seven in the morning in Westminster Hall. Despite her royal surcoat and train of crimson velvet, it would have been shoeless that Anne followed the king into the abbey, flanked by two bishops and followed by two duchesses and her ladies, knights, and esquires. Prostrating herself on ground carefully carpeted and cushioned, she was anointed after her husband, ringed, crowned, and invested with a scepter and rod. Her ceremony, however, deliberately fell slightly short of his. The couple then celebrated mass, and at the climax of the mass they both drank from the same chalice in "a sign of unity" (says the *Liber Regalis,* which had laid down provision for this rare event) because in Christ they were one flesh by bond of marriage. Anne was now consecrated to her country's service, and she must surely have felt as anyone would at such a moment: the dizzying, almost terrifying mix of grandeur, responsibility, and sheer fatigue.

By Saint Edward's shrine, king and queen were taken to separate closets and allowed to break their fast. The queen changed into a surcoat and long-trained mantle of purple velvet before she and Richard resumed their thrones and their regalia. They then proceeded back to Westminster Hall and to their chambers. The menu also survives for the banquet that afternoon in Westminster Hall: pheasant in train (with its tail feathers); roasted cygnet, egrets, and green geese; roe deer "reversed in purple" (literally turned inside out and the meat dyed); glazed kid; baked oranges; fresh sturgeon with fennel; and fritters flavored with rose and jasmine. In all as many as three thousand guests may have been fed, and the proceedings lasted so long that the third course could not be served. Everyone who was anyone, after all, was in town for the Parliament that had been summoned to greet not this king, but Edward V. Almost everyone, anyway.

A number of prominent Yorkists were nowhere to be found at Richard's coronation, while others played a tellingly active part. Not only was Cecily Neville not there, but neither—though her husband was especially prominent—was the Duke of Buckingham's Woodville-born wife. Richard's sister Elizabeth, Duchess of Suffolk, however, walked behind the queen, leading Anne's ladies. Archbishop Bourchier, who had promised Elizabeth Woodville her younger son's safety, had officiated but, says Mancini, unwillingly—and apparently he abstained from the banquet. Margaret Beaufort, by contrast, carried the new queen's crimson train.

Before the coronation, Margaret's husband, Stanley, had been in trouble with the new regime: Thomas More described him as having been attacked by the same men who arrested Hastings at the council meeting, and Vergil has him being placed under arrest. But Richard quickly changed tactics with the great landowner; when Richard had arrived at the Tower before his coronation, he had appointed Stanley steward of his household. Margaret's own intentions at this point seem to have been merely to come to an accord with Richard and get her son home, on the terms agreed upon with Edward IV the year before. She had opened negotiations in June through Buckingham, and again the possibility of a marriage between Henry and one of Edward IV's daughters had been mooted; this was, however, to be subject entirely to Richard, "without any thing to be taken or demanded for the same espousals but only the king's favour."

Margaret and her husband appeared close to the new regime, but the events of the next few months would force the couple—or at least its female half—to reveal their true colors. On July 5, the day before the coronation ceremony, she and Stanley had met Richard and his chief justice at Westminster. It is possible that Margaret might even then have been two-faced in her approach (just as Richard was concurrently also conducting independent and less well-intentioned negotiations with Brittany to get Henry handed back to him). So much had changed in so short a time. A month before Richard and Anne's coronation day, that of Edward V was still assumed a certainty; three months before it, Edward IV had still been alive, the future of his dynasty apparently ensured. All the same, Richard's speedy takeover seemed to be accepted not only by Margaret Beaufort but also by Margaret of Burgundy (who probably saw this as a simple transfer of power without contemplating any fatal consequences). But in any case, the latter Margaret had her own fish to fry. By the terms of the Treaty of Arras of December 1482 (that same treaty that had so distressed Edward IV), the daughter of Margaret of Burgundy's stepdaughter, Mary of Burgundy, was to marry the Dauphin in place of Elizabeth of York, and indeed the Burgundian infant had been handed over to the French on the same day, April 24, as the putative Edward V left Ludlow. Mary's young son and heir, Philip, was in Ghent, where the authorities refused to give him up. As his father, Maximilian, struggled to regain control of the duchy and the motherless child, Margaret was preoccupied by the need first to aid him, and then to care for the little boy in a spirit of almost surrogate maternity. She does not seem to have upbraided her brother Richard for having deposed their nephews—instead, she appealed to him for aid.

Richard, however, was more concerned with establishing himself in his own kingdom. Soon after the coronation, the new king and queen set out on progress, one of the regular royal tours designed to exhibit the monarch to his people. From Greenwich, on July 19 they traveled to Windsor, where Anne stayed while Richard went westward, the couple meeting again in Warwick as the second week of August dawned. Anne seems not to have taken part in the whole of Richard's exhausting program. But on August 15, she joined him for the rest of the fortnight's progress north to York, where they stayed for three weeks.

The highlight of the York stay was to be the investiture of Richard and Anne's son Edward as Prince of Wales. Young as he was—perhaps no more than seven—he would still be the figurehead representing his father's rule in the North. Such ceremonies were all the more important for a regime still trying to demonstrate its legitimacy—and besides, York had always been true to Richard. Its citizens deserved to see their new, their own, king and queen, wearing their crowns and walking through the streets, holding the hands of their newly honored son.

The young Edward had been left in the North when his mother came southward. But the same document that at such length records the silks and ostrich feathers, the bonnets and the furs, the reins and the cruppers for the coronation also records the delivery of blue cloth and crimson velvet to cover a saddle "for my Lord Prince against his noble creation"—that is, the boy's investiture—as well as crimson or tawny satin to make doublets for the king's henchmen on the same occasion, and murrey (mulberry) cloth and white sarcenet lining to make their gowns.

Anne and Richard traveled with their son from Pontefract to York, where the city dignitaries met them outside the walls, to escort them past a series of pageants to the archbishop's palace. It was September 8, the day of the Feast of the Nativity of the Blessed Virgin, when a celebratory mass, at which the cathedral's relics were displayed, was followed by the knighting of the prince (along with Richard's nephew Warwick and his own bastard son) and Edward's investiture. If one consistent theme of this story is women's anxiety to promote the interests of their children, or those they regarded as such, then whatever her feelings about her husband's actions, Anne's heart, like the candles at the banquets, must have flared with pride.

The couple left York on September 21 to escort their son back to Pontefract, before moving on to Lincoln on October 11. At Lincoln, however, news of a fresh crisis of Richard's reign would greet them. It was a problem that Richard might perhaps have expected, for it involved his young nephews, the "Princes in the Tower."

As Richard (and Anne) consolidated his rule, Elizabeth Woodville's young sons had presumably remained in the Tower. Mancini wrote that "after Hastings was removed"—in the second half of June—all the attendants who had waited upon the young Edward were denied access to him. He and his brother were "withdrawn in the inner apartments of the Tower proper, and day by day began to be seen more rarely behind the bars and windows, till at lengthy they ceased to appear altogether."

Mancini adds that young Edward's doctor, a man called Argentine, "the last of his attendants whose services the king enjoyed," reported that the twelve-year-old king, "like a victim prepared for sacrifice, sought remission of his sins by daily confession and penance, because he believed that death was facing him." Fabian's report of the boys seen "shooting and playing in the gardens of the Tower by sundry times" might seem to run on into later summer or early autumn, but More provides a rather wintry embroidery for Mancini's story, describing how after a time of captivity, the elder boy "never tied his points, nor ought wrought of himself"—a lassitude and disregard of his clothing that sounds very much like a state of depression. Continental chronicler Jean Molinet (who had replaced Georges Chastellain at the Burgundian court) gave a dramatic description of the younger boy urging his brother to learn how to dance, and the elder replying they should rather learn how to die, "because I believe I know well that we will not be in this world much longer."

Polydore Vergil—that unabashed Tudor apologist, writing well after the event—was very sure he knew just what had happened, from the first days of August on. He has Richard arriving at Gloucester on progress, and there "the heinous guilt of wicked conscience" so tormented him that he determined to be free of his anxieties once and for all. It was from there, Vergil says, that he sent word the Princes were to be killed while Richard himself proceeded on to York, presumably relieved of care. But the lieutenant of the Tower, Robert Brackenbury, refused to obey such wicked instructions, so Richard was forced to find another instrument.

Vergil's account, written in the sixteenth century, can no longer be distinguished from pieces of information or disinformation put out in the interim: it is likely he had been spoon-fed a party line on the all-important question of the Princes' fate. But as Vergil points out, it is interesting that at York, Richard founded a college of a hundred priests, a huge gesture of expiation or reparation. Vergil says also that

Richard purposely let it slip out that the boys were dead, "[so] that after the people understood no issue male of king Edward to be now left
alive, they might with better mind and good will bear and sustain his
government." He describes, moreover, the reception of the news by
"the unfortunate mother," Elizabeth Woodville, to whom it was "the
very stroke of death":

> for as soon as she had intelligence how her sons were bereft this life,
> at the very first motion thereof, the outrageousness of the thing
> drove her into such passion as for fear forthwith she fell into a
> swoon, and lay lifeless a good while; after coming to her self, she
> weepeth, she cryeth out aloud, and with lamentable shrieks made all
> the house ring, she struck her breast, tore and cut her hair, and,
> overcome in fine with dolour, prayeth also her own death, calling by
> name now and then among her most dear children, and condemn-
> ing herself for a mad woman, for that (being deceived by false
> promises) she had delivered her younger son out of sanctuary, to be
> murdered of his enemy.

Her only resource was to beg God for revenge.

There is no need to take Vergil's timing as sure, or even the agency
he attributes to Richard in the disappearance of his nephews. Crowland suggests only that while Richard was on his progress, rumors began to spread, and he adds that in those same months, it was advised
that "some of the [late] king's daughters should leave Westminster in
disguise and go in disguise to the parts beyond sea; in order that, if any
fatal mishap should befall the said male children of the late king in the
Tower, the kingdom might still, in consequence of the safety of the
daughters, one day fall again into the hands of the rightful heirs."
Richard apparently responded to this by ordering a blockade around
the Tower, under the command of one John Nesfield.

All the same, there is a reason Richard's attitudes toward the
"Princes" might indeed have been hardening in late July: there had
been a rescue attempt. In late July, a number of men were arrested because "they were purposed to have set on fire diverse parts of London,
which fire, while men had been staunching, they would have stole out
of the Tower, the prince Edward, & his brother the Duke of York."

The report comes from the antiquarian John Stow a century later—but the contemporary Thomas Basin confirms it.

Interestingly, there seems to have been a connection between Margaret Beaufort's Tudor relations and the plot to spring the two boys from the Tower. According to Stow, the men had planned also to "have sent writings to the earls of Richmond and Pembroke"—Henry and Jasper Tudor. In early August, Margaret Beaufort's half brother John Welles led a rising, at her childhood home of Maxey. Her connection to the rebels is enough to suggest to many that Margaret Beaufort may have given her support to the ploy; the seventeenth-century antiquarian George Buck believed her negotiations with Richard had been a feint, on the part of the "cunning countess." But it is a little hard to be sure just where Margaret's advantage would have lain in freeing the Princes. It is easier, of course, to imagine Richard—when the news had reached him, in the West—deciding that the boys were not, as he had hoped, altogether neutralized by the declaration of bastardy or their incarceration in the Tower.

If it was now that rumors of the boys' deaths began to spread, then it may also have been now that Margaret recast her hopes for her son, Henry. And if it was now that Elizabeth Woodville—possibly influenced by Margaret's agents?—became convinced her sons were dead, then it is no wonder she gave her consent to a joint conspiracy.

There is ample reason to believe that, around this time, Margaret Beaufort was beginning to actively promote her son, Henry Tudor, as a contender for the throne—or, as Vergil put it, "she, being a wise woman, after the slaughter of king Edward's children was known, began to hope well of her son's fortune." The go-between keeping the two ladies in touch was Margaret Beaufort's physician, the Welshman Lewis Caerleon—"a grave man and of no small experience," says Vergil, with whom "she was wont oftentimes to confer freely."* Margaret, according to Vergil, suggested to Caerleon that a marriage might be arranged between Edward IV's eldest daughter, Elizabeth of

---

*A noted, and Cambridge-educated, astronomer and mathematician, he would still be in the records as employed by Elizabeth of York a decade later.

York, and her son, Henry. She "therefore prayed him to deal secretly with the queen" and broach the idea to her. Elizabeth Woodville, fortuitously, was also in the habit of consulting Caerleon, "because he was a very learned physician." Vergil says that Caerleon, presumably on Margaret's instruction, pretended this idea was "devised of his own head" when he mooted the notion to Elizabeth Woodville.

Elizabeth Woodville, Vergil reports, was "so well pleased with this device" that she sent Caerleon back to Margaret promising to recruit all Edward IV's friends for a rebellion to topple Richard, if Henry would be sworn to take Elizabeth of York in marriage as soon as he had the realm (or else Cecily, the younger daughter, "if th' other should die before he enjoyed the same").

Margaret sent out her man Reginald Bray to gather her friends for the coming fight; Elizabeth Woodville sent word to hers. Margaret was on the point of sending a protégé of Caerleon's, a young priest called Christopher Urswick whom she had taken into her household, to her son, Henry, in Brittany, when she had news that halted her in her tracks. Hers was not the only conspiracy afoot.

The Duke of Buckingham had played a leading part in placing Richard on the throne but had since become disaffected—a discontent purposefully fostered (when Buckingham left Richard at Gloucester that early August week and returned to his own home of Brecon Castle) by the man he had been asked to hold in custody there: Margaret's old associate John Morton, Bishop of Ely. Richard had surely hoped that such an arrangement would keep his old foe Morton from causing him any trouble, but now the bishop made himself meddlesome in other ways, urging Buckingham that "if you love God, your lineage, or your native country," he should himself take the crown.

Buckingham was eagerly receptive to Morton's scheme. He responded that only recently, he had indeed "suddenly remembered" his own lineage through the Beaufort line; on his way home to Brecon, however, he had happened to meet Margaret Beaufort on the road, which reminded him of her superior claim (superior *if* you ignore the legitimacy question). This picture conjured up of a chance meeting is likely to be disingenuous, but at some stage the various conspirators must have decided to pool their resources. In the seventeenth century,

George Buck declared that Margaret was the brain behind the final plans, "for she was entered far into them, and none better plunged in them and deeply acquainted with them. And she was a politic and subtle lady."

So Margaret Beaufort and Elizabeth Woodville were both deeply involved in the general outlines of the plot, but of the three main conspirators, it was inevitably Buckingham, the man, who took charge of the armed rebellion launched on October 18. Leading his men from Wales, he was to have joined up with the other forces Margaret and Elizabeth had been able to rally, but freak weather conditions made it impossible for his army to cross the swollen Severn. His men began to desert—and, probably contrary to his expectations, there was no sign of Margaret Beaufort's husband, Stanley, coming to join the rebellion, as the conspirators must surely have hoped he would.

Henry Tudor's attempts to sail from Brittany with a fleet provided by the Breton duke had likewise repeatedly been thwarted by the weather, and by the time he saw the English coast, it was evident that his only option was to flee back across the Channel again. Buckingham was captured—betrayed by his servant for the reward—and summarily executed on November 2. Others (including Elizabeth Woodville's son Dorset) fled abroad to join Henry. But as so often with stories from this era, that clear and simply told version is not the whole tale.

IT IS OFTEN SAID that Elizabeth Woodville must have known the Princes were dead, or she would never have gone along with a plan to marry her daughter Elizabeth, with her valuable York blood, to the Lancastrian Henry Tudor. But her late husband had, at the end of his life, promoted the same plan of a marriage between Elizabeth and Henry: a way to bring Henry Tudor safely into the Yorkist fold. It is, moreover, possible that she first agreed to throw her weight behind the rebellion in the belief that her sons were still living and that the insurrection would have a chance of placing Edward V on the throne. The Crowland chronicle suggests that the rebels first contemplated arms in the Princes' name and then, after "a rumour arose that King Edward's sons, by some unknown manner of violent destruction, had met their fate," turned to Henry Tudor in their need for "someone new at their head."

Margaret Beaufort's position is more equivocal. If Margaret's sole goal was to bring her son safely home, subject to some friendly sovereign, she might simply have continued negotiating with Richard—unless she mistrusted him and feared treachery. On the other hand, if she knew or believed the Princes were dead when she committed herself to the rebellion, her rationale would have been significantly clearer. The Princes' deaths would have made Henry Tudor's chances for assuming the throne much better—and would also have made Elizabeth of York more important, since she would now be the main inheritor of her father's bloodline. If Henry could but marry Elizabeth, then many Yorkist supporters, dismayed by Richard's seizure of the throne, might rally behind Henry, Lancastrian though he may be.

Buckingham's position is yet more puzzling. Most now dismiss the idea (Vergil's) that he had quarreled with Richard over lands promised and not granted. It is theoretically possible that he was belatedly defending the rights of Princes he believed to be still living; no manifesto for the rebels survives, but it seems that some of the minor risings in the South and West were indeed popular ventures aimed at freeing the Princes. (Crowland reports that "in order to deliver them from this captivity, the people of the southern and western parts of the kingdom began to murmur greatly, and to form meetings and confederacies.") But as word of the Princes' deaths filtered out and the goal changed, Buckingham's involvement becomes anomalous. He may possibly have been genuinely disinterested enough to wish, while avenging the Princes, to elevate Henry Tudor to the crown. But from everything that is known of him, this seems unlikely.

Buckingham may well have been an opportunist, taking advantage of the Princes' deaths to promote his own claim. If so, he probably hoped to dupe Margaret Beaufort into believing he supported her son's claim—striking a deal with Margaret to get the Tudor and Woodville supporters as allies, while always planning himself to step into Henry Tudor's place. But it is just as conceivable that he was himself the dupe—that Margaret (his aunt, through her marriage to Stafford) invited him to join a rebellion nominally in support of the Princes, while actually interested only in her own son.

John Talbot, in his Garter robes, presents a copy of the beautifully illustrated Shrewsbury Book to Marguerite of Anjou, shown hand in hand with her new husband, Henry VI. Daisies—Marguerite's personal emblem—decorate the lavish borders.

The stained glass Royal Window in Canterbury Cathedral shows the figures of
Edward IV and Elizabeth Woodville, with their sons and daughters to either
side, kneeling at prayer desks. The royal figures originally flanked an image of
the Crucifixion, but the window was damaged by Puritan iconoclasts in 1642.

Above: Believed to have been painted by Rowland Lockey in the last years of the sixteenth century, this image of the aging Margaret Beaufort reflects her reputation for piety. *At right:* Margaret's emblems—the mythological beast called a Yale, the portcullis, and the red rose— adorn several Cambridge colleges of which she was patron.

Cecily Neville's father, the Earl of Westmorland, flanked by the many children of his second marriage, in a French illustration from the fifteenth century.

Portraits of Elizabeth Woodville—mostly sixteenth- or early seventeenth-century copies of one original portrait type—show the high forehead and elaborate headdress that were a fashion of the day.

Anne Neville, depicted here in the *Rous Roll*, is shown in her coronation robes with orb and scepter.

Portraits of Richard III often show a more personable figure than his later reputation might suggest.

RICARDVS · III · ANG · REX ·

Opposite: This lovely miniature shows a vision in which the risen Christ appeared to Margaret of Burgundy in her bedroom, so silently that even her sleeping dog was not aroused.

ELIZABETHA · VXOR
HENRICI · VII ·

Like that of her mother, Elizabeth
Woodville, this portrait of Elizabeth of
York is a later version of a single earlier
painted portrait type. She holds the
white rose symbol of York in her hand.

Opposite: This depiction of the
birth of Julius Caesar reflects not
only the childbirth customs of the
late fifteenth century but also the
high quality of illumination found
in Burgundian books and
manuscripts at the time.

haſcun home
a qui dieu a
donne raiſon
et entendement
ſe doibt pener
quil ne gaſte
le temps en oiſiuete et quil ne vi
ne comme beſte qui eſt encline et
obeyſſante a ſon ventre tant ſeu
lement. ¶ La vertu et la force
de lhomme eſt en lame et ou corp

enſamble. lame doibt comman
der et le corps ſeruir et obeir. car
lame a en ſoy lymage de dieu
et la ſamblance purement. et
le corps eſt plus commun a beſte
alle foibleſſe. ¶ Et pour ce q
veult acquerre gloire il la doibt
plus conuoittier par richeſſe de
ſens et denom que par richeſſe
de force ne dauoir. La vie de lho
me eſt briefue. mais vertu raiſo

This tapestry of a hunting scene also shows the courtly pastimes of fishing and falconry. From the marguerites woven into some of the ladies' hats, it may have been a wedding present for Marguerite of Anjou.

The funeral procession of Elizabeth of York. Margaret Beaufort's husband, Lord Stanley, walks directly in front of the bier.

The preparations for a tournament, in the *Livre des Tournois* written by Marguerite of Anjou's father, René.

Margaret of Burgundy's crown may have been made for her wedding, or possibly as a votive offering. The white roses around the rim could suggest the Virgin Mary, as well as being a Yorkist emblem.

A French collection
of love songs, made
with heart-shaped
pages, c. 1475.

This illustration for a volume of poems by Charles, Duke of Orléans reflects his twenty-five-year imprisonment in the Tower of London. Behind the Tower itself is a panorama of the city.

Opposite: Elizabeth of York has inscribed her name—"Elisabeth the quene"—on the lower margin of this page from a Book of Hours passed down through her family.

ius in adiutozium meum intende:
Domine ad adiuuandum me festi
na. Glozia patri. Sicut erat. yn
Seu orator. Memento salutis.
ana mater. Glozia tibi domine. usq ad. eii.
Germinauit radix yesse. psalmus.

A conuertendo dominus captiuitate syon:
facti sumus sicut consolati. Tunc repletum e gau
dio os nostrum et lingua nostra exultacione. Tuc
dicunt inter gentes magnificauit dominus facere
cum eis. Magnificauit dominus facere nobiscum

Taken from the *Troy Book* of the mid-fifteenth century, the image of the Wheel of Fortune, with a crowned king poised at its apex, would prove all too prophetic for the years ahead.

And there is another possibility—that Buckingham knew that a rebellion could safely be raised in the Princes' names, without in the end placing an Edward V on the throne. Rightly or wrongly, he was to some contemporaries, and remains, a favorite outside candidate for villain of the story—the murderer of the Princes. Buckingham's execution, perhaps, just makes him even more convenient a scapegoat.

But just as the reasons for Buckingham's involvement in the plot against Richard may never be truly understood, so too the fate of the Princes in the Tower may have been forever lost to history. The majority of historians from Vergil and More onward have believed that Richard III murdered his nephews. It has, moreover—thanks largely to Shakespeare—become the accepted view among many who care nothing for history. But in truth, it is impossible (barring new—and probably scientific—evidence) to be certain what happened to the boys and who is to blame. And until that conclusive evidence is discovered, it is wrong to declare Richard guilty.

If Richard did not kill the boys, the question must be, why did he not simply produce them, when rumors of their murder began to spread? One conceivable answer is that he knew they had died—by someone else's hand, or indeed by natural causes—and that he would be blamed for their deaths, even if he was not in fact guilty.

Richard, of course, certainly had both motive and opportunity. So too did others—such as the adherents of the young Henry Tudor. Candidates suggested include Margaret Beaufort's ally Bishop Morton; her husband, Lord Stanley; and Margaret Beaufort herself. It seems almost, sometimes, as though assumptions about her gender have insulated Lady Margaret from suspicion, but the early-seventeenth-century antiquarian George Buck claimed to have read "in an old manuscript book" that it "was held for certain that Dr Morton and a certain countess, [conspirin]g the deaths of the sons of King Edward and some others, resolved that these treacheries should be executed by poison and by sorcery." Unfortunately—as shall soon be seen—allegations from Buck have to be treated with caution.

Yet despite the unreliability of the historical record, Margaret Beaufort cannot be wholly discounted as a suspect. Henry Tudor and his family, after all, stood to gain tremendously from the deaths of the Princes. And although Henry himself was out of the country around the time the Princes were last sighted, it is hard to ignore the fact that he had a highly able and totally committed representative in England, in the person of his mother. And indeed, the Tudor party had even more motive than the principal suspect in the case. For Richard to rule, it was technically necessary only that the boys should be declared illegitimate, and this he had arranged soon after his brother's death (albeit this hadn't proved the end of the story). If, by contrast, Henry was to bolster his own genealogically weak claim with that of Elizabeth of York, he would have needed them actually to be dead. No other solution would have sufficed; if the whole family was declared illegitimate, then Elizabeth had no claim. And if they were legitimate, then her brothers' claim would take precedence over hers for as long as they lived.

What is more, while the assumption of Richard's guilt depends on a posthumous reputation for savagery, it was the first two Tudor monarchs who would, one by one, eliminate all the rival Yorkist line with chilling efficiency. Of course, if we are to go by track record, then practically any ruler of the era could have done it. (Edward IV had had his own brother Clarence executed and had probably had both Henry VI and Henry's son murdered.) Nor does savagery have to be a prerequisite for the crime, per se. The fact that the Princes were underage makes all the difference in modern minds, but their youth may not have been such a charged issue in the fifteenth century. Henry VII would proclaim, with curious vagueness, that Richard was guilty of the shedding of infants' blood—but in fact childhood ended early in the medieval era, and if Edward V did die soon after his uncle's accession, then he was nonetheless not much younger than Margaret Beaufort at the time of her pregnancy.

Public opinion then, as now, was not indifferent to the boys' fate. But death was only one possible reason for the Princes' disappearance. The Silesian visitor Nicolaus von Popplau reported hearing the rumors in 1484 but added, "Many people say—and I agree with them—that they are still alive and kept in a very dark cellar." Even Vergil reported rumors they had been sent to "some secret land." It is worth noting that the usually reliable Crowland does not say Richard killed the boys, but mentions only the rumor.

Rumors, of course, are no substitute for hard evidence, which remains in short supply. Many over the centuries have taken as conclusive the dubious confession to the murder supposedly made in 1502 by one Sir James Tyrell, in 1483 an officer in Richard's household. Whatever its veracity, Tyrell's testimony could not have been known to the women directly affected by the affair in 1483. If this leaves modern viewers in a state of uncertainty, then the consolation must be that we are probably only in the same state as these women. The Princes' mother and sisters may not have known what to believe. They may have had to persuade themselves to believe whatever would prove necessary for them to be able to make their way through the difficult times ahead.

"LOOK TO YOUR WIFE"

Stanley, look to your wife. If she convey
Letters to Richmond, you shall answer it.

THE TRAGEDY OF RICHARD THE THIRD, 4.2

W hen, following the rebellion of October 1483, Richard III called a Parliament, Henry Tudor was inevitably among those attainted. He was, however, beyond reach of actual punishment, safe back in Brittany. His connections in England—Henry's mother, Margaret Beaufort, and Margaret's husband, Stanley—were in a less comfortable position. Margaret may have been going behind her husband's back, but it is also possible that he approved of her actions as a sort of insurance policy—part of his lifelong strategy of having a foot in both camps.

Indeed, there is some evidence that Stanley secretly but actively continued to support Margaret's ongoing efforts to win Henry the crown. Stanley escaped censure—just too powerful (and perhaps too close to being genuinely uncommitted) for punishment to be the best option, while any other remained. Margaret herself, however, was attainted at the end of 1483: "Forasmuch as Margaret Countess of

Richmond, Mother to the king's great Rebel and Traitor, Henry Earl of Richmond, hath of late conspired, 'confedered,' and committed high Treason against our sovereign lord the king Richard the Third, in diverse and sundry wises," the official charges declared. But in the end (as so often with women), the full lethal penalties were not enacted, not even the total alienation of Margaret's goods.

Her property was indeed to be taken away from her, but it would be given over to her husband for the term of his life. Richard (like Edward before him) hesitated altogether to alienate such a powerful and chancy magnate as Stanley. Margaret had chosen her latest husband well. She was, however, to be held in Lord Stanley's charge, so strictly that she was to be deprived of "any servant or company," effectively jailed under her husband's jurisdiction—the instructions making it clear that this was less a punitive measure than a step intended to disable her from further action. According to Vergil, Stanley was ordered to "remove from his wife all her servants, and keep her so straight with himself that she should not be able from thenceforth to send any messages neither to her son, nor friends, nor practise anything at all against the king." Margaret's immediate future lay in the North, probably in Stanley's residences of Lathom and Knowsley.

Henry Parker, a member of Margaret's household toward the end of her life, wrote that "neither prosperity made her proud, nor adversity overthrew her constant mind, for albeit that in king Richard's days, she was often in jeopardy of her life, yet she bare patiently all trouble in such wise, that it is wonder to think it." That is later hagiography: at the time, even she must have been in a tumult of regret and fear. But while she must in the short term have been utterly cast down by the failure of her rebellion, the very fact of an uprising in her son's name must have underlined the fact of how close he now was to the throne.

In Brittany on Christmas Day, in Rennes Cathedral, Henry Tudor made a public declaration of his intention to marry Princess Elizabeth—aiming to catch the disaffected members of the now-divided Yorkist party—and his supporters swore homage to him as if he were already king. Elizabeth of York, however, was still with her mother, increasingly isolated in sanctuary (where Buckingham's widow,

Elizabeth Woodville's sister, now joined the family of women). The Yorkist heiress was now nearing her eighteenth birthday.

While Henry Tudor was moving ahead with his challenge, Richard III began—or, rather, renewed—an offensive of his own. On January 23, 1484, Richard's Parliament put out the bill of *Titulus Regius*, declaring that "the said pretended marriage betwixt the above named King Edward and Elizabeth Grey, was made of great presumption, without the knowing and assent of the Lords of this Land." More to the point, it declared also that at the time of Edward IV's marriage to Elizabeth Woodville, "and before and long time after, the said King Edward was and stood troth plighted to one Dame Eleanor Butler," and that thus Edward and Elizabeth "lived together sinfully and damnably in adultery." It was the old line about Edward IV's marriage to Elizabeth Woodville being invalid, an argument aimed at illegitimating all the descendants from the marriage— including, now, Elizabeth of York.

But Richard took his standard attack against his brother's family a step further. The bill declared also that the marriage had been made "by Sorcery and Witchcraft, committed by the said Elizabeth, and her Mother Jacquetta, Duchess of Bedford." Jacquetta of course was dead, and her accusers too, so the sorcery allegation was credited "as the common opinion of the people and the publique voice and fame is through all this land." Any allegations of the living Cecily's adultery were not repeated—unless something is implied in Richard's having himself described as "the undoubted son" of York.

If Elizabeth Woodville's young sons were truly dead by now, then the real point of *Titulus Regius* must have been the political disabling of her daughter Elizabeth of York. Richard had never reached the point of being able to feel secure in his rule. In February, says Crowland, "nearly all the lords of the realm, both spiritual and temporal, together with the higher knights and esquires of the king's household . . . met together at the special command of the king, in certain lower rooms, near the passage which leads to the queen's apartments; and here, each subscribed his name to a kind of new oath . . . of adherence to Edward, the king's only son, as their supreme lord, in case anything should happen to his father."

Since the turn of the year, the pressure on Elizabeth Woodville had been mounting. Now she was officially no longer recognized as a former queen, she was no longer entitled to the dowager's rights, and she would be without income if she and her daughters stayed in sanctuary. Horrible as it must have been for her to contemplate, she was eventually going to have to make some sort of deal with her brother-in-law.

Richard now ratcheted up the pressure even more. On March 1, in the presence of lords spiritual and temporal and the mayor and aldermen of the City, Richard put his hand on holy relics of the Evangelists and swore that "if the daughters of dame Elizabeth Grey, late calling herself Queen of England, that is to wit Elizabeth, Cecily, Anne, Katherine and Bridget, will come unto me out of the Sanctuary of Westminster, and be guided, ruled and demeaned after, then I shall see that they be in surety of their lives, and also not suffer any manner hurt by any manner person."

They would be safe from "ravishment or defiling contrary their wills," nor would any of them be incarcerated "within the Tower of London or other prison." The mention of the Tower may imply that, as Richard was well aware, Elizabeth was still suspicious of him. Instead, Richard said, he would put the girls "in honest places of good name and fame" and make sure they were provided with "all things requisite and necessary for their exhibition and findings as my kinswomen." He would, moreover, arrange for them marriages "to gentlemen born." It was not much of a deal for the former princesses, but expectations had sunk, and a union with a simple gentleman was better than no marriage at all.

The declaration was first about the daughters, not Elizabeth Woodville herself. But Richard's promises went one step further. He would pay Elizabeth's own maintenance for the term of her natural life, "at four terms of the year, that is to wit at Pasche [Easter], Midsummer, Michaelmas, and Christmas . . . the sum of seven hundred marks of lawful money of England."

Elizabeth relented. Vergil wrote of how Richard sent messengers to her in sanctuary, "promising mountains." The messengers were tactless enough to "wound the queen's mind" by "reducing to memory the slaughter of her sons"—by, presumably, suggesting that what was done was done and she should put the fate of her boys behind her. Horrified by this, Elizabeth's grief "seemed scarce able to be comforted." But the messengers persisted, trying so many different appeals, and making so many promises, that Elizabeth began to be mollified—for (as Vergil, with the misogyny of the age, could not resist glossing) "so mutable is that sex." Finally, Elizabeth promised that she would "yield herself unto the king."

Sometime that month, Elizabeth's daughters left sanctuary. No one knows for sure where they went, or in what company. The younger ones at least may have been placed elsewhere in the country for some time—may even have been among the royal children (unnamed) at Sheriff Hutton in Yorkshire about whose maintenance instructions were given in July. Emotionally speaking, it would be better, surely, if they did all go to the country for a while, rather than face those at court who had known them in their glory. But it is also possible that the girls went straight to court, and it is this possibility—the idea of their blithely enjoying the gaieties provided by the man who may have killed their brothers—that has done much to damage the reputation of the women of Edward IV's family.

If Elizabeth Woodville believed her sons dead at Richard's hand, she may nonetheless have felt she had no other option but to come out of sanctuary and come to some sort of terms with him. Her duty to her daughters and their future demanded it. Elizabeth may have been afraid that Richard, willing to break so many other mores, would not respect the laws of sanctuary; she must also have known that she had no means of financial support there and that her clerical hosts must have been growing desperate for her to leave. She may have been enough of a pragmatist to accept that her boys were gone and her responsibility now was to make the best deal for her girls (though if she believed Richard had killed her sons, then surely she would have felt as if she were sending her daughters into the lion's den). Or she may have been such a venal woman that she couldn't resist the chance of better living conditions, even if the donor was her sons' murderer.

But there are several other very intriguing possible explanations for Elizabeth Woodville's decision. It seems possible (given her earlier plots and her imminent conversion to Henry's cause) that Elizabeth Woodville's compliance was only superficial and that she was secretly working against Richard. There is yet another possibility, however: that when Elizabeth Woodville herself left sanctuary in 1484, possibly sometime after her daughters, she had reason to know that Richard was *not* guilty of her sons' deaths.

It is this latter interpretation that is perhaps the most provocative and is—in light of at least one theory in particular—perfectly compatible with the fact that Elizabeth Woodville simply disappears from the historical record for the rest of Richard's reign. It has been suggested that either or both "Princes" left the Tower alive and that when Elizabeth Woodville emerged from sanctuary, it was because she had been promised her sons, or at least the younger of them, would be quietly allowed to join her. The elder boy has been said to have been ill in the summer of 1483, and it is possible he had died from natural causes. (It is worth noting that none of the later pretenders to Henry VII's throne—and there would be several—claimed to be the elder prince, suggesting he, unlike his brother, was known by then to be dead.) The boys were, in any case, no longer "Princes"; their uncle had seen to it that in official terms at least, they were merely royal bastards, of whom there were several around already. But any such theory, of course, still leaves the boys' true fate a mystery.

The real mystery about the Princes in the Tower, ultimately, concerns the behavior of the women in the case. That the Princes' mother and sisters might have, within months of the boys' deaths, made friends with their murderer has been put down to fear, in a brutal age, and to pragmatism, in a harsh one. But one wonders if human nature has really changed that much. Of course, it can be assumed that if Richard gave assurances of his innocence, the women were eager to be convinced; they had, after all, few other options than compliance. But if Elizabeth Woodville believed her boys were not murdered—or not murdered by Richard—it would explain everything even more simply.

As the dead king's wife and daughters quietly left sanctuary, the kingdom seemed for a brief moment—a few weeks—to settle down. Richard in many ways was proving himself an admirable ruler; his Parliament had passed a notable amount of socially beneficial legislation, making, for example, the legal system more accessible to the poor. But once again, as so often, unforeseen events were to change the situation completely, and again it was the fate of a son that determined that of a dynasty.

On April 9, the new Prince of Wales, young Edward of Middleham, the only child of Richard and Anne, died after what Crowland calls "an illness of but short duration." It took some days for the news to travel from Middleham to the court, then at Nottingham, but then, says Crowland, "you might have seen his father and mother in a state almost bordering on madness, by reason of their sudden grief." Anne's state must have been truly pitiable. Looking at the extremely limited records as to Anne's short life as queen, it is striking just how isolated she seems. The various shenanigans over her parents' estates had left her alienated from the interests of those powerful relations who survived, while those northerners who might once have been regarded as her family's supporters now gave their allegiance to her husband, who was indeed granting away some of her family lands to bolster his network of support.

The death of Richard and Anne's son may also have struck a fatal blow to their relationship, isolating the queen even further. Vergil seems to suggest it was now that Richard began to complain of Anne. Any other problems apart, the couple must both have been aware—as must their subjects—that although Anne had given him an heir, that heir was gone and there was no spare.

Richard, as the Crowland chronicler points out, had at least the concerns of the kingdom to distract him. Personal grief apart, the death of Richard's only heir had made the political situation more dangerous for the relatively new king. The succession was again in doubt. There was of course Warwick, Clarence's son, who had been brought to London and, for a time at least, placed in Anne's charge. Clarence's attainder theoretically removed all rights of inheritance from his son; attainders, however, could be reversed or ignored. But if that was done, then as the son of Richard's elder brother, Warwick's claim to the throne would be stronger than Richard's own.

Warwick, however, passed into manhood, apparently placidly, in a kind of genteel captivity; Vergil later spoke of his simplicity, and there is a received impression, so widespread it may suggest a grain of truth, that there was something wrong with Clarence's son. It cannot have been a flamboyant, a readily visible, disability—but while his name served for pretenders, no one ever seems to have considered placing Warwick himself on the throne. It has even been suggested that Richard, after the death of his own son, planned eventually to rehabilitate the Princes as his heirs. Warwick apart, another good candidate for heir apparent was his sister's son John, the Earl of Lincoln, a grown man able enough for Richard to entrust him with the task of controlling the North. But Henry Tudor was of course another notable figure in the royal lineup, and he certainly gained in importance by Anne's son's death. And so, naturally, did Elizabeth of York.

In the summer of 1484, Richard was in the North, once Anne's own family turf; in addition to the usual business of kingship, there was other trouble there. A letter Richard wrote to his mother, Cecily, in the summer sounds almost as though he felt the need of family support. "Madam I recommend me to you as heartily as is to me possible, Beseeching you in my most humble and effectuous wise of your daily blessing to my Singular comfort & defence in my need. And madam I heartily beseech you that I may often hear from you to my Comfort."

Things were going sour for Richard. This was a waiting time. The rebellion of the past autumn and its suppression had in some ways lanced a boil, forcing those who secretly disapproved of Richard's rule to reveal their true colors, but it had also made it clear Henry Tudor was a significant threat (especially if he could be coupled with Elizabeth of York) and revealed Margaret Beaufort to be a continuing source of danger. Richard, so Vergil says, "yet more doubting than trusting in his own cause," was so "vexed, wrested, and tormented in mind" with fear of Henry's threat that he had "a miserable life." That is why he decided to "pull up by the roots" the source of his trouble and sent messages to the court of Brittany, where Henry Tudor was still living, something between a guest and a prisoner.

At first, Richard's tactic seemed successful. Duke Francis was sick with what seems to have been some kind of mental trouble. This left negotiations in the hands of his treasurer, who was less honorable and more amenable. By June Richard had been able to announce a treaty of cooperation with Brittany. Margaret must have feared that Henry's being handed back to England would be a side effect of the deal. In September her fears were realized: Henry would be handed over in return for England's backing in Brittany's quarrels.

But that same month, the deal was also thwarted. Vergil describes how John Morton in his Flanders exile, whose friends in England had passed him the news, sent word to Henry "by Christopher Urswycke, who was come to him out of England about the same time." Not only was Morton a longtime associate of Margaret Beaufort, but Christopher too had been one of her household: the same young priest and protégé of Caerleon whom Margaret had recently taken into her home. Henry and his friends sent an urgent message to France to confirm they would be welcome there, and Vergil tells a dramatic tale of a dashing escape and a chivalrous finale when Duke Francis, recovering his health and sanity, paid the expenses for Henry's fellow exiles, under Edward Woodville, to join the Tudor pretender in France.

The move to France gave fresh impetus to any attempt to promote Henry's claim. France was bound to seize on him as a pawn both in their ongoing negotiations with Richard and in their own power struggles—the struggles that had followed the death of King Louis at the end of summer 1483 and the accession of the thirteen-year-old Charles VIII to the throne. The tussle for control of the young king resulted in victory for Charles's elder sister Anne of Beaujeu. Ironically, yet another woman (and a Frenchwoman at that) would play a significant part in English political affairs. From the time Charles was informed, on October 11, that Henry had crossed his border, the Tudor claimant was treated with a sympathy that gave him every hope the French would fund another invasion attempt.

It was probably November 1484 when Henry began sending letters to England, trying to garner support, in a style that suggested he was already king. "Being given to understand your good devoir and entreaty to advance me to the furtherance of my rightful claim, due and lineal inheritance of that crown, and for the just depriving of that homicide and unnatural tyrant, which now unjustly bears dominion over you." The letters were signed "H. R."—Henry Rex—in a gesture that must have maddened Richard when he heard of it. He would have been even more concerned to hear Henry had instructed Morton to seek the papal dispensation necessary for him to marry Elizabeth of York.

In retaliation, on December 7 Richard's proclamation against Henry Tudor poured scorn on Henry's pretensions to a royal estate "whereunto he hath no manner interest, right, or colour" and warned of "the most cruel murders, slaughters, robberies and disinheritances that were ever seen in any Christian Realm." It must have felt like an insult also to Margaret Beaufort in isolation. Richard was trying to chip away at her alliances and accessories. Her useful tool Reginald Bray had been given a pardon at the beginning of the year; now pardons were extended also to Morton and, next spring, to Elizabeth Woodville's brother Richard.

But Richard's enemy was also strengthening his position in England. Henry's band in exile had for some time now included a number of Stanley affiliates. And when, toward the end of 1484, Henry's party was joined by the dedicated Lancastrian Earl of Oxford, who for some years had been a high-profile (and, as he would soon demonstrate, militarily experienced) prisoner of the Yorkist regime, the French chronicler Molinet claimed that it was Lord Stanley's advice that had persuaded his custodian to let the earl escape. Henry Tudor's stepfather, it seems, was beginning to abandon—however secretively—his long-standing policy of neutrality.

There must have been a perverse, edgy, reassurance for the Lancastrians in the very importance Richard had come to give the Tudor threat. The kingdom still held quiet under Richard's rule, but it would have been increasingly clear that something had to break, some way.

"ANNE MY WIFE"

The sons of Edward sleep in Abraham's bosom,
And Anne my wife hath bid this world good night.

THE TRAGEDY OF RICHARD THE THIRD, 4.3

On January 6, 1485, the English court celebrated the festival of the Epiphany with special splendor. There would have been the seasonal rituals—the licensed revelry of the fools and the edgier clowning of whichever young courtier had been appointed Lord of Misrule for the day and allowed to give his own fantastical orders as to the conduct of the party. The oak log burned, to draw heat back to the earth, and the toasting of the fruit trees in a wassail cup—that they might bring forth good crop.

Epiphany—the celebration of the revelation of Christ to the Magi, or wise men, and the end of the Christmas season—was an important event in the medieval calendar, and the king made a point of appearing "with his crown." But it is easy to guess that Richard was not naturally lively that day. Crowland wrote that "while [Richard] was keeping this festival with remarkable splendour in the great hall . . . news was brought to him on that very day, from his spies beyond sea, that, notwithstanding the potency and splendour of his royal state, his adversaries would, without question, invade the kingdom during the following summer."

This must have been everything the king had feared, yet—on the outside, at least—Richard didn't seem perturbed. Richard's reaction to having definite news—after months of suspicions—was to declare that "there was nothing that could befall him more desirable, in as much as he imagined that it would put an end to all his doubts and troubles." But among the other courtiers, the news must have sent a ripple of unease throughout the party.

Perhaps the women of the royal household were trying to keep things merry. Not that Richard's queen, Anne Neville, could have found it any easier than he. Anne had been in poor health for months, and in the hotbed of rumor that was a palace, she could hardly fail to have known that courtiers and ambassador alike were speculating on what would happen if (as looked increasingly likely) she were to die. She had the company of her elder nieces: Elizabeth of York and at least her older sisters had spent the festive season at court. Buck says that Anne Neville "entertained also the young ladies with all her courtesies and gracious caresses, and especially the Lady Elizabeth, whom she used with so much famil[iarity] and kindness as if she had been her own sister." They were, after all, hardly a decade apart in age. "But the queen had small joy and little pleasure in the festi[val and] pompous time, because she was sick and was much in languor and [sorrow] for the death of the prince, her dear and only son, and the which grieved her sorely."

Indeed, the company of Elizabeth must have been a very mixed pleasure for Anne. At the festivities (where, as the author of the Crowland chronicles disapprovingly relates, "far too much attention was given to dancing and gaiety"), there were "vain exchanges of clothing" between Anne and Elizabeth, "being of similar colour and shape; a thing that caused the people to murmur and the nobles and prelates greatly to wonder thereat." Crowland seems to suggest some point was being made by those exchanges of garments—clothing was an important signifier of rank. Despite that official declaration of bastardy, many still regarded Edward IV's children as the natural inheritors of the country. And for Anne Neville, the competition from Elizabeth of York would have hit even closer to home.

It was already being whispered that if anything were to happen to Anne, then a marriage between Richard and Elizabeth would square the circle of inheritance nicely. To be sure, she was his niece, but was there anything a papal dispensation could not legitimize? Anne and Richard's marriage had also needed a papal dispensation, which, modern research suggests, might not have arrived when they went through their wedding ceremony. That might provide grounds for an annulment, and Richard may have already been considering this as an option. Rumors were rife that "the king was bent, either on the anticipated death of the queen taking place, or else, by means of a divorce, for which he supposed he had quite sufficient grounds, on contracting a marriage with the said Elizabeth." Vergil described it as a plan "the most wicked to be spoken of, and the foulest to be committed that ever was heard of."

At that Epiphany party, no one surely spoke openly of the possibility of such a relation between Richard and his niece. But the rumors were there already, and the reasons for the union would have been clear. Such a marriage would be a severe blow to Henry Tudor. And Richard might have had other incentives, as Anne must miserably have realized. Elizabeth was a buxom eighteen-year-old. Later in her life, the Portuguese ambassador noticed her "large breasts"; a Venetian one called her "very handsome."

This quiet competition from her friend and niece seems to have pushed Anne Neville over the brink. Soon after the Christmas festivities, Crowland wrote, "the queen fell extremely sick, and her illness was supposed to have increased still more and more, because the king entirely shunned her bed, declaring that it was by the advice of his physicians that he did so. Why enlarge?" the chronicler asks, maddeningly. But perhaps he trusted readers to understand that—while Anne's illness may simply have been infectious—Richard may have had other reasons for leaving her alone.

The feelings of Elizabeth herself—apart, that is, from the normal eighteen-year-old's pleasure in a party—are even harder to discern. But a few weeks ahead—perhaps in mid-February—there would come an extraordinary clue. It was recorded by Buck, who in 1619, in his *History of King Richard the Third*, set down a précis of a letter in which, he said, Elizabeth of York expressed her own passionate longing to marry her uncle. Elizabeth, said Buck, was toward the end of February writing to John Howard, Duke of Norfolk, an influential magnate and once her father's friend:

> First she thanked him for his many courtesies and friendly offices, and then she prayed him as before to be a mediator for her in the cause of the marriage to the king, who, as she writes, was her only joy and maker in this world, and that she was his in heart and in thoughts, in body, and in all. And then she intimated that the better half of February was past, and that she feared the queen would never die. And all these be her own words, written with her own hand, and this is the sum of her letter, whereof I have seen the autograph or original draft under her own hand.

Well! If real, Elizabeth of York's letter would not only be surprising but also damning in several different ways, including the callousness of the fear that Anne would never die and the possible sexual implications of the assurance that "she was his . . . in body, and in all." There have long been doubts, however, over Buck's rendition of the letter. Some suggest that Buck could simply (especially when blinded by his prejudices) have misinterpreted a letter that he did indeed see or that it was not written by Elizabeth—or not written at this juncture and in relation to this match. Indeed, as shall be seen, there was another, far less controversial, marriage proposed for Elizabeth very soon after this time, and the words could be made to fit. At the most extreme, it has even been suggested that Buck invented the letter in its entirety.

But it does not seem wholly impossible that Elizabeth of York should have wanted to marry Richard. The question of consanguinity could be left to a higher, papal, authority; there was enough uncertainty in the air for her to have been able to convince herself that he was not responsible for her brothers' deaths. Power is an aphrodisiac, and this was the destiny for which she had been reared—not to mention a chance to come back from the wilderness. Possible further evidence that Elizabeth of York had an affection for Richard can be found in the inscription she wrote on a copy of Boethius's *Consolations of Philosophy*, most likely at this time: "*Loyalte mellye*" (Loyalty binds me). It was Richard's favorite motto. She also wrote, on a copy of the French prose *Tristan,* "*sans re[mo]vyr*" (without changing) above her signature, "elyzabeth."* She wrote on the page with the mark that showed it was Richard's property—but is that enough to show the unchanging loyalty she was expressing was loyalty to Richard? Not really.

And of course Polydore Vergil, the Tudor historian, sees it differently. In his telling, Elizabeth of York is an unhappy pawn—a martyr, even—in Richard's twisted game. "Richard had kept [Elizabeth] unharmed with a view to marriage," Vergil writes. "To such a marriage the girl had a singular aversion. Weighed down for this reason by her great grief she would repeatedly exclaim, saying, 'I will not thus be married, but, unhappy creature that I am, will rather suffer all the torments which St. Catherine is said to have endured for the love of Christ than be united with a man who is the enemy of my family.'"

But Vergil would say that. He was writing a quarter of a century later, when Richard had become the antagonist in the creation story of the Tudor dynasty. And "the enemy of my family" might have applied to Henry—a representative of the Lancastrian family that had so long opposed the house of York—as easily as to Richard; Richard also kept Elizabeth's sisters "unharmed," even those who were nearing maturity. What is more, if Richard wished to keep Elizabeth of York away from Henry Tudor, all he had to do was marry her to somebody else—not necessarily to himself.

Whatever the truth about Richard's plans, there were certainly rumors of the possible marriage, if not necessarily of Elizabeth's complicity. Henry across the Channel heard them and feared loss of Yorkist support if the two York factions could thus be reunited. Vergil wrote that the stories "pinched Henry by the very stomach," so much so that he began to seek an alternative match—a daughter of William Herbert, Earl of Pembroke, the loyally Yorkist supporter of Edward IV who had cared for Henry when he was a child. But the message he sent suggesting the match, says Vergil, never reached its destination, and soon he must have heard that a marriage between

---

*In Malory, Tristan is an Arthurian knight fatally in love with a lady, whose mother's brother he has unfortunately killed.

Richard and his niece was no longer a possibility—unless, that is, the rumors of the marriage—rumors so discreditable to Richard—were being spread by Henry Tudor's own party, which is another possibility impossible to discount.

Whatever the sources of the rumors, they seem to have had one immediate effect: Anne almost certainly heard them. Over the next few weeks, Anne's condition worsened, and the suggestion is that Richard hoped it would do so—and perhaps even helped the process along. Richard, said Hall, "complained to divers noble men of the realm, of the unfortunate sterility and barreness of his wife"; he was especially vocal in his complaints to the Archbishop of York, upon whom he relied to spread the word to Anne, "trusting the sequel hereof to take his effect, that she hearing this grudge of her husband, and taking therefore an inward thought, would not long live in this world." Vergil even has a story that Anne, hearing rumors of her own death, went to her husband "very pensive and sad, and with many tears demanded of him what cause there was why he should determine her death. Hereunto the king, lest that he might seem hard hearted if he should show unto his wife no sign of love, kissing her, made answer lovingly, and comforting her, bade her be of good cheer."

The reassurance did Anne little good. On March 16, 1485, during a great eclipse of the sun, she died. Since her illness was lingering—and possibly, if the doctors really warned Richard to avoid her, infectious—the best modern guess is tuberculosis. But then and now, there would be other rumors, and her death would be linked to that of the princes, whether in fact or in the art of black public relations (as current in the fifteenth century as in the twenty-first). Vergil wrote that she died "whether she was despatched by sorrowfulness or poison," Rous that "Lady Anne, [Richard's] queen, he poisoned." Commynes wrote that "some say he had her killed," and Hall: "Some think she went her own pace to the grave, while others suspect a grain was given her to quicken her in her journey to her long home."

Anne was buried on the ninth day after her death—March 25, the Feast of the Annunciation. She was interred, says Crowland, "at Westminster, with no less honours than befitted the interment of a queen." Pro-Ricardian stories of his weeping copious tears at her funeral prove to have no original source, but the signs of Richard's lack of grief are deceptive, too. The fact that there is no tomb for Anne at Westminster conveys, now, an impression of lack of care or lack of ceremony, but it is probably erroneous, for Richard's own reign would end before he had time to commission one.

It is difficult not to feel some relief at the end of Anne Neville's long suffering. The Doge of Venice, some six weeks later, after the news had reached him, assured Richard that "your consort led so religious and catholic a life and was so adorned with goodness, prudence, and excellent morality, as to leave a name immortal." But Anne's life seems to have been a hard one, even by the harsh standards of the fifteenth century.

Richard seems by now to have abandoned any plans he might have harbored for himself and his niece. On March 29, only four days after Anne's death, an emissary, Sir Edward Brampton, was sent to Portugal, to negotiate a marriage between Richard and the Portuguese king's sister, the Infanta Joana. The infanta was not only determinedly religious and averse to marriage, but also thirty-three and old for childbearing by the standards of the day. It is likely, therefore, that her appeal was her descent from John of Gaunt—a descent that made her the senior representative of the legitimate Lancastrian line, and in some ways, therefore, a better candidate than Henry Tudor.

By marrying the foremost Lancastrian then living, Richard was setting himself up to reunify the splintered Plantagenet family, thereby shoring up the foundation of his regime in a way that even his Yorkist opponents would find hard to undo. The Portuguese council urged Joana that it was her duty to agree "for the concord in the same kingdom of England that will follow from her marriage and union with the king's party, greatly serving God and bringing honour to herself by uniting as one the party of Lancaster, and York"—and urging, moreover, the danger that if she refused, Richard might look instead to the next most senior marriageable representative of the Lancastrian line, the Spanish Infanta Isabel, another great-great-granddaughter of John of Gaunt.

The idea must have maddened Margaret Beaufort if she heard of it, for such a marriage would neatly cut out her (and her son's) Lancastrian claim. Both Joana and Isabel were descended from John of Gaunt's earlier, uncontroversial, marriages to foreign princesses, while the Beaufort line came from his liaison with Katherine Swynford, only later regularized by marriage. To make matters worse, Richard's emissary to Portugal, Sir Edward, was to negotiate a double marriage—an alliance also between a daughter of Edward IV (presumably Elizabeth) and the king's cousin the Duke of Beja. This, it is suggested, may have been the marriage Elizabeth herself was discussing in the Buck letter. (The speed with which the embassy set out shows that in a pragmatic age, the matter must surely have been under discussion before Anne's death.) Since the marriage proposed for Elizabeth was dependent on the one proposed for Richard, this would explain if not excuse any fear that Queen Anne would never die.

The prospect of a royal foreign marriage for Elizabeth of York may (like the pardons granted to various Woodvilles) have been part of the general sweetening that, eventually, had persuaded Elizabeth Woodville to write, summoning her son Dorset home. Dorset that spring tried to escape from the exiled Tudor "court" and was making for Flanders and the coast when Henry's representatives (with French connivance) caught up with him and persuaded him to return. Perhaps Elizabeth Woodville had been rattled by Henry's declaring himself king before he had married her daughter; on the other hand, of course, she may have been coerced by Richard. Shakespeare has Elizabeth, asked by Richard how he should woo her daughter, sarcastically advising him to send her a token "by the man that slew her brothers." In a long recitation, she counters each promise he makes for the future with some wrong from the past. But, in the course of some 150 lines, she also changes her mind and agrees to put his proposal to her daughter—"Relenting fool, and shallow, changing woman!" as Richard apostrophizes her. Historians have not always felt able to disagree, with those writing near Elizabeth's own day making much play on women's mutability.

But in deciding to marry his niece off abroad rather than marry her himself, Richard may have been succumbing to popular pressure. Indeed, whoever else may have been complicit in his reputed plan to wed Elizabeth of York, it was Richard who attracted the most opprobrium for it. The king's closest advisers felt forced to warn him of the unpopularity of such a union. Crowland writes that "by these persons the king was told to his face that if he did not abandon his intended purpose, and that, too, before the mayor and commons of the City of London . . . all the people of the north, in whom he placed the greatest reliance, would rise in rebellion against him." The northerners might even, so the advisers said, be tempted to blame him for the death of Anne—one of their own—"through whom he had first gained his present high position."

The union between Richard and Elizabeth was opposed on other grounds, as well. Certain of Richard's advisers, Crowland added, also wheeled in a dozen or so doctors of divinity "who asserted that the Pope could grant no dispensation in the case of such a degree of consanguinity." (Other such marriages had been known, abroad, but the legality of thus defying or evading Leviticus is still discussed today.)

Richard's advisers may even have been afraid that the girl whom later commentators have always taken to be a placid and gentle woman would have sought retribution for the suffering that Richard had caused her family, or so Crowland suspected. "It was supposed by many, that these men, together with others like them, threw so many impediments in the way, for fear lest, if the said Elizabeth should attain the rank of queen, it might at some time be in her power to avenge upon them the death of her uncle, Earl Anthony, and her brother Richard [her half brother Richard Grey]."

The rumors of Richard's plans appear to have been so explosive that it took more than his Portuguese marriage proposal to defuse them. Only two weeks after Anne's death, just before Easter and days after the royal emissary had left for Portugal, in the great hall of the Hospital of St. John, Richard was forced to take the extraordinary step of making a public repudiation of any desire to wed his niece. He spoke, says Crowland, "in a loud and distinct voice; more, however, as many supposed, to suit the wishes of those who advised him to that effect, than in conformity with his own." The records of the Mercers' Company describe how, in the presence of many of his lords, and of the City hierarchy, Richard "said it never came into his thought or mind to marry in such manner wise nor [was he] willing or glad of the death of his queen but as sorry and in heart as heavy as man might be."

He could not altogether quell the whispers. The *Great Chronicle* recorded "much whispering among the people that the king had put the children of King Edward to death, and also that he had poisoned the Queen his wife, and intended with a license purchased [a dispensation] to have married the elder daughter of King Edward. Which rumours and sayings with other things before done caused him to fall in great hatred of his subjects."

The stage, as Margaret Beaufort must have known, was set for her son, Henry.

19

"IN BOSWORTH FIELD"

Here pitch our tent, even here in Bosworth field.

THE TRAGEDY OF RICHARD THE THIRD, 5.1

W hile Richard's regime was struggling in England, Henry Tudor's cabal in France was looking more robust than ever. Henry had now every hope of support from the teenage Charles VIII—or at least from his sister and regent, Anne of Beaujeu. And as the spring of 1485 warmed up, Margaret Beaufort's servant Reginald Bray—whose recent pardon by Richard seems not to have swayed him—was collecting money to fund mercenaries and sending messages across the Channel.

Richard's unpopularity had given a fresh chance to Margaret's son. Even her cautious husband, Stanley, the ultimate political weathercock, was beginning to rate her son's chances higher. If this particular coup was due to Margaret's influence, it would prove to be the most important thing she could possibly have done to aid Henry. For all she was in theory debarred from any political activity, immured on Stanley's estates, Margaret may have been more active than ever during this time.

Through the spring, Richard continued to hear rumors of an impending rebellion—perhaps heard too that in France Henry Tudor was being described as a younger son of Henry VI. The descriptions were of course erroneous (and alienating to the Yorkist Woodvilles, the enemies of the previous Henry and the clan whose support this new Henry so badly needed). But they did suggest the French were seriously promoting him as a royal heir.

After the scandal of the spring, Elizabeth of York may have been sent straight to the northern castle of Sheriff Hutton, already the residence of several other royal children—but one source has her in Lord Stanley's London house for a few weeks at least, where her furious resentment against her uncle swung her to the opposite political side. The *Ballad of Lady Bessy,* the long early-sixteenth-century verse narrative chronicling the events of these crucial months, survives in different versions. On one thing, however, the versions agree: Elizabeth of York played an extraordinarily active role in this story.

The *Ballad* describes how as the spring began to ripen, Elizabeth of York waylaid Lord Stanley in the palace corridors and asked him to send a message to his stepson, Henry Tudor, promising she would marry him and thus greatly strengthen his cause. "For an [if] he were King, I should be Queen; / I do him love, and never him see."

She tears her hair in her fury when Stanley refuses to help her, sinking into a swoon, lamenting that she would never be queen. But her determination, in this account, has also a more practical aspect: the ballad has her raising money, rallying supporters, and detailing the Stanley military strength with considerable precision. "Lady Bessy" volunteers to write letters to Stanley's adherents, which she boasts she can do as well as the scrivener who taught her. Presented as a "lady bright," as spirited and beautiful as she is able, Bessy successfully brokers a contact with Henry, and he responds with his own verse:

> Commend me to Bessy, that Countess cheer [or, clere],—
> and yet I did never her see,—
> I trust in god she shall be my Queen,
> For her I will travel the sea.

Did Elizabeth in truth hate Richard—and if she did, was it for trying to seduce her, or for repudiating her? It depends on what we think her feelings for her uncle were, or had been. But it is certain she must have awaited events with more than uncommon tension: once more, in a way, she had been cheated out of a royal match, and maybe she now feared losing another, if she had heard Henry was pursuing a Herbert heiress—or, as Francis Bacon would suggest, that he contemplated marriage to the heiress of Brittany.

After having had to make that embarrassing declaration of his marital intentions, Richard himself had left London first for Windsor and then, on May 17, to spend some three days at the home of his mother, Cecily Neville, in Berkhampsted. Possibly he wished to update her on his European marriage plans—or, of course, to explain the other, less flattering, marriage stories as best he could.

But war was coming, and Richard must have heard that as spring edged toward summer, Charles in France was openly raising money for Henry. And now, the king began to make preparations of his own.

In the second week of June, Richard set out for Nottingham Castle, not only a comfortable residence but also a military power base, strategically placed in the heart of England. From there he began to raise his army and to prepare for an invasion everyone knew would soon be on the way.

In late June, Richard's proclamation against Henry was reissued, with two important changes. The first saw the omission of the name of the Marquess of Dorset, Elizabeth Woodville's eldest son, from the list of rebels and traitors; Richard was again trying to placate her and her family, dividing and conquering the opposition. The second laid out Henry Tudor's—Margaret Beaufort's—bloodline: "descended of bastard blood, both of father's side, and of mother's side . . . [John of Gaunt's and Katherine Swynford's children being] indouble avoutry gotten."

As Richard continued to try to undercut Henry's claim to the throne, the young claimant's stepfather removed himself from the preparations at Nottingham. The same week that Richard issued his latest proclamation, Thomas Stanley requested leave to withdraw from court and return to his estates "in order to rest and refresh himself." His estates in Lancashire were the site of Margaret Beaufort's enforced residency. Richard agreed—but only on the condition Stanley left his son behind, as a guarantee of his continued loyalty.

On August 1, Henry Tudor set sail from France, though without all the backing he might have hoped for. The French had wobbled in their support, granting money as a loan only; Henry was forced to pawn his household possessions and leave two Yorkist lords, Dorset and another, behind as a guarantee of the loan. Elizabeth Woodville's brother, however, unlike her son, would ride with Henry's army. With him were a hired band of expert French pikemen and the two supporters—the Earl of Oxford, a powerful nobleman and experienced commander, and Henry's uncle Jasper Tudor, an equally battle-hardened leader whose presence compensated for his nephew's lack of military knowledge.

Henry and his force landed on August 7 at Milford Haven in Wales—far away from Richard in the Midlands, but the country of his birth and ancestry, where he might hope to attract most support. Falling to his knees, Henry kissed the soil of a country he had not seen for fourteen years. He is said to have recited the psalm "Judge me, O Lord, and defend my cause."

Then the two-week march eastward began along, as Crowland described it, "rugged and indirect tracks." It would have taken several days for galloping messengers to bring Richard the news, but on August 11 the summons to his supporters went out: "orders of the greatest severity" threatening reprisals on all who refused to take up arms. Crowland declares that on hearing news of Henry's landing, Richard "rejoiced, or at least seemed to rejoice, writing to his adherents in every quarter that now the long wished-for day had arrived, for him to triumph with ease over so contemptible a faction." Henry's arrival meant the waiting was over and that the fate of England—and of Richard's own regime—would finally be decided.

All through Wales, Henry rallied supporters. But he was a virtual stranger in England. Vergil reports that he wrote to his mother, Margaret Beaufort, along the way: it was his mother on whom, directly or indirectly, he had had to rely to raise support in the country.

Margaret was presumably still under house arrest at Stanley's home of Latham in Lancashire, some hundred miles from the eventual conflict point. Stanley had been summoned back to the king's side for fear, says Crowland, that his wife "might induce her husband to go over to the party of her son." But, extraordinarily, Stanley seems still to have been refusing to commit to either side. Richard was holding Stanley's own son hostage to ensure his good behavior, which may have had something to do with his hesitation.

Nonetheless, when the summons from Richard came, Stanley had sent word he was ill and unable to travel. Instead, he took his forces south, toward the area where the armies were likely to meet, but by an independent path, there to wait until the eve of battle, unattached to either party. His brother Sir William Stanley, on the other hand, took his three thousand or so men to meet up with Henry along the route. But William too refused to commit directly, pending further consultation with his brother.

Richard left Nottingham for Leicester around August 19; on the twenty-first, with all pomp and wearing his crown, he rode with his forces from Leicester toward what would prove to be the conflict point—Bosworth, or, as contemporaries called it, Bosworth Field. Camped near Bosworth, so some of the often-contradictory reports have it, Henry Tudor at last met Lord Stanley, the stepfather he had probably never seen, as well as Sir William. Shakespeare in *Richard III* pays brief tribute to Margaret as the link between them, an unspoken presence of which they must both have been aware. Polydore Vergil would later report that Henry's battle plan the next day had been agreed upon "in counsel" with Lord Stanley, which suggests that Henry came away from the meeting with the firm promise of Stanley support—or at least thought he did. Certainly, the Stanleys sent away with Henry two of their kinsmen backed by a force of their retainers, but they themselves remained in their own, detached, camp. Whatever decision they made on the day of battle, it would be vital. With the Stanleys, Henry's army would not fall far short of Richard's. Without them, he was massively outnumbered.

The fields around Bosworth are disputed now as thoroughly as they were trampled then. Recent archaeological work has relocated the scene of the battle and cast a different light on its strategies—and, as a sideline, perhaps given a fresh glimpse into the women's background role in what is this day the men's story. Found in the ground where Richard's army may have camped the night before the battle were two

Burgundian coins. These were legal currency in England, so it is certainly going too far to trace a link from Richard's camp back to Duchess Margaret's home of Burgundy—Burgundian mercenaries had fought in other battles of the wars. But it is a useful reminder that people and places far from the action might yet influence the progress of events.

Polydore Vergil—and, before him, the Crowland chronicler—reported that the Yorkist king slept badly on the eve of battle. Crowland says that in the morning, Richard complained of "a multitude of demons" surrounding him and that although his face was always drawn, it "was then even more pale and deathly." Vergil says he "thought in his sleep that he saw horrible images as it were of evil spirits haunting evidently about him . . . and that they would not let him rest." Later, of course, his unease would be put down to guilt over his reputed crimes, but at the time Richard seems to have made no secret of his feelings. He himself described the dream to his men in the morning, to explain away his evident "heaviness."

The ill portents were mounting. Richard, Vergil continued, could not manage to "buckle himself to the conflict with such liveliness of courage and countenance as before." It did not help that, so Crowland reported, he roused so early, his chaplains could not be found to celebrate a propitiatory mass, nor did the servants have his breakfast ready.

Richard, Crowland said, had had a presentiment that, whoever won the day, the outcome of this battle "would prove the utter destruction of the kingdom of England." In this he was no prophet. But when a Spaniard called Salazar, a mercenary commander, warned the king that those he trusted would betray him that day, he knew the man could be speaking the truth. He answered (or so it was later reported to the Spanish sovereigns), "God forbid that I yield one step. This day I will die as a king or win." He chose to wear the royal diadem above his helmet, an encouraging sight for his soldiers, but one that would mark him out as a target for the enemy.

As Polydore Vergil tells it, Richard pulled himself together and "drew his whole host out of their tents, and arrayeth his vanward, stretching it forth of a wonderful length, so full replenished both with footmen and horsemen that to the beholders far off it gave a terror for the multitude, and in the front were placed his archers." After that long vanguard came the king himself, with a "choice" force of cavalry.

In Henry Tudor's camp, meanwhile, a few grassy fields away, the mood was hardly more cheerful. Even on the morning of the battle, Henry's nerves were kept on edge by the fickle Stanleys. When he sent word to Lord Stanley to get his troops ready, Stanley sent word back that Henry should look to his own men; his stepfather would do what he had to do, when he was ready. Henry could not but notice that the Stanley force was now drawn up exactly halfway between the two opposing armies.

Although Henry, Vergil says, was "no little vexed, and begun to be somewhat appalled" at Stanley's obduracy, he put his troops in order. A slender vanguard with the archers went first, with Henry—or perhaps, rather, his uncle Jasper and supporter the Earl of Oxford—making the best of the "small numbers" of his people. He still had scarcely five thousand, if one left out the three thousand Stanley men. Richard III had "twice so many." But when both the vanguards were assembled, Vergil continues, "they put on their head pieces and prepared to the fight, expecting th' alarm with intentive ear." It was perhaps eight in the morning. The fighting would be over by ten.

The armies' actual tactics are hard to gauge, when the very site of the battle is still debated so urgently. But the traditional view has it that Richard's troops were drawn up on higher ground. Henry, learning there was a marsh between the two armies, determined to keep it on his right as he advanced, "that it might serve his men instead of a fortress." This also meant the sun was behind him—and in his enemies' eyes—on what promised to be a scorching day.

When Henry's troops moved out from the protection of the marsh, Richard saw his chance and gave the order to advance. As the lines drew together, and the exchange of arrows became hand blows, Henry's commander, the Earl of Oxford, gave the order that no one should move more than ten feet from the standards, lest their smaller force should be lost amid the greater one. This restriction on movement created a brief pause in the fighting and seemed also to confuse the enemy. The Tudor historian Vergil later suggested that Richard's men seized gladly on the break, having no great desire for his victory.

Propaganda or not, Vergil's theory would explain why, when Richard espied Henry himself, surrounded by only a small guard, the king set off "inflamed with ire" to finish the fight himself, in single combat. Perhaps, after all, Henry's long march through Wales had been less trying on the nerves than the waiting game that had been Richard's lot—waiting, with the dawning suspicion that his support was ebbing away.

In what seems almost a quixotic gesture now, Richard was surrendering the advantage of high ground and moving beyond the protection of his forces. But his decision almost won the day. Richard's own horse thundered down the gentle slope with perhaps as many as a thousand knights riding behind. It would be the last time a king of England led a charge of armored cavalry. The noise—on a battlefield already ringing with the thunder of primitive cannon, with the voices of the fighting and the dying, with the screams of horses as the foot soldiers' billhooks ripped open their bellies—must have been terrifying. The force of Richard's lance killed Henry's standard-bearer, and, drawing his ax, the king began to hack his way toward his adversary.

When Henry saw Richard spurring his horse toward him, Vergil says, he "received him with great courage." Vergil adds that Henry "abode the brunt longer than ever his own soldiers would have weened, who were now almost out of hope of victory." But it was not the personal courage of either man that would decide the day. It was probably at this point—acting, crucially, for Henry's side—that Sir William Stanley threw his troops into the fray. Richard, knowing the battle was lost, resolved (as even the Tudor historian Vergil admitted) to die "fighting manfully in the thickest press of his enemies." His own men brought him fresh horses, but he refused to flee, swearing again that that day he would make an end either of war or of life.

As Richard fought on, his horse foundered in the marshy bog, stained red with the blood of friends and foes. It is unlikely his end was either quick or easy, but at least he died, as even the normally unsympathetic Crowland put it, "like a brave and most valiant prince," "while fighting, and not in the act of flight." At last an anonymous Welsh soldier jabbed home a final weapon, ending the ill-starred life of Richard III.

Vergil describes how Richard's body was stripped naked and slung dangling across a horse to be taken back to Leicester to be buried without ceremony;* Crowland states that many insults were offered to the corpse. If Richard's mother, Cecily, heard of the indignities, she, and Richard's sisters, must have been hideously reminded of other deaths, other ignominies: when Richard, Duke of York's, body, for instance, was mockingly decked with a paper crown.

Richard III had been not only the last English king but the first since the Norman Conquest to die in the red heat of battle. The fighting had lasted just two hours, but Vergil says that a thousand men had been killed, nine-tenths of them, it is estimated, on Richard's side. John Rous tells that Richard's last words were "treason—treason." Well they might be: it was a Stanley who placed the crown on Henry's head after the battle, once it had been stripped from Richard. But the legends of Bosworth add one other telling detail—that the crown had been found on a thornbush by Reginald Bray, steward to Margaret Beaufort. The origins of the story can be traced back only to an eighteenth-century antiquarian, but, given the part Margaret Beaufort had played in bringing her son to this point, it has a poetic authenticity.

-----

*His grave was lost for centuries, but, famously, the excavation under a Leicester car park in 2012 revealed a skeleton now known to be Richard's. The identification was made from the mitochondrial DNA, carried only through the female line, which can be traced from Cecily Neville via her oldest daughter Anne to descendants still living today.

PART V

1485–1509

20

"TRUE SUCCEEDERS"

O now let Richmond and Elizabeth,
The true succeeders of each royal house,
By God's fair ordinance conjoin together.

THE TRAGEDY OF RICHARD THE THIRD, 5.5

The battle of Bosworth Field in 1485 has often been regarded as the starting place of the early modern age, but that is the result of hindsight. In the wake of the slaughter, there would have been no indication that anything substantial had changed for the average man or woman in England. As Henry Tudor assumed the throne, any adult would remember not only Richard III's overthrow of the expected order, and Edward IV's coup, but also Henry VI's brief resumption of the throne. There was not necessarily any reason to think Henry VII's dynasty would be any more durable. And while Henry had been welcomed by many in England, there were many others who were invested in the Yorkist power structure and had much to lose over a seeming twist of fate. Bosworth could so easily have gone the other way.

Henry did have one important advantage. There had been a comprehensive clearing of the decks (and the Tudors would make sure it became ever more comprehensive in the years ahead). Any previous Lancastrian comeback had been shadowed by the knowledge that the sons of York were waiting, prolific and power hungry. But now, of Cecily Neville's six adult children, four—her three sons and one of her daughters—were dead. The surviving daughters would not make life easy for Henry in the years ahead; Margaret of Burgundy would, as shall be seen, still repeatedly attempt to intervene in English affairs, and the descendants of Elizabeth, the Duchess of Suffolk, would later be an issue as well. But for the moment, they were in no position to prevent Henry from seizing power in the land.

The next generation of Yorkists—at least those males who might have stood between Henry and the throne—had been all but obliterated, as well. Even if there were some questions as to whether one or both "Princes in the Tower" had survived, they themselves—like their cousin Warwick, Clarence's ten-year-old son and the only unquestionably legitimate surviving member of the Plantagenet male line—would have been simply still too young to have mounted a credible challenge themselves, and with Buckingham and the senior Woodvilles dead, it is hard to see who would have done it for them. What is more, it would take time for any opposition to rally after the shock of defeat.

Time is one thing that Henry's opponents would not have. Henry, mindful that one Plantagenet heir still lurked nearby, immediately moved to have Warwick brought south from Sheriff Hutton and given into Margaret Beaufort's charge, or custody. If there was one person who could be trusted to keep a close eye on this potential threat to Henry, it was his mother.

Everything had changed for Margaret Beaufort, certainly. Her world had effectively been turned upside down; the man whom she had opposed—openly and otherwise—for so long was vanquished, and her son was on the cusp of power. Henry sent her from Bosworth the *Book of Hours* that had been with Richard in his tent—an appropriate tribute, for someone of Margaret's piety. But the book, already an old one when Richard began using it, had been transformed into something more personal by the addition, on blank pages, of prayers for Richard's use and mentioning his name—one prayer, particularly. A prayer seeking comfort in sadness by emphasizing the goodness of God, but more specifically seeking protection against enemies. Deleting Richard's name from what was now her book, she added the jingle on the endpapers: "For the honour of God and St Edmunde / Pray for Margaret Richmonde." For a woman of her temperament—so prone, as her confessor would later recount, to see disaster lurking behind the greatest triumph—even so wonderful a turn of Fortune's Wheel as she had just experienced could not have come altogether easily. Margaret would have set out south when she heard the news of Henry's victory, to be reunited with the son she had not actually seen since he was in his teens.

Henry Tudor reached London by September 7 and spent two weeks at Baynard's Castle—Cecily Neville's former home. (She herself was presumably still at Berkhampsted, where her son Richard had visited her only a matter of weeks before.) The task facing him was immense: to take hasty control of a country that had not only had every opportunity, in recent years, of learning to regard kings as interchangeable, but he himself hardly knew, since even his early boyhood had been spent not in England, but in Wales. He had had few direct opportunities of learning systems and making allies. But he did have advice.

From London Henry went with Margaret to her palace of Woking for a two-week stay. We may surmise that as mother and son grew to know each other again and shared memories—it was at Woking that they had last been together, all those years before—it was also time for an extended briefing. Henry across the Channel would have been kept informed of events in the realm he needed now to rule, but he was too distant in exile to understand the competing identities and agendas. Each new recruit to his band of exiles might have brought information, but each had his own ax to grind, and the others closest to him, such as his uncle Jasper, had been away as long as he. As they walked in the late-summer orchards, surely Henry drew information from the one person he could trust completely and who knew the fault lines of England as well as anyone, and perhaps this process gave Margaret Beaufort a role in her son's reign that would not easily be forgotten.

It seems never to have occurred to Margaret Beaufort to make a bid for the crown herself. She—and her future daughter-in-law,

Elizabeth of York—were in a different position to the other women in this story: they had, by blood at least, their own claims to the throne. But even her son was reluctant to stake his claim first on her blood right, preferring instead a three-pronged justification of marriage (the long-planned marriage to Elizabeth of York), birth (his descent from John of Gaunt, son of Edward III), and right of battle. "The first of these was the fairest, and most like to give contentment to the people," for whom, said Francis Bacon, Edward IV's reign had suggested the Yorkists were the natural rulers.

But Henry, says Bacon, was all too aware that if he seemed to rely upon his wife's title to the throne, he could never be anything more than "a King at courtesy," with the real power residing in Elizabeth. And then, what is more, if Elizabeth were to predecease him, he would have "to give place and be removed." Bacon was writing in the early seventeenth century, and by then the country had known two reigning queens: the entire right of Elizabeth of York may not in fact have seemed quite so clear at the time. But Henry was persuaded, Bacon said, "to rest upon the title of Lancaster as the main"—to stake his claim chiefly on his mother's bloodline—and, flaunting his God-given military victory, took care from the beginning that his prospective bride should not have too much importance.

WHAT COMPENSATION could be given to Margaret would be. One of Henry's first actions was to see that his mother was declared a *feme sole:* a woman able to act independently of a husband, as queens were allowed to do, and able to own property. An Act of Parliament ordained that she "may from henceforth [for the] term of her life sue all manner of actions . . . plea and be impleaded for . . . in as good, large and beneficial manner, as any other sole person not wife nor covert of any husband." She could take and receive "states, leases, releases, confirmations, presentations, bargains, sales, gifts, deeds, wills and writings." It made Margaret an independent financial entity and potentially a real power in the land. This was unprecedented for an aristocratic woman (queens were often allowed this privilege, and it had occasionally been used in lower ranks, to allow a woman to operate a business). Over the next couple of years, elaborate arrangements would be set up to apportion the revenues of land Margaret had inherited or would now be given between her and her husband. Stanley was treated with separate generosity—created Earl of Derby and honored as the new king's stepfather—but Margaret's power and property were not to be at his disposal, as would be normal in the fifteenth century.

That property would be substantial. While mother and son were still at Woking, orders had gone out for repairs and improvements to the fine house of Coldharbour on the Thames (the same Margaret of Burgundy had used during her stay) for "my Lady the King's Mother." In what was to be her London home, Margaret's arms were set into the windows, to be displayed to anyone passing on the water. Over the next few weeks, the king's "most dearest mother," as even the official documents described her, saw the return of her own estates, now that the attainder against her was reversed. She was also given power to appoint officers in certain areas, as well as effective use of the estates of the heirs of the executed Duke of Buckingham, whose son became her ward. From the "great grant" of March 22, 1487, came the "Exeter lands" in Devonshire, South Wales, Derbyshire, and Northamptonshire, as well as the Richmond estates in Lincolnshire and Kendal.

Tangible benefits were given also to those close to Margaret: her trusted servants Reginald Bray (who would become Henry's great officer) and Christopher Urswick (another whom Bacon described as a man the king "much trusted and employed"); her Stanley connections, led by the new king's stepfather; and Jasper Tudor, who became Duke of Bedford. Her half brother John Welles would be allowed to marry Edward IV's second surviving daughter, Cecily, while Jasper Tudor would marry Buckingham's widow, Katherine, the former Woodville girl. It was of course a favor to the men concerned—but it is also an example of how marriage could be used to bring potentially dissident bloodlines into the fold. Margaret's old associate John Morton, the Bishop of Ely, soon became her son's Archbishop of Canterbury and Lord Chancellor soon after that.

At the end of October 1485, Henry was crowned, under the book of rules laid down for Richard III. Powdered ermine and black furs were ordered, as were crimson velvet and crimson cloth of gold. Margaret's confessor, John Fisher, later recalled that "when the king her son was crowned in all that great triumph and glory, she wept marvellously."

On November 7, Parliament reenacted the 1397 statute legitimating the Beauforts, making no mention of the 1407 document barring them from the throne. The Parliamentary Rolls that incorporated *Titulus Regius* were ordered to be burned—"cancelled, destroyed, and . . . taken and avoided out of the roll and records of the said Parliament of the said late king, and burned, and utterly destroyed," because "from their falseness and shamefulness, they were only deserving of utter oblivion." Not only were the attainders against Henry VI and Marguerite of Anjou (and Jasper Tudor) reversed, but Elizabeth Woodville was restored to her "estate, dignity, pre-eminence and name."

On December 10, Parliament, surely at his instigation, begged Henry to "unify two bloods" by marrying Elizabeth of York, who had by now probably been brought south from Richard's castle of Sheriff Hutton. Care, however, was taken all around to stress that Henry's rule was valid, as Crowland put it, "not only by right of blood but of victory in battle and of conquest"; the Speaker declared that it was because the hereditary succession of the crowns of England and France "is, remains, continues, and endures in the person of the same Lord King, & in the heirs legitimately issuing from his body" that he wished to take Elizabeth for a wife, for the "continuation of offspring by a race of kings."

Still, the bride-to-be was to find herself in a strange position—at once needed and repudiated. Crowland added that Henry's marriage to Edward IV's eldest daughter merely filled in the gaps, or "whatever appeared to be missing in the king's title elsewhere," but Bacon wrote that he "would not endure any mention of the Lady Elizabeth" in any of the documents asserting his kingship. There was, however, no question but that the marriage would go ahead, and on December 11, Henry gave order that preparations for the wedding should begin.

The marriage plan was founded on the assumption that it was in Elizabeth of York that the best Plantagenet claims to the throne were now embodied; that Elizabeth's rights, in other words, were not superseded by those of any living brother. When Henry took control of London, he would have taken control also of the Tower, which begs the question of what—or who—he found or failed to find there. Was the fate of the Princes still a question, or did the denizens of this new Tudor age think of it as a certainty? The answer cannot be known because (insofar as any records can reveal) no one said, but that silence is itself suggestive. If Henry Tudor and his adherents knew that Richard had definitely, demonstrably, had his nephews killed, it is inconceivable that they would not have declared it, and made capital out of the fact, as soon as they had proof of the deed.

If, however, Henry believed the boys dead at Richard's hands, but had no way to prove it, his silence makes perfect sense; to have declared them simply missing would have been to invite pretenders. By the same token, the Princes' mother and sisters must surely have known something, or at least felt as if they did, since now would have been the moment for a hullabaloo of inquiry, and they seem to have made none. It is very possible Elizabeth Woodville and her daughters believed, like Henry, that the boys were killed, and presumably by Richard, but that they too had no proof. That dearth of evidence might allow future doubt to creep in, but for the moment at least, it could have been enough to stop them from speaking out. A measure of silent uncertainty was, it seems, everybody's friend.

The two young Princes cannot have been far from Elizabeth of York's mind when she arrived in London to meet her future husband. One of the new king's first acts, said Vergil, had been to send a messenger to Sheriff Hutton, summoning Elizabeth. She had progressed southward, "attended by noble ladies," to stay with her mother and later with Henry's. The betrothed couple met for what was almost certainly the first time. Elizabeth, happily, would have seen not the pinch-faced miser of later imagery but a man still in his twenties, already with something of his mother's hooded eyes, perhaps, but tall and slim, with blue eyes set in a cheerful face and a general appearance Polydore Vergil could describe even some years down the line as "remarkably attractive."

Henry would have seen an even more agreeable picture. Elizabeth of York does seem really to have had the blonde ("yellow") hair conventionally ascribed to queens: from later descriptions of plumpness, we can guess that she was already buxom—certainly a comely nineteen-year-old, whether or not she was a true beauty like her mother. (Vergil did describe her as "intelligent above all others, and equally beautiful"—but that can probably be put down to tact.) And if, when Henry looked at her, he saw the girl who had caused so much trouble with rumors of attachment to her uncle—if she saw the man who had long been an enemy to her family—such compromises were far from rare in the marriage of royalty. The two had, after all, one thing in common: a shared experience of uncertainty, of the swift turns that Fortune's Wheel could bring. It is likely they were both well-enough pleased, and more than that, maybe. Probably Elizabeth of York, like Margaret Beaufort, had never envisaged ruling in her own right. To be queen consort was the destiny for which she had been raised to aspire—and she had achieved it without the need to leave her own country.

Henry applied for a second papal dispensation to allow two relatives to marry. One had been issued in March 1484, to cover a marriage between "Henry Richmond, layman of the York diocese, and Elizabeth Plantagenet, woman of the London diocese," but perhaps that might not now cover Henry's changed status. Margaret's husband, Stanley, had to swear that his wife had discussed all necessary questions of lineage before any arrangement was made between the pair. The second dispensation was issued on January 16, but the couple clearly assumed it would arrive, since by that time the wedding ring was purchased and the wedding only two days away.

On January 18, 1486, came the wedding itself, almost exactly a year after Elizabeth's name had first been coupled with that of another king of England. Not much is known in comparison with other ceremonies; it is not even certain that the records describing it as taking place at Westminster meant the abbey rather than a subsidiary church, though Bacon wrote that "it was celebrated with greater triumph and demonstrations (especially on the people's part) of joy and gladness than the days either of his entry or coronation, which the King rather noted than liked." On the one hand, the great outpouring of enthusiasm for the marriage was a sign of support for the regime; on the other, the very effusiveness may have suggested to Henry that Elizabeth with her York blood might eclipse him in the public eye.

The officiating archbishop, Thomas Bourchier, was the man who had persuaded Elizabeth Woodville to send her younger son out of sanctuary; she, presumably, must have been relieved to see the final confirmation of a marriage she had long planned. The usual long list of presents and celebrations has not survived, but the records do show Henry ordering a huge quantity of ermines that would make his new wife's Easter gown. He also ordered a third papal dispensation, one dispensing with any impediment caused by the couple's relation through marriage, rather than through consanguinity; over the succeeding months, the pope was obliging enough also to threaten excommunication for anyone who challenged the right of Henry's heirs to succeed, and to issue a papal bull confirming the legitimacy of the union.

Not that the people seemed to have any doubts that this was truly a marriage made in heaven. The Tudor poet Bernard André wrote that "the people constructed bonfires far and wide to show their gladness and the City of London was filled with dancing, singing and entertainment." Bacon wrote that whereas Bosworth had given Henry the bended knee of his subjects, this marriage gave him their hearts.

The couple may not have waited for the marriage ceremony to begin living together—a common-enough practice in the fifteenth century. That third dispensation at the beginning of March may even have been because they knew Elizabeth was pregnant, and court poets hastened to link Henry's victory at Bosworth with this speedy proof of virility. Bernard André's version has to be the most oleaginous: "Then a new happiness took over the happiest kingdom, great enjoyment filled the queen, the church experienced perfect joy, while huge excitement gripped the court and an incredible pleasure arose over the whole country."

Not everyone, however, had taken Bosworth as the final verdict on the future. Easter saw rebellion in Yorkshire, and for the first full year of his reign Henry was off around the country, putting out fires and displaying himself in the guise of majesty. Meanwhile, the women— Elizabeth of York, her sister, her mother, and her mother-in-law— summered at Winchester, in St. Swithin's Priory within the cathedral precincts. Elizabeth Woodville, besides being restored to her rank as queen dowager, had been awarded a grant for life of six manors in Essex and an annual income of £102. There were, however, problems inherent in the situation, not least the fact that there was bound to be a certain amount of jostling for place between the two senior in-laws, the queen dowager and Margaret Beaufort. The former had lived through a lot but, in her late forties, wasn't necessarily ready to give up all hope of power; the latter, in her early forties, had only just arrived, and would surely be reluctant to see the real authority she wielded in her son's kingdom cast in the shade by the ceremonial status of a woman who technically outranked her.

But it is possible Elizabeth Woodville had tired of court. On July 10, she had arranged with the Abbot of Westminster to take out a forty-year lease on "a mansion within the said Abbey called Cheyne gate," an odd choice for a residence, because it might well have brought back bad memories of her time in sanctuary. But it was a practical location, and though her worldly image might sometimes have masked it, Elizabeth Woodville's behavior as queen had always been that of a conventionally devout woman. Then again, her negotiations for a London home may also have been her response to other plans first mooted for Elizabeth just a few days earlier that July. Henry had proposed that his new mother-in-law should marry the Scots king, as part of a peace treaty (a proposal that would never come to fruition).

On September 20, 1486 ("afore one o'clock after midnight," noted Margaret Beaufort in her *Book of Hours*), to widespread rejoicing, Elizabeth of York gave birth to a prince in whose veins ran the blood of both dynasties. Either the baby was a whole month early, or the date is evidence that the couple had indeed slept together before the actual marriage ceremony.

No account survives of this birth as such, but Margaret Beaufort laid down the rules for the royal confinement and for the subsequent christening. Her ordinances decreed that Winchester Cathedral should be carpeted and hung with arras, that soft linen should be folded inside the font, which was placed on a stage in the middle of the church to give the crowds a better view. Margaret and her son were both good at publicity. But Elizabeth's own maternal relations were well to the fore: her sister Cecily carrying the baby to the font with their sister-in-law the Marchioness of Dorset bearing the train, with Dorset himself as well as the Earl of Lincoln, the queen's cousin, beside her. The queen's sister Anne carried the robe, while the queen dowager—Elizabeth Woodville, the godmother—carried the little prince onto the high altar and gave the baby a covered cup of gold.

But, of course, it was Margaret whose ordinances also laid down orders for the baby's rearing—decreeing that the wet nurse should be observed by a doctor at every meal to see that the child was getting "seasonable meat and drink" and describing the leather (and presumably dribble-proof) cushion on which she should lean and the two great basins of pewter needed for the nursery laundry. The ordinances encompass both practicality and grandeur—the pommels on the cradle, the counterpane furred with ermine, and the "head sheets" of cloth of gold—and they go on forever. Court ceremony was important, and a new dynasty had to show it could do these things magnificently—but all the same, there is something a little frightening in the thoroughness with which Margaret laid down every detail. The years of her misfortunes had obviously bred in her an urgent need for control, but one wonders if through her daughter-in-law's accouchement she were not also reaching after the kind of experience she herself had been denied when she gave birth to Henry all those years before. It's almost as if Elizabeth was her surrogate, not the only such case in this story.

Elizabeth of York was ill with an ague just after the birth; she did suffer from childbed fevers and would cling to those who had seen her through one birth to help her through another, like her midwife, Alice Massy. She would in any case have had to stay at Winchester until she was churched, and the court stayed with her until All Hallows, today's Halloween. The precisely ordered ceremonials for the churching show Margaret once again stage-managing the scenario—a duchess or countess to assist the queen out of bed, two more to receive her at her chamber door. For Elizabeth of York, her relationship with Henry's mother—like that of Cecily Neville and her daughter-in-law Elizabeth Woodville—was an issue never to go away.

The choice of Winchester for the new prince's birth and the decision to name him Arthur were a conscious attempt to link the new Tudors with the ancient Arthurian tale. This was, as anyone who read Caxton's newly printed edition of the *Morte d'Arthur* knew, the city that still held the Round Table. But there may have been a more serious reason for staying on in Winchester, away from any troubles that might shake the capital. Troubles were brewing, as the court made its way back to Greenwich for the winter season.

The problem, not unpredictably, had to do with those of the Plantagenet heirs who were still unaccounted for. Francis Bacon, a century later, wrote that from the very start of Henry's reign, there were "secret rumours and whisperings (which afterwards gathered strength and turned to great troubles) that the two young sons of King Edward the Fourth or one of them (which were said to be destroyed in the Tower), were not indeed murdered, but conveyed secretly away, and were yet living." And the young Princes were not the only objects of such rumors. Earlier that year, in the summer of 1486, stories had begun to spread that Clarence's son Warwick had escaped from the Tower and was in the Channel Islands. The subject of these stories was later identified as Lambert Simnel. As a matter of fact, Simnel seemed at first to be claiming that he was Richard, Duke of York, Elizabeth Woodville's younger son, but by the time he reached Ireland by the turn of the year, he had changed his story.

What can Elizabeth Woodville have felt? To pretend this boy was her nephew Warwick was absurd, and Elizabeth must have known it. Henry soon brought the real Warwick briefly out of the Tower and sent him through the London streets in a public display. But when Simnel's supporters claimed he was Richard, the pressure on Elizabeth Woodville must have been intense (even assuming she could be *sure* that he was not). The people rallying around the pretender would need only a word from Elizabeth to endorse his claim. And the events of the next few months might suggest that, in the eyes of the authorities at least, there was a real possibility that Elizabeth would give that word.

On February 2, 1487, Henry met with his council, and, as Polydore Vergil reported after the fact, "among other matters, Elizabeth the widow of King Edward was deprived by the decree of the same council of all her possessions." This, unconvincingly, was supposedly punishment for the fact that she had, three years before, left sanctuary and made a deal with Richard III. Nevertheless, Parliament on February 20 did indeed endorse the alienation of Elizabeth's property. This step has often been seen as evidence that the dowager queen was being punished for having supported the pretender Simnel, with all that might imply about her beliefs as to her son's fate. Or, less drastically, it could have been a precautionary measure.

It may have been that the decision to take away Elizabeth's lands and the rise of Lambert Simnel bore no relation to each other. It was a time of reorganization all around: this indeed was the season of the "great grant" of lands that benefited Margaret Beaufort. A separate establishment had been set up for Prince Arthur at Farnham in Surrey, and Elizabeth of York visited in January, to check on her son. Furthermore, the lands lately belonging to Elizabeth Woodville were, after all, simply being transferred to her daughter, the new "lady queen," whose position would traditionally be kept up by income from these properties. In return, the older lady got an annuity of four hundred marks. This, however, might well be called paltry; indeed, it was less than the income Richard had promised her. What is even more curious is the fact that it was precisely now, around the middle of February, that Elizabeth Woodville took up more or less permanent residence in Bermondsey Abbey, the great convent on the Thames already equipped with accommodation for royalty. (Katherine of Valois, Henry V's widow, had been forced to retreat there after it was discovered she had married Owen Tudor.)

There is not necessarily anything strange about Elizabeth Woodville's decision to retreat to an abbey—many widows did choose a religious retirement in this era—though this does revise the standard image of Elizabeth as a wholly worldly creature. If her first choice had fallen on the more central residence of that house in Westminster Abbey, then Bermondsey was still a convenient residence—even a thrifty one, since the association of an ancestor of hers with the place meant that she could board for free. But the timing is suggestive—the more so since the lease of Cheyneygate shows she had only recently made quite different plans. It does look as though Elizabeth Woodville was at the least being urged to take up a temporary retirement—if not because of anything she had done, then because of what she might do. Francis Bacon wrote that the queen's mother was so deeply suspect, "it was almost thought dangerous to visit her, or see her."

A real threat to the young Tudor dynasty was brewing, however, and—on its surface, at least—it had nothing to do with Elizabeth

Woodville. Soon after Henry VII had paraded the real Warwick through London, John Earl of Lincoln (son to Edward IV's sister Elizabeth and trusted lieutenant and potential heir to Richard III) made a dramatic flight from England. He had been received with favor into the new Tudor court and had been prominent at the christening of Prince Arthur. But now he fled and turned up in the Low Countries. By Easter, it was clear that an invasion force was getting under way.

In April Lincoln took an army from the Low Countries to Ireland, where Simnel was given an impromptu coronation ceremony and declared King Edward VI. But the involvement of Lincoln is curious: when his aunt Margaret of Burgundy had occasion to write about the expedition, it was his name she invoked, not Simnel's. It seems possible Simnel was just a stalking horse for Lincoln's own attempt to take over the country.

In May Henry, at Kenilworth Castle in the safety of the Midlands, heard that Simnel had landed with an army and sent word that his wife and mother, still at Greenwich, should come to him there. But when Henry set out to confront the rebels, Elizabeth hotfooted it south to Farnham, where her baby was being reared, with a plan made for them to move, if necessary, on to a house of Benedictine nuns at Romsey in Hampshire—not far from the coast—in case the worst happened and they had to flee. For the young queen, it must have been a terrifying reminder of traumas past.

On June 16, at the battle of Stoke, perhaps the last familial battle of the Wars of the Roses, Lincoln was killed. The boy Simnel—in what may have been natural clemency on Henry's part, but was more certainly intended to emphasize the absurdity of his pretensions—was put to work in the royal kitchen. Lincoln's parents, the Suffolks, whatever their personal loss, suffered no further penalties.

The battle of Stoke had ended the threat of Lambert Simnel, and perhaps of the Earl of Lincoln too, but, as Henry would surely have been aware, the real question was which if any Yorkist women had been a key player in the affair. Simnel's immediate sponsor, Polydore Vergil said, was an Oxford priest called Richard Simons. But there had to have been some greater personage waiting in the wings, someone better able to coach an impostor in the things he should know about the person whose identity he would assume. Bacon believed that Lambert Simnel had been schooled, and by a Yorkist lady. "So that it cannot be, but that some great person, that knew particularly and familiarly Edward Plantagenet [Warwick], had a hand in the business." He was inclined to allot some of the blame to Elizabeth Woodville, "a busy negotiating woman" who was at this time "extremely discontent with the King, thinking her daughter, as the King handled the matter, not advanced but depressed [that is, lowered in status, suppressed]." No one, he said, in a metaphor tellingly drawn from the theater, "could hold the book so well to prompt and instruct this stage-play as she could."

But whatever Elizabeth Woodville's involvement, there was another Yorkist woman who certainly did support, and possibly coach, Lambert Simnel: Margaret of Burgundy, whom Bacon described as "the sovereign patroness and protectress of the enterprise." When her only remaining brother, Richard, had been killed at Bosworth, Margaret was fully occupied with Burgundian affairs. Perhaps she might have let well enough alone if Henry had taken care to conciliate either Burgundy or its dowager duchess. He was, after all, a novice king and one, moreover, reared in the traditions of France and Brittany, often Burgundy's enemies.

Henry had, in 1486, been careful to renew (in at least some, diminished, form) the rights Cecily Neville had been accorded by her sons— but Cecily Neville was there in his country, and therefore someone whom he would do well to appease to some degree. But the trading privileges Edward had granted his sister Margaret of Burgundy, and which her brother Richard seems to have continued, now lapsed—and it is probable that Margaret's actions in the years ahead were governed by enlightened self-interest as well as by emotion.

Margaret may also have played a more fundamental role in the Lambert Simnel drama than even Bacon suspected. As early as the summer of 1486, a donation was made in Burgundy for the feast of Saint Rombout's Day, on behalf of "the son of Clarence from England"; in the same year, the city of Malines gave Margaret money for her "reyse" (venture) to England. If it was Margaret who in fact fulfilled the coach's role Bacon ascribed to Elizabeth Woodville, then she may not have been acting solely on her own behalf, but in the interests of her adopted land. Her efforts, moreover, seem to have worked, if perhaps not in quite the way Margaret intended. After the recent rebellion, Henry began to be more conciliatory toward Burgundy.

Elizabeth Woodville, by contrast, had lost through the rebellion— assuming there was some connection between it and the reduction in her income. Henry's records, over the next few years, do show regular, almost yearly, payments to his "right dear" mother-in-law: fifty marks for Christmas here, and there the gift of a ton of wine. But it was not the kind of wholesale funding that would allow her to play any kind of political role in her son-in-law's kingdom. Her public career was over. She would, indeed, thenceforth be recorded as making only occasional appearances in public and would otherwise live a reduced life in the convent at Bermondsey.

"GOLDEN SOVEREIGNTY"

Put in her tender heart th'aspiring flame
Of golden sovereignty; acquaint the princess
With the sweet silent hours of marriage joys.

THE TRAGEDY OF RICHARD THE THIRD, 4.4

The first rebellion of the Tudor reign was over, though other ripples of armed discontent would plague Henry's next years. But he heeded a complaint voiced among the rebels that Elizabeth of York was being treated too casually—that, extraordinarily, she had not yet been crowned, an affront to Yorkist sympathies. September was full of plans for the splendid ceremony. In October the royal couple set out from Warwick to London. His plans for Elizabeth notwithstanding, the entry into the city was Henry's moment—the first time he had been there since the Stoke victory—and the craft guilds were out in number, lined up along the packed streets, "hugely replenished with people." An anonymous manuscript preserved in the collection of the sixteenth-century antiquarian John Leland describes how Elizabeth and Margaret Beaufort secretly watched the grand event from the window of a house near the City walls.

The ladies withdrew to Greenwich for the weeks before the coronation: Elizabeth was to be presented to London afresh, almost as though she were a new-arrived foreign princess. When the time came, they would leave the palace at Greenwich by boat, accompanied by a whole flotilla of barges, each resplendent with silken banners, spelling out a careful message of pageantry. Especially fine was the Bachelors' Barge, with a dragon spouting flames into the Thames. Landing on Tower Wharf, Elizabeth was greeted by the king; while he created fourteen new Knights of the Bath, she prepared for the next day.

The next morning, Saturday, November 26, she dressed in the traditional kirtle of white "cloth of gold of damask," a mantle furred with ermine and tasseled with gold. The writer of the anonymous document noticed the "fair yellow hair hanging down plain behind her back"—that symbol of virginity, suggesting anointed queenship as new territory. Elizabeth's sister Cecily carried her train as they formed for the procession.

Lengthy descriptions survive of the progress through the City, the litter and canopy. After the horse of state and the henchmen decked with white York roses came the ladies in horse-borne litters. The first had Katherine Woodville (Elizabeth Woodville's sister, the former Duchess of Buckingham, now Duchess of Bedford) and Cecily. The second had Duchess of Suffolk (Elizabeth's royal aunt, prominent despite the fact that her son had been Lincoln, the recent rebel), the Duchess of Norfolk, the Countess of Oxford, and all their various gentlewomen behind.

The night was spent at Westminster, and on Sunday, coronation day, Elizabeth was dressed in purple velvet furred with ermine. She walked to the abbey over a carpet of woolen cloth that the watching crowds would be allowed to take. It was a sign of the people's love for her, perhaps, that this traditional procedure nearly resulted in a riot, when so many pressed to take their souvenir that some were actually killed and the procession of the queen's ladies thrown into confusion. England had become used to bloodshed—but not under these circumstances.

Nothing, however, could be allowed to disturb the solemnity of the abbey ceremony itself, and as Elizabeth lay prostrate in front of the archbishop, for him to anoint her with the holy oil—as he set the crown upon her head and gave her the scepter and the rod, praying the whole while—it must have been a kind of vindication for all her, and her mother's, former sufferings. Margaret Beaufort watched with her son, the king—and with Clarence's daughter Lady Margaret Pole—from an elevated stage built at the side of the abbey and concealed by lattice and draperies. One can only speculate about what she felt, seeing another woman transformed into a quasi divinity. Any queen might validate and contribute to her husband's kingship: an almost mystical symbol. But Elizabeth's bloodline meant that she was more fundamentally necessary to Henry's legitimacy—something that must (whatever their personal feelings toward her) have struck both her husband and her mother-in-law as a potential threat, as well as an opportunity.

Next came the banquet, as the writer of Leland's manuscript describes. After grace was said, "Dame Katherine Gray and Mistress Ditton went under the table, where they sat on either side [of] the Queen's feet all the dinner time." She had the Duchess of Bedford and Cecily on her left (the Archbishop of Canterbury was on her right), while the Countess of Oxford and the Countess of Rivers (Anthony Woodville's widow) knelt on either side of her and held up a cloth as she ate. It was the same parade of homage that Elizabeth Woodville had received, and reading the descriptions of it—remembering the royally born Jacquetta on her knees before her daughter—one can guess why Margaret Beaufort was not there. Again, "the high and mighty princess his mother" watched with her son from a window at the side.

After all the banquet menus that had come before, it is hard to guess what would have impressed. The game birds were standard, and the fatted rabbits ("Coneys of high Grece"—grease) and even the swan in a chawdron sauce of its own spiced guts and the peacock in its feathers were no more than one might expect on such an occasion. The whole seal, "richly served"? The fritters, the marchpane, the castles of jelly, the subtleties? Two courses only: perhaps the royal officials organizing the feast remembered that at the coronation of Richard and Anne, no one had had time to eat three. After the alms were given and the queen's high rank was "cried" around the hall, the ceremony was almost over, barring, of course, the fruit and wafers, the ritual washing, the grace, the trumpets, and the "void" of hippocras and spices. Elizabeth left "with God's blessing and to the rejoicing of many a true English man's heart."

At mass the next day, Margaret Beaufort sat at the queen's right-hand side; so she did too when Elizabeth sat in state in the Parliament chamber. The Duchess of Suffolk was still present, and all the lessons of the wars were surely there: divide and conquer, bring past and potential enemies into the fold, and make the defeated (especially the placatory, conciliatory figures of the women) part of the victory. The one person who does not appear to have been at any part of the coronation ceremony was Elizabeth's own mother. It seems the strongest evidence that she was in some degree of disgrace. But perhaps Elizabeth of York's relations with her husband, her role as queen, would get easier as her own loving but (from all the past evidence) forceful mother moved out of the way.

With the coronation ceremony behind her, Elizabeth of York seemed ever more secure in her role as queen. Visiting the queen unexpectedly eight months later, in July 1488, the Spanish ambassador, De Puebla, found Elizabeth of York "with two and twenty companions of angelical appearance, and all we saw there seemed very magnificent, and in splendid style, as was suitable for the occasion." Already, the envoy of Ferdinand of Aragon and Isabella of Castile was in England to negotiate the marriage treaty between Prince Arthur and their daughter Catherine, which would be ratified the following spring at the Treaty of Medina del Campo. (The haggling had gone as far as quibbles over who should, when the time came, provide the grand wardrobe necessary for Catherine's arrival. "Husbands," said Ferdinand and Isabella firmly, "provide the dresses of their wives.")

Elizabeth knew how to be a queen of England; she had learned it at her mother's knee. Ten years later, De Puebla would see Elizabeth and Henry walking in procession to mass and notice that her ladies "went in good order" and were much adorned. The Venetian envoy once wrote that she was "a very handsome woman and in conduct very able"—or as the original Italian has it, "*di gran governo.*"

Elizabeth of York's motto was "humble and reverent"—but that is not necessarily the entire story. Her mother had surely known the value of informal, closet influence over the king—pillow talk, if you like—and maybe Elizabeth of York had learned something from observing the different styles of queenship exercised by Elizabeth Woodville and Marguerite of Anjou and the varying degrees of warmth with which they were received.

There is some evidence, albeit scanty, to suggest Elizabeth did exercise a behind-the-scenes influence on her husband. There was a letter, for instance, from the pope to Margaret Beaufort saying that Henry had promised to appoint Elizabeth's candidate to the bishopric of Worcester. Another letter, one of only two intercessionary letters from Elizabeth surviving, written in 1499, recommended to Ferdinand one "Henry Stuke, who wishes to go and fight against the Infidels." ("Though he is a very short man, he has the reputation of being a valiant soldier.") And there was a letter concerning the nomination of a chaplain to a vacant position.

Another, later, Spanish report has Elizabeth receiving two letters from Ferdinand and Isabella and two from their daughter Catherine: "The King had a dispute with the Queen because he wanted to have one of the said letters to carry continually about him, but the Queen did not like to part with hers," the ambassador relates. It has been taken as evidence of Elizabeth's independence—and though in fact it may sound more like a thoroughly stage-managed display, intended to show how highly missives from the Spanish court were valued, that too would show Elizabeth as a conscious player in the diplomatic game.

But against that are reports—like Bacon's comment that Elizabeth of York was "depressed" in status, or like the Spanish report that she was beloved "because she is powerless"—suggesting that Henry's queen had been sidelined, like Anne Neville before her. It may well have been that a cannier husband had subsumed her rights and powers into his own, while diverting her into a life of ceremonies, interspersed by as many as eight pregnancies. Bacon, indeed, even claimed that the king's "aversion toward the house of York was so predominant in him as it found place not only in his wars and councils, but in his chamber and bed." (Bacon did also say, more mildly, that although Henry was "nothing uxurious, nor scarce indulgent" toward his queen, he was nonetheless "companionable and respective [considerate], and without jealousy.") These reports make curious the fact that she is nonetheless widely assumed to have been happy.

There are two distinct strands of information concerning Elizabeth's personality and situation, and the two do not altogether match up. One describes Elizabeth's peaceful and satisfactory marriage with Henry, her apparent acceptance of a purely domestic role; the other looks back to the perhaps more ambitious figure of her youth. Writers have traditionally reconciled her apparent contentment, and her husband's dominance, by making her into a woman without ambition and almost without volition.

But the trouble with that judgment is that it sets up another anomaly: that this placid ruminant of a woman had once, only a few years before, been the passionately proactive girl of Richard's reign (unless, that is, the Buck letter is to be regarded as a *complete* forgery and *The Ballad of Lady Bessy* is to be completely ignored—along with the apparent fears of Richard III's henchmen that she might avenge her family's wrongs on them). Perhaps the truth is that the early Tudor chroniclers' construct of successful monarchy leaves no room for evidence of dissent, and any dissents of Elizabeth's were, moreover, probably of the private, domestic kind. A happy marriage—and this marriage does seem to have been basically happy—has no story.

On August 25, 1498, the Spanish ambassador gave another set of letters from Spain to Elizabeth, "the most distinguished and the most noble lady in the whole of England." She immediately sent for the Latin secretary to write replies; he claimed to have been always obliged to write such letters to Spain three or four times, because the queen always found some defects in them.

It is possible that Elizabeth's cultural influence has been underestimated. After all, the chivalric influence at her husband's and her son's courts derived from her Burgundian family. When renovations were later made at the Greenwich palace, displaying a Burgundian influence, the queen herself devised part of the plan. From certain similarities in their handwriting, it may have been she who taught her second son and her daughters to write, and in the spring of 1488 Elizabeth's influence could perhaps be seen when a lady mistress was chosen for Prince Arthur (at a hefty fee of more than twenty-six pounds a year):

Elizabeth Darcy, who had presided over the nursery of Elizabeth's brother Edward V.

Elizabeth had a measure of literary interest, which she shared with her mother. She owned or used several *Books of Hours,* and the placing of her signature upon them would seem to indicate that she appreciated their exquisite illustrations, as well as giving them to favored ladies. One is inscribed, "Madam I pray you remember me in your good prayers your mistress Elizabeth R." A copy of the devotional *Scala perfectionis,* the Scale of Perfection, presented to her lady Mary Roos was signed both by her ("I pray you pray for me / Elizabeth ye queen") and by Margaret Beaufort. Elizabeth shared with her mother-in-law an interest in religion that led them particularly to Saint Bridget of Sweden, whose *The Fifteen Oes* (or *O's*) took pride of place in the collection of English and Latin prayers they commissioned together from Caxton.

One of the big questions about Elizabeth of York is her relationship with Margaret Beaufort. The 1498 report from another Spanish envoy, de Ayala, saying that the queen is "beloved because she is powerless," continued: "The King is much influenced by his mother and his followers in affairs or personal interest and in others. The Queen, as is generally the case, does not like it." He also spoke of Elizabeth's "subjection" to Margaret. There is a strong received impression that the two were antagonistic (or that antagonism was averted only by the supposed placidity on Elizabeth's part), and perhaps it is true that there was bound to be an element of rivalry between the queen and her strong-willed mother-in-law.

Henry certainly seems to have tried to ensure that the degree of ceremony accorded to his mother was not too far below that given to his wife. In 1493, when Henry drew up household ordinances, demonstrating the concern he shared with his mother for the dignity and order of the court, they stipulated that a bishop dining in Margaret's house would be served "as he is served in the king's presence" and that when Margaret went to church with the king and queen, she too should have her own cloth of estate. When the king took wine and spices after Evensong, it should be served with equal state to him, his mother, and his sons—the queen presumably residing in her own household, separately.

It must not be forgotten that part of the anxious parade of state and intimacy accorded to Margaret rather than to Elizabeth was because the queen had her own separate establishment and status already, whereas a place had to be created for the sort of "king's mother" Margaret was determined to be. Perhaps if Margaret had become a queen, a role that she clearly felt Fortune had denied her, she would not have felt the need to press for her rights quite so stridently.

Cecily Neville had likewise played an active part in the first years of Edward IV's reign, but Cecily, while possibly as determined a woman as Margaret, had herself been newly arrived at the independence of widowhood when her son became king. She had not spent years imagining her future role as Margaret must have done; she had not played such an active part in bringing her son to the throne.

Yet the picture of Elizabeth of York and Margaret Beaufort only as rivals may be slightly too simplistic. The Spanish envoy apart, the picture of their hostility depends largely on one particular well-known story of Margaret Beaufort's intervening to block a man who was trying to petition the queen and his resulting complaint that he had been set aside by "that strong whore," the king's mother. Margaret's action could be seen as officious, or protective—a little bit of both, maybe. Perhaps de Ayala had expectations unrealistic in England, having seen how his joint employer, Isabella of Castile, could exercise power quite openly. But the fact that Elizabeth and Margaret's contentious relationship is sketched in so few sources does draw its veracity into question.

Perhaps, too, Elizabeth and Margaret were able to utilize to some degree the fact that between them they represented two very different faces of queenship, or quasi queenship. Certainly, the two women could work together when necessary, joining together to receive the license to found a chantry or to apply for the rights to the next presentation to a deanery, though one might wonder how large a part Elizabeth really had to play in the actions—the more so because both of those partnerships also included, among other participants, her mother-in-law's old employee Reginald Bray. In 1501 the names of several of Margaret's trusted connections were among Elizabeth's officers—but this may mean only that, after all this time, their relationships were simply entangled to a degree, rather than displaying Margaret's dominance.

Elizabeth and Margaret probably collaborated more naturally on family matters. In the years ahead, they acted in concert to try to prepare for Catherine of Aragon's smooth passage into English life upon her marriage to young Arthur and to protect Elizabeth's daughter Margaret from the perils of too early marriage. But all the same, if Elizabeth of York's life was spelled out in big ceremonies and childbirths, then in very many of them she had her mother-in-law by her side, a situation that would certainly have displeased some of the other daughters-in-law in this story.

For the first decade or so at least, reports of the royal couple's movements almost always show Margaret with them—if, indeed, she was not with her son when the queen was absent. Margaret was, of course, a woman now past the pressures of childbearing and child rearing, which left her free to act almost like a male counselor. At the Oxfordshire palace of Woodstock, Margaret's lodgings were linked to the king's by a withdrawing chamber where the two could be together, for work or leisure. In the Tower, again, her rooms were next to the king's bedchamber and the council chamber.

It is hard to imagine how Margaret's extensive involvement in the royal family could not to some degree have grated on her daughter-in-law. A letter from William Paston describes how the royal trio—the king, his wife, and his mother—"lie at Northampton and will tarry there till Michaelmas," as though they were one indissoluble entity. A letter of Margaret's from 1497 wrote that the king, the queen, and all "our" sweet children were in good health.

By this time, however, Queen Elizabeth would perhaps be able to act more independently. As Henry VII found his feet, Francis Bacon would later claim that he reverenced but did not heed his mother. Nonetheless, to keep the two women closest to him placated must always have been a juggling act.

Henry's balancing of his wife's and his mother's claims can be seen in operation immediately after Elizabeth's coronation, at the end of 1487, when the court spent Christmas at Greenwich. On Twelfth Night, the king and queen wore their crowns, though the closest thing

Margaret Beaufort could be allowed was (as another manuscript preserved by John Leland records) "a rich Coronal." But when the king wore his formal surcoat and the queen hers, Margaret dressed "in like Mantel and Surcoat as the Queen."

There were, of course, distinctions made between the two royal women. Margaret had to walk slightly behind and "aside the queen's half train." After mass, as the king and queen dined in state, the king's marshal ended the formalities by making "Estate," or a formal reverence, to the king and queen and "half Estate" to the king's mother, the same as to the Archbishop of Canterbury. A letter from Henry VIII's day, after the divorce, would concede that Catherine of Aragon could keep the royal privilege of holding a Maundy Thursday, not as queen, but only "in the name of Princess Dowager, in like manner as my Lady the Kings graunt-dame did in the name of the Countess of Richemount and Derby."

As the court moved on to Windsor for Easter that spring, and the royal trio wore their Garter robes to chapel on Saint George's Day, the queen and the king's mother were censed after the king (though only the king and queen kissed the pax). Elizabeth of York was in one sense the senior partner here, having ridden in her first Garter procession decades before. Here once again, her ceremonial presence was probably more important for Henry's legitimacy than was usual for a queen, irritating though that may have been to Margaret. When they were accorded the Order of the Garter together, a song was composed to celebrate the two women's togetherness: it was as if everyone needed to parade, and to reassure the protagonists about, this odd duality.

Windsor, Westminster, Greenwich, Eltham, Sheen—despite his later reputation for miserliness, Henry made frequent and generous payments to dancers, entertainers of all kinds, and especially musicians. Music seems to have been an interest he and Elizabeth, who kept her own minstrels, shared. The pair traveled together perhaps more often than was usual, which could be variously ascribed to affection or possibly even to suspicion, if Henry felt he needed to keep an eye on Elizabeth—or on any Yorkists who might be drawn to her, anyway. But it was certainly an economy, since a second household functioning quite independently would inevitably cost more. The Great Wardrobe accounts show Henry not only making Elizabeth presents such as robes furred with miniver, but also supplying household essentials such as beds and hammers. The gifts of cash and communion cloths, gowns and gold wire may seem like evidence of intimacy and affection, but they could be seen another way. Despite the lands settled on her, Elizabeth's finances were not run like those of preceding queens, and Henry often had to bail her out, undermining her independence, even though her signature on each page of her Privy Purse accounts shows that she had by no means chosen to abnegate responsibility for her own finances. Her lands and fee farms, yielding some nineteen hundred pounds in 1496, plus an annuity the king had extracted on her behalf from the town of Bristol of another hundred, still amounted to less than half the income Elizabeth Woodville had enjoyed in her day. Often in debt, borrowing money on the security of her plate, Elizabeth of York was dependent on an ongoing stream of other gifts and loans from the king.

The only surviving records of Elizabeth's Privy Purse expenses date from later in the reign. Nonetheless, many of the sums dispersed must have been duplicated every year. The records show monetary recognition of presents of food: pippins and puddings, peasecods and pomegranates, warden pears and chines of pork, wine and woodcocks, rabbits and quails and conserves of cherries, a wild boar and tripes. They also show small practical purchases a great household requires: baskets and bellows, bolts and barehides, two barrels of Rhenish wine and the perpetual "boathire," for transporting people and property from one palace to another along the great watery highway that was the Thames. Her purchases for clothes included a gown of russet velvet and white fustian for socks. Further sums included upkeep for her horses and greyhounds, expenses to the keeper of her goshawk for meat for his bird and his spaniels (27s 8d), and three doublets of Bruges satin for her footmen at 20d apiece.

In Lent, almond butter was brought to Elizabeth—the rich man's substitute for dairy, at a time of year when fats were not allowed. In April and November, she gave money to nuns in the Minories, by the Tower, whose abbess had sent her rose water. There were many acts of charity. Elizabeth paid for the burying of a man who was hanged and gave money to another whose house had burned down. She paid support for one of the children who had been "given" to her, made contributions toward the enclosed life of an anchoress, and provided funding for one John Pertriche, son of "Mad Beale," right down to payment for the man who cured him of the French pox.

But the records also suggest that Elizabeth's income did not fit her expenditures. A great many of the entries record only part payment from Elizabeth—to tailors, saddlers, goldsmiths—and some of the money was long due. Her gowns were being mended, and she bought shoes with cheap tin buckles; she was pledging plate and borrowing money. This may be the result of Henry's habit of keeping her dramatically short of funds—or it may just reflect the casual relationship with cash of the aristocracy in any century.

One story in the Venetian state papers does fit with the conventional picture of Henry's miserliness. On May 9, 1489, the papal envoy wrote to the pope, "We have, moreover, opened the moneybox which the king was pleased to have at his court: we found in it 11 pounds 11s, which result made our heart sink within us, for there were present the King, the Queen, the mother of the King and the mother of the Queen, besides dukes, earls and marquises, and other lords and ambassadors, so that we expected to have far more."

The mention of Elizabeth Woodville as being present at the royal court in the spring of 1489 is particularly interesting. It is usually said that after her exile or retreat to Bermondsey, she visited court on literally only one or two specific occasions, one of them being the visit of a kinsman, the following November 1489, at the time of her daughter's next confinement. But this extra, less well-known, record of her presence some six months earlier suggests that while she undoubtedly did live largely retired, her appearances might have been more frequent, if not always conspicuously noted.

In the autumn of 1489, Elizabeth of York did indeed take to her chamber again.* She did so in state—"royally accompanied; that is to say, with my lady the Queen's mother, the Duchess of Norfolk, and many other going before her." The chamber itself was hanged with

---

*It is possible she had also given birth, the year before, to another son, Edward, who lived only a few hours. Other sources suggest the birth of such a child, but set the date considerably later.

rich cloth of blue arras, decorated with gold fleurs-de-lis—no other, more exciting, images, which were "not convenient about women in such case." But this time Elizabeth flouted protocol—the protocol her mother-in-law had enshrined—by receiving a great embassy from France after her retreat into her chambers. The party included a member of her mother's Luxembourg family.

This child, a daughter, was born just as her tiny son Arthur was being made knight and invested Prince of Wales. The baby was named for her godmother and grandmother Margaret Beaufort.

Eighteen months later came another, even more significant, confinement for Elizabeth. Prince Henry, the future Henry VIII, was born on June 28, 1491. But the months immediately following brought the start of a new trouble, which would haunt the new dynasty for the rest of the decade.

22

"THE EDGE OF TRAITORS"

Abate the edge of traitors, gracious Lord,
That would abate these bloody days again,
And make poor England weep in streams of blood

THE TRAGEDY OF RICHARD THE THIRD, 5.3

The autumn of 1491 saw the appearance of a pretender to the throne far more dangerous than Lambert Simnel. Simnel's story had been shaky from the beginning, and even the royal personage he had tried to impersonate— Clarence's young son Warwick—was not a figure to inspire much confidence in opponents to the new Tudor regime. Even with the rumored counseling of the queen's mother, Elizabeth Woodville, Simnel had been easily dispatched. This new pretender, however, would be far harder to get rid of—and his challenge would shake the young dynasty to its very foundations.

The pretender's name was Perkin Warbeck, and his early life was shrouded in a mist of uncertainty. Ironically, that just left observers all the more free simply to appreciate the princely looks and bearing that, from the start, gave him an air of legitimacy. Bernard André and

Polydore Vergil, with their Tudor-inspired hatred of Margaret of Burgundy, suggest that Warbeck may have had his birth in that country—possibly even physical birth, but certainly in his adult, royal identity (since they suspect Margaret might have been behind him even before his official arrival at the court of Burgundy in 1492, to launch a serious claim to the English throne). Bacon tellingly uses the imagery of witchcraft, saying that "the magic and curious arts" of Lady Margaret "raised up the ghost" of the boy Duke of York to walk and vex King Henry.

Warbeck's origins may be a mystery, but his entrance onto the English political stage was swift and well publicized, and his claim was, ingeniously, impossible to disprove. It had once again been Ireland that, in 1491, had first seen the princely looking lad who was Perkin Warbeck hailed as Richard, Duke of York, Elizabeth Woodville's younger son who had disappeared into the Tower during the reign of Richard III—a claim that, however improbable, cannot be conclusively disproved even today. As Perkin would later tell it, he was simply strutting the streets to display the handsome wares of his master, a silk merchant, when he began to be hailed as self-apparent royalty, and it is true that Ireland, chafing under the yoke of English governance, was always ready to foster dissent. But needless to say, Perkin's opponents saw a less naive story.

Warbeck quickly returned to the Continent after unveiling himself on England's doorstep. By the summer of 1492 (when Elizabeth of York was already preparing to give birth to a fourth baby), Perkin was in France, treated as an English prince and used by King Charles VIII (just as Henry Tudor had been used before him) as a tool of diplomacy. Indeed, the tall, glowing young man—so like his supposed father, Edward IV—seems to have owed a lot of the credence he received to the fact he looked and behaved like a king, or at least a prince. The same, at the beginning of his reign, had been said of Henry.

At this timely moment, in early June 1492, just before Whit Sunday, Elizabeth Woodville died, still at her convent in Bermondsey. The event cannot have been wholly unexpected; now in her midfifties, she had been predeceased by almost all of her many siblings. She had made her will on April 10: "Item. I bequeath my body to be buried with the body of my lord at Windsor, without pompous interring or costly expenses done thereabout. Item. Whereas I have no worldly goods to do the queen's grace a pleasure with, neither to reward any of my children according to my heart and mind, I beseech God Almighty to bless her grace, with all her noble issue; and, with as good a heart and mind as may be." She willed that "such small stuff and goods as I have" should be spent on repaying her debts and on prayers for the repose of her soul. It is hard not to remember, less than a decade before, the walls having to be broken down to get Elizabeth Woodville's extensive goods into sanctuary.

A surviving manuscript record shows that her burial was certainly as unostentatious as she had asked. "On Whit-Sunday, the queen-dowager's corpse was conveyed by water to Windsor, and there privily, through the little park, conducted into the castle, without any ringing of bells or receiving of the dean . . . and so privily, about eleven of the clock, she was buried, without any solemn dirge done for her obit." The only gentlewoman to accompany her body on its journey along the river was one Mistress Grace—"a bastard daughter of king Edward IV," which might seem to show Elizabeth Woodville had enough generosity of spirit to make a friend of a girl she might well have resented.

Elizabeth of York was not able to take any charge of her mother's obsequies, having entered her fourth confinement. (She would call her new daughter Elizabeth, perhaps the only form of commemoration available to the grieving queen.) Her next eldest sister, Cecily, was also absent and so was represented at the funeral by her husband. The three remaining, unmarried, daughters of Elizabeth Woodville did arrive—Anne, Katherine, and even eleven-year-old Bridget from the Dartford convent, where she had already been placed.* With them came Elizabeth Woodville's daughter-in-law the Marchioness of Dorset, Elizabeth's niece, and others, as well as the gentlemen, led by Dorset himself.

---

*Bridget seems to have been placed in the Dartford convent, famed for strict observance of Dominican rule, before she was ten, and it may have been that she was cloistered so early because she suffered some sort of physical weakness or frailty.

Finally, the dirge got under way, though instead of the twelve poor men neatly clad in black that custom would have dictated at the ceremony, there were only "a dozen divers old men, and they held old torches and torches' ends." Still, the queen dowager herself had said that she wanted it that way.

The grave had spared Elizabeth Woodville the agonizing doubts that Warbeck's mounting credit and credibility might have inspired. Any private conversations Elizabeth of York and her husband had about the pretender could never have been recorded, but a century or so later Bacon would have Perkin in his character of Richard declaring that on his delivery from the Tower, he resolved to wait for his uncle Richard III's death "and then to put myself into my sister's hands, who was next heir to the crown." It is interesting that Bacon suggests the alleged Duke of York would have sought refuge with the wife to a king from a new dynasty, a hint, possibly, that Elizabeth's feelings about this putative brother were a matter for speculation even in this near-contemporary day.

At the beginning of October 1492, Henry launched an expedition against France, both to protect his former refuge of Brittany from possible annexation by the French and to punish France's support for Perkin. Unsurprisingly, Margaret Beaufort made a major financial contribution to the campaign. As it turned out, though, Henry spent only a brief time across the Channel; like Edward years before, he was happy to be bought off by a sizable French pension. But before he left for France and a possible fight, while putting his affairs in order, he did acknowledge that Elizabeth of York's finances were "insufficient to maintain the Queen's dignity," giving her reversion rights to her grandmother's property whenever Cecily Neville would at last die.

Elizabeth of York was left as her mother had been left when Edward IV too went to a French war, and again government was nominally vested in her six-year-old son. Arthur was at Westminster while Elizabeth seems to have been with her other children at Eltham, the site of what was becoming the royal nursery for all her younger children. Within easy reach of London, the palace was an old favorite of her father's and near her own favorite residence of Greenwich. But her absence from Westminster at this moment shows that Elizabeth of York did not have even the limited powers that had been invested in

Elizabeth Woodville long before. Nor did Margaret Beaufort, presumably; the times were changing and not, for half a century yet, in favor of a woman's authority.

But women still had other avenues of influence open to them, as was demonstrated in November 1492 when a new major player appeared in the Perkin Warbeck story. It was, predictably, Margaret of Burgundy, who some believed had been behind Perkin from the very start, but who now met him openly. The Low Countries had, despite Maximilian's accord with Henry, never ceased to be a refuge for Henry's enemies. Nor had Margaret ceased to have contact with Ireland and Scotland, those springboards for an English invasion. She had, indeed, been planning to take the battle to the Tudors—spreading the rumors a prince had survived—even before Perkin publicly appeared.

Perkin was, it seems, exactly the sort of weapon that Margaret of Burgundy was looking for to avenge her brother Richard and their house of York. Vergil said that she had found the boy herself; he was a suitable candidate for instruction. Bacon wrote that she had long had spies out to look for "handsome and graceful youths to make Plantagenets." The French king told the Scottish that Perkin had been "preserved many years secretly" by Margaret. In a letter to the pope, begging for recognition of her "nephew's" claims, Margaret herself supported her petition with a garbled version of a story from the first book of Kings, in which the prince Joash is snatched from harm to be brought up secretly in the house of an aunt.

Margaret, indeed, may have been convinced of Perkin's legitimacy. Whatever those in other countries believed, Perkin had been welcomed in Burgundy as a prince and as Margaret's close kin. Indeed, Vergil wrote that Margaret received him "as though he had been revived from the dead . . . so great was her pleasure that the happiness seemed to have disturbed the balance of her mind." Margaret wrote to Queen Isabella in Spain that when Perkin appeared in Burgundy, she had at once recognized him as her nephew. She had been told of his existence when he was in Ireland but had then thought the tale "ravings and dreams," until in France he had been identified by men she sent who would have recognized him "as easily as his mother or his nurse." When Margaret herself at last met him, she said, "I recognised him as easily as if I had last seen him yesterday or the day before. . . . He did not have just one or another sign of resemblance, but so many and so particular that hardly one person in ten, in a hundred or even in a thousand might be found who would have marks of the same kind." However ardent they were, Margaret's claims, of course, need to be taken with a hefty grain of salt; she had last seen the actual Duke of York in England when he was a child, some dozen years before.

Margaret seems to have used no such caution in her embrace of Perkin. "I indeed for my part, when I gazed on this only male Remnant of our family—who had come through so many perils and misfortunes—was deeply moved," she wrote to Isabella ecstatically, "and out of this natural affection, into which both necessity and the rights of blood were drawing me, I embraced him as my only nephew and my only son." It was perhaps emotionally important that she would now, after Elizabeth Woodville's death, have been the prince's only mother. She intended—as the Latin is translated—to nourish and cherish him. The language was that one might use for a young child.

Perkin also wrote to Isabella, with a vague description of how a "certain lord" had been told to kill him but, "pitying my innocence," had preserved him. He seemed, however, to have gotten his own age slightly wrong, though his praise of his "dearest aunt" rang true enough.

Isabella was unimpressed and concerned about the fresh potential for unrest in the country where her daughter Catherine of Aragon was to marry. She wrote, woman to woman, to Margaret, suggesting she should not be taken in. But Isabella's caution would not necessarily be followed by the other rulers of Europe: a prince or pretender could always prove an invaluable pawn of diplomacy.

The news that the Duke of York was alive "came blazing and thundering over into England," said Bacon, breeding murmurs of all sorts against the king, suggesting that by rights he should be ruling only through Elizabeth, and so "God had now brought to light a masculine branch of the house of York," who could not be overlooked as easily as Elizabeth, his "poor lady."

In 1493 Henry was writing about "the great malice that the Lady Margaret of Burgundy beareth continually against us," in sending first the "feigned boy" Lambert Simnel and now another "feigned lad." He was invoking a conception popular at the time: that of the she-wolf or, as Edward Hall would later imagine Margaret, the "dog reverting to her old vomit." Hall memorably described Margaret as being "like one forgetting both God and charity" in her malice against Henry, seeking "to suck his blood and compass his destruction," not just a she-wolf like Marguerite of Anjou, but a vampire as well.

Hall (and Bacon after him) followed Vergil in this, claiming Margaret, driven by "insatiable hatred and fiery wrath," continually sought Henry's destruction—"so ungovernable is a woman's nature especially when she is under the influence of envy," he glossed. Vergil was probably swayed by Henry VII's own perception of events, and Henry may well have been influenced by Louis of France: he who had cast doubts on Margaret's chastity even before her marriage, just as he had impugned the chastity of Cecily.

Margaret of Burgundy, Bacon sneered, had "the spirit of a man and the malice of a woman."* Being "childless and without any nearer care," he said, she could devote herself to her "mortal hatred" of Henry and the house of Lancaster—a hatred, Bacon claimed, she now extended even to Henry's wife, her own niece. Certainly, Margaret did not seem to regard Elizabeth's role as queen consort as elevating the family's status in any way. Her letter to Isabella had spoken of how her family had "fallen from the royal summit," suggesting the situation could be redeemed only by a "male remnant." Or perhaps she thought that for one who had been, in Vergil's words, "the means of the king's ascent to the throne," a mere consort's role was inadequate.

Margaret's hopes, however, were already on shaky ground. By 1493 Henry had discovered an alternative identity for the supposed prince: Perkin Warbeck from the French border city of Tournai, a boatman's son. That summer an embassy was sent to Burgundy, warning Philip (now old enough to hold at least theoretical rule when his father, Maximilian, succeeded to the grander title of Holy Roman Emperor) that he was giving houseroom to an impostor. One of the envoys

---

*Impossible not to think of Marguerite of Anjou—but perhaps also of Cecil's famous dictum that Elizabeth I was "more than a man, and in truth sometimes less than a woman."

(Warham, a future archbishop) joked unpleasantly to the childless Margaret that in Simnel and Warbeck, she had produced "two great babes not as normal but fully grown and long in the womb." Henry's efforts were unsuccessful: while Philip, and probably Maximilian behind him, raised men for the pretender, Margaret provided money. She had not lost her head over the affair entirely. Her "nephew" was to pay his "aunt" the remaining part of her dowry as soon as he won the English throne: her promised wool rights, the manor of Hunsdon, and the town of Scarborough.

In October 1494, in England, Henry VII created his second son, Henry, Duke of York—the title the younger Prince in the Tower had borne and the one Warbeck had since claimed for himself. (Arthur, as Prince of Wales, had the year before been sent to take up residence in Ludlow, just as Elizabeth of York's eldest brother had done.) Prince Henry's new title was a riposte to Perkin, and also perhaps a sop to any disaffected Yorkists—a reminder that through his wife, the king had annexed also the Yorkist claim. The celebratory tournaments for the younger Henry's investiture were set up as a chivalric fantasy centering on the queen, just as earlier tournaments had centered on Elizabeth Woodville and her jousting family: "The Queen's grace and the ladies, remembering themselves that ancient custom of the [the king's] noble realm of England . . . besought the King's grace to license and to permit them at the said feast to hold and to keep a 'justes royall' [a royal joust]." Margaret Beaufort was with the king and queen as they left Woodstock to move toward the capital for the ceremonies; she was still with them three weeks later as they processed away from Westminster.

The queen was prominent in her state, the jousters on the first day wearing her crest as well as the king's livery. But subsequent challengers could also be seen in Margaret Beaufort's blue and white livery, and she was one of the ladies who advised on the prizes, which were presented by her namesake, the "high and excellent princess," little Margaret.

Other changes around this time were also designed, in part, to tighten the security of the regime. In January 1495, Henry offered his daughter Margaret in marriage to the king of Scotland—the son of

Elizabeth Woodville's erstwhile prospective bridegroom. Henry was busy securing his flanks.

The queen's sisters were also being married off: Anne to the grandson of one of Richard III's leading adherents who might thus be reconciled to Henry's regime and Katherine, by way of reward, into the notably Lancastrian Courtenay family. Connections of the various women, after all, were still involved in machinations against Henry. In February 1495, Sir William Stanley—Margaret Beaufort's brother-in-law, the man whose intervention had made all the difference at Bosworth—was found to have had contact with Warbeck and was executed.

But the royal women's troubling connections did not end there. A servant of Edward's sister Elizabeth had also been among those indicted in these years, and several of those in trouble over the Warbeck affair had been neighbors or servants of Cecily Neville's. But any question of active involvement on Cecily's part would soon be over. Her long life was drawing to a close.

On May 31, 1495, at Berkhampsted, Cecily died, being, as her will declared, "of whole mind and body, loving therefore be it to Jh'u [Jesus]," surrendering her soul into God's hands and the protection of the saints. Her body, subject to Henry VII's permission, was to be buried at Fotheringhay beside that of "my most entirely beloved Lord and husband, father unto my said lord and son [Edward IV]." She left a series of bequests to the Fotheringhay college—everything from mass books to ecclesiastical vestments—and to the abbey at Syon "two of the best copes of crimson cloth."

In her will, Cecily asks, as was usual, that any debts should be paid, rather touchingly "thanking our Lord at the time of making of this my testament [that] to the knowledge of my conscience I am not much in debt." But it is the personal bequests that are the interesting ones. An acknowledgment to the king, legacies to officers of her household, to "my daughter of Suffolk" her chair of litter with all the "cushions, horses, and harnesses" belonging to it, and to her granddaughter Anne a barge with all its accoutrements and "the largest bed of bawdekyn [a silk fabric with metal threads, like a less costly cloth of gold], with counterpoint of the same." (Her great-grandson Prince

Arthur, heir apparent to the Tudor dynasty, got a bed of arras with the Wheel of Fortune—an unsettling, if salutary, reminder that nothing in royal life was ever fixed.)

Cecily's granddaughter and godchild Bridget was left the *Legenda Aurea* on vellum and Cecily's books on Saint Katherine and Matilda. A Psalter with a relic of Saint Christopher went to Elizabeth of York, a breviary "with clasps of gold covered with black cloth of gold" to Margaret Beaufort. It was yet another exemplar of how religion forged links between women who, perhaps, might find in God a new, a separate, lease on life after their years of marriage and childbearing were over and after they were freed from their husbands' enmity.

But even as the royal family mourned the passing of the matron of the house of York, there were troubling reminders that the old divisions still lingered. When Cecily died, her will left money to Master Richard Lessy, who had been involved in the plotting against Henry, specifically to help him pay the fine, with the request the king might curtail the charge. Several of the others to whom she left legacies had connections with Burgundy and with Duchess Margaret. It would have been just one more reminder that Henry could never really feel secure about his wife's Yorkist connections, however amicable their personal relations might be.

23

"CIVIL WOUNDS"

Now civil wounds are stopped; peace lives again.
That she may long live here, God says amen.

THE TRAGEDY OF RICHARD THE THIRD, 5.5

In late June 1495, nearly a month after Cecily Neville died, Perkin Warbeck's fleet set sail across the Channel for a first invasion attempt. His men landed on the coast near Deal on the southeastern coast of England, but, for lack of support, were forced to set sail again for Ireland, and in November made for Scotland and the court of the young King James.

James and Warbeck took to each other, and, as Perkin settled into the Scottish court, the king even married him to the beautiful Katherine Gordon, his own "tender cousin." Perkin was awaiting more arms from Margaret in Burgundy, but financial support even from that quarter seemed to be drying up, since Burgundy's new young ruler, Philip, now withdrew his support. It is a salutary reminder that cooler issues of broader Burgundian policy and of pay ran alongside Margaret's emotional enthusiasm. In the treaty that, in February 1496, restored the damaged trading relation between Burgundy and England,

Margaret was bound over not to give aid to Henry's enemies, and she at least seemed to comply.

It was a time of mixed emotions back in England. In that autumn of 1495, Elizabeth of York's daughter and namesake had died of "atrophy," aged three—or "passed out of this transitory life," as her monument in Westminster Abbey described it. The next spring, on March 18, 1496, another daughter, Mary, was born.

In 1496, amid fears of an invasion, Margaret Beaufort and Henry toured her Dorset estates, winding up at the improved and impressive castle of Corfe, traditionally a Beaufort property. Tensions were still running high. It was that year Margaret Beaufort sent a letter to the Earl of Ormond thanking him for a gift of gloves sent from Flanders—"right good," she said, but too big for her hand. "I think the ladies in that parts be great ladies all, and according to their great estates they have great personages"—a crack from the petite Margaret Beaufort about the solidly built Margaret of Burgundy.

An invasion of sorts came later that year, when in September 1496 James of Scotland and his protégé, Perkin, rode south with an army fourteen hundred strong. It was little more than a raiding party, however, and they soon returned across the border. Henry surely wanted to focus on this continuing threat from the North—he had instituted new forms of taxation to fund a campaign against Scotland—but his attention was soon to be split between Warbeck and a new, unexpected danger.

In the early summer of 1497, news came of trouble at the opposite corner of the kingdom. The Cornishmen were in rebellion against Henry's new tax and calling for the dismissal of the king's money raisers, Morton and Bray—Margaret Beaufort's former men. The news caught the royal party at Sheen, but now the queen, with her son Henry, moved to London and Margaret Beaufort's house of Coldharbour. A week later, as news came that the Cornish rebels were as close as Farnham, Elizabeth of York—like her mother before her, and with her own memories—took to the Tower for refuge. The main battle was at Blackheath, only a mile or two from the royal nursery palace of Eltham—but, on June 17, it was Henry who won the victory.

At the end of the summer, however, Perkin (urged on by James) was back, not this time attacking across the northern border, but leaving Scotland by sea. His wife set sail with him—shades of Anne and Isabel Neville—which may show that Scotland too was finally tiring of its puppet princeling and that this was to be a last throw of the dice. The couple landed in Cornwall, the site of the recent May rebellions, where, sending the ladies to Saint Michael's Mount for safety, Perkin declared himself king. As Henry marched west, Elizabeth (with her young son Henry) went on pilgrimage to Walsingham, getting out of the way of danger without looking too panicky.

But Perkin seems to have been the one who was really unnerved—unnerved by the first fighting, along with the news that Henry was on the way. Fleeing into sanctuary, he was persuaded to surrender and confessed to being a fraud. The confession was widely circulated in Europe; Margaret in Burgundy must have heard it. Coincidentally or otherwise, that summer she was taken ill. Vergil wrote that news of the capture "made her weep many tears for her prince."

Perkin wrote to his real mother, Katherine Warbeque, telling her the story of how he had left home for Antwerp and there been taken into the service of Sir Edward Brampton—the man sent to negotiate a marriage for Richard III in Portugal—who had taken him to that country. From Portugal a new employer, Pregent Meno, had taken him to Ireland, where he was first taken for a Plantagenet. It was a curious story, made more curious by the fact that both Brampton and Meno had come into King Henry's service, and by the fact that many still doubted a boatman's son could so convincingly play the prince—and, perhaps, by the treatment the pseudoroyal couple received once they surrendered to Henry.

Perkin's wife, Katherine Gordon, is an interesting figure—interesting in the light her treatment casts upon Henry VII, and perhaps on Elizabeth too. Katherine—like Elizabeth Woodville before her—had to be "much talked to" before she would relinquish the privileges of sanctuary. But from the start, it was obvious that her treatment would be kindly. This may be the single most striking example of the way in which women were often regarded as exempt from the penalties levied on their menfolk—but it may also be a sign of something more personal, a reputation that had gone before her for beauty. Henry's letter's spoke of her as being "in dole"—that is, mourning, and literal mourning, rather than just grief for her husband's capture—and this may have been for a lost or stillborn child. When Katherine was finally able to travel, Henry sent black clothes in which she could do so: satin dress, riding cloak—everything down to hose and shoes. Vergil said that when Henry saw her, he was much taken, or, as Hall put it, he "began then a little to fantasy her person." His concern took an overtly paternal form, providing sober matrons to accompany her "because she was but a young woman," as well as everything practical from money to (so the wardrobe accounts record) "night kerchers"—sanitary wear.

Henry, too, took care to extricate Katherine from her relationship with Perkin. When Henry (so his pet writer, blind Bernard André, wrote in a private volume for the king's own pleasure) arranged a meeting with her husband, Katherine "with a modest and graceful look and singularly beautiful, was brought into the king's presence in an untouched state." Henry, as André tells it, made a long speech to this quasi maiden—apparently considered, since the man she thought she married never existed, to have attained the state of honorary virginity almost as a queen did before her coronation—telling her life ahead would have "many possibilities." As Perkin was forced to repeat his confession to her, Katherine burst into a torrent of lamentation and recrimination, "soaked through with a fountain of tears." Only one man now could be her savior—Henry himself, naturally.

On one level, it was natural that Katherine should be taken into the queen's household, the obvious place for one of her own, undisputed, noble birth. Perhaps something was being implied about Perkin's pretensions—that there had never been any smidgen of truth in them and that there was thus no danger in putting Katherine into a position where she could give Elizabeth dangerous information, or conspire with her Yorkist connections in any way. But it is probably also true that Henry could now feel sure his wife was too committed to the future of her own offspring to be moved by any older loyalty. Certainly, Elizabeth (just returned from that pilgrimage to Walsingham) seems to have accepted Katherine as one of her ladies, with the high place her Scottish rank entailed. If Elizabeth had any other reason for warmth toward the girl who had thought to be her sister-in-law, then she concealed it. And if, conversely, she had any suspicion of her husband's feelings for Katherine, then it would seem she was prepared, as her mother had done, to turn a blind eye.*

It was, of course, one thing to treat the noble Katherine with kid gloves, but, extraordinarily, Perkin too was brought to court and treated with a surprising leniency. The Venetian ambassador reported only that he and Katherine were forbidden to sleep together, suggesting that otherwise he was handled courteously.

It has often been suggested over the years that "Perkin Warbeck" did indeed have Plantagenet blood in his veins—not perhaps as the legitimate Duke of York, but as a Plantagenet bastard. True, Edward IV (and his brother Richard) had acknowledged other illegitimate children, but their decisions to do so must to some degree have depended on the mothers' position—as well, of course, as on the fathers' knowledge of the pregnancies. What is more, whereas it would have been relatively acceptable for the king to admit to a liaison, for a royal woman to have borne a bastard child would have been a very different story.

It was even suggested at the time that Perkin was Margaret of Burgundy's actual, illegitimate, son. In 1495 Maximilian had apparently said so, and Maximilian was close to Margaret. This may well have been just another example of a man using a woman's reputation as an expendable tool of political expediency, and the suggestion has to be put in the context both of earlier slurs on her reputation and of the regularity with which such slurs were cast upon a woman who transgressed in any way. But the time of a pregnancy, later historians have suggested, would have been in 1473, when she had disappeared for two months to the palace of Ten-Noode, commonly used for recuperative purposes. If the allegations were true, Margaret, of course, could have simply declared the bastard to be her husband's child—but that option would obviously have been unavailable if she and her husband

---

*After the queen's death—and the funeral at which she laid the fourth pall, right after the queen's sisters—Henry was said to keep Katherine so close it was rumored they had now married. Remaining in England after Henry's death, she made three more marriages with English gentlemen, retaining a particular friendship for the daughter of Queen Elizabeth's sister Cecily.

were both aware that a lack of physical relations between them, in the right period of time, made this an impossibility. It must go down as another mystery.

If Perkin Warbeck was truly a Plantagenet, there is, of course, a possibility that Elizabeth of York would pick up on their family connection—but Elizabeth, who must have seen him in person, though not necessarily at close quarters, appears never to have commented publicly (unless her kindness to Katherine Gordon can be interpreted as a tacit comment). Indeed, she seems to have continued to stand firmly by her husband. On October 11 at Woodstock, the family certainly put on a good, united, display for the visiting Venetian envoy, who found Elizabeth "at the end of the hall, dressed in cloth of gold," with Margaret on one side of her and Prince Henry on the other.

Margaret Beaufort, meanwhile, was still traveling incessantly with the king. In the summer of 1498, mother and son were together at London, Westminster, Sheen, and Windsor (where Margaret ordered brooches for her grandchildren), then on a tour of eastern counties. Her house was now a gathering place. Henry Parker, her carver as a teenager, remembered how, when serving her at New Year's, he had twenty-five knights following behind him. "In her hall from nine of the clock till it was seven of the clock at night as fast as one table was up another was set, no poor man was denied at that said feast of Christmas if he were of any honesty." It was an almost royal liberality. Her household had its lighter side. She employed a fool named Skyp, for whom high-heeled shoes had to be bought, and "Reginald the idiot." She would give money to visiting dancers, and she would have a "house of boughs" built, one April, in which she could dine. Once she paid a man to go on pilgrimage for her—because she herself was too busy playing cards.

In 1498 the ongoing negotiations for a marriage between Prince Arthur and Catherine of Aragon showed how far into the club of European royalty the Tudors had come. Elizabeth herself wrote to Queen Isabella, her "cousin and dearest relation," wishing her "health and the most prosperous increase of her desires"; she described Catherine as "our common daughter."

Elizabeth's own initiative apart, the details of the match between Arthur and Catherine of Aragon had also been a much-cited instance of she and her mother-in-law working together. In July 1498, the Spanish ambassador reported, "The Queen and the mother of the King wish that the Princess of Wales [Catherine] should always speak French with the Princess Margaret [the daughter of Mary of Burgundy, raised in France] who is now in Spain, in order to learn the language, and to be able to converse in it when she comes to England. This is necessary, because these ladies do not understand Latin, and much less, Spanish. They also wish that the Princess of Wales should accustom herself to drink wine. The water of England is not drinkable, and even if it were, the climate would not allow the drinking of it." In the letter, Margaret and Elizabeth speak as if with one voice, commanding from a position of greater unity and cohesion than they perhaps had enjoyed in the earlier years of Elizabeth's queenship.

Not all the potential royal marriage arrangements, however, were going as planned. Also in 1498, the Spanish envoy de Ayala was reporting to Ferdinand and Isabella that a marriage between the Scottish king and Henry's daughter had many "inconveniences." The English king said that his wife, Elizabeth, and her mother-in-law joined forces to protect their daughter and granddaughter Margaret, who "has not yet completed the ninth year of her age, and is so delicate and weak [*femi-nina*] that she must be married much later than other young ladies. Thus it would be necessary to wait at least another nine years." Besides his own doubts, Henry said, "The Queen and my mother are very much against this marriage. They say if the marriage were concluded, we should be obliged to send the Princess directly to Scotland, in which case they fear the King of Scots would not wait, but injure her, and endanger her health." If her granddaughter and namesake took after Margaret Beaufort in stature, the elder lady was clearly determined the child should not share her fate. And as with the instructions concerning Catherine of Aragon, both Margaret and Elizabeth of York seemed to be reconciled, to a degree, by their common interests.

The year 1498 also saw an attempt by Perkin Warbeck to escape. Vergil wrote that friends pushed him into it, and his wife, Katherine Gordon, may have urged it—but it is also possible that he had been lured into it by servants of King Henry, anxious now (since the threat represented by Perkin's continued existence was concerning the parents of Catherine of Aragon and proving a hindrance to the Spanish match) to have an excuse to do away with him. Afterward, he was kept under much stricter conditions and indeed moved to the Tower—an ill portent for the debunked prince.

Perkin's incarceration in the Tower was shortly followed by the arrival of a trade delegation from Burgundy, headed by the Bishop of Cambrai and bearing (so said the Spanish ambassador) a formal apology to King Henry from Margaret, perhaps humbling herself in a last throw to get clemency for her protégé. The bishop asked if he might see the young man. When taxed with having deceived his benefactress, Perkin "swore to God that Duchess Madame Margaret knew as well as himself that he was not the son of King Edward." The Spanish reported that Henry wanted to proceed against the duchess, but that Philip of Burgundy and his new wife (Juana, a sister of Catherine of Aragon) would not allow it. If Margaret was a mother of sorts to Perkin, she had played that part, too, to Philip, and now Burgundy's ruler stood by her.

At the end of February 1499, Elizabeth of York gave birth to another son at Greenwich. Margaret Beaufort was again the godmother, making generous presents to the midwife and nurses and a christening gift worth one hundred pounds. But maybe some frailty in the baby, Edmund (who would die some sixteen months later), was allied to some concern over the state of his mother's health. The Spanish envoy wrote to his monarchs that "there had been much fear that the life of the Queen would be in danger, but the delivery, contrary to expectation, has been easy. The christening was very splendid, and the festivities such as though an heir to the Crown had been born." It is possible that Henry and Elizabeth here decided—having, as it seemed, the heir and two spares—to settle for what family they had. After Edmund's birth, Elizabeth's pregnancies ceased—for the moment, at least.

With their brood of robust children, Elizabeth and Henry had laid an auspicious foundation for the new Tudor dynasty. In 1499 the great Renaissance scholar Erasmus was taken by his friend Thomas More to visit the royal nursery at Eltham. He described what he found: nine-year-old Henry ("already with a certain royal demeanour"), flanked on his right by eleven-year-old Margaret, and "on the left Mary was playing, a child of four. Edmund was an infant in arms." It sounds as solid a family group as, a generation before, the York family—although, as in the York family, the eldest son had been drawn apart, to live outside his mother's direct care. Prince Arthur in distant Wales had his own household, with all the tutors necessary to train him to be a king.

With the threats from pretenders receding, it did seem as though the Tudors were breaking through into a new era of stability. Perhaps now Margaret Beaufort felt she could safely turn her attention elsewhere, to the task of shoring up other, more immediately practicable, dimensions of the regime.

In 1499 to 1500, Margaret spent more than a hundred pounds on a new series of buildings against the gates of her principal residence, Collyweston, in Northamptonshire: a council house, a chamber where those coming in legal suits could receive attention without impinging on the domestic side of the household itself, and a prison. Margaret Beaufort's house was becoming not only a palace—with a jewel house and a presence chamber, a library, and pleasure grounds—but an administrative center for the king's authority in the Midlands and in the North.

In earlier reigns, a measure of control in the North had been delegated by Edward IV to his brother Richard and by Richard to his nephew John. But Henry VII was an only child, and in the absence of other near relations, he turned, as so often before, to his mother. Her task may have been different from the one given to those men and soldiers, but no one can doubt that Margaret's was the ultimate authority in deciding the fate of every litigant who came before her council, whether it was a question of money owed between individuals or alleged disrespectful remarks made about the Tudor dynasty. She made a powerful and lasting impression. In the early sixteenth century, and again in the early seventeenth, debates in the Inns of Court in London cited Margaret's example as suggesting that a *feme sole* could, through royal commission, be made a justice of the peace; the king's attorney declared that he had seen "many arbitraments" made by her.

With men like the old "Kingmaker," Earl of Warwick, and Lord Hastings gone, power in the Midlands had fallen largely into the hands of the Stanley family. But now the Stanleys were proving themselves dubiously trustworthy—with Sir William Stanley having thrown in his lot with the recent rebellion and been executed for his pains—despite being in-laws to the king's mother and despite having made the decisive contribution at the battle that swept the Tudors into power.

Henry needed someone on whom he could completely rely. That may be—partly—why in 1499 Margaret Beaufort was able to take another step toward independence. At the beginning of the year, with the permission of her husband, Stanley, the Earl of Derby, she undertook a vow of chastity (technically, stating it as a "purpose," since to do such a thing in her husband's lifetime was unheard of and might, surely, seem to counteract the other vows she had taken in matrimony). It would not have been an unusual choice for a widow; an increasing number, in these years, were choosing to become vowesses, undergoing a ceremony of cloaking and veiling before a bishop, taking a vow of chastity, but without going to live in a convent, taking vows of poverty and obedience, or renouncing the goods and concerns of the lay state. But for a woman with a living husband, Margaret's action was unusual to a degree.

She was now basing her establishment clearly in Collyweston rather than in Lathom or Knowsley, the houses she had shared with her husband. There is no evidence as to how Stanley felt about this, but although there was no actual breach—rooms were reserved for him at Collyweston—he also was in no position to resist. Not only was Margaret's move a recognition of a state of affairs that had probably long existed, but it was also to some degree a matter of state, since Margaret's new administrative role required that she should be associated only with those of certain loyalty.

Also from this year, instead of signing her letters "M Richmond," Margaret took to signing them with the quasi-regal "Margaret R"—the R, of course, capable of being interpreted either as Richmond or as Regina. A letter to Henry, which has tentatively been dated to January 14, 1499,* is indeed so signed, by "your faithful true bedewoman, and humble mother, Margaret R." But even if Margaret at this point in her life did feel able to claim a higher title in her own right, there was certainly no diminution in the ardently expressed devotion that breathes

---

*Many letters of the period have the day and the month, but no year.

from the document itself—addressed to "My own sweet and most dear King and all my worldly joy." The bulk of the letter is concerned with "my matter which so long hath hanged"—a decades-old attempt to extract from the French ducal house of Orléans a sum of ransom money the Beauforts believed was still owed to Margaret's grandfather. But there was still time among the necessary pieces of information and instruction to assure Margaret's "dear heart" that if she should finally get any of the money, "there shall never be that or any good I have but it shall be yours. . . . And Our Lord give you as long good life, health and joy, as your most noble heart can desire, with as hearty blessings as our Lord hath given me the power to give you."

In May 1499, the proxy marriage between Arthur and Catherine of Aragon had taken place, but Catherine's parents, still worried about any threat to the English throne from "doubtful royal blood," were reluctant to send their daughter to that country. Nor, all too visibly, were all the old York interests reconciled to the Tudor dynasty: in July 1499, Suffolk—the younger son to Edward IV's sister Elizabeth and younger brother to the Earl of Lincoln, who had died fighting for Lambert Simnel—decamped abroad. He was persuaded back, and just as well, maybe. Bacon would later say that although Suffolk went to Flanders, Margaret of Burgundy was growing weary of her attempts to replace Henry. Presumably, therefore, she gave him less than a wholehearted welcome. But shortly afterward, another young man appeared claiming to be Clarence's son the Earl of Warwick. Henry realized his only safety lay in ridding himself, once and for all, of any such threat.

On November 23, 1499, Perkin Warbeck was executed, as shortly afterward was the real Warwick, Queen Elizabeth's cousin; his death was a political necessity not for anything he had actually done, but for what had been, and still might be, done in his name. Henry said the executions were necessary "because the Duchess Margaret of Burgundy and the King of the Romans [Maximilian] would not stop believing that Perkin was the true and legitimate son of King Edward, and Duke of York; and the duchess had given him so much authority and credit, that it had to be done." The fact was, of course, that it had to be done to facilitate the Spanish marriage, which, it was hoped, would move the Tudor dynasty into the next century, but would not come off with either Perkin or the hapless Warwick—perhaps the most innocent victim of these disputes—still providing a rallying point for opposition to the Crown.

To Margaret in Burgundy, Henry's words must have cut deep—as, of course, they were meant to do. She had lost the young man whom she had once considered her nephew and son, and Henry claimed to have executed him because of her. What's more, with Perkin had died Margaret's hopes for reinstalling a Yorkist on the throne of England. For a woman who had spent so much of her life looking northward across the Channel, it would have been a devastating blow.

At some point in that year of 1499, Margaret commissioned a painting, derived from Rogier van der Weyden's painting of Christ's body being lifted down from the cross. One figure bears Margaret's long-nosed face—she is the Mary Magdalene lamenting at the feet of the deposed Christ, her crimson velvet cloak and cloth-of-gold robe caught by a belt trimmed with daisies—marguerites—and ornamented by a white rose. Indeed, her whole posture seems designed to draw attention to the flower, the white rose of York, which had become Perkin's symbol in his royal—if perhaps assumed—identity.

24

LIKE A QUEEN INTER ME

yet like
A queen and daughter to a king inter me.

THE LIFE OF KING HENRY THE EIGHTH, 4.2

As the new century dawned, a new generation of Tudor royalty was moving to the fore. Among Henry VII and Elizabeth of York's children, Prince Arthur was now thirteen and even Margaret ten, fast approaching the age of marriageability. While Elizabeth's childbearing seemed to have ceased, for the moment at least, the increased geographical distance of Margaret Beaufort from the court may also well have come as a relief to the queen.

In May 1500, Elizabeth went with Henry to Calais (the only part of France the English still held) on a forty-day trip. It was partly to escape the plague (especially bad that year) and partly a matter of diplomacy; they were going to a meeting with Philip of Burgundy. They sailed on May 8 and arrived the same night. The king took ushers, chaplains, squires, herald, clerks, grooms, pages, as well as guards—and so did his queen.

A month later, the royal couple met Philip at St. Peter's Church outside Calais's walls, especially decorated for the occasion with tapestries and scented flowers strewn on the floor. Philip's recent marriage to Catherine of Aragon's elder sister Juana had forged a new tie between Burgundy and the new English dynasty. The Spanish envoy reported that "the King and the Archduke had a very long conversation, in which the Queen afterwards joined. The interview was very solemn, and attended with great splendour." The royal couple landed back in Dover on June 16, but any pleasure they felt at returning home would be short-lived. On June 19, their baby son, Edmund, died at Hatfield, and the heartbreakingly tiny coffin had to be carried through the London streets to a royal burial in Westminster Abbey.

Margaret Beaufort, probably in one of her own residences, must only later have heard the news. There is, for once, no record of Margaret having joined the Calais party. The Spanish ambassador had commented on the speed with which the trip was arranged, so perhaps Margaret was simply at Collyweston, too far away to join the party, and in any case outside the plague zone. But if there was any element of her being left behind to "mind the shop," as it were, she may nonetheless have been determined not to be wholly left out.

Early the next year, Margaret was writing her own letter from Calais, commemorating her son's birthday: "This day of St Anne's, that I did bring into this world my good and gracious prince, king and only beloved son." Margaret's life was as peripatetic as ever, but not necessarily based around the court, since other letters in roughly the same year were signed from other of Margaret's regular residences, Hatfield and Buckden. Once again, her letter from Calais was addressed to "My dearest and only desired joy in this world" and signed as from Henry's "humble servant, bedeswoman, and mother." But the first part of the document was—again—about what Henry had next to do in support of his mother's long-standing Orléans claim, pursuance of which may have been what brought her across the Channel. "I wish, my dear heart, an [if] my fortune be to recover it [the money], I trust you shall well perceive I shall deal towards you as a kind, loving mother; and, if I should never have it, yet your kind dealing it is to me a thousand times more than all that good I can recover." It was almost as if the common pursuit of money (and the power—or security—that came with it) was a shared language between mother and son.

They had, however, other ways of speaking freely; in the same letter, Margaret also asks her son to enter into a small subterfuge to help her maintain good relations with her husband, Stanley. Stanley's son, who held offices on her lands in Kendal, had himself been claiming the allegiance of Margaret's tenants; rather than claim her own rights directly but tactlessly, she suggested the king send her a letter ordering that all her tenants should be retained only in the name of little Henry, Duke of York—"a good excuse," Margaret noted, "for me to [give to] my lord and husband." Perhaps Stanley, now Margaret was officially independent of him, was feeling a little jealous of his rights.

Elizabeth too was having troubles with her extended family. In August 1501, her cousin Suffolk decamped again, this time permanently, inevitably making his way into the Burgundian sphere of influence. Caught up in the fallout were Elizabeth's nephew Dorset (the son of her half brother, now succeeded to his father's dignities) and her brother-in-law Courtenay, who was arrested and sent to the Tower. The queen's financial records show her taking on responsibility for her sister Katherine and her sister's Courtenay children: payment for their "diets" and servants (two women and a groom at 14s 4d per week), for their journey to London, for their rockers, for their doctor—and, when medicine failed, for the burying of one small boy. Foreign observers had not yet ceased speculating whether the queen might have further children of her own; in May 1501, the Portuguese ambassador had been writing home, "The queen was supposed to be with child; but her apothecary told me that a Genoese physician affirmed that she was pregnant, yet it was not so; she has much embonpoint and large breasts."

But Elizabeth still had children enough to worry about, and Suffolk's timing was particularly galling in that 1501 also saw Catherine of Aragon's long-awaited arrival in the country. Her sea voyage had been stormy even in comparison with those of other royal brides, but her ship finally entered the harbor at Plymouth in early October. As Catherine's grand arrival into London was planned, Elizabeth's officers were involved every step of the way, the queen's chamberlain selecting the ladies who should accompany the new princess and her master of horse providing the henchmen who would ride behind Catherine, himself leading the palfrey of state. The ceremony was to be extraordinary, but Henry the puppet master couldn't wait for the curtain to go up on his play.

The king took his son Arthur, rushing south to intercept the Spanish bride on her journey, against the protests of her scandalized staff, who declared she had gone to bed. On his return to Richmond, the king immediately reported back to Elizabeth (so an account of Catherine's arrival published by John Leland recounts): "He was met by the Queen's Grace, whom he ascertained and made privy to the acts and demeanour between himself, the Prince, and the Princess, and how he liked her person and behaviour." Margaret Beaufort was presumably not present, but her *Book of Hours* recorded the progress of Catherine's journey, and her town house at Coldharbour was being fitted out with almost seven hundred pounds' worth of fabrics and luxuries to entertain the wedding party. (The additions included new ovens, freshly glazed windows, new liveries and Beaufort badges for the servants, as well as a carpet of "imagery work" for Margaret's own chamber. Coldharbour boasted even a conservatory, to provide fresh herbs in the winter.)

On November 10, the king and queen, on their separate barges, left Richmond for Baynard's Castle, to be at hand for the festivities. On November 12, Catherine entered London, with an escort of lords. The king and Prince Arthur watched from a haberdasher's house, as did a number of the royal women, according to another contemporary document, *The Receyt of the Ladie Kateryne*: "In another chamber stood the Queen's Good Grace, my Lady the King's Mother, My Lady Margaret, my Lady her sister [Mary], with many other ladies of the land, not in very open sight, like as the King's Grace did in his manner and party." What Elizabeth would have seen as she peeked out of the window was a blooming fifteen-year-old dressed with "fair auburn" hair, "rich apparel on her body after the manner of her country," and "a little hat fashioned like a cardinal's hat of a pretty braid with a lace of gold."

It was the afternoon of the thirteenth that Catherine was taken to Baynard's Castle, with a "right great assembly," actually to meet Queen Elizabeth, who welcomed her "with pleasure and goodly communication," dancing, and "disportes." On November 14, the king and queen—with the king's mother—stood "in secret manner" in St. Paul's to watch the wedding ceremony from behind a lattice. It was arranged that the bridal couple should process along a walkway six feet above the ground to the specially constructed stage where their marriage would be solemnized—so that everyone could see.

Elizabeth watched while her son Henry escorted the bride into the church and her sister Cecily carried Catherine's train. The Duchess of Norfolk led those who prepared the bed. Later, what did or did not happen in it would become a source of great controversy. Arthur (so it was reported almost thirty years afterward) boasted the next morning that he had "been this night in the midst of Spain," but Catherine declared that she had remained as "untouched and pure" as when she came from her mother's belly. But at the time, no one seems to have doubted that everything had gone swimmingly. Next morning the princess kept her chamber with her ladies, while the Spanish delegation was entertained by Margaret Beaufort.

There was Solemn Mass the next day, Tuesday, and a move to Westminster; on Thursday, the usual tournaments began. The queen shared the stage built to accommodate the royal party with her daughters, her new daughter-in-law, and, inevitably, the king's mother, Margaret Beaufort—a third generation of royal ladies on the dais, heading as many as several hundred other ladies and gentlewomen. Elizabeth's cousin and nephew Buckingham and Dorset led the challengers. Friday saw more pageants—reluctant ladies successfully assaulted by Knights of the Mount of Love—and afterward the company danced: Arthur with his aunt Cecily and Catherine with one of her ladies (women often partnered with other women) and Henry with his sister Margaret. The ten-year-old Henry, "perceiving himself to be encumbered with his clothes," cast off his gown and danced in his jacket "in so goodly and pleasant manner that it was to the King and Queen right great and singular pleasure." At the Sunday banquet, Elizabeth, with her sisters and of course her mother-in-law, sat at a table in the upper part of the Parliament Chamber on, as the report preserved by John Leland has it, "the table of most reputation of all the tables in the Chamber"—another reminder that this chivalric world was her terrain, by virtue not only of her sex, but also of her family history. More tournaments, more spectacles, until the following Friday saw a veritable armada of barges transport the royal party, each in their own craft, and their attendants to Richmond.

The new Tudor palace of Richmond—built on the site of the old palace of Sheen, destroyed by fire in 1497—was an architectural monument to the young dynasty, its royal apartments offering both luxury and a new measure of privacy. Its richly decorated rooms looked out onto gardens of topiary and statues of heraldic beasts, with a gallery set upon the walls and tables set out ready for guests to play games of chance. On Sunday afternoon, Henry took a party out there, and among the surprises they found was a specially rigged platform where a Spaniard showed off "many wondrous and delicious points of tumbling, dancing and other sleights." The account, in Leland, was written to praise, but it does paint an impressive picture. After Evensong and supper, the hall was once again decked out with carpets and cloth-of-gold cushions, and a great display of plate; a richly decorated portable stage in the shape of a tower was dragged in by sea horses and occupied by disguised ladies and singing children of the chapel. Coneys and white doves were set free to run or fly about the hall, to everyone's "great laughter and disport." After "courtly rounds and pleasant dances" came the void of "goodly spices and wine," served by a host of nobles. The revelers were ages away from the days when a fleeing Marguerite of Anjou, another foreign princess brought over to become England's queen, had been reduced to living off a single herring. That was the point, presumably.

The new couple set out for Arthur's seat at Ludlow just before Christmas, and only a few weeks later, in January 1502, Richmond saw the celebration of Princess Margaret's marriage to the king of Scotland. After mass in the new palace chapel, the queen's Great Chamber was the site of the proxy wedding. The description written by John Younge, the official called the "Somerset Herald" and again preserved by John Leland, makes, once again, no mention of Margaret Beaufort being present, though the party did include little Princess Mary.

King, queen, and princess were asked whether they knew of any impediment to the match, Margaret "wittingly and of deliberate mind having twelve years complete in age" affirming that she contracted the match; "incontinently," after the ceremony was concluded, Elizabeth "took her daughter the Queen of Scots by the Hand," and they went to dine, both served as queens. Two queens together: it is a pity Elizabeth Woodville could not be there. There were jousts, followed by a supper banquet, and the next morning the twelve-year-old Margaret came into her mother's Great Chamber and "by the voice of" the officer of arms gave thanks to all the noblemen who had jousted for her, and distributed praise and prizes "by the advice of the ladies of the court." Margaret was still left in her mother's charge, but it was agreed she would be sent northward by the beginning of September 1503.

But three months after Margaret's wedding came tragedy. On April 2, 1502, Prince Arthur died at Ludlow after a short illness; the letter with the news arrived at Greenwich so late in the night of the fourth that the council did not immediately inform the king but summoned his confessor, who broke the news early the next day.

Henry sent for his wife, saying that "he and his Queen would take the painful sorrows together." Elizabeth, seeing her husband's distress, rallied herself to speak to Henry with "full great and constant comfortable words." She urged that he should "first after God, remember the weal of his own noble person, the comfort of his realm, and of her. She then said that my Lady his Mother had never no more children but him only, and, that God by his Grace had ever preserved him, and brought him where that he was." God had, she pointed out, still left him a fair prince and two princesses, and "God is where he was and we are both young enough [to have more children]." But after Elizabeth had left Henry, her own enforced composure crumbled. "After that she was departed and come to her own Chamber, natural and motherly remembrance of that great loss smote her so sorrowful to the heart, that those that were about her were fain to send for the king to comfort her." Now it was Henry's turn to "relieve" her. He "showed her how wise counsel she had given him before; and he for his part would thank God for his son, and would she should do in like wise." It was positive evidence of Henry and Elizabeth's relationship.

Catherine of Aragon, the youthful widow, was left in painful uncertainty about her fate, and she herself was "suffering"—ill, though perhaps only with distress. Elizabeth sent "a litter of black velvet with black cloth" to bring her back to the capital by slow stages (there was, after all, the possibility of a pregnancy). She reached Croydon by late May, and Elizabeth was careful to remain in reassuring contact, although she herself was planning to journey the other way.

That summer Elizabeth of York went on a progress into Wales, although—at thirty-six, and after multiple childbirths—she must surely have known that she was once again pregnant. Even if she and Henry had earlier decided to content themselves with their existing family, they must both have been acutely aware that the situation had now changed. They had now lost two of their three sons. It was the old situation, an heir but no spare, and even if she really had decided that the time for childbearing was past, it may now once again have appeared worth the risk. The timing of her journey does seem odd, given that she had no particular history of long, solitary trips, but perhaps all the arrangements were in place before she knew of her condition.

An event in the late spring may possibly have had a part in Elizabeth's desire for some time away from court. On May 6, one Sir James Tyrell was privately executed, in connection with the Suffolk conspiracies, and his death paved the way for subsequent declarations that he had in his last days made a confession of having, at Richard III's instigation, murdered the Princes in the Tower. Such a declaration was never published, nor seen by any of the chroniclers who mention it.

In early to mid-August 1483, the tale runs, Richard had ordered Sir Robert Brackenbury, the man in charge of the Tower, to put the boys to death. Brackenbury had refused, but he did agree to turn the keys over for one night to a less scrupulous man—Tyrell, who enlisted two ruffians called Miles Forrest and John Dighton—to do the actual deed.

There are both indications and counterindications as to the truth of the tale. In March 1484, Richard rewarded Brackenbury for deeds unspecified, reappointing him to his post for life, "considering his good and loyal service to us before this time, and for certain other considerations especially moving us"; Tyrell too prospered under Richard's rule. But in fact Tyrell was not in 1483 the needy man on the make Thomas More depicts—we have indeed heard his name, as a successful court official, several times in this tale. Some theories that have the younger Prince, at least, released alive also have him hidden at the Tyrell family seat, while the fact that in late 1484 Richard sent Tyrell to Flanders "for divers matters greatly concerning the King's weal" could be taken as suggesting that Tyrell had escorted the boy to safer hiding there.

Indeed, almost every piece of evidence can be taken two ways (even, indeed, the fact that Tyrell had once been in Cecily Neville's wardship, and a Miles Forrest was listed as being one of Cecily's attendants). In June 1486, Henry VII issued Tyrell with a general pardon for anything he had done before that date; on July 16, he issued him with another one, almost as if, in the intervening month, Tyrell had, with Henry's knowledge, committed some other heinous crime. (Why, if Henry found the boys alive after Bosworth, should he have kept them alive for almost a year and then murdered them? Perhaps the answer is that Elizabeth of York's pregnancy gave an urgent reason to remove any threat to his dynasty. It has even been suggested that Elizabeth Woodville found out what Henry had done and that this was why she was dispatched to her convent so abruptly.)

After that time, Tyrell continued to thrive under Henry's rule, albeit the posts Henry gave him kept him out of the country. When Tyrell was finally attainted in 1504, it was only for treasons in connection with Suffolk, while Dighton (both Forrest and Brackenbury being already dead) was left at liberty. Bacon says that Henry "gave out" word of Tyrell's guilt, but there is no sign of his having actually published any confession—an incomprehensible oversight, if it is true. It must go down as yet another mystery—but also as one of those stories that do not necessarily reflect well on the Tudor dynasty.

In any event, if such a confession was indeed made, and if Elizabeth believed it, it would have stirred up painful memories. If she had any cause to doubt it—as many have since—then it could have operated on her yet more powerfully.

Before Elizabeth even set out from Woodstock, she was unwell, but she still managed to depart in early August. Modern psychological theory might suggest that her choosing this moment to visit Wales, where her son the Prince of Wales had died a few months before, was linked to her grief for him. But the question of whether a premodern parent had in any sense the same relationship with their children that we now expect is one of the more vexed in history. And in any case, Elizabeth did not visit Ludlow, where Arthur had died, but instead was headed to Raglan, home of the Herbert family, into which her cousin Anne had been married.

From Woodstock the queen traveled to Langley, to Flaxley Abbey, to Mitchel Troy near Monmouth, and the sprawling modern comfort of Raglan Castle itself. There she must have found, perhaps, some escape from recent strains, but her Privy Purse expenses record what must have fallen first on her servants—the myriad minor complications of the actual journey: repairs for her "chair" (or litter), local guides, twenty pairs of shoes for her footmen on her first setting out for Wales (it was a long way to walk), the grooms and the hostlers, the wine and meat to be provided along the way, and a cart and "load of stuff" that had to travel overland on the journey home, rather than crossing the Severn (had Elizabeth been buying souvenirs?). The effort it took to carry a queen and her retinue was staggering, not just the provisioning of what was effectively a small army on the march, not just the hasty upgrading of the houses where she was to sleep, but also the arrangements for the jewels and robes that maintained the queen's majesty.

These Privy Purse expenses, from the spring of 1502 to that of 1503, form an extraordinary document. They in no sense give— despite the lists of wages and receipts—a complete picture of the queen's finances. But they do provide a glimpse into daily life of the kind modern observers have not often been able to see—and, tangentially, an equally rare glimpse into an emotional reality.

Particularly interesting is the support the records show Elizabeth giving to fellow members of the house of York and those who had served her natal family. In December by Elizabeth's "commandment," three yards of cloth were given "to a woman that was norice [nurse] to the Prince brother to the Queen's grace." In the same month, twelve pence went to a man who said that Earl Rivers (Elizabeth Woodville's brother Anthony) had lodged in his house just before his death. Alms, twice that year, were provided for an old servant of King Edward's and upkeep for the queen's sister Bridget in her convent. A messenger was paid for carrying a command from the queen in April 1502 that the Duchess of Norfolk should receive the wife of Edmund de la Pole, "late Earl of Suffolk"—Elizabeth's traitorous cousin, who had rebelled against Elizabeth's husband. There were payments, of course, for the maintenance of the Courtenay children, whose mother was the queen's sister Katherine but whose father had been implicated in the Suffolk rebellions. A queen was supposed to be the caring face of her husband's regime, and of course Elizabeth would care for her family; there is no need to suspect any insurgency was going on. But all the same, one wishes that comparable records had survived for other years, so that we could know whether this kind of support to old Yorkists had been her standard practice, or whether it was new in any way.

Through the lists of Privy Purse expenses, it is possible to disentangle a whole volume of stories and a web of women's connections, too. The expenses end with a list of women's fees: a pension to the queen's sister Katherine, a sum to her sister Anne's husband for her keep. Salaries to some half dozen more ranging downward from Elizabeth Stafford (£33 6s 8d) to Agnes Dean, the queen's laundress (66s 8d) and the rockers of Katherine Courtenay's children. (There were wages, too, for messengers and minstrels, attorneys and auditors, the clerk of the queen's council and the man who surveyed her lands.) Besides payments recorded there to those who had been kind to her mother's family, there are payments to some who would ease her daughters' way. Dame Jane Guildford who had £23 6s and 8d in Elizabeth's final wage bill would become one of Margaret Beaufort's close attendants and then, a decade later, would escort Elizabeth's daughter Mary to marry the old king of France; she would be the same "mother Guildford" for whose continued company and counsel Mary, feeling isolated and alone in a foreign court, would beg, hysterically.

Black clothing was paid for in June, after the death of Prince Arthur, and, in connection with the expected birth of another child, offerings were made on the eve of and the feast of the Blessed Virgin on December 7 and 8. December 13 brought a reward to a monk who brought "Our Lady girdle" to the queen, an item believed to protect a woman who wore it in childbirth. Elizabeth had ordered a "rich bed" with decorated red and white roses and with clouds, purchased linen, and interviewed childbed attendants. Then she took a boat to Richmond for Christmas; she played cards, listened to music, and paid a messenger who had brought a gift from her mother-in-law. That season, Henry's pet astrologer, William Parron, had beautifully illustrated and bound up what must at the time have seemed a suitable and seasonal prophecy: that Henry would father many sons and Elizabeth live until she was eighty.*

It was not to be. Elizabeth spent a January week at Hampton Court, but on January 26 she went to the Tower. On February 2 she gave birth to a baby girl in what would seem to be a premature delivery. The Privy Purse expenses record a payment for "iii yards of flannel bought for my Lady Katherine," the daughter who would not long survive her mother, and also the payment that gives the first urgent alarm: "Item to James Nattres for his costs going into Kent for Doctor Hallysworth physician to come to the Queen by the King's commandment," boat hire from the Tower to Gravesend and back (3s 4d), two watermen to wait there while the doctor was hastily fetched, and horse hire and guides "by night and day." We have no record of whether the birth itself went smoothly, of how any fever first came upon her, of what remedies—if any—were attempted. But on February 11, 1503, she died. It was her thirty-seventh birthday.

Death in childbirth can never have been wholly unexpected in the fifteenth century. But this one seems to have struck all those around Elizabeth a devastating blow. Nonetheless, the practicalities had to be gone through. Sir Thomas Malory described what happened after the death of Queen Guenivere. "And then she was wrapped in cered cloth of Raines [waxed cloth from Rennes], from the top to the toe, in thirtyfold; and after she was put in a web of lead, and then in a coffin of marble." Elizabeth's body was placed only in a wooden chest for its progress through the London streets, but that does not mean that any expense was spared for the ceremony, or for the velvet-clad effigy that would be placed on Elizabeth's coffin. "Item to Master Lawrence for carving of the head with Fedrik his mate, xiijs iiijd. Item to Wechon Kerver and Hans van Hooh for carving of the two hands, iiijs. . . . Item for vij small sheep skins for the body . . . ijs iiijd."

Elizabeth was to have the grandest of resting places, albeit work on the building that was to house her tomb was begun only weeks before. At the beginning of the century, Henry VII had given the orders for a wonderful new Lady Chapel, a monument to his family that would, he

---

*After the events of the next few weeks, Parron sensibly fled abroad.

hoped, ultimately house the body of Henry VI, canonized into a Lancastrian saint. The old chapel on the site had been pulled down, as had, claimed the sixteenth-century writer John Stow, an adjoining tavern called, ironically, the White Rose. The first stone had finally been laid on January 24, 1503. It would be another fifteen years before the tomb Elizabeth would share with her husband was finally completed, but meanwhile her body was placed in a temporary vault in the crossing of the abbey, in front of the high altar.

As always, there are stories to be deduced from the records of the burial ceremonies. Though the queen's sisters Katherine and Anne took a prominent part in the funeral procession, Bridget the nun, the youngest, must still have been at her convent at Dartford, and Cecily, though next in age to Elizabeth herself, was absent either because of the offense her unsanctioned second marriage (to a man of lower rank called Thomas Kyme) had caused the king or perhaps because of the sheer distance of her residence. Instead, place in the procession after Katherine and Anne went to Lady Katherine Gordon, the widow of Perkin Warbeck, by virtue of her own connections to Scottish royalty.

King Henry's retreat into his grief was a profound one. He was never likely to indulge in the swooning grief Malory imagines for Lancelot after Guenivere's death: shunning food and drink, "evermore, day and night, he prayed, but sometime he slumbered a broken sleep; ever he was lying grovelling on the tomb of King Arthur and Queen Guenivere." But he became seriously ill, so much so that Margaret Beaufort moved into Richmond to take charge of his sickbed, ordering medicines for him and a sustaining supply of sweet wine for herself. Thomas More's *Rueful Lamentation of the Death of Queen Elizabeth* vividly imagined Elizabeth's farewell to the world:

> *If worship might have kept me, I had not gone.*
> *If wit might have me saved, I needed not fear.*
> *If money might have helped, I lacked none.*
> *But O good God what vaileth all this gear?*
> *When death is come thy mighty messenger,*
> *Obey we must, there is no remedy,*
> *Me hath he summoned, and lo now hear I lie.*

Besides having Elizabeth bid a respectful farewell to Margaret Beaufort, and a heartbreakingly affectionate one to her children, More's poem also warned King Henry, in curiously modern terms, that "Erst were you father, and now must ye supply / The mother's part also." The bereaved king may not have found it an easy task. His son Henry still in adulthood remembered his mother's death bitterly enough to recall that "hateful intelligence" as a standard for melancholy. In the wake of Elizabeth's death, there must have been readjustments all around, in a diminished family party. But as the months passed, life went on.

In the summer of 1503, young Princess Margaret was sent north, as promised, to marry James of Scotland—he who had so recently harbored the pretender Perkin Warbeck. On June 27, she and her father, the king, traveled from Richmond to Collyweston, Margaret Beaufort's house, where the gardens were enlarged and fitted out with new summerhouses to entertain the royal party. On July 8, the younger Margaret set out north, to be crowned in Edinburgh on August 3. She was not yet fourteen years old. Out of the six children she bore James, five would die in infancy; perhaps her mother and grandmother had been right to worry about her health.

The almost forty-page account of the young Margaret's journey north, written by the same "Somerset Herald" who had described her proxy marriage ceremony to James eighteen months earlier, makes fascinating reading. Everything was splendidly done; Margaret was sent off "richly dressed, mounted upon a fair palfrey," "very nobly accompanied, in fair order and array." The procession of towns, of official receptions and leave-takings (Margaret always "richly dressed"), makes exhausting reading. Margaret must have been tougher than she was reputed to have been, for she survived it, even if she hadn't "killed a buck with her bow" at Alnwick, as the chronicle claimed. But there is no doubt the ceremonial must have been impressive; this was of course a publicity exercise, not only for the new Scottish queen, but also for the father who was sending her off so lavishly equipped.

Minstrels were sent along to attract the populace and make sure no one missed Margaret's entry into and departure from all the various towns, and a party of gentlemen was ordered "to make space, that more plainly the said Queen and her company might be better seen."

As she passed into Scotland, her servants had sometimes to force a way for the carriage through the crowds that thronged the route, but the "great quantity" of people flocking to see her had at least brought "plenty of drink" for those prepared to pay for it. It was truly a great public spectacle.

The description of Margaret's initial meetings with her husband at Hadington Castle shows, with unusual clarity, the stages of two people getting to know each other under these trying circumstances. As James was brought to what was now Margaret's Great Chamber, she met him at the door, and the two "made great reverences, the one to the other, his head being bare, and they kissed together." The greeting to the rest of her party being done, they "went aside, and communed together by long space." But one wonders how much a thirteen-year-old and an experienced womanizer of thirty can really have had to say to each other.

The next day, James found Margaret playing cards in her room, and she kissed him "of good will"; after she had danced with the Countess of Surrey, a lady of her retinue, and bread and wine had been brought to James, he served her before himself and played for her on the clavichord and the lute, "which pleased her very much." Every day saw a visit, and on the next occasion, seeing the stool where she was seated for supper "was not for her ease," he gave her his chair. Things were looking good, surely. The two did have some things in common—an interest in music as well as in hunting.

But this was an account written to glorify the couple, and although Margaret may have been lucky by comparison with her grandmother Margaret Beaufort, married at an even earlier age, a letter back to her father, Henry, in England nonetheless breathes homesickness. After expressing her formal thanks to all the ladies and gentlewomen who had accompanied her, and asking her father to take care of one Thomas, who had been her mother's footman, Margaret describes the intimacy sprung up between the Earl of Surrey and her new husband, the king of Scots, and how her own chamberlain, committed to "my cause," gets hardly a look in. "I pray God," she writes plaintively, trying to make sense of the internal politics in the new world in which she found herself, "it may be for my poor heart's ease in time to come." A teenager trying to negotiate the politics of a foreign court, she wishes "I would I were with your Grace now, and many times more." It was the common lot of princesses, but that cannot have made it easy.

Among the older generations of York women, the year 1503 ended on the same sad note with which it had begun. On November 23, Margaret of Burgundy died. But although her last few years saw her decline in health, hers is by no means a story of decay. Whatever personal grief she had felt for the loss of Perkin, she remained a central figure at the Burgundian court: the dowager whose presence was in demand for diplomatic functions, the devoted mother figure who would care for the children of the new duke and duchess whenever they were called away. Indeed, Duke Philip spoke of "how, after the death of our late lady mother, she behaved towards us as if she were our real mother." She had become, almost, the Plantagenet who got away, safe from the precautionary violence that in decades to come the Tudors would continue to wreak on other remaining scions of the family.

Some unrecorded time between January 1503 and May 1504, Edward IV's other sister Elizabeth also died—the mother of Lincoln and Suffolk, the last of Cecily Neville's brood. The ground was being cleared. Of the women who had earlier occupied the stage, there was only one survivor. It was Margaret Beaufort, inevitably.

25

"OUR NOBLE MOTHER"

Tell me, how fares our noble mother?

THE TRAGEDY OF RICHARD THE THIRD, 5.3

I t was an end, of course, but perhaps it was also a beginning, and a long-awaited one at that. Lady Margaret Beaufort had now—with Elizabeth of York dead, Princess Margaret gone north, and Princess Mary still a child—become England's first lady. Perhaps she no longer felt she had to struggle so hard, now that there were no other contenders for that position.

But Margaret Beaufort would not have long to enjoy her new prominence. Before the end of the decade, John Fisher, the cleric with whom she developed an increasingly close relationship in the last years of her life, would be called on to preach a memorial sermon (the month-mind sermon, or *Mornynge Remembraunce*) for Lady Margaret, and in it he painted a picture that was at least partly hagiography. All England, he would say, "had cause of weeping" for her death: "The poor creatures that were wont to receive her alms, to whom she was always piteous and merciful. The students of both the universities to whom she was as a mother. All the learned men in

England to whom she was a very patroness. . . . All the good priests and clerks to whom she was a true defenderess. All the noble men and women to whom she was a mirror and exemplar of honour. All the common people of this realm for whom she was in their causes a common mediatrix, and took right great displeasure for them."

Fisher, perhaps inevitably under the circumstances, painted the portrait of a saint, and whatever Margaret Beaufort's virtues, she was not that. Fisher's assurance that she was never guilty of avarice or covetousness carries less conviction than his description of how her servants were kept in good order, suitors heard, and "if any factions . . . were made secretly amongst her head officers, she with great policy did bolt it out and likewise any strife or controversy." The picture of Margaret ruling her household with a rod of iron and a measure of surveillance is not hard to conjure. More personal still, perhaps (even in an age when the specter of death was considered a good companion for the living), was Fisher's description of how Margaret would not only comfort in sickness any of the dozen poor people she maintained, "ministering unto them with her own hands," but "when it pleased god to call any one of them out of this wretched world she would be present to see them depart and to learn to die."

Fisher also provided in the sermon a description of Margaret's daily round of devotions, evocative of those recorded for Cecily Neville some years before. They began before dawn with the matins of our lady and the matins of the day "not long after v [five] of the clock." Four or five masses a day, she was "upon her knees" before the early dinner (at ten on "eating days" and eleven on fasting days); after dinner she "would go her stations" to three different altars and say her diriges and commendations and her Evensongs before supper. "And at night before she went to bed she failed not to resort unto her chapel, and there a large quarter of an hour to occupy her in devotions." She seems to have followed this rigorous schedule assiduously, although so much kneeling was difficult for her, "and so painful that many times it caused in her back pain and disease."

Fisher describes her habit of saying every day—when she was in health, at least—the crown of our lady "after the manner of Rome," kneeling each of the sixty-three times she heard the word *ave*, and recounted her meditations from French devotional books "when she was weary of prayer." He describes her "marvellous weeping" at confession, which at many seasons she made as often as every third day and how when she was "houselled," or received the Eucharist, nearly a dozen times a year, "what floods of tears there issued forth from her eyes."

It is the picture of what was for the time a perfect piety: wholly obedient to Rome and partaking of all the old rituals though perhaps not uninfluenced by the more individual, more interior style of religious practice beginning to make its way over from the Continent. Margaret participated in all the old popular practices and would surely have been horrified by any suggestion that the inevitably questioning nature of her own intelligent interest—her readiness to challenge church authorities over matters of property and patronage where necessary—could have sown the seeds of her grandson Henry VIII's eventual break from the Roman Catholic Church and his creation of an independent Church of England. But it is hard not to see Fisher's words also as the picture of a woman who had learned the hard way that life was not to be trusted, even if you might still rely on God's mercy. And it is hard not to be touched when Fisher recalls how the "merciful and liberal" hands that gave comfort to the poor were so afflicted with (arthritic?) cramps as to make her cry out, "O blessed Jesu help me. O blessed lady succour me."

Margaret's onetime carver Henry Parker confirmed Fisher's picture of Margaret's extraordinary devotions: "As soon as one priest had said mass in her sight," he remembered, "another began." But he adds also that at dinner (and "how honourably she was served I think few kings better"), she was always "joyous" at the beginning of the meal, hearing tales to make her merry, before hearing readings from some spiritual work. Nonetheless—despite her fondness for muscadel, her habit of keeping wine and spices in a locked cupboard of her own chamber for a nightcap—Fisher wrote of her "sober temperance in meats and drinks," eschewing banquets and tidbits between meals. For "age and feebleness," he wrote, she might have been exempted from the fast days appointed by the church, but chose instead to keep them "diligently and seriously," and especially all through Lent "restrained her appetite to one meal and one fish" a day. She mortified herself in other ways, as well. "As to hard clothes wearing she had her shirts and girdles of hair, which when she was in health every week she failed not certain days to wear . . . [so] that full often her skin as I heard her say was pierced therewith."

In her faith, Margaret was at one with the women of the old Yorkist regime. Like Cecily Neville, Margaret owned—and commissioned Wynkyn de Worde to print—Walter Hilton's writing on the "mixed life," which combined a spiritual program with more worldly concerns. Like her frequent opponent, Cecily's daughter Margaret of Burgundy, she was particularly attached to the reformed order of Franciscans, the Observants. Margaret of Burgundy had probably been responsible for their establishment in England after 1480; in 1497 Margaret Beaufort was granted confraternity by the order.

A disproportionate amount of the information that has survived about Margaret Beaufort seems to come from these last years of her life, thanks in part to her involvement with the Cambridge colleges, in whose archives much of it is preserved. But perhaps that ever more active engagement was not coincidental; perhaps it was now, when she had been shaken by the death of a woman who—whatever their personal relations had been—she could never have expected to predecease her, that Margaret became aware that it was time to follow her own interests and make her own legacy.

King Henry's retreat immediately after Elizabeth's death showed he was indeed devastated. He would continue, religiously, to keep the anniversary of her demise, and from this time on there would be a marked lessening in the cheer of his court. He had loved her . . . But Henry was now a widower, just as his son's wife Catherine of Aragon was now a widow. The coincidence seems to have struck Henry as opportune. Marrying Catherine may have seemed for a moment like a good way of resolving the equation and keeping her dowry and the Spanish connection in the country. But Catherine's mother, Isabella, in Spain, was horrified when she heard the rumors. Such a marriage between father and daughter-in-law would, she said, be "a very evil thing—one never before seen, and the mere mention of which offends the ears—we would not for anything in the world that it should take place." It is an interesting reflection on Henry's character that his instructions to his ambassadors, when later he was considering other candidates, made it plain he was not prepared to marry an ugly second wife. They were to make a careful note of breath, breasts, and complexion—a roundabout tribute to Elizabeth of York.

Henry VII soon conceived of anther way to keep Catherine of Aragon in England. Shortly after the idea of marriage to her father-in-law was mooted, Catherine was instead betrothed to Prince Henry, amid an extended debate as to whether she was betrothed as Arthur's widow in the fullest sense, or as the virgin survivor of an unconsummated marriage. It was a debate that would display its full ramifications later in the next century, when the younger Henry, Henry VIII, would begin casting about for reasons to cancel his marriage to Catherine so he could take a new bride. Henry VII negotiated—bickered—indefatigably over the question of Catherine's dowry, but in this and other negotiations, he was now maneuvering from a position of decreased security.

The Tudor dynasty now faced an uncertain future. The death of Elizabeth of York, so soon after that of the expected, the near-adult, heir, Prince Arthur, put fresh question marks over a regime that had, after all, been in power for less than twenty years. Anyone tethered to the Tudors by loyalty to the old Yorkist dynasty—of which Elizabeth had been, pretenders apart, the last embodiment—might now consider themselves free to explore other options.

Too many of the men (and women) who had been involved in the rebellions against Henry had surnames like Neville, or else were under the young Duke of Buckingham's sway. Margaret Beaufort's onetime ward, son to Richard III's nemesis, Buckingham had turned out to be another who gazed toward the throne itself with covetous eyes. Henry VII was known to be sickly, and his sole surviving son was at this point only eleven years old. Had the infections that wracked the king's lungs and throat actually carried him off, it would have been the question of another minority—that, or another, older, man's opportunity.

In 1504 Henry's officers were discussing a conversation that had earlier taken place between "many great personages" about the succession and the future of the country. Some spoke of Buckingham as a possible next king, some of Suffolk, but none of them "spoke of my lord prince." An agent of Suffolk's at the imperial court had been assuring Maximilian that, should Henry VII die, young Prince Henry could in no way prevail against Suffolk's own claim.

This insecurity probably affected the way Henry VII comported himself once the warmth and influence, and the political authority, he had gained from his wife had vanished. That summer of 1503, Reginald Bray—Henry's greatest officer and one who had had his start under Margaret Beaufort—had also died. Rather than replace him by giving any other individual the same authority, Henry increasingly kept power in his own hands, raising new men but trusting none completely. He was also becoming ever more obsessed with money, an accusation that could of course also be brought against his mother. Perhaps Elizabeth had been instrumental in his earlier comparative liberality.

In the summer of 1504, Margaret's husband, Stanley, died, allowing her even greater access to her own funds. She also took the opportunity to confirm her vows of chastity. "In the presence of my Lord God Jesu Christ and his blessed Mother the glorious Virgin Saint Mary and of all of the whole company of Heaven & of you also my ghostly father I Margaret of Richmond with full purpose and good deliberation for the weal [welfare] of my sinful soul with all my heart promise from henceforth the chastity of my body. That is never to use my body having actual knowledge of man after the common usage in matrimony the which thing I had before purposed in my lord my husband's days."

But despite her powerful religious interests, Margaret did not turn to a semiretired and contemplative life, as others had done. She had different duties. In 1505 she felt it necessary to abandon her recently established power base of Collyweston for a variety of houses often borrowed from the bishops whose perks of office they were; here too Margaret was prepared to take advantage of everything the church had to offer. She wanted to be nearer to Henry and his court, even if there were some new frictions between mother and son. Henry was in the process of taking her beloved, and convenient, Woking away from her to convert it to royal use. Shades of Cecily and Fotheringhay—which, indeed, was one of the properties Margaret now used, cleared and cleaned for her convenience. A letter Henry wrote to his mother around this time makes excuse that he had "encumbered you now with this my long writing, but me thinks that I can do no less, considering that it is so seldom that I do write."

Margaret had after all her other, ever more absorbing, field of independent interest: her patronage of colleges and universities, especially the University of Cambridge. Her benevolence had originally been a little more widely spread; in the closing years of the last century, Oxford too had hailed her as the princess "of rank most exalted and of character divine" who would exceed all others in her patronage. However, the influence of John Fisher led her to the other establishment—as did, perhaps, its proximity to her geographical areas of influence.

Margaret's support for Queens' College in Cambridge (which Marguerite, Anne, and Elizabeth Woodville had supported before her) could be taken as part of her ongoing bid for the regal role. Her long-standing interest in Cambridge's Jesus College, too, was a concern shared by the whole royal family. But what came next was all her own. She took the underfunded "God's House" in Cambridge and turned it into Christ's College: not her only enduring legacy in that city, but the one that can be most clearly identified with her. The college statutes of 1506 show that she reserved for her own use a set of four rooms there, located between the chapel and the hall and with windows giving a direct view down into either, a position from which she could partake of the college devotions in privacy, perhaps fancy herself part of this masculine seat of learning, and from which she could also keep an eye on the college business as it progressed day to day. Her heraldic devices are still prominently modeled on the oriel window outside her former lodgings. One is a portcullis, the other a "yale"—a mythical creature with the ability to twist its horns in different directions, to keep one of them safe in a fight, and a symbol of proud defense appropriate for the wary Tudors.

Margaret is known to have visited Cambridge in 1505, 1506, 1507, and (less certainly) 1508, and her work there did not cease with the foundation of Christ's. Her careful arrangements extended not only to ensuring that Fisher could use her rooms when she was not doing so, but to arranging a country property (one of her many bequests to the college) to which the scholars could retreat when plague came to the city. As early as 1505, Fisher also drew her attention to the lamentable state of the ancient hospital of St. John the Evangelist, and though in the event it would be her executors who oversaw the difficult process of converting it into St. John's College (a place that was to be "as good and as of good value" as Christ's), here too her arms can still be seen resplendent above the porter's lodge today. There is a story of how, looking out of her windows at Christ's once, Margaret saw the dean punishing a lazy scholar and cried out, "*lente, lente*" (gently, gently). That softer side of her character is elusive; life had not taught her to display it readily.

After Elizabeth of York's death, Margaret was certainly involved to some degree in the upbringing of Prince Henry, though her interventions sound more like those of a formidable organizer than of a doting grandmother. The excessive interest his father now took in the young prince meant he was never going to be sent off to Ludlow where his brother had died, but as heir to the throne he was nevertheless in need of a more adult and masculine establishment than he had hitherto been provided. Here, as everywhere, his grandmother's hand can be seen, and the composition of his new household showed a considerable degree of cross-fertilization with hers. His bede-roll—a portable prayer manual, meant to be pored over daily—suggests not only a genuine piety but a particular interest, which Margaret shared, in the Crucifixion itself: the wounds and the holy name of Jesus. His love of chivalry might have come first from the York side of the family, but here too Margaret played a role: in 1504 two of the four young men added as "spears" to the prince's household came from hers.

There is no evidence of Margaret having fulfilled any sympathetic function toward Catherine of Aragon, however much the girl may have stood in need of it. Catherine was caught between her father's and her father-in-law's diplomacy, an unenviable position and one that soon became even more uncomfortable. At the end of 1504, the death of Catherine's mother, Isabella of Castile, reduced Catherine's diplomatic value; thenceforth, she represented only a less valuable alliance with her father's Aragon, rather than with a united Spain. In June 1505, Prince Henry was instructed to repudiate his official marriage with her, leaving Catherine once again without clear prospects in a strange land.

Isabella's own kingdom of Castile, her share of Spain, descended not to her husband, Ferdinand, but to her daughter Juana, Catherine's older sister. This development created a battle for control between Juana's husband, Philip of Burgundy, and her father, Ferdinand, who had no intention of giving up so easily. Though there is evidence Juana made valiant if ineffectual efforts to take control into her own hands and rule as her mother had done, the real tussle was between the two men. History knows Juana as "the Mad," but modern scholarship suggests that although her behavior could sometimes be erratic, the slur was little more than a pretext used by the men of her family to set her aside—a decision apparently acquiesced in by most contemporary opinion.

In January 1506, the wintry weather gave England a firsthand view of Juana and her problems and blew an unexpected bonus onto Henry's shores. Juana and Archduke Philip, on their way to Spain to claim her inheritance, were shipwrecked on the Dorset coast. Hearing the news at Richmond, King Henry immediately sent word to his mother at Croydon and set about preparing a dazzling reception. The reluctance of her male connections to take up cudgels for the isolated Catherine was dramatized when she invited her brother-in-law Philip to join her in dance and got only a resounding snub. It was the precocious Princess Mary, not yet in her teens, who saved the situation by dancing with Catherine herself. Philip's attitude to Juana was also made plain. He purposely kept her away from Henry's court until he himself was firmly established as the star visitor, which left Catherine only a few hours to spend with the sister she was never likely to see again. Other factors apart, the last thing Philip would have wanted was for Catherine either to encourage Juana in independence or, maybe, to get too much evidence of her sister's sanity.

Philip was taken also to visit Margaret Beaufort at Croydon, where the archduke's minstrels would perform for the king's mother. Prince Henry would receive a grandmotherly present of a new horse with fine gold and velvet trappings, the better to show off in front of a Burgundian guest who was a leading exponent of martial chivalry.

King Henry's main topic of negotiation with his guest was a treaty of mutual defense between England and Burgundy (something that would make an Aragonese alliance with Catherine even less necessary). One subtext was Henry's determination to regain custody of the fugitive Suffolk, still enjoying Burgundian hospitality. He won Philip's promise to send Suffolk back to England, for all that Philip initially demurred, apparently invoking the memory of Margaret of Burgundy, to whom he said he still owed a loyalty. And King Henry, when he met her, appeared to have been considerably more impressed with Juana than Juana's own husband, lending her, when the time came to resume her journey, Elizabeth of York's "rich litters and chairs."

Suffolk was brought back to imprisonment in England; he would eventually be executed but by Henry VIII, not by his father. Indeed, a number of those caught up in the fallout of his dissent were treated with a leniency that may owe something to their female connections.

In other directions, however, the king was proving himself a harsher ruler than in earlier days. He had now two new and dauntingly aggressive money collectors, Richard Empson and Edmund Dudley, who used every tactic of law and intimidation to extract revenue and who caused, so Bacon heard from an earlier chronicle, "much sorrow" from the autumn of 1506. Was this what John Fisher was referring to when he wrote that Margaret Beaufort detested avarice and covetousness in anyone, but most especially in any that belonged to her? Her own love of money was tempered by possibly a softer heart, and surely a stronger morality, than her son's.

But if there were any differences of opinion between Margaret and her son, they would now regularly be eclipsed by concerns over the king's health. Early in 1507, he fell ill with a disease of the throat or chest—perhaps quinsy (an abscess) or else tuberculosis. Lady Margaret moved into Richmond to be by his side, just as she had done in 1503, and, just as she had done then, she buried her worries in practicalities, ordering not only a supply of medicinal materials but also mourning garb—attire that, for the moment, proved unnecessary.

Also in February 1507, Margaret in Scotland gave birth to a son— several years after her marriage, so it is possible her husband, James, unlike Edmund Tudor long ago, had indeed waited until she was rather older to consummate the marriage. She was dangerously ill after the birth, but her husband went seven days on foot to a famous shrine to pray for her recovery. Despite the presence of his illegitimate children—despite the early death of this and other of her babies—this Margaret was lucky in her marriage. She was lucky, that is, until her husband's early death at Flodden in 1513, fighting against an English army—her brother Henry Tudor's army.*

Henry and Mary, the Tudor children still in England, were beginning to come into their own. That spring, in May 1507, the tournaments with their elaborate springtime pageantry were all about the young Prince Henry and the ravishing sovereign of the joust, his budding sister Princess Mary. After Elizabeth's death, Mary had probably spent some of her time in Margaret Beaufort's care, whether at court or at Eltham (where the very swans in the moat now wore enameled badges with the Beaufort portcullis around their necks).

That summer, the elder Henry was sufficiently recovered to be set on a new and promising courtship. Philip of Burgundy had died unexpectedly in the autumn of 1506, leaving Juana, the queen of Castile, a widow. From Henry's viewpoint, she was almost as desirable a prospect as Elizabeth of York had been—beautiful, and carrying with her a kingdom. The Spanish ambassador wrote that the English "seem little to mind . . . her insanity, especially since I have assured them that her derangement of mind would not prevent her from bearing children." It was a realistic but nonetheless brutal reminder that a queen consort's first duty was childbearing and that mental strength—even mental stability—was not regarded as necessary in a woman.

Ferdinand, of course, was never going to be prepared to give England such a controlling hand in Spanish affairs, and within two years Juana had been confined by her father in a convent near Valladolid, nominally because of her mental health—an incarceration, attended only by a small retinue of Ferdinand's servants, that would last almost a half century. But the negotiations did afford a more prominent role in the English court to Juana's sister Catherine, who got involved, at Henry's request, in the negotiations.

---

*After James's death, Margaret would be appointed regent for her baby son, albeit some argued this was against Scottish tradition. But after making a controversial second marriage to the Earl of Angus, she was demoted to a lesser title, albeit one with resonance in her family—that of "My Lady the King's Mother."

Catherine of Aragon obtained from her father, Ferdinand, a "letter of credence," making her officially his ambassador to her father-in-law, Henry. Catherine, of course, had every reason to desire her sister's presence at Henry's side, which might not only help her free herself from limbo but also relieve her endless money worries. The disputes about her dowry had dragged on, and she sent frantic pleas to her father that she was spending what money she could obtain—money from selling her plate and jewels, the odd handout from Ferdinand himself or from Henry—not on frivolities but only on necessities. (The Spanish ambassador De Puebla was famous for eating at court to save money; Margaret Beaufort as well as her son found that funny.) The desperate tone of her letters in these last years of Henry VII's reign recalls that of Elizabeth of York, seemingly writing of her burning desire to marry her uncle Richard more than twenty years before.

But while Henry VII was making every effort to secure Juana's hand, it would soon become clear that he was in no state to contemplate anything so arduous as another marriage. In the next chill of the early spring of 1508, his illness returned, and soon Margaret Beaufort was back in Richmond with her orders and her sweet wine. Once again Henry recovered—he was strong enough by summertime to resume normal activities—but the writing was on the wall. The Spanish envoy Fuensalida wrote that the young Prince Henry was still kept "in complete subjection to his father and his grandmother and never opened his mouth in public except to answer a question from one of them." But whether or not this was a true picture, it was clear the young boy who turned seventeen at the end of June would soon be called upon to carry forward the Tudor dynasty.

The great diplomatic game of arranging marriages went on, with Prince Henry and Princess Mary the two cards Henry VII had still to play. Three marriages had been discussed while Philip of Burgundy was on English shores: one between Prince Henry and Philip's daughter, another between King Henry and Philip's sister, and a third between Mary and the son of Juana and Philip, a boy named Charles who was destined to become the most powerful ruler in Europe, since Charles was heir through his mother to the Spanish territories and through his father to the Holy Roman Empire. The first two proposed matches never took on much color of reality, but on December 17,

1508, a betrothal between Charles and Mary was celebrated, amid great festivities. This would be a match indeed (and though in the end the planned marriage would never take place, no one knew that at the time). The bride made, in perfect French, a lengthy speech from memory, and the king kept his watchful eye on even the smallest detail of the pageantry. As the printed souvenir from the ceremony had it, the red rose (the recently conceived sign of the house of Lancaster) looked set to bloom throughout the Christian world.*

The times were repeating themselves again. Not long before, another father, Edward IV, had been obsessed by his daughter's marriage as the last months of his life approached. Henry, too, was drawing close to the grave, as those around him—and perhaps he himself—surely knew. But in spite of that fact, or perhaps because of it, he poured himself into his daughter's marriage to the young Charles.

In January 1509, as the air of triumph died away, so too did this last spurt of the king's energy. The annual pattern must have been horribly familiar, but this time there was a difference: there would be no rally as the dank, sapping air of the early spring warmed into new life at last. Henry seemed to know it. His religious observance took on a hysterical note; observers recorded how he "wept and sobbed by the space of three quarters of an hour in penance, how he would crawl to the foot of the monstrance to receive the mass." It was the end of March when Margaret Beaufort had herself rowed downriver from her own house of Coldharbour, where she had been nursing her own health. She brought to Richmond her favorite bed and a quantity of "kitchen stuff," clearly prepared for a long stay. It would not, in the end, be that long: on April 21, Henry died.

The king's death was followed by what was in essence a massive cover-up—a two-day pretense he was still alive, until a smooth succession of power could be established. There can be no doubt Margaret Beaufort was at the heart of it. Henry had named his mother chief executrix of his will, and she moved quickly to take the reins of power

---

*Mary's marriage to Charles would not in the end proceed. She would instead be married by her brother Henry VIII to the aging French king, and dance him into his grave.

from her late son. The account left by Garter herald Thomas Wrio-
thesley made that clear: the busy councilors were being "over seen by
the mother of the said late king." Here was another woman, like Elizabeth Woodville after Edward IV's death, who could not afford the
time to mourn her private loss. She was another woman having to
cope with what was once again in a sense a minority—though this
time, blessedly, there was only a matter of weeks to go before, in June,
Henry VIII would reach his eighteenth birthday.

As the young King Henry VIII—once his father's death was publicly admitted and he was proclaimed—moved to the Tower in preparation for his coronation, his grandmother briefly stayed behind at
Richmond, from whence, notable even amid this stream of business,
were sent out the orders to arrest Empson and Dudley. The seizure of
these hated officials would be one of the defining moments that set the
seal on the new king's popularity. And it is tempting to speculate that
the arrests may have been in part the handiwork of the new king's
grandmother; coincidentally or otherwise, Margaret Beaufort had
once been crossed in a property deal by Dudley.

Similarly, the interim council that would keep firm hands on the
reins of government until Henry VIII was crowned is likely to have
had Margaret Beaufort's fingerprints all over it. Stow's *Annales* would
state that the young king "was governed by the advice of his grandmother in the choice of the privy council he appointed at the com-
mencement of his reign." Edward Herbert in the seventeenth century
would write that Henry trusted his grandmother's choices for councilors "and took their impressions easily," suggesting even that it was
she who held the group together during her life, though afterward its
members might fall out among themselves.

One wonders what Margaret would have felt if, as Fuensalida reported, the death of her beloved son had made people "as joyful as if
they had been released from prison." But that was not the real point.
As Henry VII was buried as he had ordered beside "our dearest late
wife the queen," Elizabeth of York, it was the future of the dynasty
that mattered. And Margaret Beaufort, in ensuring her grandson's
smooth accession, had struck another blow for the Tudor monarchy.

It is interesting to speculate whether, had she lived longer, Margaret would have won lasting influence, but it must be unlikely. The

influence she had enjoyed under Henry VII had been based not only on a similarity of temperament (and sheer gratitude on her son's part) but also on the fact that he arrived in England as an outsider, in urgent need of trusted allies.

It was very different with Henry VIII. Margaret had a vital role to play in that tense moment of succession, but young men do not usually wish to be governed by old women, as Elizabeth I would discover in the last years of her reign. The new king seemed, moreover, to take after his mother and his mother's York ancestors, right down to his height and splendid appearance. In the long term, he, like his father, would move remorselessly to stamp out any Yorkist threats to his throne, but his first instinct on reaching the throne seems to have been to treat his Yorkist relations kindly. That heritage may have been more inviting for a young man.

Perhaps it was memories of his mother, and of the happiness she had brought his father, that made Henry so anxious to be married himself. His wedding to Catherine of Aragon took place fast and privately. The joint coronation less than two weeks later was to be huge and public, a fit celebration of what some see as the end of the long war. It was effectively the end of a long battle for control of the English throne. "The rose both red and white / In one rose now doth grow," as Henry's onetime tutor, the poet John Skelton, put it.

The coronation ceremony took place on June 24, the crowd hacking up the carpet just as they had done when Henry VIII's mother was crowned twenty-two years before. Just as before, Margaret Beaufort, with Princess Mary, watched the procession from behind a lattice, in the window of a hired house in Cheapside, with "full great joy," as Fisher recorded, though the old lady kept up her usual reminders that "some adversity would follow." (She had, at least, set aside her usual conventual black and white and ordered dresses of tawny silk for her entourage to wear on the occasion.) Maybe she felt vindicated when a sudden shower forced the drenched bride to shelter under the awning of a draper's stall. Margaret enjoyed the coronation banquet. Henry Parker records that "she took her infirmity with eating of a cygnet." But Margaret was now sixty-six, and it was soon clear that this was no mere case of surfeit, but a serious illness. She seems, predictably, to have been prepared for the end. Having always sought so desperately to control all the details of her life, Margaret had not neglected her own obsequies. In fact, some of her instructions and bequests would be a source of controversy, not least among her servants unhappy with the leading role John Fisher was given in handling her legacy. But her tidy mind and attention to detail were reflected even in the date of her death. Margaret Beaufort died on June 29, the very day after her grandson's eighteenth birthday.

Tidily again, Margaret died in the precincts of Westminster Abbey, where she would also be buried—in Cheyneygate, that section of the abbot's lodging that Elizabeth Woodville had once planned to occupy. Fisher, in his memorial sermon, described Margaret's deathbed, "how with all her heart and soul she raised her body . . . and confirmed assuredly that in the sacrament was contained Christ Jesu." If prayers, pity upon the poor, and pardons granted by diverse popes could ensure her future in the next world, her confessor said, then it was a "great likelihood and almost certain conjecture" that she was indeed in the country above. But even as Margaret Beaufort found peace, Fisher touched too on that other side of her personality, the side that lived always in fear, "for that either she was in sorrow by reason of the present adversities, or else when she was in prosperity she was in dread of the adversity for to come." The theme of his sermon was to compare Margaret to the biblical Martha: he cited the nobleness of her nature and the excellence of her endeavors and compared the painful death of Margaret's own body to the way Martha "died for the death of her brother Lazarus."

It is true, of course, that the one Margaret loved most—her only son, Henry—had gone before her. But one cannot but wonder whether Fisher was not responding also to some echo in Margaret of Martha's resentment; she was the woman, after all, who complained to Jesus that her sister Mary, whose life was so much easier, was more appreciated than she.

In Fisher's long character analysis of Margaret, hagiographical though it is, there are flashes that reveal her true personality. He recalled that she was never forgetful of any service done to her and wary of "any thing that might dishonest [dishonor] any noble woman" and that she was of a wisdom "far passing the common rate of women," "good in remembrance and in holding memory," and "right studious" in books in French and English, even the ones that were "right dark." Fisher touched on the way that, "for her exercise and for the profit of others," she was herself responsible for translating several devotional works from the French: *The Mirror of Gold for the Sinful Soul* as well as the fourth book of the *Imitation of Christ.* Her linguistic ability is reminiscent of that of her multilingual great-granddaughter Elizabeth I, while as a bulk purchaser and a patron she did much to popularize translations of religious literature and to encourage printing in England, giving a seal of royal approval—celebrity endorsement—to the new industry.

Despite Fisher's repeated assurances of her generosity, liberality, and freedom from concupiscence, Margaret died hugely wealthy. The paperwork from her executors in the weeks after her death mentions bequests to the "King's good grace that now is, King Henry VIII; the queen that now is, the princess of Castile" (as Mary was now called). The truly extensive list of memorandums concerning her various properties shows just how far Margaret's grasp had stretched: from Kent to Kendal, from Devon to Dartford. There are memos concerning "the profits of rabbits in Upton Dorset" and "three tenements in the market place of Boston Linc." Annuities were made in consideration of services already rendered and appointments of stewards and auditors whose services were to come. There were executors' assessments of portable property: "plate and great jewels to the value of £4,213. 4s. 3 and a half d.," "Chapel stuff £1,193. 18s. 2d," "Wines left in the cellar £28. 3s. 4d.," and "Ready money £3,595. 8s. 9 and a half d. Obligations £783. 6s. 8d." It was a comforting balance tipped the right way: in the financial realm at least, Margaret had known how to find her security.

An inventory made of the goods in her closet, hard by her bedchamber, at the time of Margaret's death shows her interests and concerns, her physical frailty, and her ability to command luxury: spectacles, but made of gold, and combs of ivory; cramp rings worn to ward off pain and silver pots for powdered medicines; a small gilt shrine to hold reliquaries; two service books bound in velvet and a small gold goblet with the Beaufort emblem of a portcullis on the cover; and a pile of paperwork—bonds, details of the jointure made to her by Thomas Stanley, annuities arranged for dependents, and the king's patent for founding a preacher's position in Cambridge.

In her wardrobe at her death were seven gowns of black velvet with ermine trimming as well as an old scarlet Garter gown: the nunlike (to modern eyes) appearance of her late portraits, with the widow's wimple and white barb, should not deceive us into thinking that the pleasure and pomp of dress were something Margaret had put away. Black fabric was expensive, because to produce a true color required a large quantity of dye. In the keeping of one of her gentlewomen were pearls and rubies, "a serpent's tongue set in gold garnished with pearls," two books whose images were mounted in gold leaves, and a piece of the holy cross set in gold and one of "unicorn's horn."

Shakespeare never wrote a voice for Margaret Beaufort, and indeed it is hard to envisage her fitting into his parade of betrayed and bitter women. But instead, as well as her papers and her writing, we have, in her accounts, what records from this period often lack—the tangible, day-to-day details of a full human life.

EPILOGUE

T he tomb Lady Margaret's executors commissioned in Westminster Abbey looks oddly austere today, but it is among the most convincingly human of the abbey's monuments. Its bronze-gilt portrait effigy was, ironically, constructed for a woman who in life might sometimes have seemed to command either pity or respect rather than any warmer sympathy. But the qualities she defied in life are evident in the architecture of her death. The hands are those arthritis-ridden hands John Fisher described—the hands of an old lady. Old, too, are the deep brackets around the mouth.

Margaret's head rests on a cushion; at her feet is (so the contract for the carving stated) "a beast called a Yale," that fitting symbol of Tudor defensiveness. The arms around the base of the tomb speak to her fierce loyalty to family: there are the arms she shared with her first husband, Edmund Tudor; those of her son, Henry VII, and his queen; of her dead grandson Arthur; of her grandson Henry VIII and Catherine of Aragon; of her parents and of her grandparents; those she shared with her third and final husband, Stanley; those of Henry V and Katherine of Valois, even; but no visible sign of her second husband, Stafford, happy though her life with him seems to have been. He was commemorated in the masses she had ordered for him at the abbey, but the tomb was about the dynasty.

Margaret in her will had given instructions—a controller to the last—for the religious services that should take place in the church of the parish and the fifteen parishes around it and in every parish

through which her body should pass in its Westminster-bound journey. Since she died in Westminster itself, the instructions proved unnecessary. But someone else got to choose the sculptor who would do
her figure—the quarrelsome Italian Pietro Torrigiano, the man who
broke Michelangelo's nose—and, for a fee of twenty shillings, Erasmus composed the Latin inscription around the ledge.

This tomb was not finished until well into Henry VIII's reign. The
contract for the figure of Margaret was drawn up only on November
23, 1511, and her executors' accounts record the transaction: "First
paid the 27th day of December in the 4th year of the reign of King
Henry VIII to M. Garter the king of heralds for making and declaring
my lady's arms in viii 'scochyns' [escutcheons] for my lady's tomb, and
delivered to the Florentine: 8s 4d." It was probably his figure of Margaret that won Torrigiano ("the Florentine") the commission to create
the figures for an even more important royal tomb—that of Henry VII
and Elizabeth of York—which is one of the glories of Westminster
Abbey.

Elizabeth and her husband, Henry, lie side by side in unemotional
gilt splendor, on a plinth of Italian marble. They are gazing upward to
God, and God sees them clearly: two gold images, almost sanctified by
their beauty. Static, stationary, in their tranquillity, emphasizing the
message of Henry VII's Lady Chapel, prominently placed to the east
of the high altar: the Tudors were here to stay.

Look upward above the tomb of Henry and Elizabeth, and you see
the Beaufort portcullis, the Tudor rose, and the French fleur-de-lis.
Leland called the chapel "*miraculum orbis universali*," the wonder of
the entire world, not only for its myriad carvings—the saints in their
ranks, the beasts of heraldry—and its stained glass, now long lost, but
also for the soaring arches of the roof. Henry VII's dream of seeing
Henry VI canonized and "translated" here had never to become reality,
but both Henry and Margaret Beaufort had poured money into the
project—some twenty thousand pounds, or roughly seven million
pounds today.

Elizabeth lies with eyes open and hands folded in prayer, in a fur-
lined robe and with her feet resting on a royal lion. Torrigiano can
never have seen Elizabeth of York—the image was only completed fifteen years after her death—so this may be a standardized royal image,

or may be guided by her effigy. The result has been called the finest Renaissance tomb north of the Alps, with gilded putti and curling foliage jostling the greyhound and the Tudor dragon. But the point—the point of the whole chapel—was not Elizabeth herself, but rather the dynasty she helped to found.

In the south aisle of the Henry VII Chapel are three freestanding tombs, those of Margaret Beaufort and two of her descendants: her great-great-granddaughter Mary, queen of Scots, and her great-granddaughter Margaret Lennox, the mother of Mary's husband, Lord Darnley. It's a distinctly crowded setting, given the quantity of white marble beneath which the Scots queen was reinterred in the seventeenth century. In the north aisle are two more of Margaret Beaufort's great-granddaughters, the two English ruling queens Elizabeth and Mary. Since Henry VIII lies at Windsor—with his son Edward VI merely placed beneath the altar in Henry VII's chapel—this has wound up being a monument not only to the Tudors as such, but also to the female side of history: a "Lady" Chapel—a chapel in honor of Our Lady, of the Virgin Mary, appropriately.

None of the other women in this story has a tomb as visible as the ones in this chapel of Westminster Abbey. Elizabeth Woodville, interred with so little ceremony, at least got to share, almost unnoticed, her husband's tomb at Windsor; Anne Neville is at least known to be buried in Westminster Abbey, although the site is not recorded. Although Cecily Neville is buried as she desired at Fotheringhay, the place never became the memorial to the Yorkist dynasty she had planned; indeed, by Elizabeth I's day, the tombs had fallen into such disrepair she ordered them removed and replaced by a simple plaque elsewhere in the church. Even Margaret of Burgundy's tomb in Malines was ransacked in the sixteenth century—by local iconoclasts, Spanish troops, or English mercenaries—so that no trace of any memorial can be seen today. Marguerite of Anjou was buried as she requested with her parents at Angers, her final resting place serving as evidence that the war in the country that should have been her marital home had not gone her way.

But everything we know about these women suggests that their main imperative was dynastic—genetic. And the blood of Elizabeth Plantagenet and Henry Tudor—and therefore the blood of Margaret

Beaufort, Elizabeth Woodville, and Cecily Neville—still runs in Britain's royal family. The establishment of this legacy, surely, for them, outweighed whatever personal price they had to pay. It is the urge of our age to hunt for other legacies, for tokens of a personal existence. It was not necessarily a need they would have recognized. Among the women of this Cousins' War, Margaret Beaufort fought hardest and most successfully for her bloodline. She is also the only one to leave another sort of legacy—a legacy of works—but even for her, that can only have been a secondary matter.

The deadly dispute between cousins continued for the next century, with its contests mostly fought away from the battlefield, in arenas where women could compete more visibly. Elizabeth of York's granddaughter "Bloody" Mary would dispute the throne with her kinswoman Jane Grey (descended from Elizabeth's younger daughter Mary); Elizabeth Tudor would be forced to execute the queen of Scots, descended from Elizabeth of York's elder daughter Margaret. But out of these women's combined experience, out of the different models of female agency they embodied, would be born something more productive.

If you look at England's consort queens, from the Conquest to the Tudors, you may see a move toward confinement—toward mere domesticity, from the time when a strong woman "will be counted among the men who sit at God's table" to one when any sign of such "manful" strength was a source of profound unease. Yet in the century that followed the Cousins' War, the idea of the strong woman (something then seen almost as a third sex) was about to reach its apogee. Elizabeth I played upon all the ambiguities of gender, not least in the famous speech at Tilbury where, in the face of the oncoming Armada, she assured her soldiers that although she had the body "of a weak and feeble woman," she also had "the heart and stomach of a king." She reconciled, at least for her own lifetime, the problem with which Marguerite of Anjou had grappled in vain: that of reconciling the requirements of rule and the pressure to be "womanly."

In that later Elizabeth, of course, we have also a woman whose signal contribution to history was not genetic or dynastic. The so-called Virgin Queen confounded all the expectations of her own day by reigning in her own right, while the years of her rule saw the expansion of England's interests, the securing of its borders, the regularization of its currency, the great flowering of the Renaissance, and the establishment of the religious settlement Britain still knows today. (She had effectively made possible a Protestant northern Europe.) In her reign began the adventures of exploration and trade, the mechanisms of political and religious toleration, that gave Great Britain its future prosperity.

The achievements of that later Elizabeth have been, to all women since, her lasting legacy. And if Elizabeth of York was Elizabeth I's physical progenitor, then perhaps she could trace back to Marguerite of Anjou a different kind of ancestry. Perhaps, even—however cruelly the wars had told upon her—that fact gives to Marguerite, too, a share in the ultimate victory.

ACKNOWLEDGMENTS

This book began with two conversations, each with writers more familiar than I with the pleasures and pitfalls of the fifteenth century. I was discussing with Alison Weir the possibility of basing a book around a place or an event, rather than a person, when the idea of a book on the battle of Bosworth first occurred to me—one from the viewpoint of the women affected. I was discussing that idea with Ann Wroe when she mentioned that she had always thought how interesting it would be to try to build an entire book around the Privy Purse expenses of one of those women, Elizabeth of York. I wasn't quite courageous enough to take that on, but it did start me thinking about how the surviving records for the lives of the royal ladies might be used in a new way. It was George Lucas of Inkwell Management in New York who, eyeing my first proposal on Bosworth, said that since it was clearly the women who really interested me, why didn't I just write about the women? But even since then, it has been a long journey.

Along the way I have encountered the most extraordinary generosity. Susan Ronald most kindly made available to me her own research on Richard III. Besides Alison Weir, my text was read and improved by Ceri Law, while Julian Humphrys and George Goodwin corrected my blunders on military history, and Dr. David Wright checked my interpretation of certain Latin texts. What errors remain are all my own. Above all, thanks are due to Margaret Gaskin who, as so often before, answered the call of old friendship and came to my rescue over everything from questions of attribution to the family tree.

I want to thank my commissioning editor, Lara Heimert, and all the team at Perseus. I owe much, also, to those authors whose work on the individual subjects and strands that combine to make up this book has been of such assistance to me. Every effort has been made to contact the owners of any copyrighted material reproduced, but if any have been inadvertently overlooked, the publishers would be glad to hear from them so that the mistake can be corrected in future editions.

A NOTE ON SOURCES

There is very little, from the cupidity of Elizabeth Woodville to the culpability of Richard III, on which the historians of the middle and late fifteenth century agree. There is just one subject, however, on which they speak with remarkable unanimity: the inadequacy of their sources. J. R. Lander wrote that these were "notoriously intractable"— and it is especially true when it comes to dealing with women who fought in no battles and passed no laws. Charles Ross, biographer of Edward IV, lamented that "any discussion of motive and the interplay of personality in politics [were] matters generally beyond the range of the unsophisticated and often ill-informed and parochial writers of the time."

The sources for this period are sketchier even than one might find for eras considerably earlier. This was in part because the fifteenth century saw great change in the very writing of history. The monastic Latin chronicle, with a couple of honorable exceptions, was in decline; and though the baton was being passed to secular chroniclers—City merchants and the like, writing in the vernacular and often anonymously—their records were erratic and often confusing. In an age that showed few signs of anything we would recognize as a sense of authorship or provenance, the chroniclers and antiquarians frequently repeat and adapt each other. The writing of humanist history in the Italian style really came to England only at the beginning of the sixteenth century with Polydore Vergil and Sir Thomas More, as did the keeping of state papers of the kind on which students of Henry VIII onward rely. And though the records of state departments like Chancery, the Exchequer, and the law courts have been the subject of extensive study in recent decades, they do not satisfy the biographer's thirst for motive and feeling.

The records of royal life provide few personal letters of the kind we do find in, for example, the Paston papers. (Perhaps the fact that aristocratic letters were usually dictated militated against the written expression of intimate feeling—especially when the times were so very edgy, when you knew a friend could become an enemy.) There is, too, the fact that in the difficult days of the civil war, most reports were written very definitely from one side or the other. As Lander put it, introducing his book on the Wars of the Roses, "Many of the letters and narratives quoted in this book purvey biased opinion, wild rumour, meretricious propaganda and the foulest of slander as well as historical truth." It was not just what someone, writing after the event, thought had happened, but, even more invidiously, what they wanted others to think had happened. Brief introductions will be given below to some of the most important contemporary writers, in an attempt to offer the reader some idea of their likely starting point, but for a far more extensive discussion of these points, see Keith Dockray's introductions to his *Source Books* or the chapter "Writing History" in *English Historical Documents*, vol. 5.

Any work of synthesis, such as this largely is, inevitably owes a great deal to the individual studies already published on its protagonists. Six of the seven women here have already been the subject of individual biographies, from the great Victorian works of Cooper, Hookham, and the like (see the Bibliography) to the sometimes less considerable works of the mid-twentieth century. More recently, Michael K. Jones and Malcolm G. Underwood in *The King's Mother: Lady Margaret Beaufort, Countess of Richmond and Derby* have produced a wealth of new detail on Margaret Beaufort, while Helen Maurer's book *Margaret of Anjou: Queenship and Power in Late Medieval England* explored the whole question of queenship and power. Both Elizabeth Woodville and Elizabeth of York have benefited from new biographies by Arleen Okerlund, while Christine Weightman was able to bring a knowledge of continental sources to bear on her biography of Margaret of Burgundy (or "Margaret of York"). With these I would couple, as of prime importance, Joanna Laynesmith's book *The Last Medieval Queens: English Queenship, 1445–1503,* while Lisa Hilton's *Queens Consort: England's Medieval Queens* and Helen Castor's *She-Wolves: the Women Who Ruled England Before Elizabeth* provide an invaluable context.

Michael Hicks has been brave enough to confront the sometimes-daunting lack of information for a biography of Anne Neville, but there has, at the time of writing, been no published study of Cecily Neville, though Joanna Laynesmith (née Chamberlayne) has written several valuable articles, and Michael K. Jones used his book on the psychological background of Bosworth to explore his controversial but fascinating theories. It is possible that the uncertainty surrounding several crucial points is enough to prohibit a biography as such; therefore, the source notes given here for Cecily are more extensive than for the other women in this book.

NOTES

Prologue

xviii **the anonymous manuscript:** Printed in *The Antiquarian Repertory: A Miscellaneous Assemblage of Topography, History, Biography, Customs, and Manners,* 4:655–663.

xxi **the "Wars of the Roses":** The beginning and end points are themselves a matter for dispute. The preferred option now tends to be from 1455 to 1485—the battle of Bosworth—or possibly 1487 and the battle of Stoke. Nonetheless, some have seen this conflict as starting as early as 1399, with the seizure of Richard II's throne by Henry IV, while others point out that 1471, with the death of Henry VI and his son, saw the end of any conflict between York and what could properly be called the house of Lancaster.

xxv **matter as much as the battles:** Henrietta Leyser, *Medieval Women: A Social History of Women in England,* 167, cites Philippa Maddern in the *Journal of Medieval History* 14 (1988) on the important role of the Paston women in the "bloodless battles of land transactions, county rumour-mongering and client maintenance."

PART I: 1445–1460

Chapter 1: Fatal Marriage

3 **seasick fifteen-year-old:** Earlier writers have Marguerite born in 1429 rather than 1430, but this perception was corrected in an article of 1988 by C. N. L. Brooke and V. Ortenberg, "The Birth of Marguerite of Anjou," *Historical Research* 61:357–358.

4   **Polydore Vergil:** Vergil (ca. 1470–1555) was an Italian Renaissance scholar who came to England in 1501–1502 and was a few
years later invited by Henry VII to write a history of England—
the *Anglica Historia,* not completed until the reign of Henry VIII.
When considering his views on, for example, events as controversial as those of Richard III's reign, it is disconcerting to realize he
can have had no firsthand knowledge of them, the more so since
his writings have been among the most influential in blackening
Richard's name. Nonetheless, although writing in a Tudor, which
effectively meant a Lancastrian, age, Vergil set conscientiously
about his task, collecting memories and canvassing opinions, and
his work is widely seen as marking a turning point in the writing
of English history. (Keith Dockray, moreover, points out that
where the civil wars are concerned, so high a percentage of the
surviving records were written from a Yorkist viewpoint that
Vergil serves as a useful corrective in re-creating the Lancastrian
perspective.)

5   **ominous sign:** Shakespeare in *The Second Part of Henry the Sixth,*
3.2, has Marguerite herself later recalling the "well forewarning
wind" that, by twice beating her ship back toward France, seemed
to be urging her away from the "scorpion's nest" waiting on England's "unkind shore."

6   **chivalry:** This concept, embodied in the courtly tournament and in
popular literature, recurs time and again in the lives of the women
of the late fifteenth century, one that served at once to elevate and
to contain them. It was once a standard practice to contrast the
bloody epics of the early medieval period with the later, "heroine-
centred," romances, "showing women in the courtly worlds of the
later Middle Ages as the privileged and adored mistresses of all
they surveyed. More recent criticism has come to make this view
seem singularly naive; the romance heroine on her pedestal is, if
anything, worse off than her epic predecessor who had at least
some part to play in the thick of the fighting." Henrietta Leyser,
Medieval Women: A Social History of Women in England, 248. Many
of Marguerite's problems would come from the uncertainty of her
position between these two worlds. See also the notes for the
Epilogue.

Chapter 2: "The Red Rose and the White"

18 **Crowland Abbey chronicles:** "Crowland" will be a convenient way of referring to the important chronicles compiled at Crowland—or Croyland—Abbey in the Fens. The chronicle begun by one "In-gulph," and giving the history of the abbey from 655, was later taken over by a series of "continuators"; the identity of the second continuator who chronicled the years from 1459 to 1486 (which, he declares, was the time of writing) is a matter of debate. The most popular candidate is John Russell, Bishop of Lincoln (Richard III's chancellor for much of his reign, but needing now to ingratiate himself with the new king, Henry VII), or possibly, as an alternative, a member of Russell's staff. Other candidates, however, have been suggested: from a clerk in Chancery whose writings only later found their way to the abbey to an unknown Crowland monk working from a secular source. It has often been pointed out that the second continuator, whoever he was, displays a certain animus against Richard III. Nonetheless, the more one reads the records for this period, the more a certain amount of bias comes to seem inevitable, and Crowland must rank as a very significant source.

19 **by way of the male line:** The question of inheritance through a fe-male line would prove a recurrent issue in this century, albeit one that had already long ago provided the basis for the Neville family's power when one Robert Fitz Meldred of Raby married the daugh-ter of Geoffrey de Neville and their son took the rich mother's Neville name and founded this branch of the Neville family. See Charles R. Young, *The Making of the Neville Family, 1166–1400* (Boydell Press, 1996).

20 **jointly to choose a confessor:** For what information exists on Ce-cily's early married life, see Anne Crawford, *Yorkists: The History of a Dynasty*, 1, 3, 5.

20 **Cecily's expenditures:** For Cecily as a "late medieval big spender," see Michael K. Jones, *Bosworth, 1485: Psychology of a Battle*, 59.

21 **debate about . . . Edward's birth:** These are the facts on which Michael K. Jones bases his argument that the suggestion Edward

was not York's son was in fact true: he points out (ibid., 67) that York was away from Rouen on campaign exactly nine months before Edward's birth on April 28, 1442; he has, indeed, found new documentation that shows the duke was away for longer than had been previously thought—from mid-July until after August 20. But the baby would have had to be only a matter of weeks late or premature to put the argument in jeopardy, even disregarding the possibility of conjugal visits, during a campaign fought only fifty miles away. See Crawford, *Yorkists*, 173–178, for the facts that weigh against the theory. Jones also suggests that Cecily's later piety was that of the reformed rake; this theory, though fascinating, can only be speculative.

21   **Edward simply took after his mother, Cecily:** Edward's different appearance would later be held up as evidence of his illegitimacy—but the same grounds would also be used by Richard III to infer the bastardy of Edward's brother Clarence, who himself had been the first to accuse Edward of bastardy, and Clarence was born some years and several siblings down the line, and in a different country.

21   **no sign of querying his son's paternity:** This was the all-important heir. As Horace Walpole put it in the eighteenth century, a time of notably lax aristocratic morality, while writing his *Historic Doubts on the Life and Reign of King Richard III:* "Ladies of the least disputable gallantry generally suffer their husbands to beget the heir."

21   **Mancini:** Dominic Mancini was an Italian visiting England for the first half of 1483 and writing a report on English affairs for his patron, Angelo Cato, one of the advisers of King Louis of France. These comprised Richard III's takeover of the country, as well as a certain amount of backstory. He left England in July 1483, though he seems to have tried to update his information right up to the point when he handed in his report at the beginning of December. It is unclear how good his sources were—though one may possibly have been John Argentine, physician to the boy king Edward V— or even how much English he spoke. Nonetheless, as a man writing in the year the events he described took place, his testimony is invaluable. It is perhaps worth noting that although his report is usually known as the "Usurpation" of Richard III, its Latin title

actually referred to the *"occupatio,"* that is, occupation or seizure of the throne, rather than to its *"usurpatio."*

Chapter 3: "A Woman's Fear"

24   **Jean de Waurin:** Jean or Jehan de Waurin (ca. 1398–ca. 1474) was born a Frenchman, but wound up at the court of Burgundy, where he was commissioned to write a history of England, ending in 1471. A single copy of his *Recueil* survived in the library of Louis de Gruuthuyse.

27   **Shakespeare has Marguerite pleading:** *Henry VI, Part 2*, 3.2.

30   **a high-spending queen:** A. R. Myers in *The Crown, Household, and Parliament in Fifteenth Century England* (coedited with Cecil H. Clough) has studies on the household of Queen Margaret of Anjou, 1452–1453, and on "some household ordinances of Henry VI," as well as on the household of Queen Elizabeth Woodville, 1466–1467.

31   **Margaret Beaufort . . . had been raised at her own family seat:** Another theory suggests that she was at least partly raised in Alice Chaucer's household at Ewelme. Christina Hardyment, *Malory: The Life and Times of King Arthur's Chronicler*, 244.

Chapter 4: "No Women's Matters"

35   **Cecily wrote to Marguerite:** Anne Crawford, *Letters of Medieval Women*, 233–235. On the birth of her son Richard, Cecily writes of an "encumberous labour, to me full painful and uneasy, God knoweth."

36   **Thomas More:** Sir Thomas More's *History of King Richard the Third* brings into sharp focus many of the issues that bedevil the historical sources for the late fifteenth century—a focus all the sharper not only for More's own later reputation as a figure of probity, but for the extremely attractive (and quotable) nature of his writing, full of lengthy reported speeches and the kind of human drama not always found in other sources of the day.

The first question must be to what degree More can be regarded as a contemporary at all, given that he—born in 1478—is describing the events of 1483. (His mention of Richard's birth, like his descriptions of Richard's brother's marriage, are all part of the backstory to his main theme.) But this apart, the long, impassioned speeches he gives to Elizabeth Woodville and her opponents over the surrendering of the younger of the Princes in the Tower could in any case not credibly have been relayed to him verbatim even by someone who was present and reinforce the observation that his *History* is in fact as much a matter of literary creation as factual narrative, a conscious warning against the dangers of tyranny owing a good deal to classical models (unless—a suggestion mooted by R. S. Sylvester, editing the sixteen-volume Yale edition of More's works—he was drawing on a now-lost piece of writing by that someone, possibly John Morton, in whose household the youthful More spent some time).

Morton (whose own experience would help account for More's anti-Richard bias) is most often suggested as More's probable source of information; other theories, however, have also been raised. Michael K. Jones (*Bosworth, 1485: Psychology of a Battle,* 63–64) postulates that "Jane" Shore, whom More evidently knew, may have given him some information, though she would hardly have been privy to the speeches mentioned above. Alison Weir (*The Princes in the Tower,* 170) points out that More was in close touch with a nun in the Minoresses' convent of Aldgate, the inmates of which included several women who might have had important information to give him concerning the fate of the Princes in the Tower (including the daughter of Sir Robert Brackenbury and two female relatives of Sir James Tyrell; see note in Chapter XXIV for Tyrell's supposed confession). It is More's testimony concerning the fate of the Princes that has been more influential even than Vergil's in blackening the reputation of Richard III; nonetheless, supporters of King Richard can choose between simply blaming him for calumny and speculating that the reason he left his narrative unfinished, ending at the point of the murder, may have been because he had come to realize this version of events was a lie, assuming, of course, that he did indeed abandon it at this point. *The History of King Richard III* was printed only two decades after his death, at which time it was described merely as having been found among More's papers and in his hand, so that even the authorship could—the crowning uncertainty—be seen as unclear.

39   **"honour or dishonour":** Helen Cooper writes in her introduction to Malory's *Morte Darthur:* "Malory's Arthurian world operates by the principles of a shame culture, where worth is measured in terms of reputation, 'worship,' rather than by the principles of a guilt culture."

39   **several of the early Norman queens:** The two Matildas—the Conqueror's wife and daughter-in-law—exercised this kind of power, as of course did Eleanor of Aquitaine, while in 1253 Henry III had named his queen, Eleanor of Provence, regent during his absence.

42   **process was completed:** "There has been a tendency among historians to acknowledge Margaret's [*sic*] emergence as a political actor but then to shy away from looking at it too closely. A part of the problem lies in the traditional habit of regarding the Wars of the Roses from the perspective of its male protagonists." Helen Maurer, *Margaret of Anjou: Queenship and Power in Late Medieval England*, 78; see also 81–82.

43   **two sides of the same unnatural coin:** This is the trope by which Richard, in *Henry VI, Part 3*, 5.5, accused her of having usurped her husband's breeches, that is, his masculinity.

45   **Anne Neville:** Another aspect of Neville power was northern: Anne Neville was, of course, great-niece as well as, eventually, daughter-in-law to Cecily.

Chapter 5: *"Captain Margaret"*

50   **Bernard André:** André, a.k.a. Andreus (1450–1522), was a French Augustinian friar who was appointed poet laureate in the first few years of Henry VII's reign, became his official "historiographer" (and inevitably apologist), and played a role in the education of his sons. See André, *Vita Henrici Septimi,* in *Memorials of King Henry VII.*

50   **held maidenhood . . . virginity to be the most perfect time:** The
famous thirteenth-century tract *Holy Maidenhead* paints a horrify-
ing picture of maternity: "a swelling in your womb which bulges
you out like a water-skin, discomfort in your bowels and stitches in
your side . . . the dragging weight of your two breasts, and the
streams of milk that run from them. . . . Worry about your labour
pains keeps you awake at night. Then when it comes to it, that
cruel distressing anguish, that incessant misery, that torment upon
torment, that wailing outcry; while you are suffering from this, and
from your fear of death, shame [is] added to that suffering." Henrietta Leyser, *Medieval Women: A Social History of Women in England,* 123. The same tract paints an equally damning picture of a
wife's lot—the child screaming, "the cat at the flitch and the dog at
the hide, her loaf burning on the hearth and her calf sucking, the
pot boiling over into the fire—and her husband complaining."
Ibid., 146. But at least that is a position with which Margaret
Beaufort would not have to cope. The tract may have been written
specifically for an audience of enclosed religious women; later in
life, Margaret Beaufort would be recorded as fitting out a cell for at
least one anchoress, at Stamford in Lincolnshire, and making her
gifts of wine and apples.

50   **a new marriage had to be arranged for her:** Perhaps—since she
did, after all, ride out to be present at the negotiations—her modern biographers are right to suggest she took a hand in arranging it
herself. Earlier biographers of Margaret Beaufort preferred to
stress her piety and resignation.

54   **"entreated and [de]spoiled":** *An English Chronicle of the Reigns of
Richard II, Henry IV, Henry V, and Henry VI,* 83.

54   **submitted herself:** *Gregory's Chronicle,* 206.

54   **"relief of her and her infants":** *Calendar of Patent Rolls: Henry VI,
1452–61,* 542.

54   **the Countess of Salisbury was personally attainted:** This was a
comparatively novel procedure, where a woman was concerned.
From the parliamentary rolls of 1442: "Also pray the commons . . . that it may please you, by the advice and assent of the

lords spiritual and temporal in this present parliament assembled, to declare that such ladies (duchesses, countesses, or baronesses) thus indicted . . . of any treason or felony . . . whether they are married or single, should be held to reply and set for judgement before such judges and peers of the realm as are other peers of the realm."

Chapter 6: "Mightiness Meets Misery"

58 **chair of blue velvet:** Christine Weightman, *Margaret of York: The Diabolical Duchess*, 45; *The Paston Letters*, 3:233.

60 **Hall and Holinshed:** Edward Hall, *The Union of the Two Noble Families of Lancaster and York*, originally published in 1548. Hall (ca. 1498–1547) drew heavily on Vergil and on More; in fact, when Thomas More's *History* was first printed, it was described as having appeared earlier in Hall but "very much corrupt . . . altered in words and whole sentences." Raphael Holinshed (?–1580) first published the *Chronicles* containing his *History of England* in 1577; his work, more directly even than Hall's, which in large parts it reproduces (a modern age would say plagiarizes), is the major source for Shakespeare's history plays. John Stow (1525–1605, mentioned subsequently in text), who contributed to a later edition of Holinshed's work, was also an antiquarian who transcribed a number of manuscripts.

61 **The pillaging did much:** There is, of course, a theory that the whole saga of Marguerite's indifference and her soldiers' outrage itself originated as Yorkist propaganda. See B. M. Cron, "Margaret of Anjou and the Lancastrian March on London, 1461."

62 **The ladies were Ismanie, Lady Scales:** That, at least, is the consensus view, though Cron's article demonstrates how this is in fact a good example of how information has often to be pieced together from diverging sources: The *Great Chronicle* mentions Jacquetta and Lady Scales but not Anne; the *Annales*, once attributed to the antiquarian William Worcester, and the Milanese *State Papers* mention Anne and Jacquetta but not Lady Scales; another source, the so-called *English Chronicle*, edited by J. S. Davies, has Anne alone.

62   **her eldest daughter, Elizabeth:** The name of Domina Isabella (the Latin "Elizabeth") Grey occurs among the ladies attending Queen Marguerite, at a point when (insofar as the records allow us to guess the dates) the young Elizabeth Woodville had probably recently been married to the Lancastrian John Grey. This reference may well describe another lady; nonetheless, Thomas More would mention Elizabeth's service with Marguerite as a fact. The nineteenth-century writer Prévost d'Exiles relates a romantic story that Elizabeth had accompanied her husband on the campaign and was, before St. Albans, persuaded by Marguerite to visit Warwick's camp as the queen's spy.

65   **The Bishop of Elphin:** *Calendar of State Papers: Venetian,* 1:103. See also *Calendar of State Papers: Milan,* 1:65–66.

PART II: 1460–1471
Chapter 7: "To Love a King"

71   **the lands held by his father:** See *Calendar of Patent Rolls: Edward IV, 1461–67,* 131 (June 1, 1461), an extremely extensive list of properties (with their "advowsons, wards, marriages, escheats . . . warrens, chases, fairs, markets, fisheries, liberties, wrecks of sea") granted to Cecily for life "in full recompense of her jointure." A later grant describes her holding properties, which carried with them the right to hold a regular court, "as fully as the king's father had them." See also *Calendar of the Close Rolls: Edward IV,* 1:73.

81   **it *may* have been . . . bigamous:** See Chapter 8. The possibility of Edward's having been already married is explored at length in John Ashdown-Hill's *Eleanor: The Secret Queen.* See also Anne Crawford, *Yorkists: The History of a Dynasty,* 178–179.

82   **The only Englishwoman to become queen consort:** The closest comparisons would probably be with Matilda of Scotland, wife to Henry I, whose mother came from a Saxon royal house, and Joan of Kent, who made a controversial marriage with the Black Prince, son of Edward III. It could not, however, be said against Matilda that she was not of royal stock, while the Black Prince died before he became king or Joan queen.

83   **Cecily elaborated her title:** Joanna L. Chamberlayne, "A Paper Crown: The Titles and Seals of Cecily Duchess of York." See also Crawford, *Yorkists*, 175–176.

Chapter 8: *"Fortune's Pageant"*

86   **until de Brézé found her:** Nor were her dramatic adventures over. When she and her son, with de Brézé, had ridden back into Scotland, they fell into the hands of an English spy named Cook, who planned to take her to Edward IV. Cook's confederates overpowered the men, dragged them all into a rowing boat, and put out to sea where, as dawn light came up, Marguerite was able surreptitiously to loosen de Brézé's bonds, so that he overpowered Cook and they got away.

91   **to exercise influence:** Men, of course, exercised influence as well, but they also had more formalized rules, which meant that the dangerous, mistrusted interaction of the political and the personal was one step further away.

95   **instructions from Marguerite:** Malory biographer Christina Hardyment postulates (*Malory: The Life and Times of King Arthur's Chronicler*, 419ff.) that he may have been employed as a go-between.

Chapter 9: *"Domestic Broils"*

98   **John Rous:** John Rous, Rows, or Roos (d. 1491) was a Warwickshire cleric and antiquarian, the chronicler of Anne Neville's family. His *Rous Roll,* a history of the Earls of Warwick, warmly praised Anne's husband, then on the throne as Richard III; later, however, his *History of the Kings of England* vilified the dead king just as ardently. It was this work that first saw the portrait, seized upon by Shakespeare, of a Richard who spent two years in his mother's womb, emerging complete with teeth and long hair.

98   **Worcester:** The chronicler once mistakenly identified as the fifteenth-century antiquarian William of Worcester, now often known as "pseudo-Worcester."

98   **Clarence's mother, Cecily, had recently told him:** Michael K. Jones, *Bosworth, 1485: Psychology of a Battle,* 73. Militating against

the theory that Cecily here fell out with Edward is (as Joanna Laynesmith points out in "The Kings' Mother") the fact that in a time of danger soon afterward—a time when he had, however, been reconciled with Clarence—Edward took his family for safety to his mother's house, and Cecily was recorded as taking part in several family ceremonies in the years ahead. As several writers have also reflected, however, within the context of a family, irritation is not the same thing as total alienation—now or in the fifteenth century.

101   **Cecily and her daughters were surely working:** Like so much concerning Cecily's role in the Clarence saga, this seems to be, as Jane Austen put it, "a truth universally acknowledged" rather than one for which it is possible to produce actual proof. For discussion of that role, see Laynesmith, "The Kings' Mother." See also Jones, *Bosworth*, chap. 3, for his theory as to Cecily's motives in traveling to Sandwich to see Clarence as he set off for Calais and marriage with Warwick's daughter.

103   **Marguerite held out for fifteen days:** Shakespeare (*Henry VI, Part 3*, 3.3) takes full dramatic license to have Warwick change his allegiance, and Marguerite accept it, in a half-dozen lines, or the blink of an eye.

Chapter 10: "That Was a Queen"

109   **Philippe de Commynes:** Philippe de Commynes or Commines (1447–ca. 1511) made the opposite journey to that of Jean de Waurin: born in Flanders, he eloped into the service of King Louis of France (at which court he may have met the exiled Henry Tudor). His *Mémoires* reflects the insider's view of international relations he gained in his career as a diplomat, while his analytical style has seen him dubbed "the first truly modern writer."

110   **his force met Warwick's at Barnet:** The reports of the battle serve as a good example of how news spread: The battle of Barnet started at dawn twelve miles outside London; wild rumors were abroad early, and by ten the city was hearing tales of Edward's victory, but these were disbelieved until, the *Great Chronicle of London* says, a rider raced through the streets displaying one of Edward's own

gauntlets, sent as a token to his queen. A Norfolk man claimed to have seen the bodies of Warwick and Montague at St. Paul's that morning. Wanting to be the first to deliver the news back home, he took a boat after dinner, about noon, but was captured at sea by merchants of the Hanseatic League and carried to Zealand, where his story was quickly taken to Margaret of Burgundy at Ghent. Margaret wrote a letter describing it to her mother-in-law and presumably also to her husband—who, however, was also getting erroneous news that Edward IV had been killed.

111   **"womanly behaviour and the great constance":** Agnes Strickland's early-Victorian *Lives of the Queens of England* wrote that Elizabeth's "feminine helplessness" had produced a "tender regard" for her throughout the realm, in contrast to the effect produced by the "indomitable spirit" of Marguerite of Anjou. We might now phrase the comparison differently, but contemporaries clearly agreed.

PART III: 1471–1483
Chapter 11: "My Lovely Queen"

120   **Cecily . . . "sore moved" Sir John to sell her the place:** Helen Castor, *Blood and Roses: The Paston Family and the Wars of the Roses,* 119. She had, after all, grown up in far less commodious establishments: Raby was a palace-cum-fortress rebuilt almost a century before, with towers and apartments irregularly grouped around courtyards.

123   **disguised as a kitchen maid:** If that sounds too much like Cinderella in the fairy story, we should remember not only that Marguerite is supposed to have traveled disguised as a servant, but that in the turmoils of the 1440s Alice Chaucer had had to go to Norwich disguised "like a housewife of the country."

123   **the dispensation failed to arrive:** Anne's biographer Michael Hicks (*Anne Neville: Queen to Richard III,* 143ff.) has written on the invalidity of the dispensation and therefore of the marriage, clearly not a subject of debate at the time, but casting an interesting light on Richard's attitudes.

123 **any other choices:** Hicks, for example (ibid., 111), though without citing actual evidence, portrays it as her own decision to marry Richard.

123 **George Buck:** Sir George Buck (1560–1622), James I's master of the revels and Richard III's first determined apologist. His *History of King Richard the Third* was edited by A. N. Kincaid for Sutton in 1979. Buck's account plays a significant part in the history of the next reign (see Chapters 16 and 18) at which time it will, however, become clear that information from this source must be treated warily.

128 **a declaration of trust:** Cecily, by contrast, spent the summer well away from the seat of power. A letter from Margaret Paston to her son John describes how "my Lady of Yorke and all her household is [*sic*] still here at St Bennet's [an abbey near the Paston home of Mautby in Norfolk] and purposed to abide there still, till the king come from be yonder the sea, and longer if she likes the air there." *The Paston Letters*, 5:236. *The Paston Letters* contain a number of references to Cecily; see, for example, 3:110, 233, 266.

Chapter 12: "Fortune's Womb"

131 **the reburial . . . at Fotheringhay:** Anne F. Sutton and Livia Visser-Fuchs, *The Reburial of Richard, Duke of York, 21–30 July 1476*.

136 **simply watched the ceremony:** Sutton and Visser-Fuchs (ibid.) say Cecily was certainly conspicuous "for her absence, or for the failure of the texts to refer to her." They speculate that it is possible: "Her status as the widow of a man who was being buried almost as a king may have created problems of precedence that were best resolved by her merely watching," suggesting alternatively that she may have been absent from sickness "or choice."

137 **Elizabeth Stonor writes:** Anne Crawford, *Letters of Medieval Women*, 75–77; Stonor Letters, 269–271.

137 **letter of Cecily's perhaps written in 1474:** Crawford, *Letters of Medieval Women*, 133–134. For the possible significance of Syon

in the family dynamics, and the shared piety here reflected as a bond between Richard and Cecily, see Michael K. Jones, *Bosworth, 1485: Psychology of a Battle*, 78. Anne Crawford, *Yorkists: The History of a Dynasty*, 66, however, sees Edward IV's later decision to call one of his youngest daughters Bridget, "a name almost unknown in England," as a reflection of Cecily's devotion to Saint Bridget of Sweden and the Bridgettine abbey of Syon.

138   **Cecily's daughter Elizabeth . . . access of independence:** The Paston letters suggest that John was perhaps dominated by his mother, Alice, as possibly, at least in her younger years, was Elizabeth herself, who in any case would have been fairly well occupied with her childbearing. In 1468 the Pastons reported that Queen Elizabeth had been persuaded to write to "my lady of Norfolk and another letter unto my lady of Suffolk the elder"—Alice. It is noticeable that the Pastons first found it worth petitioning Elizabeth herself, to intercede in a land dispute, right after Alice's death in 1475. But Elizabeth's awareness of the need for status and finery continued to be at war with her and her husband's comparatively low financial standing. Present when Edward made one of his few gestures to education, at Oxford in 1481, she could be found writing (in, most unusually for any fifteenth-century noblewoman, her own hand) to John Paston, asking if she might have the use of his rooms at Windsor. "For God's sake, say me not nay."

Chapter 13: Mother of Griefs

142   **the ever-troublesome Scots:** Edward had the option of other marital plans as a peaceable way of dealing with those same Scots: a letter of 1477 to his ambassador in Scotland replies to the Scots king's suggestions that Clarence and his sister Margaret should marry a sister and brother of his own, with Edward pleading that both were still in their period of "doule," or mourning, and that until they were out of it he would not be able to "feel their dispositions." It is, however, again a moot point whether he would have wished thus to advance his dangerous brother.

146   **daughter to the great Earl of Shrewsbury:** Eleanor Butler was also, through her mother, niece by marriage to Warwick, and Shakespeare only echoes other sources in having Warwick cast up

against Edward, "th' abuse done to my niece" (*Henry VI, Part 3,* 3.3), speaking also of the difficulty of this king's being "contented by one wife" (ibid., 4.3).

147   **Thomas More . . . muddied the waters:** More also has Cecily, at the time of Elizabeth Woodville's marriage to Edward and "under pretence of her duty towards God," sending for Elizabeth Lucy and putting considerable, though ultimately unavailing, pressure on the unfortunate Elizabeth Lucy to stake her prior claim. The idea of precontract was a regular trope: the *Mirror for Magistrates* of 1559 would suggest that Humfrey, the old Duke of Gloucester, had attempted to disrupt Marguerite of Anjou's marriage on the grounds that Henry VI was precontracted to another lady.

148   **loyalty to the family:** Michael K. Jones, whose theory this is, writes in *Bosworth, 1485: Psychology of a Battle,* 35, of "a far more collective sense of identity held by medieval society. . . . As custodians of an historical pedigree, a family would together determine where the interests of its lineage lay and act to defend it."

148   **good ladyship:** Both letters are in Anne Crawford, *Letters of the Queens of England,* 142–143. See also Anne Crawford, *Letters of Medieval Women,* 238, for Cecily's exercise of influence.

148   **[Cecily] can be glimpsed:** See, for example, *Calendar of Patent Rolls: Edward IV, 1461–67,* 89, 151; and *Calendar of Patent Rolls: Edward IV and V and Richard III,* 218, 441, 459, 522. See also *Calendar of Papal Registers,* vol. 13, pt. 1, 106, 260.

149   **A few years later:** *English Historical Documents,* 4:837 (from *A Collection of Ordinances and Regulations for the Government of the Royal Household,* edited by J. Nichols [1790]), a record believed to have been made sometime around 1485, which leaves it open to interpretation whether the events that first pushed Cecily to a religious retirement (if that was indeed the sequence of events) were those of 1478, 1483, or 1485 itself. It is the dwindling trace of her presence at court that inclines me to the earlier date.

149   **Cecily had chosen . . . the mixed life:** See C. A. J. Armstrong, "The Piety of Cicely [*sic*], Duchess of York, a Study in Late

Medieval Culture." See also Jonathan Hughes, *The Religious Life of Richard III: Piety and Prayer in the North of England;* and Joanna L. Laynesmith, "The King's Mother: Cecily Neville."

150 **great female mystics:** Matilda had been a nobly born nun in thirteenth-century Germany whose visions, recorded by her companions, were translated into English as the book of Saint Maud, or *The Book of Ghostly Grace.* (Cecily's son Richard and his wife, Anne, also owned a copy.) The *Revelations* of Saint Bridget, a fourteenth-century Swedish princess who founded the Bridgettine order, was very influential in England—not least in the institution of Syon, with which Cecily had connections—as a great double foundation for men and women living under the Augustinian rule reformed by Saint Bridget. Saint Catherine of Siena was widely celebrated for her mystical marriage with Jesus and for the zest with which she set aside the trappings of a woman's worldly life, cutting off her hair and fasting to a degree that seemed excessive even to the most devout among her contemporaries—the latter a phenomenon that has been called *anorexia mirabilis,* tellingly.

Chapter 14: "A Golden Sorrow"

154 **She also had the encounter painted:** This work and a number of others mentioned, including the *Shrewsbury Book* and the *Beaufort Hours,* were gathered together in a British Library exhibition in 2011–2012. See the catalog by Scot McKendrick, John Lowden, and Kathleen Doyle, *Royal Manuscripts: The Genius of Illumination.*

161 **their mother too was a patron of Caxton's:** Philippa Gregory, David Baldwin, and Michael Jones (*The Women of the Cousins' War: The Duchess, the Queen, and the King's Mother,* 135) suggest she may be the noble lady who, in the interests of her daughters' moral education, commissioned from Caxton a translation of the manual for young ladies called *The Book of the Knight of the Tower.*

165 **with a grant to the king's mother:** *Calendar of Patent Rolls: Edward IV and V and Richard III,* 441. See also *Calendar of Papal Registers,* vol. 13, pt. 1, 106, 260.

166 **her Victorian biographer Mary Ann Hookham:** Hookham (*The Life and Times of Margaret of Anjou*) also quotes the local historian of the nineteenth century J. F. Bodin: "Her blood, corrupted by so many sombre emotions, became like a poison, which infected all the parts that it should nourish; her skin dried up, until it crumbled away in dust; her stomach contracted, and her eyes, as hollow and sunken as if they had been driven into her head, lost all the fire, which had, for so long a time, served to interpret the lofty sentiments of her soul."

PART IV: 1483–1485
Chapter 15: "Weeping Queens"

173 **his wishes no longer paramount:** This begs the question of whether deathbed codicils to Edward's will (mentioned by both Crowland and Mancini but, if made, since lost) had in any case removed the powers formerly given to her.

174 **even female:** The hint of Richard's double prescience—both as to Edward V's fate and as to Elizabeth of York's future importance—cannot necessarily this time be put down to hindsight, since Mancini's narrative ended, with his visit, in the summer of 1483.

175 **confided to his wife:** Anne's role in events is one of the great imponderables. Shakespeare, in *The Tragedy of Richard III*, 4.1, would have a scene of mutual lamentation when the three women—Elizabeth Woodville, Anne Neville, and Cecily—get the first inkling of Richard's plans. But there is no reason to assume this was the reality (it certainly failed to reflect the dissent between Elizabeth and her mother-in-law). Janis Lull, introducing the Cambridge University Press edition of the play, notes that the triad has been compared to the lamentations of Helena, Andromache, and Hecuba in Seneca's *Troades* and explores also the motif of the three Marys—Mary Magdalene, Mary Salome, and Mary the mother of James—in the medieval Resurrection plays.

179 **already an ally of Margaret Beaufort's:** Morton had been one of the protectors involved in the negotiation of Margaret Beaufort's

marriage settlements, as well as mediator to Edward IV in her attempt to get her son home.

180 **On June 16 the council sent a delegation:** Some sources, Mancini, Vergil, and More among them, seem to suggest that the younger boy was surrendered before Hastings's execution; however, the dispassionate evidence of a contemporary letter and an account book suggests the sequence of events followed here.

180 **"womanish frowardness":** Elizabeth had, Buckingham said, no need to fear, since there was "no man here that will be at war with women," and as for the rights of sanctuary: "What if a man's wife will take sanctuary because she list to run away from her husband? I would ween if she can allege no other cause, he may lawfully, without any displeasure to St Peter, take her out of St Peter's church by the arm."

181 **More's pages have . . . to be decoded:** See notes for Chapter 4.

184 **Another theory:** See that of Michael K. Jones in *Bosworth, 1485: Psychology of a Battle:* "The painful turmoil of 1469 was to be mirrored in 1483, as Richard succeeded where Clarence had failed. And as King Richard struggled to overcome the threats from those who opposed this new Yorkist settlement, it was Cecily to whom he appealed for daily blessing in his enterprise. Her role was crucial." See chapter 4, "The Search for Redemption." It is Jones who cites as evidence the archbishop's register: *Registrum Thome Bourgchier, Cantanuariensis Archiepiscopi, AD 1454–1486,* edited by F. R. H. DuBoulay (Canterbury and York Society, liv, 1957), 52–53. Michael K. Jones also states (*Bosworth,* 91) that several decades later, in 1535, a conversation between the Spanish ambassador Chapuys and Henry VIII's minister Thomas Cromwell showed Cecily had made a written confession. The actual statement from Chapuys (*Calendar of State Papers Foreign and Domestic: Henry VIII,* 8:281) is that he had told Cromwell that Henry, in seeking a divorce from Catherine of Aragon, was wrong to rely on the statutes of the realm, "which only depended on the prince's wish, as might be seen by the Acts of King Richard,

who . . . caused King Edward himself to be declared a bastard, and to prove it, called his own mother to bear witness, and caused it to be continually preached so." From this Jones concludes that Cecily did indeed bear written evidence, that she did so before Shaa preached his sermon, and that she was in London to do it. But this may apportion more weight than Chapuys's statement can really bear. Joanna Laynesmith in her article "The King's Mother: Cecily Neville" for the *Ricardian* of autumn 2005 suggests as her own suspicion that Cecily "did not actively promote Richard's accession, but equally did not oppose it either." I would be inclined to agree.

185   **The right of inheritance to the throne:** Even a hundred years later, when Elizabeth I was dying, there was, to quote the succession historian Howard Nenner, no agreement as to how the next ruler should be chosen, let alone as to whom he or she should be. No one knew "whether the crown ought to pass automatically at the death of Elizabeth to the next in the hereditary line; whether the next in the hereditary line might be passed over because of a 'legal' incapacity to rule; whether the next monarch ought to be determined in parliament; or whether the queen should be exhorted in the waning days of her life to nominate her own successor." Nenner, *The Right to Be King: The Succession to the Crown of England, 1604–1714,* 13.

186   **the grant of [Cecily's] manors and lands:** *Calendar of Patent Rolls: Edward IV and V and Richard III,* 459.

Chapter 16: "Innocent Blood"

188   **The list of accounts:** Anne Sutton and P. W. Hammond, eds., *The Coronation of Richard III: The Extant Documents.*

192   **young Edward had been left in the North:** The fact that some documents (believed to have been prepared in advance) describe him as present on his parents' coronation day suggests that he might have been expected.

196   **Elizabeth Woodville . . . was "so well pleased":** A phrase from Crowland is often cited that might seem to suggest Elizabeth had

taken a very active and early part in the plotting: that "many things were going on in secret . . . especially on the part of those who had availed themselves of the privilege of sanctuary." But a fuller quotation describes specifically the people "of the South and of the West" of the kingdom, "especially those people who, because of fear, were scattered without franchises and sanctuaries."

196   **Margaret was on the point of sending . . . Christopher Urswick:** In the end, another messenger would be sent to Brittany, with "a good great sum of money" raised by Margaret in the City. This next messenger, interestingly, was a man, Hugh Conway, with connections not only to Edward IV's household but also to the Stanleys.

199   **a favorite outside candidate for villain:** If the Duke of Buckingham had had the boys killed then (as Buckingham would surely have calculated), Richard might indeed have hesitated at least in the short term to publish the deaths, though one must still ask, why did he not do so later? Henry VII, when the time came, might well have kept a similar silence. If this was true, the guilty man, after all, was nominally one of Henry's supporters—one of his mother's close allies.

199   **historians from Vergil and More onward:** This is true *unless* we agree with the suggestion that More broke off his history at the crucial point because he could no longer subscribe to what he had become convinced was a lie.

199   **Margaret Beaufort herself:** See Helen Maurer's article "Whodunit: The Suspects in the Case" for an analysis of the evidence for the different candidates mooted (who in fact include even the boy's mother, Elizabeth Woodville). Margaret Beaufort is her personal favorite for the role.

200   **not indifferent to the boys' fate:** There *was* a mounting body of rumor. Weinreich's *Danzig Chronicle* of 1483 claimed that "later this summer Richard the king's brother seized power and had his brother's children killed, and the queen secretly put away." French chancellor Guillaume de Rochefort, in a speech to the Estates-General on January 15, 1484, warned the French (faced with their

own minority rule): "Look what has happened in [England] since the death of King Edward: how his children, already big and courageous, have been put to death with impunity, and the royal crown transferred to their murderer by the favour of the people." Not everyone, however, had Richard as the sole culprit. The *Historical Notes of a London Citizen* declared that "King Edward the Vth, late called Prince of Wales and Richard Duke of York, his brother . . . were put to death in the Tower of London by the vise [advice] of the Duke of Buckingham." This last comforting theory—that the blame belonged to Buckingham—may have been the one to which Margaret of Burgundy persuaded herself to subscribe. Of the chroniclers associated with Burgundy, Molinet blamed Richard, but Commynes put at least part of the guilt on Buckingham. She may, alternatively, have assumed any rumors of murder were exaggerated.

Chapter 17: *"Look to Your Wife"*

207 **Sometime that month, Elizabeth's daughters left sanctuary:** Vergil says, "When the queen as thus qualified, king Richard received all his brothers' daughters out of sanctuary into the court," which might seem to show that they went to court immediately. But a precise timescale was not necessarily the priority of the contemporary chroniclers. Vergil also implies that all of this happened after the queen's writing to bring her son Dorset home, which other evidence shows to have happened a year later. Crowland writes that Elizabeth Woodville ("after frequent entreaties as well as threats") "sent all her daughters out of the sanctuary at Westminster before mentioned to King Richard"—that is, into his charge—implying, however, that this happened rather earlier than other evidence suggests.

208 **quietly allowed to join her:** Even a location for the family's secret residence has been suggested by one of Richard's modern supporters, Audrey Williamson: Gipping Hall in Suffolk, seat of the Tyrell family, whose own tradition suggests that royal children lived "by permission of the Uncle." Williamson, *The Mystery of the Princes: An Investigation into a Supposed Murder*, 122–124. We will, of course, be hearing of Sir James Tyrell later: this would not only

cast a new light on his relations to the Princes, but also explain why
Henry Tudor might later feel the need to put a very different spin
on them.

208   **died from natural causes:** This may be another case of arguing
from effect to cause: Professor Wright, who in the 1930s examined
two children's skeletons found within the Tower, noted that the
skeleton of the older child bore the symptoms of what has been
tentatively diagnosed as the progressive bone disease osteomyelitis.
But we do not know these skeletons were those of the Princes, and
though the older boy was known to have been visited by his doctor
that summer, any royal person might have a physician in precautionary attendance anyway.

208   **true fate a mystery:** We cannot wholly rule out the possibility that
the younger boy at least *may*—with or without Richard's connivance—eventually have been sent abroad (just as Cecily sent her
sons abroad in time of danger), given a new identity, or both.
Francis Bacon, writing a century later, has Perkin Warbeck, the
pretender who claimed to be Elizabeth Woodville's younger son,
saying that he would not reveal details of his escape from the
Tower, but "Let it suffice to think I had a mother living, a Queen,
and one that expected daily such a commandment from the tyrant
for the murdering of her children." The clear implication is that
Elizabeth Woodville smuggled her younger son away, and though
the words of a pretender may lack credibility, it shows the idea was
in currency.

If this were done with Richard's connivance, the intention
might have been to get the boy out of the way of Henry, to whom
he might have figured as either a tool or a threat. If so, it would not
only explain Elizabeth Woodville's sudden accord with Richard,
but at least help to clear up one minor mystery: why Elizabeth was
lying so low during all these months that her very whereabouts are
uncertain, from the time she left Westminster Abbey right
through to the time she starts appearing in documents as one of
the new King Henry's beneficiaries.

209   **granting away some of her family lands:** Some of them, however,
were to the "Queens'" College that honors her as a patron. The

Great Chronicle some thirty years later would call her "a woman of gracious fame," but of that too there is very little evidence.

Chapter 18: "Anne My Wife"

214 **"of similar colour and shape":** For consistency I have used the older translation of the complete Crowland chronicle, *Ingulph's Chronicle of the Abbey of Croyland with the Continuations by Peter of Blois and Anonymous Writers.* Here, however, the more recent translation of the work of the "second continuator," *The Crowland Chronicle Continuations, 1459–1486,* differs in significance as well as wording. Their translation from the Latin (*eisdem colore et forma*) is "who were alike in complexion and figure," which clearly indicates the women rather than the garments. (Dress was an important signifier of rank.) Interpretation had hitherto varied—but the real point is that nothing in the original necessarily compels the popular assumption that Richard had given the garments; Buck indeed says that Anne herself instituted the swap.

216 **damning in several different ways:** Shakespeare's wooing (*The Tragedy of Richard III*, 1.2) by Richard of a Lady Anne still lamenting the first husband Richard killed in a sense represents a dramatization of our reaction to this different, but equally, shocking marriage. It might have been unwise for him to comment more directly on the behavior of one who was grandmother to Elizabeth I.

216 **invented the letter in its entirety:** *Against* that theory is the fact that Buck gave a specific source for the letter—in the collection of Thomas Howard, Earl of Arundel, in a "rich and magnificent cabinet, among precious jewels and more monuments"—and he would have been taking a huge risk that other scholars might have called his bluff. But Buck, a determined apologist for Richard, was not above "suppressing evidence and altering record," so one modern historian, Alison Hanham, declared. N. Harris Nicolas in the nineteenth century put it even more directly: "The character of Buck as a faithless writer is well known." The great Victorian James Gairdner, on the other hand, was disgustedly inclined to accept the letter, writing that "the horrible perversion and degradation of domestic life which it implies in only too characteristic of

the age"—so different, one can't but add, from the home life of his own dear queen.

Buck himself may be the victim of an inadvertent injustice here. What we think of as "Buck" is the version of his manuscript printed several decades after he wrote it under the auspices of his great-nephew (confusingly, another George Buck), and the extensive work done by Buck's modern editor, Arthur Kincaid, reveals among other things that this branch of the Buck family had a track record for forgery.

The surviving manuscript versions of Buck's original show revisions not only by Buck himself but also by his great-nephew; even more important, the earliest of them has been very considerably damaged by fire. In an article for the *Ricardian,* Kincaid transcribed precisely what was (and was not) left:

< st she thanked him for his many Curtesies and friendly>
                    as before   in the cause of<
>d then she prayed him ^ to bee a mediator for her to the K<
>ge
whoe (as she wrote) was her onely ioye and her maker in<
                                in
Worlde, and that she was [in] his, harte, in thoughts in<
and \ in / all, and then she intimated that the better halfe of
      Ffe<
was paste, and that she feared the Queene would neu<

In other words, the choice of the word *body* and the fear the queen would *never die* were inserted by the younger George Buck: guided, admittedly, by the space that must have been left on the paper, but writing with the goal more of producing a sensational and salable text than of historical accuracy. The gaps leave it unclear in quite what cause the recipient was to intercede—as mediator for the writer's marriage *to* the king or as mediator to the king for her marriage to someone else? These circumstances were explored in an article in the *Ricardian:* Arthur Kincaid, "Buck and the Elizabeth of York Letter." See also Livia Visser-Fuchs, "Where Did Elizabeth of York Find Consolation?," and of course Kincaid's introduction to his edition of Buck's work: George Buck, *History of King Richard the Third.* The conclusion presented in

Kincaid's own edition of the text was that "Elizabeth in her letter was referring to a hoped-for marriage—though not necessarily with the king," and it is hard to disagree.

220   **a double marriage:** Details of the Portuguese proposal, and Elizabeth of York's role in it, are from John Ashdown-Hill's book *The Last Days of Richard III*, 32, who suggests that rumors about a foreign match for her and for Richard were (by contemporaries as well as later historians) misunderstood as a match between her and Richard.

222   **the *Great Chronicle* recorded:** It is often said—supported by some internal evidence—that this entry refers to the spring of 1484, but that is surely impossible to reconcile with the mention of Anne's death.

Chapter 19: "In Bosworth Field"

224   ***Ballad of Lady Bessy:*** The *Ballad of Lady Bessy* (or, *The Most Pleasant Song of Ladye Bessiye*) is believed probably to have been written by Stanley's officer Humphrey Brereton—chiefly because it is hard otherwise to account for the large part Brereton himself plays in the narrative.

225   **Francis Bacon:** Bacon (1561–1626), best known as Elizabeth I's counselor and James I's attorney general and lord chancellor, turned wholly to writing after being indicted by Parliament on charges of corruption. His *History of Henry VII* was published in 1622.

225   **at the home of his mother, Cecily Neville:** John Ashdown-Hill (*The Last Days of Richard III*, 53) cites R. Edwards, *The Itinerary of King Richard III* (Richard III Society, 1983).

PART V: 1485–1509
Chapter 20: "True Succeeders"

235   **the starting place of the early modern age:** "Historians have claimed that a 'new' monarchy arose with the coming of Henry VII, that a new age was inaugurated. . . . But wise readers should

be wary of the 'new.' . . . Most change, deep change, occurs more slowly, experimentally, cautiously, and through deliberation. It thus often goes unnoticed by those who live it and make it happen." Miri Rubin, *The Hollow Crown: A History of Britain in the Late Middle Ages*, 322.

238 **said Francis Bacon:** See his *History* of Henry VII. The question of whether a woman's rights of inheritance to the throne should automatically skip over her to her sons was of course still an issue in the mid-sixteenth century when Edward VI attempted to will his crown to "Lady Jane's heirs male," before being forced by the imminence of his own death to alter it to Jane Grey and her heirs male. See also Helen Castor, *She-Wolves: The Women Who Ruled England Before Elizabeth*, 28–29.

241 **silent uncertainty was . . . everybody's friend:** According to David Baldwin, "It is impossible to believe" that those women closest to them—women in positions of power—remained in complete ignorance as to the boys' fate. He concludes not only that "the implication is that they did know but chose to remain silent, something that would not have been necessary if both boys were dead and threatened no one," but also that "the most likely scenario" is that the younger son at least may have been sent to a secure place. Philippa Gregory, David Baldwin, and Michael Jones, *The Women of the Cousins' Wars: The Duchess, the Queen, and the King's Mother*, 210.

248 **Lincoln's own attempt:** According to Francis Bacon, "As for the daughters of King Edward the Fourth, they thought King Richard had said enough for them [that is, the people thought that Richard's example showed they were not the inevitable heirs], and took them to be but as of the King's party, because they were in his power and at his disposing."

249 **"discontent with the King":** Elizabeth Woodville's biographer David Baldwin suggests as one possibility that she envisaged a papal dispensation allowing Elizabeth of York, with Henry out of the way, to marry her cousin Warwick while she herself became the power behind a monarch believed to be of feeble personality. There is, as he says, no evidence. Another possibility is

that Elizabeth knew that one of her sons was alive and intended, should the rebellion succeed, then to assert his prior claim in place of Warwick's, though this might suggest that she had not been sure of her sons' fate earlier, when she allowed her daughter to marry herself and her valuable royal rights into the opposing dynasty.

249 **fundamental role in the Lambert Simnel drama:** Christine Weightman, *Margaret of York: The Diabolical Duchess*, 153.

Chapter 21: *"Golden Sovereignty"*

251 **John Leland:** Best known for his *Itinerary*, describing his findings on journeys through England and Wales, John Leland (1503?– 1552) was also the antiquarian whose *De Rebus Brittannicis Collecteanea* includes a number of the most important descriptions of key ceremonies of Henry VII's reign. Narratives quoted from this source include Margaret Beaufort's ordinances for the confinement of a queen and the christening of her child (4:179–184), the christening of Prince Arthur (204–215), Elizabeth of York's coronation (216–233), the Twelfth Night celebrations of 1487 (234–237), Elizabeth's taking her chamber (249), and the proxy marriage of Princess Margaret and her journey into Scotland (258–300).

254 **evidence that she was in some degree of disgrace:** Theories that Elizabeth Woodville's health had gone into some sort of major decline, necessitating her retirement, are contradicted by the fact that the negotiations for her to marry the king of Scots went on for years. See Baldwin in Philippa Gregory, David Baldwin, and Michael Jones, *The Women of the Cousins' Wars: The Duchess, the Queen, and the King's Mother*, 215. But then again, if Elizabeth was seriously suspected of treason, it seems unlikely Henry would really have contemplated giving her access to a foreign army.

256 **a purely domestic role:** Nicholas Harris Nicolas, editing her Privy Purse expenses in 1830: "The energy and talents of Henry the Seventh left no opportunity for his Queen to display any other qualities than those which peculiarly, and it may be said exclusively,

belong to her sex. From the time of her marriage she is only to be heard of as a daughter, a wife, a mother, a sister, and an aunt; and in each of these relations, so far as materials exist by which it can be judged, her conduct reflects honour upon her memory." Nicolas, *Privy Purse Expenses of Elizabeth of York: Wardrobe Accounts of Edward the Fourth, with a Memoir of Elizabeth of York*, xxxi.

256 **letters to Spain:** There was also a considerable mention in De Puebla's correspondence of Elizabeth's determination to arrange a marriage with an Englishwoman for De Puebla himself and his efforts to avoid the same. Perhaps one of the lessons Elizabeth had learned early is that marriage as a means of bringing a party onside may be the most useful tool of diplomacy.

256 **similarities in their handwriting:** David Starkey, *Henry: Virtuous Prince*, 118–120.

258 **Elizabeth of York and Margaret Beaufort only as rivals:** Joanna Laynesmith argues that between the two—both of whose royal blood had caused their past fortunes to seesaw—"there probably existed more than cordial relations," equivalent to those between Eleanor of Provence and Eleanor of Castile some 250 years before. Elizabeth's biographer Arlene Okerlund suggests that Margaret Beaufort may have substituted for the absent Elizabeth Woodville—if we really think that Margaret had that sort of warm personality.

260 **A letter from Henry VIII's day:** These are original letters illustrative of English history, including numerous royal letters, from autographs in the British Museum, the State Paper Office, and one or two other collections edited by Sir Henry Ellis (1846), ser. 1, vol. 2.

261 **Minories:** It was the same convent of Minoresses with which Thomas More was known to have been in touch.

262 **"we have, moreover, opened the moneybox":** *Calendar of State Papers: Venetian*, vol. 1, *1202–1509*, edited by Rawdon Brown, 181, May 9, 1489.

Chapter 22: "The Edge of Traitors"

272 **Henry offered his daughter Margaret:** The elder Margaret, Margaret Beaufort, had always promoted her half-blood family, and the autumn of 1494 was also when she arranged for Richard Pole—the son of her half sister Edith St. John—to marry Clarence's daughter Margaret. This would prove to be setting up trouble: for the Tudor dynasty, but also for Margaret Pole, who, as the increasingly paranoid eyes of an aging Henry VIII focused on her family, would be beheaded in one of the Tower's nastiest execution stories. At the time, however—since it may have seemed unrealistic to keep Margaret Pole forever unmarried—it may have looked like the safe thing to do, another way of using the marriage tie to secure her within the family.

273 **servants of Cecily Neville's:** Ann Wroe, *Perkin: A Story of Deception*, 178–179.

273 **as her will declared:** *Wills from Doctors Commons: A Selection for the Wills of Eminent Persons, Etc.*

Chapter 23: "Civil Wounds"

276 **another daughter, Mary, was born:** Her date of birth is often given as 1495, which is how it is described in the *Beaufort Hours*—but Margaret Beaufort followed the then-current practice of beginning a new year on March 23.

277 **Perkin declared himself king:** Among his otherwise rather vague charges proclaimed against Henry was that he had married "by compulsion certain of our sisters"—Elizabeth's younger sisters—to his own friends and kinsmen of unsuitably low degree.

277 **Katherine Gordon:** Ann Wroe, *Perkin: A Story of Deception*, 374–378.

279 **Margaret of Burgundy's actual, illegitimate, son:** There is a possible alternative identification, as suggested by Ann Wroe (ibid., 516–518). The childless Margaret took several children under her wing (and indeed even the fertile Elizabeth of York's Privy Purse expenses show upkeep for children who had been "given" to her),

but one appeared to have attracted her special interest: Jehan le Sage, a boy of about five when she adopted him in 1478, which makes him around the same age as Richard, Duke of York. Carefully educated and luxuriously clad, he was reared in some seclusion until—at the end of 1485, just when Margaret must have been swallowing the bitter knowledge of the destruction of the house of York—he vanished from the records. It may be pure coincidence that the room in the country palace of Binche in which he lived was later known as "Richard's room." Wroe notes also (ibid., 467–471) that the delegation sent to inquire into Perkin's fate was headed by the Bishop of Cambrai; among those who believed Perkin Margaret's own son, it was said (ibid., 209) he had been fathered by the incumbent of the Cambrai see, whether this man or his predecessor.

Chapter 24: Like a Queen Inter Me

293   **jousted for her:** Among the fighters, so John Younge, the Somerset Herald, who wrote the description, noted, "Charles Brandon had right well jousted." A dozen or so years down the line, Brandon would be the husband of Mary Tudor's unsanctioned second marriage.

294   **confession . . . never published:** Indeed, though both Vergil and the *Great Chronicle* (both postdating 1502) mention Tyrell's guilt or at least the possibility thereof, mention of the confession, so dramatically utilized by Shakespeare, can be traced back only as far as Thomas More.

295   **a Miles Forrest was listed:** Audrey Williamson, *The Mystery of the Princes: An Investigation into a Supposed Murder*, 178.

298   **velvet-clad effigy:** The effigy is still there in the precincts museum, or part of it, anyway—a bald head, long stripped of its wig and crown, a wooden arm and hand. It looks like nothing so much as a monstrous doll—the broken toy of some giant child. The body of straw-stuffed leather fell victim to a World War II incendiary bomb. The flames took no hold in the vaulted stone room, but the damage was done by water from the firemen's hoses. The planks of pear-tree wood around which the torso was built started to separate

after their wartime saturation, and in 1950 they were "discarded," as the restorer noted regretfully. But photographs survive and show the "ragged regiment" of the royal effigies in all their macabre glory. For more information, see A. Harvey and R. Mortimer, eds., *The Funeral Effigies of Westminster Abbey* (Boydell, 1994).

Chapter 25: "Our Noble Mother"

303 **John Fisher:** John Fisher, Bishop of Rochester (ca. 1469–1535), was the first holder of the Cambridge Lady Margaret Professorship of Divinity. Vice chancellor of that university, Fisher (like Sir Thomas More) would be best remembered, and indeed canonized, for his refusal to accept Henry VIII as head of the Church of England, a refusal that sent him to the headsman's block. For the *Mornynge Remembraunce* sermon preached a month after Margaret Beaufort's death, see *The English Works of John Fisher*.

310 **her daughter Juana:** See Julia Fox, *Sister Queens: Katherine of Aragon and Juana, Queen of Castile.*

320 **Shakespeare never wrote a voice for Margaret Beaufort:** He never wrote a *Henry VII*, of course, though the coauthored *Henry VIII* takes the story up until the christening of Elizabeth I.

Epilogue

324 **legacy of works:** In Cambridge today, her image is among the parade of academic notables who gaze down over the modern setting of the Graduate Society's café, the only other woman there besides Rosalind Franklin, the "dark lady" of DNA. Flick through the *Cambridge Guide to Women's Writing in English,* and there she is, "Beaufort, Lady Margaret, English translator of religious texts and literary patron," sandwiched between Simone de Beauvoir and American satirist Ann Beattie.

324 **toward mere domesticity:** See the conclusion to Lisa Hilton's *Queens Consort: England's Medieval Queens.*

SELECTED BIBLIOGRAPHY

PRIMARY SOURCES

A number of the following original sources are now available online, notably the different versions of the *Ballad of Lady Bessy* and the texts of the *Arrivall* and *Gregory's Chronicle*. Useful sites are those of the Richard III Society's online library (http://www.r3.org/bookcase) and British History Online (http://www.british-history.ac.uk).

Quotations from William Shakespeare are from the texts printed by Cambridge University Press.

André, Bernard. *Vita Henrici Septimi.* In *Memorials of King Henry VII*, edited by J. Gairdner. Rolls Series. 1858.

The Antiquarian Repertory: A Miscellaneous Assemblage of Topography, History, Biography, Customs, and Manners. Edited by Francis Grose and Thomas Astle. Vol. 4. 1807.

Calendar of Papal Registers. Vol. 13, pt. 1, edited by J. A. Twemlow. 1955.

Calendar of Patent Rolls: Edward IV, 1461–67. HMSO, 1899.

Calendar of Patent Rolls: Edward IV and V and Richard III, 1476–85. HMSO, 1901.

Calendar of Patent Rolls: Henry VI, 1452–61. HMSO, 1897.

Calendar of State Papers: Milan. Vol. 1, *1385–1618*, edited by Allen B. Hinds. HMSO, 1912.

Calendar of State Papers: Spanish. Vol. 1, *1485–1559*, edited by G. A. Bergenroth. 1862.

Calendar of State Papers: Venetian. Vol. 1, *1202–1509*, edited by Rawdon Brown. 1864.

Calendar of the Close Rolls: Edward IV. Vol. 1, *1461–68*. HMSO, 1949.

Chronicles of London. Edited by C. L. Kingsford. 1905. Reprint, 1977.

Commynes, Philippe de. *Mémoires.* Translated by A. R. Scoble. 1855–1856. Translated by M. Jones. Harmondsworth, 1972.

Crowland. *Ingulph's Chronicle of the Abbey of Croyland with the Continuations by Peter of Blois and Anonymous Writers.* Translated by Henry T. Riley. 1854.

The Crowland Chronicle Continuations, 1459–1486. Translated and edited by Nicholas Pronay and John Cox. Sutton, 1986.

Ellis, Sir Henry. *Original Letters Illustrative of English History, Including Numerous Royal Letters, from Autographs in the British Museum, the State Paper Office, and One or Two Other Collections.* Three series: 1824, 1827, and 1846.

An English Chronicle of the Reigns of Richard II, Henry IV, Henry V, and Henry VI. Edited by J. S. Davies. Camden Society, 1856.

English Historical Documents. General editor David C. Douglas. Vol. 4, *1327–1485,* edited by A. R. Myers. Vol. 5, *1485–1558,* edited by C. H. Williams. Eyre & Spottiswoode, 1953–1970.

Fisher, John. *The English Works of John Fisher.* Edited by J. E. B. Mayor. 1876.

The Great Chronicle of London. Edited by A. H. Thomas and I. D. Thornley. Originally published for the Library Committee of the Corporation of the City of London, 1938. Facsimile edition. Sutton, 1983.

Gregory's Chronicle. In *Historical Collection of a Citizen of London,* edited by J. Gairdner. N.s. 17. Camden Society, 1876.

Hall, Edward. *The Union of the Two Noble Families of Lancaster and York.* Originally printed 1552, 1558, and 1560. Modern edition edited by H. Ellis. 1809.

Historie of the Arrivall of Edward IV. Edited by J. Bruce. Camden Society, 1838.

Leland, John. *De Rebus Brittannicis Collecteanea.* Edited by T. Hearne. 1774.

Malory, Sir Thomas. *Le Morte Darthur [sic]: The Winchester Manuscript.* Edited by Helen Cooper. Oxford University Press, 1998.

Mancini, Dominic. *The Usurpation of Richard III (Dominicus Mancinus ad Angelum Catonem de Occupatione Regni Anglie per Riccardum Tercium Libellus).* Translated by C. A. J. Armstrong. Clarendon Press, 1936.

More, Thomas. *Complete Works.* Vol. 2, edited by Richard S. Sylvester. Yale University Press, 1963.

The New Chronicles of England and France. Also known as *Fabian's Chronicle.* Edited by H. Ellis. 1811.

Nicolas, Nicholas Harris. *Privy Purse Expenses of Elizabeth of York: Wardrobe Accounts of Edward the Fourth, with a Memoir of Elizabeth of York.* 1830.

The Paston Letters. Edited by J. Gairdner. 1904.

Pizan, Christine de. *A Medieval Woman's Mirror of Honour: The Treasury of the City of Ladies.* Translated by Charity Cannon Willard. Edited by Madeleine Pelner Cosman. Bard Hall Press and Persea Books, 1989.

Stonor Letters. Kingsford's Stonor Letters and Papers, 1290–1483. Edited by C. Carpenter. Cambridge University Press, 1996.

Vergil, Polydore. *Three Books of Polydore Vergil's English History: Comprising the Reigns of Henry VI, Edward IV, and Richard III.* 1844.

Wills from Doctors Commons: A Selection for the Wills of Eminent Person, Etc.
Edited by J. G. Nichols and J. Bruce. O.s. 83. Camden Society, 1863.

SECONDARY SOURCES

Armstrong, C. A. J. "The Piety of Cicely Duchess of York: A Study in Late Medieval Culture." In *For Hillaire Belloc: Essays in Honour of His 72nd Birthday.* Sheed & Ward, 1942.

Ashdown-Hill, John. *Eleanor: The Secret Queen.* History Press, 2009.

———. *The Last Days of Richard III.* History Press, 2011.

Bacon, Francis. *The History of the Reign of King Henry VII.* Edited by Brian Vickers. Cambridge University Press, 1998.

Bagley, J. J. *Margaret of Anjou, Queen of England.* Herbert Jenkins, 1948.

Baldwin, David. *Elizabeth Woodville: Mother of the Princes in the Tower.* Sutton, 2002.

———. *The Lost Prince: The Survival of Richard of York.* Sutton, 2007.

Buck, George. *History of King Richard the Third.* Edited by A. N. Kincaid. Sutton, 1979.

Bullough, Geoffrey, ed. *Narrative and Dramatic Sources of Shakespeare.* Vol. 3. Routledge and Kegan Paul, 1960.

Castor, Helen. *Blood and Roses: The Paston Family and the Wars of the Roses.* Faber and Faber, 2004.

———. *She-Wolves: The Women Who Ruled England Before Elizabeth.* Faber and Faber, 2010.

Chamberlayne, Joanna L. [Joanna Laynesmith]. "A Paper Crown: The Titles and Seals of Cecily Duchess of York." *Ricardian* 10, no. 133 (1996).

Chrimes, S. B. *Henry VII.* Eyre Methuen, 1972.

Cooper, Charles Henry. *Memoir of Margaret, Countess of Richmond and Derby.* Cambridge University Press, 1874.

Coss, Peter. *The Lady in Medieval England, 1000–1500.* Sutton, 1998.

Crawford, Anne. *Letters of Medieval Women.* Sutton, 2002.

———. *Letters of the Queens of England.* Sutton, 2002.

———. *Yorkists: The History of a Dynasty.* Hambledon Continuum, 2006.

Cron, B. M. "Margaret of Anjou and the Lancastrian March on London, 1461." *Ricardian* 11, no. 147 (1999).

Cunningham, Sean. *Richard III: A Royal Enigma.* National Archives, 2003.

Davies, Katharine. *Elizabeth Woodville: The First Queen Elizabeth.* Lovat Dickson, 1937.

Dockray, Keith. *Edward IV: A Source Book.* Sutton, 1999.

———. *Henry VI, Margaret of Anjou, and the Wars of the Roses: A Source Book.* Sutton, 1997.

———. *Richard III: A Source Book.* Sutton, 1997.

Duffy, Eamon. *Marking the Hours: English People and Their Prayers.* Yale University Press, 2011.

Dunn, Diana. "Margaret of Anjou, Queen Consort of Henry VI: A Reassessment of Her Role, 1445–1453." In *Crown, Government, and People in the Fifteenth Century,* edited by Rowena E. Archer. Sutton, 1995.

Fields, Bertram. *Royal Blood: King Richard III and the Mystery of the Princes.* Sutton, 2006.

Fox, Julia. *Sister Queens: Katherine of Aragon and Juana, Queen of Castile.* Weidenfeld & Nicolson, 2011.

Gillingham, J., ed. *Richard III: A Medieval Kingship.* Collins & Brown, 1993.

Goldstone, Nancy. *The Maid and the Queen: The Secret History of Joan of Arc and Yolande of Aragon.* Weidenfeld, 2012.

Goodwin, George. *Fatal Colours: Towton, 1461—England's Most Brutal Battle.* Phoenix, 2012.

Gregory, Philippa, David Baldwin, and Michael Jones. *The Women of the Cousins' War: The Duchess, the Queen, and the King's Mother.* Simon & Schuster, 2011.

Griffiths, Ralph A., and James Sherborne, eds. *Kings and Nobles in the Later Middle Ages.* Sutton, 1986.

Griffiths, Ralph A., and Roger S. Thomas. *The Making of the Tudor Dynasty.* Sutton, 1987.

Hanham, Alison. *Richard III and His Early Historians, 1483–1535.* Oxford University Press, 1975.

———. "Sir George Buck and Princess Elizabeth's Letter: A Problem in Detection." *Ricardian* 7, no. 197 (1987).

Hardyment, Christina. *Malory: The Life and Times of King Arthur's Chronicler.* Harper Perennial, 2006.

Harris, Barbara J. *Edward Stafford, Third Duke of Buckingham, 1478–1521.* Stanford University Press, 1986.

Harvey, Nancy Lenz. *Elizabeth of York.* Weidenfeld & Nicolson, 1973.

Haswell, Jock. *Ardent Queen: Margaret of Anjou and the Lancastrian Heritage.* Peter Davies, 1976.

Hicks, Carola. *The King's Glass: A Story of Tudor Power and Secret Art.* Chatto and Windus, 2007.

Hicks, Michael A. *Anne Neville: Queen to Richard III.* Tempus, 2007.

———. *Edward V, the Prince in the Tower: The Short Life and Mysterious Disappearance of Edward V.* Tempus, 2007.

———. *False, Fleeting, Perjur'd Clarence: George, Duke of Clarence, 1449–1478.* Sutton, 1980.

———. *Warwick, the Kingmaker.* Blackwell, 1998.

Hilton, Lisa. *Queens Consort: England's Medieval Queens.* Weidenfeld & Nicolson, 2008.

Hookham, M. A. *The Life and Times of Margaret of Anjou.* Tinsley Brothers, 1872.

Hughes, Jonathan. *The Religious Life of Richard III: Piety and Prayer in the North of England.* Sutton, 2000.

Hutchinson, Robert. *Young Henry: The Rise of Henry VIII.* Weidenfeld & Nicolson, 2011.

Ingram, Mike. *Battle Story: Bosworth, 1485.* History Press, 2012.

Johnson, P. A. *Duke Richard of York, 1411–1460.* Oxford University Press, 1988.

Jones, Michael K. *Bosworth, 1485: Psychology of a Battle.* Tempus, 2002.

Jones, Michael K., and Malcolm G. Underwood. *The King's Mother: Lady Margaret Beaufort, Countess of Richmond and Derby.* Cambridge University Press, 1992.

Kincaid, Arthur. "Buck and the Elizabeth of York Letter." *Ricardian* 8, no. 101 (1988).

Kingsford, C. L. *English Historical Literature in the Fifteenth Century.* Clarendon Press, 1913.

Lander, J. R. *The Wars of the Roses.* Palgrave Macmillan, 1990.

Laynesmith, Joanna. "The Kings' Mother." *History Today* 56, no. 3 (2006).

———. "The King's Mother: Cecily Neville." Autumn 2005. http://www .richardiii.net/r3_mother.htm.

———. *The Last Medieval Queens: English Queenship, 1445–1503.* Oxford University Press, 2004.

Lewis, Katherine J., Noel James Menuge, and Kim M. Phillips, eds. *Young Medieval Women.* Sutton, 1999.

Leyser, Henrietta. *Medieval Women: A Social History of Women in England, 450–1500.* Weidenfeld & Nicolson, 1995.

Marks, Richard, and Paul Williamson, eds. *Gothic: Art for England, 1400–1547.* V&A Publications, 2003.

Mattingly, Garrett. *Catherine of Aragon.* Jonathan Cape, 1942.

Maurer, Helen E. *Margaret of Anjou: Queenship and Power in Late Medieval England.* Boydell Press, 2003.

———. "Whodunit: The Suspects in the Case." N.d. http://www.r3.org /bookcase/whodunit.html.

McKendrick, Scot, John Lowden, and Kathleen Doyle. *Royal Manuscripts: The Genius of Illumination.* British Library, 2011.

Myers, A. R., and Cecil H. Clough. *The Crown, Household, and Parliament in Fifteenth Century England.* Hambledon Press, 1985.

Nenner, Howard. *The Right to Be King: The Succession to the Crown of England, 1604–1714.* Macmillan, 1975.

Norton, Elizabeth. *Margaret Beaufort: The Mother of the Tudor Dynasty.* Amberley, 2010.

Okerlund, Arlene Naylor. *Elizabeth of York.* Palgrave Macmillan, 2009.

———. *Elizabeth Wydeville: The Slandered Queen.* Tempus, Stroud, 2005.

Palmer, Richard, and P. Michelle Brown, eds. *Lambeth Palace Library: Treasures for the Collection of the Archbishops of Canterbury.* Scala, 2010.

Penn, Thomas. *Winter King: The Dawn of Tudor England.* Allen Lane, 2011.

Perry, Maria. *Sisters to the King.* Andre Deutsch, 1998.

Pollard, A. J., ed. *The Wars of the Roses.* Macmillan, 1995.

Ross, Charles. *Edward IV.* Eyre Methuen, 1974.
————. *Richard III.* Eyre Methuen, 1981.
Royle, Trevor. *The Wars of the Roses: England's First Civil War.* Little, Brown, 2009.
Rubin, Miri. *The Hollow Crown: A History of Britain in the Late Middle Ages.* Allen Lane, 2005.
Seabourne, Gwen. *Imprisoning Medieval Women: The Non-judicial Confinement and Abduction of Women in England, c. 1170–1509.* Ashgate, 2011.
Seward, Desmond. *The Last White Rose.* Constable, 2011.
————. *The Wars of the Roses.* Harper Press, 2008.
Starkey, David. *Henry: Virtuous Prince.* Harper Press, 2008.
————, ed. *Henry VIII: A European Court in England.* Collins & Brown, 1991.
Strickland, Agnes. *Lives of the Queens of England.* Vols. 3–4. 1841, 1842.
Sutton, Anne F., and P. W. Hammond, eds. *The Coronation of Richard III: The Extant Documents.* Sutton, 1983.
Sutton, Anne F., and Livia Visser-Fuchs. "The Device of Queen Elizabeth Woodville: A Gillyflower or Pink." *Ricardian* 11, no. 136 (1997).
————. *The Reburial of Richard, Duke of York, 21–30 July 1476.* Richard III Society, 1996.
Thurley, Simon. *The Royal Palaces of Tudor England: Architecture and Court Life, 1460–1547.* Yale University Press, 1993.
Tremlett, Giles. *Catherine of Aragon: Henry's Spanish Queen.* Faber and Faber, 2011.
Visser-Fuchs, Livia. "Where Did Elizabeth of York Find Consolation?" *Ricardian* 9, no. 122 (1993).
Walpole, Horace. *Historic Doubts on the Life and Reign of King Richard III.* First published 1768. In *Richard III: The Great Debate,* edited by Paul Kendall. Folio Society, 1965.
Weightman, Christine. *Margaret of York: The Diabolical Duchess.* Amberley, 2009.
Weir, Alison. *Britain's Royal Families: The Complete Genealogy.* Pimlico, 2002.
————. *Lancaster and York: The Wars of the Roses.* Pimlico, 1998.
————. *The Princes in the Tower.* Pimlico, 1997.
Williams, Barrie. "Elizabeth of York's Last Journey." *Ricardian* 8, no. 100 (1988).
Williams, Marty Newman, and Anne Echols. *Between Pit and Pedestal: Women in the Middle Ages.* Markus Wiener, 1994.
Williamson, Audrey. *The Mystery of the Princes: An Investigation into a Supposed Murder.* Sutton, 1978.
Wolffe, Bertram. *Henry VI.* Eyre Methuen, 1981.
Woolgar, C. M. *The Senses in Late Medieval England.* Yale University Press, 2006.
Wroe, Ann. *Perkin: A Story of Deception.* Vintage, 2004.

ILLUSTRATION CREDITS

Marguerite of Anjou with Henry VI and John Talbot in the "Shrewsbury Talbot Book of Romances," c. 1445. British Library, Royal 15 E. VI, f.2v (© The British Library Board).

The stained glass Royal Window in Canterbury Cathedral (© Crown Copyright, English Heritage).

Margaret Beaufort by Rowland Lockey, late sixteenth century (by permission of the Master and Fellows of St. John's College, Cambridge).

Margaret Beaufort's emblems (© Neil Holmes/The Bridgeman Art Library).

Cecily Neville's father, the Earl of Westmorland, with the children of his second marriage (Bibliothèque Nationale, Paris/Flammarion/The Bridgeman Art Library).

Portrait of Elizabeth Woodville from 1463 (© The Print Collector/ Corbis).

Anne Neville depicted in the *Rous Roll*, 1483–1485. British Library, Add. 48976 (© The British Library Board).

King Richard III by unknown artist, oil on panel, late sixteenth century; after unknown artist late fifteenth century (© National Portrait Gallery, London).

The risen Christ appearing to Margaret of Burgundy by the Master of Girard de Rousillon, from *Le dyalogue de la ducesse de bourgogne a Ihesu Crist* by Nicolas Finet, c. 1470. British Library, Add. 7970, f.1v (© The British Library Board).

Elizabeth of York by unknown artist, oil on panel, late sixteenth century; after unknown artist c. 1500 (© National Portrait Gallery, London).

The birth of Julius Caesar from *Le fait des Romains*, Bruges, 1479. British Library, Royal 17 F.ii, f.9 (© The British Library Board).

INDEX